THE BOOK OF EDIBLE NUTS

THE BOOK OF EDIBLE NUTS

Frederic Rosengarten, Jr.

DOVER PUBLICATIONS, INC.
Mineola, New York

Bibliographical Note

This Dover edition, first published in 2004, is an unabridged republication of the work originally published by the Walker Publishing Company, Inc., New York, in 1984.

Acknowledgments

Grateful acknowledgment is made to the following for permission to reprint from the material listed below:

Holt, Rinehart and Winston, Publishers, for "Evil Tendencies Cancel" by Robert Frost from *The Poetry of Robert Frost*, edited by Edward Connery Lathem. Copyright © 1936 by Robert Frost, copyright © 1964 by Lesley Frost Ballantine. Copyright © 1969 by Holt, Rinehart and Winston. U.K. and Empire rights administered by Jonathan Cape Ltd.

D. E. P. Dearnley, Brandon-Thomas Co., for *Charley's Aunt* by Brandon Thomas.

The roman numeral following each recipe name indicates its source, as described under Recipe Acknowledgments (page 363), which constitutes an extension of the copyright page.

Library of Congress Cataloging-in-Publication Data

Rosengarten, Frederic.
    The book of edible nuts / Frederic Rosengarten, Jr.
        p. cm.
    Originally published: New York : Walker Pub., 1984.
    Includes bibliographical references and indexes.
    ISBN 0-486-43499-0 (pbk.)
        1. Nuts. 2. Cookery (Nuts) I. Title.

SB401.A4R67 2004
634'.5—dc22

                                                            2004045504

Manufactured in the United States of America
Dover Publications, Inc., 31 East 2nd Street, Mineola, N.Y. 11501

To M. O. R.

Contents

CONTENTS

Preface

The author acknowledges his sincere appreciation for the help given him by many persons during the preparation of this book. Wholehearted thanks are due to Dr. Richard Evans Schultes, Director of the Botanical Museum, Harvard University; Dr. Richard A. Howard of the Arnold Arboretum, Harvard University; Dr. Ghillean T. Prance of the New York Botanical Garden; Dr. Ara Der Marderosian of the Philadelphia College of Pharmacy and Science; and to Dr. Walter H. Hodge of Trumansburg, New York—for their thoughtful editorial criticism and numerous constructive suggestions. The author is most grateful to Dr. Dennis V. Johnson of Austin, Texas, for providing useful and detailed research data concerning the literature on edible nuts, and to Mrs. Arlene M. Seeley of Southampton, Massachusetts, for her kind permission to make use of selected nut stamps from the remarkable collection of her late brother, Elmer W. Smith.

The author acknowledges with thanks the cooperation of the following individuals, institutions or companies that have provided him with technical advice, information, orientation, photographs, recipes, nut samples, or otherwise assisted him during the course of the work: Ace Pecan Company, Elk Grove Village, Illinois (Joseph C. Graziano—pine nut samples); Ira S. Agress, New York City (pistachio photos); Almond Board of California, Sacramento; American Soybean Association, St. Louis; Mrs. Margarette Andrade, Freeport, New York (several recipes from *Brazilian*

Cookery); Bobbi Angell, New York Botanical Garden, for botanical drawings of twelve selected nuts; O.L. Applegate, Sarasota, Florida; Arizona Historical Society, Tucson (Buehman Collection photo); Arnold Arboretum, Jamaica Plains, Massachusetts (Dr. Peter Ashton and Sheila Geary); Association of Food Distributors, Inc., New York (Richard J. Sullivan—Brazil nut recipes); Avitrol Corp., Tulsa, Oklahoma (sunflower photo); Michael J. Balick, New York Botanical Garden; Dr. Rupert Barnaby, Mrs. Katina Enders and Dr. Tetsuo Koyama of the New York Botanical Garden (for names of the nuts in several foreign languages); A. L. Bazzini Co., Inc., New York City (William P. Dignam—information about the nut trade); Dr. Junius Bird, American Museum of Natural History, New York City (archaeological information and photo re. peanuts in Peru); Botanical Museum, Harvard University (Kristine L. Forsgard, Scott Wilder and Wesley Wong, librarian); J. F. Braun & Sons, Inc., Lake Success, New York (Wally Huggins—nut samples and information about the nut trade); British Museum, Natural History, London (Mrs. Judith A. Diment, Botany Librarian); California Almond Growers Exchange, Sacramento (Jack Axer and Susan Valdes—photos, recipes for and information about almonds and other edible nuts); California Macadamia Society, Fallbrook, California; California Pistachio Association, Fresno; Cargill, Minneapolis (Greg C. Lauser—sunflower photo); Carver Research Foundation of Tuskegee Institute (photo of

G.W. Carver); Cashew Export Promotion Council, Ernakulam, India (cashew recipes and photos); Andre L. Causse, New York City and Findik Tarim Satis K. B., Giresun, Turkey (hazelnut photos); Continental Nut Co., Chico, California; Dr. Julian C. Crane (information about pistachios and walnuts) and Dr. Dale E. Kester (almond photos), University of California, Davis; Dahlgren and Co., Crookston, Minnesota (sunflower photos); T. M. Duché Nut Co., Inc., Orland, California (Joseph C. Edgar—photos of and recipes for almonds); Günter Enderle, Mainz-Gonsenheim, West Germany; Field Musem of Natural History, Chicago; Fisher Nut Co., St. Paul, Minnesota and the Pillsbury Company (for permission to make use of selected recipes from the Goin' Nuts Cookbook); General Foods Corporation (Max E. Ruehrmund and Doris Koch—photos of and recipes for coconuts); Georgia Agricultural Commodity Commission for Peanuts (peanut recipes); Georgia Peanut Commission (peanut recipes); Georgia Pecan Growers Association (pecan recipes); Gray Herbarium and Arnold Arboretum libraries, Harvard University (Barbara Callahan, librarian); Dr. Richard A. Hamilton, University of Hawaii at Monoa, Honolulu (information about macadamia nuts); Mrs. Harriet Healy, Palm Beach, Florida (several recipes); Dr. Charles B. Heiser, Jr., Indiana University (information about and photos of sunflower seeds); I B G E, Rio de Janeiro, Brazil (illustrations by Percy Lau); Imperial Sugar Company (pecan recipes); Inari Ltd., Lansing, Michigan (Leonard Stuttmann—information about "soynuts"); Dr. Richard A. Jaynes, The Connecticut Agricultural Experiment Station, New Haven; Dr. Arnold Krochmal, U.S.D.A., Rio Piedras, Puerto Rico; Diana Kirkbride Halbeck, Helsinge, Denmark (archaeological data and pistachio photo); Walter Kuzio, New York City; Dr. Harry B. Lagerstedt, U.S.D.A., Corvallis, Oregon (information about and photos of filberts); Lewis & Neale, Inc., New York City; The Linnean Society of London (Gina Douglas, librarian); Dr. L. H. MacDaniels, Ithaca, New York; Mrs. Jayne MacLean,

National Agricultural Library, Beltsville, Maryland; Macmillan Publishing Co., Inc., New York City (two illustrations from The Standard Cyclopedia of Horticulture); Mauna Loa Macadamia Nut Corp. (a C. Brewer company: A. A. Yort, Jr., Paul G. Bennett and Masao Nakamura—photos, recipes and information about macadamia nuts); Ian McConachie, Brisbane, Queensland, Australia (the history of the macadamia nut); Dr. Edwin A. Menninger, Stuart, Florida (several photos); Dr. Frederick G. Meyer, National Arboretum, Washington, D.C. (nut samples and photos); Michigan Nut Growers Association, Charlotte (several recipes from The Nut Jar cookbook); Dr. Julia Morton, Morton Collectanea, University of Miami (help with search of literature and several photos); Gary Paul Nabhan, University of Arizona, Tucson; Nabisco Brands, Inc., Planters Division (J. J. Edelmann and Ted J. LoCascio—selected Planters' photos and recipes); Dr. Tommy Nakayama, University of Georgia, College of Agriculture (pecan photos and booklets); Walter P. Naquin, Jr., Kihei, Maui, Hawaii (early history of macadamia nut in Hawaii); National Peanut Council, Washington, D.C.; National Pecan Marketing Council (pecan recipes); National Pecan Shellers & Processors Association (pecan recipes); Lewis Nordlinger, Roslyn, New York (Brazil nut photos); North Dakota Sunflower Council, Bismarck; Northern Nut Growers Association, Hamden, Connecticut; Nut Tree Pecan Company (pecan recipes); University of Oklahoma Press, Norman (sunflower photo from The Sunflower); Oregon Filbert Commission, Tigard (photos and recipes); Oxford University Press, Oxford, England (water chestnut illustration from The Oxford Book of Food Plants); Parker Products, Inc., Holliston, Massachusetts (Parker Halpern—samples of "soynuts"); Dr. Jerry A. Payne, U.S.D.A., Byron, Georgia (photos of and information about pecans); Pecan South Magazine, Atlanta (Mrs. Rebecca Johnson—pecan photos); Dr. John Popenoe, Fairchild Tropical Garden, Miami (information about coconuts); Red V Coconut Products Co., Inc.,

Piscataway, New Jersey (Linda I. Clark—coconut photos and recipes); Dr. R. G. Robinson, University of Minnesota (information about and photos of sunflower seeds); the staff of the Royal Botanic Gardens, Kew, England; SSI, Inc., Nixa, Missouri (Robert R. Zoppelt—sesame snack samples); Sigco Research, Inc., Breckenridge, Minnesota (Dr. Gerhardt Fick—photos of, recipes for and information about sunflower seeds); Jerome F. Smith and Jerome F. Smith, Jr., San José, Costa Rica (data on jojoba); Southeastern Chestnut Growers Association, Atlanta (chestnut recipes); *Soyfoods Magazine* (Richard Leviton); Dr. J. Benton Storey, Texas A & M University (information about and photos of pecans); Dr. William B. Storey, Riverside, California (information about and illustrations of macadamia nuts); Sun-Diamond Growers of California, San Ramon (Donald J. Soetaert, Noreen Griffee, Larry Holden and John P. Farrell, Jr.—photos of, recipes for and information about walnuts and Brazil nuts); *Sunflower and Grain Marketing*, Davenport, Iowa (Alan McGaffin—sunflower photos); Tenneco West, Bakersfield, California (Tristan E. G.

Krogius, Clyde Harter and Jerry Lemmons—photos of, recipes for and information about almonds and pistachios); H. M. Thames Pecan Company, Mobile, Alabama (Dan A. Miller—pecan recipes); Tracy-Locke, Dallas (pecan recipes and photos); the staff of the Tropical Products Institute, London; Dr. Noel D. Vietmeyer, National Academy of Sciences, Washington, D.C. (jojoba photos); Walnut Marketing Board, San Mateo, California; Dr. Thomas W. Whitaker, La Jolla, California (information about pumpkins); Harold F. Winters, Silver Spring, Maryland (U.S.D.A. data on tree nuts); Dr. Jasper Guy Woodroof, Griffin, Georgia (photos of and information about pecans).

The author is grateful to his wife for her long-suffering patience as well as for enlightenment concerning some Greek nouns; and to Mrs. Judith K. Benson for her competent typing of the manuscript.

Finally, the author wishes to express his appreciation to the staff of Walker and Company: to Michael Sagalyn for his perceptive editing; and to Ruth Cavin for her proficient selection of the nut recipes.

F. R., Jr.
July, 1983

Introduction

ARCHAEOLOGICAL RECORDS of the food of primitive man are few, but nuts must have been among the items of plant origin which he sampled, along with leaves, buds, fruits, barks and roots. Gradual improvement of the more palatable and nutritious nuts through crude selection may have taken place due to the haphazard efforts of early man. Plant debris has been found in prehistoric archaeological sites, suggesting that cavemen had at least a few nuts at their disposal. The middle Paleolithic cave-dwellers in northern Iraq at Shanidar are believed to have consumed acorns, pine nuts, walnuts and chestnuts. In Mesolithic times, before 10,000 B.C., acorns

and filberts (hazelnuts) formed part of the diet of Europeans, as evidenced by charred shell fragments discovered in the Swiss prehistoric lake dwellings and at Alvastra in Sweden. Studies of antiquity indicate that acorns were being used as food at Catal Hüyük, Turkey as early as the sixth millenium B.C. Three nuts, eaten since ancient times, are mentioned in the Bible: pistachios were carried down to Egypt by Joseph's brothers, walnuts were cultivated in King Solomon's garden, and almonds were utilized as ornaments for the candlesticks in the Tabernacle.

Stone pine nuts (pignolias) and sweet chestnuts were much sought after in the Med-

ANCIENT WILD HICKORY?

This nut, dating from the late third century B.C., was found at the site of the Agora Excavations, Athens, Greece. Its form and very thick shell suggest it may be a wild hickory.

A HIT ON THE HEAD, OR A CRACKER ON THE NUT

In 1859 a British reporter, describing a boxing match in London, observed that one of the fighters got a *cracker on his nut.* This was an early slang reference to the head as a "nut."

iterranean region during the Greco-Roman era. Two thousand years ago, the diet of Indians in North America included pecans, hickories, piñon pine nuts, beechnuts, acorns, chestnuts, black walnuts and sunflower seeds. At about the same time, peanuts were popular in southern South America: excavations in sites along the Peruvian coastal regions have unearthed ancient mummy bundles containing peanuts, as well as pottery with peanut motifs. The "youngest" important edible nut is the macadamia, which has been in cultivation for less than a hundred and fifty years, although it was known centuries earlier to the aborigines of northeastern Australia.

A logical name for this work would have been "The Book of Nuts;" however, some knowledgeable people have observed that this title would be ludicrous—and could subject the book to ridicule by the literati. The reason, of course, is that the word "nuts" for many years has been popularly associated with people who are "nutty," crazy, or have something wrong with their heads. This slang expression dates back probably to 19th century England: a keen-eyed reporter named Mayhew, describing a prize-fight in London in 1859, observed: "The first round was soon terminated, for Jack got a *cracker on his nut.*" The relationship of head and nut had an earlier origin, as we shall see in the chapter on walnuts: in the 16th and 17th centuries in medieval Europe and England, it was noted in accordance with the Doctrine of Signatures that the anatomy of the human head bore a striking resemblance to the kernel of a walnut. This doctrine theorized that the Lord had placed a definite sign or signature on every plant, pointing out its usefulness in medicine. For example, a plant with a heart-shaped leaf was believed to be helpful in curing heart disease, while one with a liver-shaped leaf could cure hepatic ailments. Thus the ground husk of the walnut was prescribed to cure a head wound, while the mentally ill were told to eat

 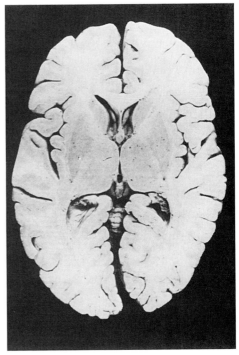

THE WALNUT   THE HUMAN BRAIN

According to the Doctrine of Signatures in the 16th and 17th centuries in medieval Europe and England, various plants were employed in herbal medicine as specific cures due to a fancied resemblance of the shape of a root, leaf or fruit to a particular part of the human body. Thus the walnut was the perfect signature of the human head, while its kernel bore an uncanny likeness to the brain. So the ground, outer husk of the walnut was prescribed to cure a head wound; and eating the walnut was recommended for the mentally ill.

walnuts for their presumed therapeutic effects on the brain.

Few botanical terms are used more loosely than the word "nut." Technically, according to Funk & Wagnalls Standard Encyclopedic College Dictionary (1968), a nut is "1. A dry fruit consisting of a kernel or seed enclosed in a woody shell; the kernel of such fruit, especially when edible, as of the peanut, walnut, or chestnut; *Bot.* A hard, indehiscent, one-seeded pericarp generally resulting from a compound ovary, as the chestnut or acorn." (Indehiscent means that the seedcase does

not split open spontaneously when ripe.) The nut has also been described as a one-celled, one-seeded, dry fruit with a hard pericarp (shell); and, more simply, as a type of fruit that consists of one edible, hard seed covered with a dry, woody shell that does not split open at maturity. Only a fraction of so-called nuts—for example, chestnuts, filberts and acorns—answer this description. The peanut is not really a nut; it is a legume or pod, like the split pea, lentil or bean—but an indehiscent one because the pod does not split open upon maturing. The shelled peanut is a seed

TWELVE SELECTED EDIBLE NUTS

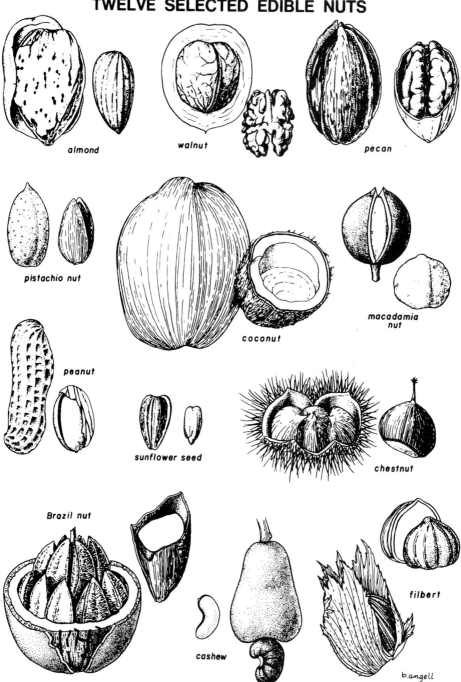

almond

walnut

pecan

pistachio nut

coconut

macadamia nut

peanut

sunflower seed

chestnut

Brazil nut

cashew

filbert

b.angell

or bean. The edible seeds of almonds, walnuts, pecans, pistachios, hickory nuts and macadamia nuts are enclosed in the hard stones of a drupe—like the stones of peaches, cherries or plums. A drupe is a soft, fleshy fruit with a spongy or fibrous husk, which may or may not split free from the inner hard-shelled stone containing the seed. In plums and peaches, we eat the fleshy parts and throw away the stones; but the fleshy part of the walnut, for example, is removed and discarded, while the kernel of the stone—the nut—is eaten. The shell of a drupe nut, like the walnut, corresponds to the hard, outer layer of the peach stone. The coconut is the seed of a fibrous drupe. The Brazil nut is a seed with a hard seed coat, as is the piñon nut. Another dry, indehiscent fruit type is the achene—a small, thin shell containing one seed, attached to the outer layer at one point only—as in the dandelion and buttercup. The sunflower seed is an achene. A true nut resembles an achene, but it develops from more than one carpel (female reproductive structure), is usually larger and has a harder, woody wall; e.g., the difference between the filbert nut and the sunflower achene.

In this book, the word "nut" will be employed in the broad, popular sense, covering a wide range of fruits or seeds, some of which would not be classified as nuts according to strict botanical definition, but which nevertheless are called nuts in everyday usage.

Nuts differ considerably in their structure. Some, such as the almond and pistachio, have a single, firm kernel; while others, like the walnut and pecan, consist of a kernel formed in two distinct halves.

Nuts also show considerable variation in the coverings which protect their edible kernels. The chestnut is protected by a spiny husk, the coconut by a thick fibrous husk, the cashew by poisonous materials in the fruit wall which are removed before the kernel is eaten. The shells of some nuts, such as almonds, pistachios and chestnuts, are usually easy to crack; but the extremely hard protective coverings of other nuts, including macadamia nuts, Brazil nuts, hickories and eastern black walnuts, require a very sharp blow or considerable pressure from special rollers in order to open them.

Most nuts are spherical, but there are exceptions: almonds and pistachios are flat and elongated; beechnuts and Brazil nuts are triangular; cashews are kidney-shaped; and Eurasian water chestnuts look like the horns of a buffalo.

It should be pointed out that not all nuts and nutlike seeds are edible. The toxic tung nut, from the Chinese tree, *Aleurites fordii*, now widely cultivated in the Old and New Worlds, is the source of tung oil—a highly effective drying agent employed in varnish and paint manufacture, which possesses superior preservative and water-proofing qualities. Another related poisonous nut, the candlenut, from the candlenut oil tree, *Aleurites triloba*, is the source of a drying oil long important in Malaysia and the Pacific islands as an illuminant, wood preservative, and ingredient of soap and paints.

Nux vomica is an even more venomous, nutlike seed of the Asiatic tree, *Strychnos nux-vomica*. The Latin binomial means "the nut that causes vomiting." The hard, grayish, disklike seeds contain the bitter, highly poisonous alkaloid strychnine, formerly used in small quantities in medicine as a heart stimulant, but better known as a deadly rat poison. Another infamous, toxic seed is the ordeal or Calabar bean of Nigeria. Up to the nineteenth century, these dark brown seeds of the woody, climbing vine, *Physostigma venenosum*, were widely used by tribes of western Africa: an individual suspected of witchcraft or some other heinous crime was forced to swallow an infusion of the crushed seeds; if he died from the effects of the poison, he was considered to be guilty; if, on the other hand, the accused merely vomited and survived, he was judged to be innocent and was set free. Today, the dried, ripe seeds of this plant are employed medicinally to produce physostigmine, an alkaloid utilized in opthalmic medicine to contract the pupil of the eye.

The twelve main edible nuts, described in detail in this book, have been selected on the

SOME POPULAR EDIBLE NUTS IN THE SHELL

From left to right: pistachios, Brazil nuts, Persian walnuts, chestnuts, peanuts, filberts, almonds and pecans.

basis of their importance from the standpoint of consumption in the United States. Sunflower seeds are assigned to this group, since they have become a very important nut snack item in recent years. It has not been easy to draw the line with reference to the nuts selected. For example, there are over one hundred tropical palms which produce edible nuts. However, as the coconut's multiple uses give it preeminence, it has been given priority.

Thirty other nuts are more briefly covered. Some are virtually unknown in the United States but are in demand elsewhere in the world and may eventually become more popular in this country. Although the betel "nut" and the cola "nut" are masticatories (they are chewed but not eaten), they have been included because they are popularly known as nuts. Similarly, the edible portion of the litchi is really the swollen aril or stalk that bears the seed, comparable to the mace and the nutmeg. Nevertheless, the litchi is commonly called a nut. The tiger or chufa "nut" is not a true nut, but a tuber. Soybeans, especially valuable as a source of vegetable protein, are included, since processed, nut-flavored soy products, resembling dry roasted split peanuts, have become a significant commodity in the snack nut trade.

Many edible nuts and seeds available in supermarkets, groceries and health-food stores are grown in this country. Almonds, for example, filberts, macadamia nuts, peanuts, pecans, pine (piñon) nuts, California pistachios, pumpkin seeds, sunflower seeds and walnuts are all cultivated in the United States. Some are imported, such as Brazil nuts, cashews, coconuts, pine (pignolias), pistachios from the Middle East and European chestnuts. Most nuts can be purchased year-round, although fresh chestnuts are usually sold during the winter. There is a strong association between the consumption of edible nuts and the holidays of Thanksgiving and Christmas.

As a general rule, nuts are available in both shelled and unshelled form. Cashews are an exception: they are never sold in the shell, since the inner, honeycomb-like structure between the kernel and the shell contains irritating juices, similar to those of poison ivy, which blister the skin.

The shell of most nuts is a perfect, hermetically-sealed package provided by nature, which shields the kernel and keeps it fresh. In-shell nuts are not usually roasted; pistachios are an exception. Peanuts can be eaten roasted or not—with slight differences in flavor. Nuts are energy-packed seeds, with as much nutrition as possible concentrated in a compact space to nourish the first stages of development of young seedling plants. The edible portion of most nuts is the embryo, in which large amounts of protein and fat are stored. If toasted, the flavor of the nut becomes more evident. The nut shell protects the kernel from contamination; few of the

THE NUT GATHERERS

A painting by Edward H. Wehnert. London, 1850.

COMPOSITION OF FOODS

	Water	Food Energy	Protein	Fat	Carbohydrate		Ash
					Total	Fiber	
	(C)	(D)	(E)	(F)	(G)	(H)	(I)
	Percent	Calories	Grams	Grams	Grams	Grams	Grams
SELECTED EDIBLE NUTS							
Almonds:							
Dried	4.7	598	18.6	54.2	19.5	2.6	3.0
Roasted and salted	.7	627	18.6	57.7	19.5	2.6	3.5
Brazil nuts	4.6	654	14.3	66.9	10.9	3.1	3.3
Cashew nuts	5.2	561	17.2	45.7	29.3	1.4	2.6
Chestnuts:							
Fresh	52.5	194	2.9	1.5	42.1	1.1	1.0
Dried	8.4	377	6.7	4.1	78.6	2.5	2.2
Coconut meat:							
Fresh	50.9	346	3.5	35.3	9.4	4.0	.9
Dried:							
Unsweetened	3.5	662	7.2	64.9	23.0	3.9	1.4
Sweetened, shredded	3.3	548	3.6	39.1	53.2	4.1	.8
Filberts (hazelnuts)	5.8	634	12.6	62.4	16.7	3.0	2.5
Macadamia nuts	3.0	691	7.8	71.6	15.9	2.5	1.7
Peanuts:							
Raw, with skins	5.6	564	26.0	47.5	18.6	2.4	2.3
Raw, without skins	5.4	568	26.3	48.4	17.6	1.9	2.3
Boiled	36.4	376	15.5	31.5	14.5	1.8	2.1
Roasted, with skins	1.8	582	26.2	48.7	20.6	2.7	2.7
Roasted and salted	1.6	585	26.0	49.8	18.8	2.4	3.8
Pecans	3.4	687	9.2	71.2	14.6	2.3	1.6
Pistachio nuts	5.3	594	19.3	53.7	19.0	1.9	2.7
Sunflower seed kernels, dry	4.8	560	24.0	47.3	19.9	3.8	4.0
Walnuts:							
Black	3.1	628	20.5	59.3	14.8	1.7	2.3
Persian or English	3.5	651	14.8	64.0	15.8	2.1	1.9
OTHER EDIBLE SEEDS & NUTS							
Beechnuts	6.6	568	19.4	50.0	20.3	3.7	3.7
Butternuts	3.8	629	23.7	61.2	8.4	—	2.9
Hickory nuts	3.3	673	13.2	68.7	12.8	1.9	2.0
Lychees:							
Raw	81.9	64	.9	.3	16.4	.3	.5
Dried	22.3	277	3.8	1.2	70.7	1.4	2.0
Pilinuts	6.3	669	11.4	71.1	8.4	2.7	2.8
Pine nuts:							
Pignolias	5.6	552	31.1	47.4	11.6	.9	4.3
Piñon	3.1	635	13.0	60.5	20.5	1.1	2.9
Pumpkin and squash seed kernels, dry	4.4	553	29.0	46.7	15.0	1.9	4.9
Sesame seeds, dry:							
Whole	5.4	563	18.6	49.1	21.6	6.3	5.3
Decorticated	5.5	582	18.2	53.4	17.6	2.4	5.3
Soybeans:							
Mature seeds, dry:							
Raw	10.0	403	34.1	17.7	33.5	4.9	4.7
Cooked	71.0	130	11.0	5.7	10.8	1.6	1.5
Water chestnut,							
Chinese (matai, waternut), raw	78.3	79	1.4	.2	19.0	.8	1.1

SOURCE: *Composition of Foods.* USDA Agricultural Handbook No. 8. 1975.

(100 Grams, Edible Portion)

Calcium	Phos-phorus	Iron	Sodium	Potas-sium	Vitamin A value	Thiamine	Ribo-flavin	Niacin	Ascorbic acid
(J)	(K)	(L)	(M)	(N)	(O)	(P)	(Q)	(R)	(S)
Milli-grams	Milli-grams	Milli-grams	Milli-grams	Milli-grams	Interna-tional units	Milli-grams	Milli-grams	Milli-grams	Milli-grams
234	504	4.7	4	773	0	.24	.92	3.5	Trace
235	504	4.7	198	773	0	.05	.92	3.5	0
186	693	3.4	1	715	Trace	.96	.12	1.6	—
38	373	3.8	15	464	100	.43	.25	1.8	—
27	88	1.7	6	454	—	.22	.22	.6	—
52	162	3.3	12	875	—	.32	.38	1.2	—
13	95	1.7	23	256	0	.05	.02	.5	3
26	187	3.3	—	588	0	.06	.04	.6	0
16	112	2.0	—	353	0	.04	.03	.4	0
209	337	3.4	2	704	—	.46	—	.9	Trace
48	161	2.0	—	264	0	.34	.11	1.3	0
69	401	2.1	5	674	—	1.14	.13	17.2	0
59	409	2.0	5	674	0	.99	.13	15.8	0
43	181	1.3	4	462	—	.48	.08	10.0	0
72	407	2.2	5	701	—	.32	.13	17.1	0
74	401	2.1	418	674	—	.32	.13	17.2	0
73	289	2.4	Trace	603	130	.86	.13	.9	2
131	500	7.3	—	972	230	.67	—	1.4	0
120	837	7.1	30	920	50	1.96	.23	5.4	—
Trace	570	6.0	3	460	300	.22	.11	.7	—
99	380	3.1	2	450	30	.33	.13	.9	2
—	—	—	—	—	—	—	—	—	—
—	—	6.8	—	—	—	—	—	—	—
Trace	360	2.4	—	—	—	—	—	—	—
8	42	.4	3	170	—	—	.05	—	42
33	181	1.7	3	1,100	—	—	—	—	—
140	554	3.4	3	489	40	.88	.09	.5	Trace
—	—	—	—	—	—	.62	—	—	—
12	604	5.2	—	—	30	1.28	.23	4.5	Trace
51	1,144	11.2	—	—	70	.24	.19	2.4	—
1,160	616	10.5	60	725	30	.98	.24	5.4	0
110	592	2.4	—	—	—	.18	.13	5.4	0
226	554	8.4	5	1,677	80	1.10	.31	2.2	—
73	179	2.7	2	540	30	.21	.09	.6	0
4	65	.6	20	500	0	.14	.20	1.0	4

chemical agents used to treat nuts can penetrate it. Processing steps for nuts may include treatment with lye or various gases, as well as bleaching and occasional coloring and waxing. Some consumers, for example, prefer imported, red-stained pistachios—colored by dyes approved by the United States Food and Drug Administration. These treatments sometimes make it difficult to pick out nuts of inferior quality, so one should look carefully for small holes (possible insect contamination) and beware of surface mold or mold inside the nuts.

In recent years, there has been an increase in the sale of raw nuts—i.e., nuts which have been shelled, but which are unroasted and unsalted. They may be available whole, broken into pieces, slivered or sliced by mechanical means. Some nuts, such as almonds, may be blanched—immersed in scalding water for a few minutes—after which their brown skins can be removed without difficulty to expose the whiteness of the kernels. Raw, unsalted cashews are now available, and are preferred by some consumers, especially those who are on special diets.

With reference to the buying and storing of nuts, the following general observations and suggestions may be of practical use:

(1) Two pounds of unshelled nuts should yield about one pound of shelled nuts, which, in turn, should make approximately three to five cups of nutmeats.
(2) Protect the shelled kernels from excess heat, light, air and moisture.
(3) Store the kernels in a covered jar or tin, below room temperature, in a cool, dark place.
(4) In-shell nuts retain their high quality longer than shelled nuts. Whole nuts do not become rancid as quickly as nuts which have been cut into pieces. Nuts keep better unroasted than roasted.
(5) Store the nuts or kernels in a closed jar in the refrigerator if a long storage period is anticipated.

Nuts still in the shell or kept in vacuum containers are usually protected against deterioration. Unpackaged, they may become rancid due to moisture, heat and other environmental conditions. Rancidity is caused by chemical changes in the oil of the nuts. The longer the exposure to excessive heat and moisture, the higher the increase of free fatty acids. Rancidity can be delayed by storing nuts in opaque, tightly-sealed jars in a cool place, preferably the refrigerator.

Nutritious nuts, rich in proteins, fats and minerals—vital for vegetarians—may be substituted occasionally for meat in normal diets, and provide a far more healthful snack than cookies and candies. The digestibility of nuts increases when they are finely ground (as in peanut butter), or well chewed; gluttonous overindulgence should be avoided.

Fats and oils are a concentrated source of calories and energy in the typical American diet, supplying some 40 to 50 per cent of the usual caloric intake. Many nuts contain a high portion of fat, such as pecans (71%), macadamias (71%), Brazil nuts (66%), Persian walnuts (64%) and almonds (54%). While most protein foods like cheese, meat and eggs add saturated fats to the diet, the fat found in most nuts is, in the main, highly unsaturated. This is beneficial, since unsaturated fats tend not to elevate blood cholesterol. One pound of nut kernels (assuming 3,000 calories of fuel value per pound) is equivalent in energy value to about 2.4 pounds of bread, 3.2 pounds of steak, 8 pounds of potatoes or 10.4 pounds of apples. Peanuts, almonds and pistachios have an especially high protein content; chestnuts are rich in carbohydrates, but low in fat. Most nuts are an excellent source of calcium, phosphorus, iron, potassium and the B vitamins, as is evident in the table extracted from *Composition of Foods*, U.S.D.A. Agricultural Handbook No. 8, 1975 on pp. xx–xxi.

Eight major tree nuts of the world may be listed in the order of their importance in terms of production on a kernel-weight basis as follows: almonds, filberts (hazelnuts), cashews,

U.S. PRODUCTION OF TREE NUTS
(1,000 tons—Inshell Basis)

	Almonds (California)	Walnuts	Pecans	Filberts	Macadamia Nuts	Pistachios (California)	Total
1965-69	86.2	90.8	106.3	8.5	4.6	—	196.4
1970	124.0	111.8	77.8	9.3	6.6	—	329.5
1971	134.0	136.4	123.1	11.4	7.2	—	412.1
1972	125.0	116.8	91.6	10.2	6.6	—	350.2
1973	134.0	175.0	137.9	12.3	6.1	—	465.0
1974	189.0	156.5	68.6	6.7	8.2	—	429.0
1975	160.0	199.3	123.4	12.1	9.1	—	503.9
1976	233.0	183.7	51.6	7.2	9.5	1.0	486.0
1977	249.0	192.5	118.3	11.8	9.8	2.3	583.7
1978	142.7	160.0	125.0	14.1	10.5	1.3	453.6
1979	303.7	208.0	105.3	13.0	13.3	8.6	651.9
1980	260.1	197.0	91.8	15.4	14.8	13.6	592.7

SOURCES: U.S.D.A. Agricultural Statistics, Crop Reporting Board; *The Edible Nut Market, a Marketing and Economic Study.* The Morton Research Corporation, Merrick, New York. February-March, 1982.

walnuts, pecans, Brazil nuts, pistachios and macadamias. The total annual world production of these major tree nuts reaches usually about 1.5 billion pounds at the present time. Almonds (primarily from the United States) are first, with about 35 per cent of the total production; filberts (mostly from Turkey) are second, with some 30 per cent; and cashews (India is the leading producer) follow with about 14 per cent.

Geography plays a significant role in nut production, which occurs for the most part in warm and temperate climates. Brazil nuts, coconuts and cashews are grown in the tropics; almonds, filberts, macadamia nuts, peanuts, pistachios and Persian walnuts are produced in the subtropics and temperate zones. From the standpoint of world trade, the colder regions of the earth provide only minor nut production.

Tree nuts, produced domestically in the United States, are ranked as follows in the order of annual kernel-weight production: almonds, walnuts, pecans, filberts, macadamia nuts and pistachios. Almond production in California grew from less than fifty million pounds in 1960 to more than 400 million

pounds in 1981. The production of macadamias and pistachios has also notably increased. Macadamia nut production in Hawaii has risen more than twenty-fold during the past twenty-five years, while the output of pistachios in California has been expanded remarkably during the past decade.

The above table summarizes tree nut production in the United States between 1965 and 1980.

The per capita consumption of edible nuts in the United States, including peanuts and dessicated coconuts, during the period 1960-1979 is summarized in the table at the top of next page (U.S.D.A. Statistical Bulletin 656, February 1981).

As may be noted, on a per capita basis about three times more peanuts were consumed in 1979 than the combined production of all tree nuts, including coconuts. The largest per capita growth, however, took place in macadamia nuts. In 1909, the per capita consumption of tree nuts was 0.8 pounds, compared to 1.8 pounds in 1979; in the case of peanuts, it increased from 2.4 pounds per capita in 1909 to 7.1 pounds seventy years later. On the whole, in keeping with an increased em-

TREE NUTS, COCONUTS, AND PEANUTS:
Per capita consumption, 1960-79[1]

Year	Tree nuts (shelled basis)							Coconut (dessi- cated[3]	Peanuts (shelled basis)
	Almonds	Filberts	Pecans	Walnuts	Macadamia	Other[2]	Total		
				POUNDS					
1960	0.30	0.07	0.36	0.32	.004	0.52	1.6	0.61	4.9
1961	.28	.07	.44	.30	.006	.53	1.6	.64	4.9
1962	.27	.05	.27	.32	.008	.56	1.5	.66	4.9
1963	.27	.05	.45	.32	.010	.47	1.6	.72	5.0
1964	.30	.05	.43	.41	.012	.56	1.8	.62	5.3
1965	.31	.06	.52	.33	.013	.56	1.8	.67	5.6
1966	.33	.07	.41	.37	.013	.54	1.7	.55	5.5
1967	.30	.07	.40	.37	.012	.59	1.7	.56	5.7
1968	.33	.07	.39	.33	.016	.68	1.8	.70	5.8
1969	.30	.05	.42	.34	.015	.58	1.7	.44	5.9
1970	.34	.06	.37	.38	.020	.60	1.8	.57	5.9
1971	.37	.07	.38	.42	.021	.62	1.9	.57	5.9
1972	.37	.07	.38	.40	.019	.72	2.0	.48	6.2
1973	.26	.10	.36	.40	.017	.58	1.7	.49	6.6
1974	.27	.04	.35	.43	.023	.46	1.6	.45	6.4
1975	.36	.08	.34	.52	.026	.61	1.9	.45	6.5
1976	.43	.08	.30	.52	.027	.56	1.9	.48	6.3
1977	.46	.08	.31	.52	.027	.34	1.7	.50	6.4
1978	.41	.09	.36	.40	.029	.48	1.8	.50	6.9
1979	.45	.08	.30	.50	.033	.48	1.8	.50	7.1

[1]Crop year beginning July of year indicated for tree nuts except for filberts and walnuts which begin in August and peanuts which are on a September-August crop year.
[2]Includes Brazil, pignolia, pistachios, chestnuts, cashews, and miscellaneous.
[3]Based on imports beginning July of the year indicated. 1978 and 1979 estimated.

phasis on natural foods and nutrition, the consumption of both tree nuts and peanuts has grown steadily in the United States during the past fifty years.

In 1980, the ranking of edible nuts in this country, determined by per capita consumption, on a shelled basis, was as follows: (1) peanuts, 7.1 pounds; (2) walnuts, 0.52 pounds; (3) almonds, 0.46 pounds; (4) pecans, 0.31 pounds; and (5) filberts, 0.09 pounds.

As shown in the following summary, the pignolias and macadamia nuts are the most expensive edible nuts in the United States at the present time, while peanuts, sunflower seeds and watermelon seeds are among the cheapest. The approximate wholesale prices per pound, raw, on a shelled basis, in New York City in mid-June 1983 were as follows:

Edible nut	Dollars, U.S. Price per pound
ALMONDS, nonpareil, supreme	1.75
BRAZIL NUTS, unblanched, midget	1.65
CASHEW NUTS, 300/320	2.15
CHESTNUTS	1.65
COCONUTS, dried, desiccated	.65
FILBERTS, unblanched, regular Turkish	1.40
LITCHI NUTS	1.45
MACADAMIA NUTS	5.50
PEANUTS, Virginia	.65
PECANS	2.75
PIG NUTS	3.25
PINE NUTS, New Mexico piñones	4.25
PINE NUTS, Chinese	3.35

PINE NUTS, Spanish & Portuguese pignolias	5.75
PISTACHIO NUTS, roasted & salted	3.30
PUMPKIN SEEDS, hulled, Georgia	2.10
PUMPKIN SEEDS, hulled, Chinese	1.60
SESAME SEEDS, hulled	.85
SUNFLOWER SEEDS, hulled	.55
WALNUTS, Persian (California)	2.00
WALNUTS, Black	3.25
WATERMELON SEEDS	.50

SOURCES: Average of prices supplied through the courtesy of Mr. Wally Huggins of J.F. Braun & Sons, Inc., Lake Success, New York; and Mr. William P. Dignam of A.L. Bazzini Co. Inc., New York City.

Flavorful nuts are still looked upon as a snack item by most consumers. Very few people use them regularly as ingredients in cooking, except as garnishes. This is unfortunate, since the crunchiness and flavor of nuts enrich and add character to food. The recipes presented in this book will be of interest to those readers who might wish to make greater culinary use of nuts in a variety of appetizing dishes.

Few trees are more versatile and desirable than nut trees. In addition to providing edible, nourishing fruits, nut-producing species add beauty to housing projects, empty lots and drab landscapes, wherever they are planted. Let us hope that more lofty pecans, as majestic as elms, will be planted in the South and Southwest; more decorative macadamias, which resemble hollies, in Hawaii, California and Florida; more bush-like filberts for hedges and screen plantings, as well as utilitarian black walnuts, for timber and nuts, in the northern regions; and more spreading Persian walnuts as well as numerous other types of nut trees throughout the country. These nut trees could play a useful role in soil conservation by preventing erosion of the soil in vulnerable areas. Grafted nut trees of selected varieties should be planted, since most nuts, like orchard fruits, do not grow true to their variety when raised from seed. Many seedling nut trees never bear at all, while grafted or budded trees may reasonably be expected to produce annual harvests within a few years after planting—as well as to adorn and beautify the rural scene, townscape or cityscape. Young, grafted nut trees might be obtained through cooperation with government or state agricultural experiment stations or purchased from reliable tree nurseries. Once planted, the nut trees require little labor and expense. If conditions of famine should ever present themselves in this country, nuts could provide a valuable reserve supply of food.

PART I

Twelve Selected Edible Nuts

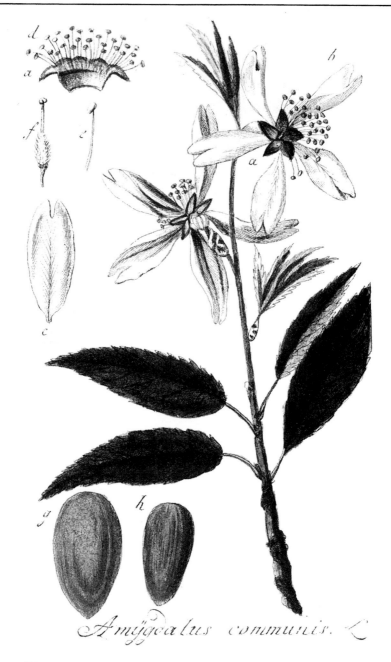

Amygdalus communis. L

ALMOND

CHAPTER ONE

Almonds
Family: Rosaceae

LATIN	*Prunus dulcis* (Mill.) D.A. Webb	ARABIC	Lōz
	Syn.: *Prunus amygdalus* Batsch	DUTCH	Amandel
	Amygdalus communis L.	ITALIAN	Mandorla
SPANISH	Almendra	PORTUGUESE	Amêndoa
FRENCH	Amande	RUSSIAN	Mindál'
GERMAN	Mandel	JAPANESE	Âmondo
SWEDISH	Mandel	CHINESE	Hsing Jen

THE ALMOND, *Prunus dulcis* (formerly called *Prunus amygdalus* and *Amygdalus communis*) is a graceful, medium-sized tree of the rose family—closely related to and resembling the peach, plum and apricot.

The peach-like almond fruit consists of the edible seed or kernel, the shell, and the outer hull. At maturity the hull splits open. When dry it may be readily separated from the shell.

The sweet, luscious outer flesh of the peach is eaten and the pit containing the seed thrown away, while the almond pit is kept and the thin, fibrous outer flesh is discarded. The almond pit, containing a kernel or edible seed, is the nut of commerce.

The bushy, round-crowned almond tree normally attains a height of twenty to thirty feet. The wood is harder than that of the peach, and the almond tree lives longer. The bark is dark gray, the branches are spreading, and the borders of the lance-shaped leaves are finely toothed.

Almonds may be grouped into two principal types: sweet almonds and bitter almonds. There are also some intermediate types. The sweet almond is grown for its edible nuts. Bit-ter almonds provide the main source of oil of bitter almond, which is used both as a flavoring and as an ingredient in cosmetic skin preparations. The bitterness in the bitter almond is due to the presence of the glycoside *amygdalin*, which readily hydrolyzes or breaks down to produce a cyanide. During extraction of the oil of bitter almond, the cyanide, also known as prussic acid, is eliminated so that the oil may safely be used for flavoring. While sweet almonds are nourishing and healthful, bitter almonds may cause cyanide poisoning when ingested. The danger of eating bitter almonds should be emphasized: it has been estimated that fifty to seventy bitter almonds with a high *amygdalin* content might constitute a lethal dose for adults if consumed at one sitting. Fortunately, the unpleasant taste of bitter almonds is usually adequate protection against an overdose.

Of obscure origin, the almond is presumed to be native to temperate, desert parts of western Asia. Gradually, it spread westward to the warm, dry regions of the Mediterranean basin. In addition to the cultivated almond, *P. dulcis*, more than thirty wild or mi-

ALMOND

nor almond species have been described. Some botanists believe that the cultivated almond is not a natural species but a hybrid of prehistoric origin, descended from several of the wild almond species found today in the warmer parts of western Asia. In Europe, the domesticated almond has been found in Bronze Age sites in Greece and Cyprus.

There are numerous biblical references to the almond. By about 1700 B. C. it was common in Palestine. In the Book of Genesis 43:11 the patriarch Israel commanded his sons to carry into Egypt gifts from Palestine, which included almonds: "And their father Israel said unto them, if it must be so now, do this; take of the best fruits in the land in your vessels, and carry down the man a present, a little balm, and a little honey, spices, and myrrh, nuts and *almonds.*"

In Numbers 17:8, there is an early reference to the fast-sprouting characteristic of almond branches. After the Exodus, the rods of the princes of Israel were placed in the Tabernacle; of the twelve staffs, only one sprouted and it was the almond: ". . . and, behold, the rod of Aaron for the house of Levi was budded, and brought forth buds, and

THE ALMOND ROD OF AARON BLOSSOMING ON THE TABERNACLE

bloomed blossoms, and yielded *almonds.*" Almond branches are still known for the quickness with which they prematurely bloom when placed in water in a warm place. In Biblical times the Hebrews looked upon the almond tree as a symbol of haste because of its sudden blossoming.

In Greek mythology, Phyllis, a beautiful Thracian queen, died of grief and was transformed into an almond tree, called *Phylla* by the Greeks. The almond was mentioned in the writings of the Greek naturalist Theophrastus about 300 B.C. In his treatises on the history of plants he called it *amugdalai.* Later when the plant was introduced to Italy, Marcus Porcius Cato referred to almonds as the "Greek nut" in his writings on agriculture about 200 B.C. Presumably the almond had been introduced to Italy from the Greek islands. Scribonius Largus named bitter almonds "Amygdali amari" in the first century A.D.

Plant remains of seeds, grains, fruits and nuts, carbonized by the intense heat of the eruption of Mount Vesuvius in 79 A.D., furnish valuable historic evidence of the staple foods utilized by the Campanians in Italy during the first century. These carbonized materials were recovered and identified in recent years by Frederick G. Meyer and Wilhelmina F. Jashemski from the archaeological sites of Pompeii and Herculaneum. They include almonds, filberts, chestnuts and walnuts

CARBONIZED ALMOND REMAINS

Found at Herculaneum, this plant material had been destroyed by the eruption of Mount Vesuvius in A.D. 79.

GREEK ALMOND-SHAPED VASE, 4TH CENTURY B.C.

From the Attica (Athens) region. This decorative vase may have contained some sort of juice, possibly olive oil or an almond extract.

among the edible nuts; other plant remains have been found of onions, garlic, figs, olives, dates, millet, oats, chickpeas, lentils, pears and grapes.

The Mohammedans associated almond flowers with hope, since the blossoms appear on bare branches.

As early as 716 A.D., almonds had been introduced to Northern Europe, and mentioned together with spices and other groceries in a charter granted to a monastery in Normandy by Chilperic II, King of France. In 812, Charlemagne ordered almond trees to be planted on the imperial farms.

By the fourteenth century, almonds were produced on the islands of the Greek Archipelago, and had become an important commodity of the Venetian trade to Alexandria. In 1411, the Knights Templar levied tithes in Cyprus on almonds, honey and sesame seed.

Almonds were popular in England, where they had been introduced by the Romans at an early date. Among the recipes in the *Form*

5

of Cury, a fourteeenth century cookbook written by the master chefs of King Richard III, mention is made of "Creme of Almand, Grewel of Almand, Cawdel of Almand Mylke," and others. The consumption of almonds in French medieval cookery was substantial. An inventory of the household goods of the queen of France in 1372 listed only 20 pounds of sugar—but included 500 pounds of almonds.

Almonds were popular, and inexpensive, in England too: the average price between 1259 and 1350 was 2 pence per pound. Between 1351 and 1400 it rose to only 3 1/8 pence per pound, hardly an inflationary quotation.

The word "almond" came to the English language from the French *amande,* which had come from the Greek *amugdalai* and Latin *amygdalus.* In practice, its precise spelling has varied widely. Alexander Neckam, an English scholar of the early thirteenth century, wrote of "Noyz de l'almande, nux Phyllidis." Chaucer, in fourteenth-century England, referred to the almond as *almandre.* Edmund Spenser in the *Faerie Queene* (1590), i. 7, 32, praised the almond:

> *"Like to an Almond tree ymounted hye*
> *On top of greene Selinis all alone*
> *With blossoms brave bedecked daintily."*

In Elizabethan England, "An almond for a parrot" was a popular proverb in which the almond was considered to be a mouth-watering temptation: thus, in Shakespeare's *Troilus and Cressida,* Act V, Scene 2, Thersites says, "The parrot will not do more for an Almond."

The almond tree played a key role in the legend of Tannhäuser, whose trials were made famous by Richard Wagner's 1845 opera. Tannhäuser, a thirteenth-century German lyric poet, or *Minnesinger,* was in disgrace with the Pope, who informed him that he was as likely to have his sins forgiven as the Pope's staff was likely to bloom. In Tannhäuser's absence, the almond wood staff blossomed. But the *Minnesinger* died before his pardon arrived.

During the Middle Ages, the almond rod became the wand of choice among professional magicians during the performance of their hocus-pocus. In Tuscany, forked almond sticks were used as divining rods for dowsing, to locate water underground, or even buried treasure.

Almonds have symbolized good luck for many centuries in southern Europe: traditionally, candied almond nuts are given away at weddings in Greece as tokens of long life and happiness. In Spain, glistening, ceremonial "Jordan" almonds from Malaga are usually sugar-coated. "Jordan" refers to a renowned Spanish almond variety, the name of

ALMONDS
1493

which is probably a corruption of the French word for garden—*jardin.*

John Gerard, publisher of a famous herbal (1597), observed that "five or six (almonds) being taken fasting do keepe a man from being drunke." This recommendation may have been the forerunner of the cocktail nut of today.

In the seventeenth century, Ninon de Lenclos, a French woman of fashion, recommended an almond-based cold cream which was said to have preserved her beauty and kept her face free of wrinkles until she was seventy. The *Ninon de Lenclos Ointment* contained four ounces oil of almonds, three ounces of hog's lard and one ounce of spermaceti (a yellowish, waxy solid obtained from sperm whale oil). After leek juice had been added, the ingredients were melted, stirred until cool and scented with rose water. Almond oil is still used today as a base for cosmetics employed in theatrical makeup.

During the four centuries following the death of Mohammed in 632, his followers developed a flourishing civilization. The great empire of the Prophet extended some seven thousand miles—from Spain in the west to the Chinese border in the east. When the Arabs conquered Persia they acquired a taste for almonds. In tenth century Baghdad, for example, a popular entree was *harisa,* a meat and vegetable stew served with a sauce thickened with powdered almonds.

When the trade routes to the East were reopened during the Crusades in the eleventh through thirteenth centuries, the Crusaders brought back to western Europe exotic Arab cooking techniques, some of which caused basic changes in European eating habits. The Europeans not only acquired a taste for spices, but also for other appetizing features of Arab cuisine such as creamy almond sauces and almond-based confections like nougat and marzipan (sweetmeats made with ground almonds stirred into a sugar paste).

Following the Arab conquests, the cultivation of almonds gradually spread from Greece and Italy to North Africa, Spain, Portugal and

ALMOND BRANCH WITH FRUITS

France. From medieval times to the eighteenth century, nuts became a major source of substitute "milk." First almonds and walnuts were blanched, that is, the thin skin ("pellicle") was removed with hot water or steam. The nuts were then pulverized and soaked in water to provide a staple "milky" beverage.

The first plantings of edible almonds in North America were made in the Spanish missions between San Diego and Santa Barbara, California, in the latter part of the eighteenth century. The damp, coastal fogs and moist conditions were unsuitable however,

7

Nonpareil almond in full bloom in California during February. The blossoms are five-petaled, similar to peach blossoms. The almond flowers are cross-pollinated by bees.

and these plantings were abandoned. Efforts were made to grow almonds in New England and the Middle Atlantic states in the early nineteenth century. These plantings also failed because the early-blooming characteristic of the almonds made the trees vulnerable to damage from spring frosts. Milder Mediterranean types of climatic conditions proved more suitable for almond cultivation.

During the 1850's almonds were introduced to California with nursery stock from New York. It gradually became apparent that selected areas of north-central California—those free from coastal fogs and spring frosts—would be suitable for commercial almond production. Today ninety-nine percent of the almonds grown in the United States come from a 400-mile long stretch of land in California extending north from Bakersfield to Red Bluff. About 420,000 acres have been

ALMOND ORCHARD IN FLOWER, KERN COUNTY, CALIFORNIA

The pipe sprinkler irrigation system is used five or six times in the summer. It is also useful in the winter for frost protection, and can be used to apply liquid fertilizer.

NONPAREIL

Over 50% of California almonds are of the Nonpareil variety. The almond is shown in shell, in cross-section, and shelled.

important exporter, accounting for over half of the world's almond production.

Because of genetic differences within the seeds, almond trees grown from seed do not reproduce true to variety. Therefore, in California, almonds are propagated asexually by budding or grafting scion material of the most desirable varieties onto rugged rootstock seedlings. Apricot roots, plum roots, peach roots, almond roots and almond-peach hybrid roots have been tried. Now, for the most part, orchardists favor peach rootstocks for irrigated orchards. Peach seedlings of the Lovell variety, or nematode-resistant peach stocks such as Nemaguard are widely employed. Almond seedlings from special sources are also used.

In field plantings, almond trees are usually spaced twenty-four to thirty feet apart. Branches are trained and pruned to shape the trees for efficient bearing, to avoid crowding and competition, and to allow space for the orchard equipment to pass under the branches.

planted with almonds by over 7,000 individual growers. The most favorable growing conditions exist in the Sacramento and San Joaquin Valleys. Almonds represent California's most important tree crop in terms of acreage, dollar value and world distribution. Years ago, all of the United States almond supplies were imported from Europe. Today California supplies the entire needs of the domestic market, and has become a most

One of the best-known almond varieties produced in Europe is the Jordan almond, which has not been grown successfully in California. However, several superior almond cultivars (i.e. clones or varieties) have been developed in California. The most im-

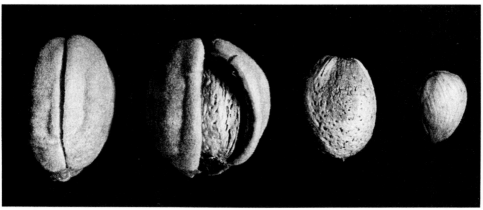

MISSION ALMOND

portant is the Nonpareil, which accounts for over fifty per cent of the total California production. This variety was first selected by A. T. Hatch in Suisun, California, in the early 1880's. Its shells are paper thin and soft. The next most important cultivar in California is the Mission, with a harder shell and a slightly bitter flavor.

Other major California almond varieties include: Merced, Carmel, Ne Plus Ultra, Thompson and Peerless. These seven cultivars account for roughly ninety percent of the almond acreage in California, where the average yield per acre is about 1,800 pounds of in-shell almonds.

Spanish almond acreage is over three times that of California, but Spanish production is less than one half that of California. For the most part, Spain's almonds are produced on thousands of small, marginal farms located adjacent to the Mediterranean Sea. The

soil is generally poor in this Spanish dry land farming which relies on natural rainfall. The bulk of the Spanish commercial almond crop consists of hard-shell almonds of the Valencia and Majorca classes. These Spanish varieties, with hard and relatively thick shells, have a very low shelling rate compared to the best

BEE HIVES IN SOUTH AUSTRALIA

The honeybee is the most important insect pollinator of almonds. Hives are brought to the orchard during the flowering period.

10

California varieties. For example, the shelling percentage of the California Nonpareil almond may be 60 to 70 per cent, while the typical Spanish almond may have a shelling percentage of only about 25. This means that 60 to 70 per cent of the weight of the average Nonpareil in-shell almond will be kernel and 30 to 40 per cent of the weight will be shell. On the other hand, in the Spanish almond, the kernel may represent only 25 per cent of the in-shell weight, while the shell amounts to 75 per cent. Furthermore, production per tree is generally smaller in Spain than in California. The shelling percentage for Spanish almonds is comparable to the rate in other Mediterranean countries, including Italy and Portugal.

Flowers of most almond varieties are "genetically self-incompatible"; in order to obtain satisfactory pollination and fertilization it is necessary to interplant two or more cross-compatible cultivars that bloom at about the same time. Commercial almond orchards in California usually have one row of the pollinizing cultivar (such as Merced or Carmel) for every two rows of the main, most desirable variety (such as Nonpareil). The sticky, heavy pollen is carried and principally transferred by honey bees. Growers bring bees to their orchards in February when the almond trees begin to bloom. The honey bee industry is an essential part of almond production.

Almonds do not prosper in the tropics. Humidity is high and there is lack of sufficient chilling to break the rest period of the buds. Moist weather during ripening may cause mold to develop on the shells and rancidity in the kernels.

Almond trees in California generally begin to bear at three to four years and enter into heavy production in about seven to eight years. Almonds respond favorably to fertilizing. Nitrogen is particularly effective when applied at the rate of two to four pounds per tree.

Almonds are subject to several diseases which adversely affect the yield and quality of the crop, and which may eventually weaken and kill the trees. Among the most common diseases are: "brown rot," which attacks the blossoms and spreads into the spurs and shoots; "shothole," a fungus disease which attacks flower buds, blossoms, young fruits and leaves; bacterial canker or "blast," a bacterium which attacks during flowering and kills both buds and blossoms; "crown rot" and "crown gall;" and *"Poria* wood rot." Almonds occasionally suffer from a genetic disorder in which vegetative buds are damaged by high summer temperatures which can cause "bud failure." Since 1974, almond growers have had to contend with another threatening disease known as almond leaf scorch or "golden death," a serious leaf disorder similar to Pierce's disease in grapes. The bacterium of both is spread by several species of leaf hoppers.

A constant program of disease and pest control is essential for almond growers in California. Fungicides are important to control the above-mentioned diseases. Selected, healthy scion wood should be utilized for propagation to reduce the spread of a disorder called "noninfectious bud failure" or "crazy top." Selected insecticides may be employed to control navel orange worms, peach twig borers, "San José scale" and various mites.

Irrigation is a necessary and important cultural practice. Unirrigated almond orchards are rare in California. If the field is level, flood or furrow irrigation may be desirable; otherwise, a sprinkler system is recommended.

As almond fruits approach maturity, the hulls begin to dehisce or split open. The nuts are usually harvested mechanically: a mechanical knocker shakes the trees, causing the nuts to fall to the ground. Mechanical sweepers place the nuts in windrows. They are then gathered by pick-up machines and transported to hullers to remove the leathery outer cover or hull. (The hulls are utilized as feed for livestock.) Drying of the nuts then takes place, which should reduce the moisture content to less than eight per cent. For long storage periods, the nuts should be fumigated

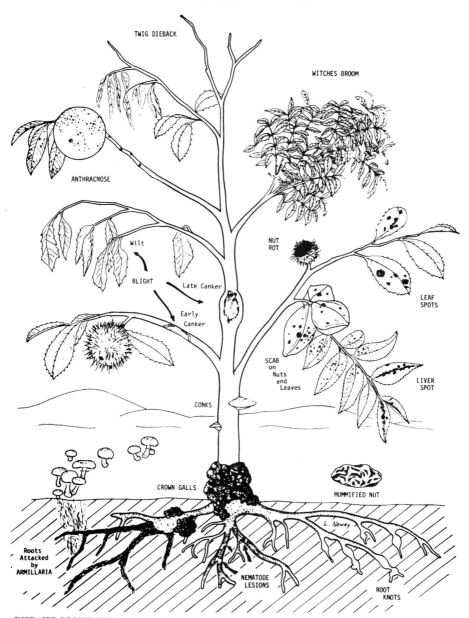

DISEASES OF NUT TREES

Plant diseases cause huge economic losses to nut growers. The causative fungi and bacteria can usually be controlled through sanitation, fungicides and bactericides. Planting resistant cultivars is also recommended. Some of the most common disease symptoms may be noted above.

12

MECHANICAL HARVEST OF ALMONDS

Shakers are attached to the primary limbs of the trees, knocking the ripe almonds to the ground—ready for collection and delivery to the hulling machines.

and kept at a temperature of less than 40 degrees Fahrenheit; otherwise, severe worm infestation may occur.

The almond crop is subsequently delivered to a packing company to be shelled, processed and packaged. The largest facilities are located at the California Almond Growers Exchange in Sacramento, a grower-owned co-operative which processes and packages almond products under the Blue Diamond label. Five thousand five hundred grower-members belong to this organization, which has been in continuous operation since 1910.

Many independent companies are also in the business of processing almonds. Of these the most important is Tenneco West, which now handles more than half of the independent tonnage, packaging its almonds under the Sun Giant label at three California plants. The almond processing activities of Tenneco West and its predecessor companies date back to the mid 1930's.

At the processing plant, the nuts are passed through cracking machines where the kernels are separated from the shells. The shells are removed by air and gravity separa-

13

tors. They are then usually sold for conversion into charcoal briquets, or used as roughage for cattle feed. At the California Almond Growers main plant in Sacramento, all shells are now conveyed directly from the shelling machines to an adjacent co-generation plant where they are burned to produce electricity. Some of this energy powers the almond processing plant. The rest is sold to the local utility—enough to supply 20,000 private homes in the area. Broken, discolored or chipped kernels are diverted for other uses, while the top quality kernels are cleaned, sorted by an electric eye, separated according to size and finally manually inspected. Chocolate bar manufacturers prefer small almond kernels, while salters require larger nuts. Salters are companies which process shelled nuts by roasting them in oil, or dry-roasting them, and then applying salt or other seasonings.

Tenneco West has recently pioneered a major advancement in almond sorting at its Bakersfield plants. New Scanray Lonescan sorting machines have been installed which scan a continuous flow of almonds. This application by Tenneco West's engineers may prove to be of considerable significance to the entire food processing industry because it permits the detection and elimination of rocks and other foreign matter which were previously virtually nondetectable.

Shelled almonds are sold according to cultivars, sizes (kernels per ounce), and grades (principally; whole, blanched, unblanched, and select sheller run). Approximately ninety-eight percent of the almond crop is sold shelled, and only two percent in the shell. Shelled almonds may be sold as whole natural almonds or be processed into various almond forms. The whole natural almonds have had their shells removed but still retain their brown skins; blanched whole almonds have had both their shells and skins removed. Other popular almond forms include sliced natural, chopped natural and blanched slivered. Almond butter and almond powder are new products developed by the California Almond Growers Exchange.

The latter is produced from blanched almonds that have been ground and spray dried to a fine powder granulation which contains the natural oxidation inhibitor, Vitamin E. It can be utilized in almond macaroon powder, almond marzipan powder, almond paste powder and almond drink powder (which is mixed in milk). Almond butter has been described by the industry as "a delightful new taste experience which offers a worthy alternative to peanut butter." Further processing produces other types, such as roasted and spiced almonds. Kernels are dry roasted, or roasted by being cooked in oil (usually almond oil) and then salted and seasoned.

The tender kernels of young almonds, picked from the tree before they are mature, are a traditional delicacy in Middle Eastern food markets.

Almonds are the most important and the most versatile of all tree nuts; they enjoy as well the largest share of the world tree nut trade. During the crop year 1982, total world almond production was estimated at about 573 million pounds, of which the United States (California) produced roughly 331 million pounds; followed by Spain with 137 million pounds, and Italy with 40 million pounds. Other almond-producing countries include Portugal, Iran, Morocco, Turkey, Greece, Algeria, China, Afghanistan, Cyprus, France, Tunisia and Yugoslavia.

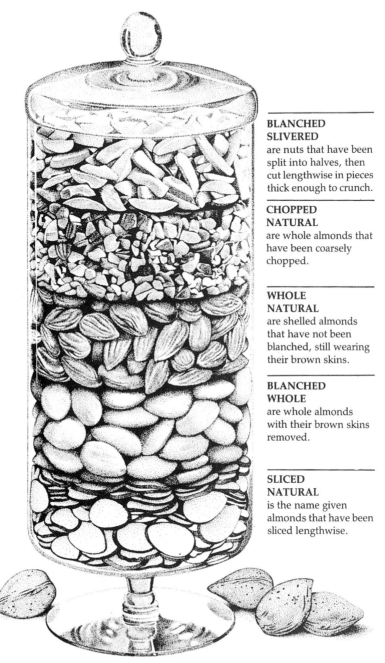

**BLANCHED
SLIVERED**
are nuts that have been
split into halves, then
cut lengthwise in pieces
thick enough to crunch.

**CHOPPED
NATURAL**
are whole almonds that
have been coarsely
chopped.

**WHOLE
NATURAL**
are shelled almonds
that have not been
blanched, still wearing
their brown skins.

**BLANCHED
WHOLE**
are whole almonds
with their brown skins
removed.

**SLICED
NATURAL**
is the name given
almonds that have been
sliced lengthwise.

FIVE FORMS OF CALIFORNIA ALMONDS

To Store Almonds (I)

To assure freshness of shelled almonds, place them in tightly sealed containers in the central portion of your refrigerator. Almonds, or almond paste, stored this way, will stay fresh for months.

To Toast Almonds (I)

Spread in single layer in shallow pan. Bake, stirring often, in 300° F (150° C) oven 15 minutes, or until they begin to turn color. *Don't wait for them to become golden brown.* After removing the almonds from the oven, their residual heat will continue to toast them slightly.

To Roast Almonds (I)

Spread about 1/2 teaspoon (2.5 ml) margarine, butter, peanut or vegetable oil over surface of shallow pan. Add almonds in a single layer. Roast, stirring often, at 300°F (150°C) for about 15 minutes, or until they begin to turn color.

Almond Arithmetic (I)

1 cup (1/4 l) sliced almonds weighs 3-1/4 oz (91 g).
1 cup (1/4 l) slivered almonds weighs 4-1/2 oz (126 g).
1 cup (1/4 l) whole almonds, shelled, weighs approximately 5 ounces (142 g).

1 cup (1/4 l) (5 oz, 142 g) blanched whole almonds will yield 1-1/4 cups (1/3 l) when ground in blender, 1-3/4 cups (420 ml) when ground in a nut/cheese grater, 1 cup + 3 tablespoons (285 ml) when ground in a food chopper.

Note: Amandine, Almondine, aux Amandes? Essentially, each means the same thing: the dish is made or garnished with almonds. The world *Almondine* is a U.S. adaptation of the French word *amandine* that has been used with increasing frequency during the last twenty years or so. (IV)

HORS D'OEUVRE

Almond Cheese Pine Cone (I)

2 packages (8 oz/224 g *each*) cream cheese, softened
2 jars (5 oz/140 g *each*) pasteurized process cheese spread with pimiento
1/2 pound (224 g) blue cheese, crumbled
1/4 cup (60 ml) minced green onion
1/2 teaspoon (2.5 ml) Worcestershire sauce
2 cups (500 ml) blanched whole almonds, toasted
Pine sprigs for garnish
Crackers

In large bowl with mixer at medium speed, beat cream cheese, cheese spread with pimiento and blue cheese until smooth. With spoon, stir in green onions and Worcestershire sauce. Cover and refrigerate about one hour. On work surface, with hands, shape cheese mixture into shape of large pine cone: Arrange on wooden board. Beginning at narrow end of cone, carefully press almonds about 1/4 inch (6 mm) deep into cheese mixture in rows, making sure that pointed end of each almond extends at a slight angle. Continue pressing almonds into cheese mixture in rows, with rows slightly overlapping, until all cheese is covered. Garnish pine cone with pine sprigs. Serve with crackers.

Yield: About 25 servings

ALMOND CHEESE
PINECONE

SOUP

Sopa de Almendras con Jerez (Almond Soup
with Sherry)

2 tablespoons (30 ml)
  butter or margarine
2 tablespoons (30 ml)
  flour
2 tablespoons (30 ml)
  finely chopped
  onion
3 cups (750 ml) chicken
  broth
1-1/2 cups (375 ml) fine-
  ly ground almonds
1/4 teaspoon (1.5 ml)
  mace or nutmeg
1/4 teaspoon (1.5 ml)
  dry mustard
Dash cayenne pepper

1/4 teaspoon (1.5 ml)
  paprika
1/4 teaspoon (1.5 ml)
  basil
1 teaspoon (5 ml) sugar
1/2 small garlic clove,
  peeled and finely
  minced
1/4 teaspoon (1.5 ml)
  salt
1 cup (250 ml) whipping
  cream
2 tablespoons (30 ml)
  medium-sweet
  sherry.

In heavy saucepan melt butter: blend in flour
to form a smooth paste. Add onions and simmer gently for 2 minutes. Gradually add
chicken broth; blend well. Cook over medium
heat, stirring constantly, until sauce begins to
boil and thickens. Stir in almonds, mace,
mustard, paprika, basil and sugar; simmer
gently for 20 minutes. Add garlic, salt and
cayenne. Remove from heat and gradually
blend in cream. Return to heat and warm but
do not boil. Stir in sherry and serve immediately. Garnish each bowl with toasted slivered
almonds if desired.

Yield: 6 servings

17

MAIN DISHES

Green Chili Steak (III)

2 dozen fresh mush-rooms, sliced	1/2 pound (225 g) package egg noodles
1/4 cup (60 ml) butter	4 tablespoons (60 ml) flour
one 4-ounce (120 g) can green chilis	3/4 cup (175 ml) white wine
1/2 onion, chopped	1 tablespoon (15 ml) sugar
1/2 teaspoon (2.5 ml) sage	1 cup (250 ml) water
1/2 teaspoon (2.5 ml) pepper	1/2 cup (125 ml) whole blanched almonds
Garlic salt	
1 flank steak (about 1-1/2 pounds/675 g)	

Cut mushrooms in 1/8" (3 mm) slices. Sauté lightly in about 2 tablespoons butter and set aside. After removing seeds, cut chilis into 1/8" (3 mm) slices; add to mushrooms uncooked. Slice onion into 1/8" (3 mm) slices and add to chilis and mushrooms.

Thinly slice flank steak across grain diagonally. Heat remaining butter in a large frying pan. Put in meat; season with sage, pepper, garlic salt, and salt to taste. Fry quickly just until browned, about 1 minute each side. Remove from pan and keep warm. Put noodles in boiling salted water, cook until tender.

Blend flour with mixture of wine, sugar, and water; pour into the frying pan and stir until smooth. Add mushrooms, chilis, and onions and cook, stirring until sauce is slightly thick. Add steak and almonds, and cook until just heated through, about 2 minutes.

Pour mixture over drained noodles and serve with a tossed green salad.

Yield: 6 servings

Poulet Farci Bon Vivant (IV)

1 cup (250 ml) sliced blanched almonds, crushed	1/3 cup (75 ml) raisins marinated in 1 ounce (30 ml) Cognac and 1 ounce (30 ml) dry white wine
1 small onion, chopped very fine	
3 chicken livers, chopped very fine	
4 medium fresh mush-rooms, chopped very fine	Salt and pepper
	Two double chicken breasts, boned (8 oz/225 grams *each*, after boning)
1 tablespoon (15 ml) parsley, minced	1/4 pound (112 g) butter, melted
1 tablespoon (15 ml) chives, minced	1-1/2 cups (375 ml) Supreme Sauce
1 egg	1/2 cup (125 ml) sliced blanched almonds, lightly roasted
3 tablespoons (45 ml) cream	
Apple, pared, diced	

Sauté crushed almonds in butter-coated pan, stirring until lightly roasted. In another pan, sauté onion until lightly browned. Add chicken livers, mushrooms, parsley and chives. Stir over high heat for a few minutes. Turn off heat. In a small bowl, mix egg with cream. Stir into chicken liver mixture. Mix in almonds, marinated raisins (drained, with the marinade reserved) and diced apple. Season to taste with salt and pepper. Cool partially, then chill.

Lay chicken breasts out flat. Place chilled stuffing on each breast. Roll each breast around stuffing. Place seam side down in roasting pan. Bake 5 minutes at 450° F (235° C); reduce heat to 325° F (165° C) and bake 25 minutes longer, basting occasionally.

Flavor Supreme Sauce with raisin marinade to taste. Spoon flavored sauce over chicken, garnish with roasted sliced almonds and sprinkle with a little additional minced parsley.

Supreme Sauce
Make a delicate white sauce with butter, flour, chicken stock and cream.

Yield: 4 servings

Baked Seafood Casserole (II)

1 pound (450 g) cooked
  crabmeat, flaked
2 cans (4-1/2 oz/135 g
  each) shrimp,
  drained
1 cup (250 ml) mayon-
  naise or salad
  dressing
1/2 cup (125 ml) (one
  medium) chopped
  onion
1 cup (250 ml) sliced
  mushrooms
2 teaspoons (10 ml)
  Worcestershire
  sauce
1 teaspoon (5 ml) salt
1/2 teaspoon (2.5 ml)
  paprika

one 8-1/2 ounce (238 g)
  can water chest-
  nuts, drained and
  sliced
2 cups (500 ml) (4 medi-
  um stalks) diced
  celery
1 cup (250 ml) (1 medi-
  um) chopped
  green pepper
3/4 cup (175 ml)
  blanched slivered
  almonds, toasted
2 cups (500 ml) buttered
  croutons
2 cups (500 ml)
  shredded Cheddar
  cheese

Heat oven to 375° F (190° C). Combine first 12 ingredients in large bowl. Arrange 1 cup croutons in greased 13 × 9-inch (32.5 × 22.5 cm) baking dish. Top with half of seafood mixture, 1 cup (250 ml) cheese, 1/2 cup (125 ml) almonds and remaining croutons. Repeat layering with remaining seafood mixture, cheese and almonds. Bake for 30 minutes.

Yield: 10 servings

SALAD

Bean Sprout and Almond Salad (III)

2 cups (500 ml) fresh
  bean sprouts
1/2 cup (125 ml)
  chopped natural
  almonds
1-1/2 cups (375 ml) juli-
  enned cooked ham

1 head of lettuce, rinsed
  and torn
2 tomatoes, chopped
2 green onions,
  chopped

Dressing

1/3 cup (75 ml) salad oil
2 tablespoons (30 ml)
  red wine vinegar
1 tablespoon (15 ml)
  lemon juice

3 to 4 teaspoons (15 to
  20 ml) sugar
Salt and pepper to taste

Blanch bean sprouts in boiling water for 1-1/2 to 2 minutes. Drain and cool. Combine with rest of salad ingredients. Combine ingredients for dressing. Pour over salad and toss well.

Yield: 6 to 8 servings

VEGETABLES

Brussels Sprouts Royale (II)

one 10-ounce (300 g)
  package baby
  Brussels sprouts,
  frozen in butter
  sauce
1/2 cup (125 ml)
  seedless green
  grapes

2 tablespoons (30 ml)
  Sauterne
2 tablespoons (30 ml)
  blanched slivered
  almonds

Cook Brussels sprouts according to package directions. Partially open pouch; drain butter sauce into small saucepan. Add grapes. Cook only enough to heat through. Remove from heat; add Sauterne and almonds. Toss with Brussels sprouts.

Yield: 3 to 4 servings

Potatoes Almandine (II)

1 lb. (450 g) potatoes
3 egg yolks
2 tablespoons (30 ml)
  minced onions
Salt and white pepper
2 whole eggs
2 tablespoons (30 ml)
  cold water

2 tablespoons (30 ml) oil
1/4 teaspoon (1.5 ml)
  salt
1 cup (250 ml) finely
  chopped almonds

Peel potatoes; boil in lightly salted water until tender; drain. Mash potatoes. Add egg yolks and onion and whip until fluffy. Salt and pepper to taste. Combine whole eggs, water, oil and salt; beat well. Drop potato mixture by rounded heaping tablespoonsful into egg mixture. Roll potato balls in almonds, coating evenly. Heat 2 inches (5 cm) of oil in large heavy saucepan or deep fat fryer. Fry a few at a time in deep, hot fat (350° F/175° C) 5 to 6 minutes or until golden brown. Sprinkle with additional salt and pepper. Serve very warm.

Yield: 4 servings

Almond Asparagus (I)

1 pound (450 g) asparagus	1/2 cup (125 ml) blanched slivered almonds, toasted
2 tablespoons (30 ml) butter or margarine	Salt and pepper
1 tablespoon (15 ml) lemon juice	

Wash asparagus, cut into 1-inch (2.5 cm), diagonal slices. Heat butter in skillet; add asparagus and sauté 3 to 4 minutes. Cover skillet and steam about 2 minutes, or until tender-crisp. Toss asparagus with lemon juice and almonds; salt and pepper to taste.

Yield: 4 servings

DESSERT

Lemon Cream in Almond Meringue (I)

Almond Meringue Shell

3 egg whites	1 cup (250 ml) blanched slivered almonds, finely chopped
1 cup (250 ml) granulated sugar	

Combine egg whites and sugar on top of double boiler; beat over hot, not boiling, water until stiff peaks form. Remove from heat; fold in almonds and spoon into heavily greased and floured 9-inch (22.5-cm) pie plate; smooth with spatula. Bake in 275° F (135° C) oven for 1 hour. Cool.

Lemon Cream

4 egg yolks	Finely grated peel of 1 lemon
1/2 cup (125 ml) granulated sugar	1 cup (250 ml) whipping cream
1/4 cup (60 ml) lemon juice, freshly squeezed	

In top of double boiler beat egg yolks; add sugar and lemon juice and continue beating until well blended. Add peel and cook, stirring, over hot, not boiling water, until mixture thickens. Cool. Whip cream until stiff; fold into cooled lemon mixture. Pour into cooled meringue shell. Refrigerate at least 1 hour.

Yield: 6 to 8 servings

BAKED GOODS

Danish Almond Apple Bars (III)

2-1/2 cups (625 ml) sifted flour	5 to 6 tart apples, pared and sliced
1 teaspoon (5 ml) salt	3/4 to 1 cup (175 to 250 ml) sugar
1 cup (250 ml) shortening	1 teaspoon (5 ml) cinnamon
1 egg, separated	
Milk	
1 cup (250 ml) sliced natural almonds	

In a medium bowl combine flour and salt. Cut in shortening. Beat egg yolk in a measuring cup. Add enough milk to make 2/3 cup (150 ml) liquid; mix well. Stir egg mixture into flour mixture to make a stiff dough. On a floured surface, roll half the dough into a 17-inch by 12-inch (42.5-× 30-cm) rectangle. Line a 15-1/2-inch × 10-1/2-inch × 1-inch (38-× 26-× 2.5-cm) baking pan with rolled pastry. Sprinkle about 1/2 cup (125 ml) sliced almonds over dough. Toss sliced apples with 3 tablespoons (45 ml) flour and arrange apples over almonds. Combine sugar and cinnamon—sprinkle over apples. Beat egg white lightly and brush on top of pastry. Bake at 350° F (175° C) for 35 to 40 minutes. Remove and brush on more egg white and sprinkle on remaining 1/2 cup (125 ml) almonds. Finish baking 5 more minutes till almonds are toasted. While warm, drizzle with powdered sugar glaze. Cut into bars.

Yield: 3 dozen bars

Swiss Peach Pie (III)

Crust

1-1/2 cups (375 ml) sifted flour	1/4 teaspoon (1 ml) salt
1/3 cup (75 ml) sugar	1/2 cup (125 ml) butter
1/2 teaspoon (2.5 ml) baking powder	1 egg

Sift together flour, sugar, baking powder and salt. Cut in the butter, add slightly beaten egg and stir until dough clings together. Press dough into bottom and sides of an ungreased 10-inch (25-cm) pie pan or 9 × 9 × 2-inch (23 × 23 × 5-cm) pan. Bake at 375° F (195° C) for 25 to 30 minutes, until deep golden brown.

Filling

1 tablespoon (15 ml) lemon juice	1/2 cup (125 ml) sugar
3 cups (750 ml) fresh peaches, peeled and sliced	1/4 cup (60 ml) flour

Sprinkle lemon juice over peeled, sliced peaches. Combine sugar and flour and add to peaches. Cook over low heat, stirring occasionally, until sauce is slightly thickened. Spread in bottom of pie shell.

Topping

2 eggs, separated	1 tablespoon (15 ml) milk
1/3 cup (75 ml) sugar	1 cup (250 ml) blanched almonds, ground
1 tablespoon (15 ml) lemon rind, grated	1/2 cup (125 ml) blanched almond slivers
1/4 teaspoon (1 ml) salt	
1/2 cup (125 ml) sour cream	

Beat egg whites to stiff peaks, set aside. Combine egg yolks, sugar, grated lemon rind and salt. Beat until thick. Blend sour cream, thinned with milk, and ground almonds. Fold in egg whites. Spread on top of peach mixture. Sprinkle with slivered almonds. Bake at 375° F (195° C) for 25 to 30 minutes, until deep golden brown.

Yield: 1 pie

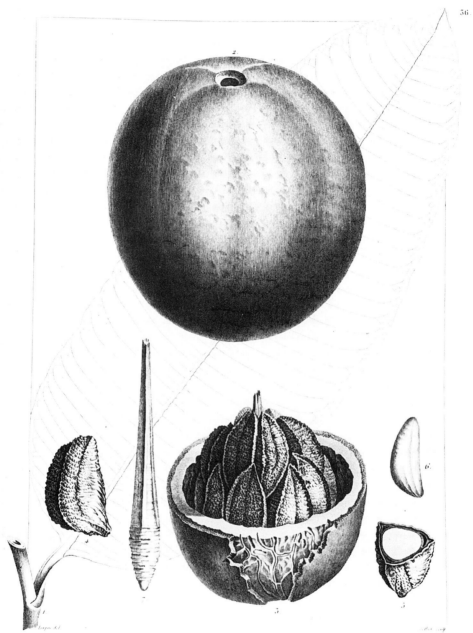

THE BRAZIL NUT

CHAPTER TWO

Brazil Nuts

Family: Lecythidaceae

LATIN	*Bertholletia excelsa* H.B.K.	DUTCH	Para-Noot
SPANISH	Castaña de Pará	ITALIAN	Noce del Para
FRENCH	Noix du Brésil	PORTUGUESE	Castanha-do-Pará
GERMAN	Paranuss	RUSSIAN	Brazil'Skiï Orékh
SWEDISH	Paranöt	JAPANESE	Buraziru Nattsu
ARABIC	Jōz Al-Birāzîl	CHINESE	Pahsi Li

"I'm Charley's aunt from Brazil
—where the nuts come from."

Charley's Aunt (1892) Act I

BRAZIL NUTS, formerly known as cream nuts and Pará nuts, are the large, hard-shelled seeds of the Brazil nut tree, *Bertholletia excelsa* H. B. K., a handsome giant evergreen indigenous to the Amazon forests of South America. It belongs to the Lecythidaceae family. With a long straight trunk branched only in the uppermost part, the tree may reach a height of 100 to 150 feet with a trunk diameter of four to eight feet. The crown spreads out to a breadth of one hundred feet or more as it towers over other tropical forest vegetation. Its large, glossy dark green leaves are twelve to fifteen inches long, about six inches wide and deeply ribbed. Pale yellow flowers, with six large petals, are borne in clusters at the ends of the branches. The spherical dark brown fruits, which take about fourteen months to mature, are four to six inches in diameter and weigh two to four pounds each. They resemble large coconuts with a hard, woody casing.

Inside the rough but fragile outer shell of the fruit is a tough, woody and fibrous inner shell about one quarter of an inch thick, which contains from twelve to twenty-four Brazil nuts, closely packed together, with the thin edge inward, like the sections of an orange. When the fruits ripen, they fall to the ground from a height of 100 feet or more, making nut collection a dangerous job, especially in windy weather and during heavy rains. Fatal accidents occur from time to time when one of these hard, four-pound fruits crashes down like a cannon ball on some unsuspecting person's head.

Virtually all Brazil nuts come from wild trees scattered throughout the Amazon Basin in a huge area of over a million and a quarter square miles, covering about forty percent of Brazil as well as parts of five other neighboring countries. The trees grow best in deep, well-drained, alluvial soils on high ground not subject to flooding; they frequently occur in groups or colonies of six or more. Most Brazil nuts are produced in the states of Pará, Amazonas, and Acre in Brazil; a smaller, less important part of Brazil nut production comes from wild trees in Bolivia, Peru, Colombia, the Guianas and Venezuela.

23

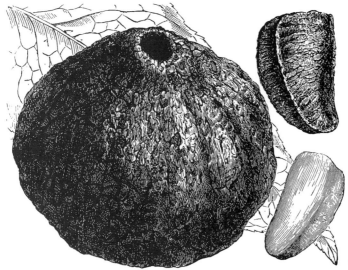

THE BRAZIL NUT

FLOWERING OF BRAZIL NUT
Detached from tree. Manaos, Brazil.

BRAZIL NUT SEEDLINGS

BRAZIL NUT PRODUCING REGIONS

Most Brazil nuts come from the states of Amazonas and Pará.

A mature, high-yielding Brazil nut tree can produce 250 to 500 pounds of unshelled nuts in a good year. High yield in one year, however, usually results in a poor yield the next. The nuts are harvested from an estimated 250,000 to 400,000 trees annually—but undoubtedly there are hundreds of thousands of inaccessible, out-of-sight wild trees from which nuts are never collected. Consequently, every year thousands of tons of Brazil nuts are not harvested by man, but rot on the jungle floor or are consumed by monkeys, rodents and other beasts of the forests.

Efforts have been made to establish Brazil nut plantations, but the results have been unsuccessful or at best inconclusive. In the

BRAZIL NUT TREES IN THE AMAZON

late nineteenth century, small scale plantings were established in Kuala Lumpur in the Malay Peninsula, Ceylon, Java and the West Indies. More recently, numerous trials have been attempted in Brazil itself. A Brazil nut plantation can hardly be classified as a "get rich quick" project: it takes twelve to fifteen years for a tree to bear fruit and at least thirty years would probably be required before a plantation could become profitable. Agricultural research is currently being carried out by Embrapa, the Brazilian Agricultural Research Organization located in Belém, on methods of growing compact, selected, grafted varieties of the Brazil nut. These would be about half the size of the normal adult tree and could start producing about seven years after planting.

An early historical reference to the Brazil nut was made in 1569: a Spanish colonial official, Juan Alvarez Maldonado, while reconnoitering in the lowlands of southeastern Peru near the Madre de Dios river, came upon a few Brazil nut trees in a village called Vinono. The *Cayanpuxes* Indians informed him that many of these wild nut trees were also growing in the adjacent region of Cavanava. The Spanish commander thereupon ordered that thousands of the nourishing nuts be collected as rations for his tired and hungry troops. The Spanish called the kernels "almendras de Los Andes" ("almonds of the Andes"). When the English pirate, Richard Hawkins, was captured by the Spanish in 1594, he became familiar with these nuts as he languished in jail in Lima.

In 1633 Dutch traders in Brazil sent a small shipment of "wild oil fruits" from the Amazon to the Netherlands. These were probably Brazil nuts. During the eighteenth century the Dutch and others continued to make Brazil nut shipments to Europe from ports in the Brazilian territory of Maranhão, so the nuts were called "castanhas de Maranhão." The earliest shipment of Brazil nuts to the United States took place in 1810 when a small lot was

LEAVES AND FRUITS OF THE
BRAZIL NUT

27

exported to New York from Maranhão, along with rubber, cocoa and cashews.

By 1818 larger quantities began to be shipped from Pará to Europe; accordingly the Brazil nuts became known as "Pará nuts." After 1866, when the Amazon river was opened up to foreign trade, Brazil nut production increased substantially. In the early twentieth century, after the price of Brazilian rubber collapsed in 1910 due to competition from southeast Asia, Brazil nuts became a vital export crop in the Amazon region.

The first official United States customs entry of Brazil nuts was recorded in 1873: during the period July 1, 1872 to June 30, 1873, 3,690,908 pounds of unshelled Brazil nuts entered the country from Brazil at an average price of 4.62 cents (U.S.) per pound. The price varied little up to 1940 and World War II. However, by 1982 the spot price for unshelled Brazil nuts in New York rose to about $1.40 per pound, while the quantity of both shelled and unshelled nuts imported into the United States increased sevenfold over that imported in 1873.

The life of the Brazil nut harvester or "castanheiro" is still harsh and miserable. If he is a local laborer, he will have a permanent

JUNGLE LABORER, CENTRAL BRAZIL

28

home nearby. On the other hand, if he is a migratory worker who also works part of the year harvesting rubber, his living quarters during the Brazil nut collecting period—from February to June in the Amazon Basin—will usually be a primitive, temporary shelter with a palm leaf roof at the edge of a stream. His floor will be the damp earth, his bed a palm-frond mat or a hammock. The adjacent creek may supply him and his family with an occasional fish, but his regular diet will probably consist of rice, wild fruits and boiled manioc (the starchy tubers of a shrubby perennial *Manihot esculenta*, native to the region). His clothing will be ragged and he will generally go barefoot. The worker will most likely be suffering from malaria, hookworm, dysentery or some other debilitating tropical ailment. He will have few domestic animals, due to the presence of jaguars, ocelots, snakes and other wild animals. Having few possessions, when the time comes to break camp he can readily load his family, his dog and a few pots and pans into a dugout canoe and push away.

Narrow trails known as "estradas," winding across streams and around swamps and fallen trees, are cut into the jungle by the castanheiros to provide access to the Brazil nut trees. The mature fruits are picked up off the ground when there is little or no wind blowing to minimize the danger of being struck by a falling pod. The fruits are known

BRAZIL NUT WORKERS KNOWN AS "CASTANHEIROS" OPENING TOUGH FRUITS WITH MACHETES IN THE JUNGLE

Each fruit contains 12 to 24 Brazil nuts.

as "ouriços" or sea urchins, due to their prickly outer shell. Sometimes they are brought back entire to the castanheiro's hut in large baskets to be split open deftly with long knives similar to machetes in order to extract the nuts. More often they are opened in the forest to avoid carrying the extra weight of the shells. Once the nuts are removed, the shells

WASHING BRAZIL NUTS IN A TRIBUTARY OF THE AMAZON

DELIVERING BRAZIL NUTS TO LOCAL TRADING POST
The nuts have been transported by canoe in the interior of the Amazon Basin.

can be fashioned into cups, household utensils, bracelets, or used as fuel.

After being washed in the stream, the nuts are given a preliminary drying in a primitive shelter. Any sort of drying is difficult since the Brazil nuts are collected during the rainy season in the Amazon Basin when there is enough water in the streams to permit travel by canoes and light boats. The nuts are then transported by canoe or mule-back to the nearest local trading post known as a "barracão," which is usually located at a strategic river junction.

There are hundreds of these trading posts in the Amazon. The trader at the barracão may have as many as 200 castanheiros who deliver Brazil nuts to him. The barracão generally consists of a few rustic houses, a store, a small landing place for river steamers and some limited storage facilities. Years ago, the trader did not pay the castanheiros for the Brazil nuts in cash, but customarily paid him with merchandise such as machetes, hardware, tobacco, cotton cloth and sugar. At the

end of the harvesting season, the wretched castanheiro often had little merchandise and no money at all to show for his efforts. More recently, many castanheiros have learned to handle money, and prefer to be paid in cash.

When the trader has collected sufficient Brazil nuts and other tropical products that he may have received in trade—cabinet woods, rotenone-rich climbing vines, rubber—he ships the goods along to other traders through whose hands the merchandise will pass en route to the port of Belem for export. Some Brazil nuts are now exported directly from Manaos, Óbidos and Itacoatiara; while smaller nuts may be shipped from southern Brazil through the port of Santos.

Years ago, transportation in the Amazon Basin was almost entirely by mules, dugout canoes, small river boats and steamers. Recent improvements in overland shipping, such as the new Transamazonian Highway and other, secondary roads, now permit trucking of substantial loads of Brazil nuts and other tropical commodities. The munici-

BRAZIL NUT FRUITS ARE COLLECTED NEAR A
NATIVE HUT IN THE AMAZON BASIN

pality of Marabá, near the Tocantins river and bordering the Transamazonian Highway in the state of Pará, is one of the most important collection and processing centers for medium-sized Brazil nuts, known in the trade as "Tocs." Other leading producing regions in Brazil are: Itacoatiara on the Amazon river in Amazonas state; Coarí near the Solimões river, also in Amazonas state; and Rio Branco in the state of Acre. The largest nuts are produced in Amazonas and processed in Manaos and Óbidos; the smallest, produced in Acre, Mato Grosso and Rôndonia, are usually shelled in Brazil, although some lots are shipped to England for shelling. After drying, Brazil nuts in the shell are graded as follows: Extra Large, 40 to 45 nuts per pound; Large, 46 to 50; Weak Large, 51 to 56; Medium "Tocs," 57 to 62; and Small, up to 110 nuts per pound.

Due to the intense heat and high humidity of the Amazon region, the heaps of Brazil nuts tend to "sweat" and must constantly be

SHELLING BRAZIL NUTS
At factory, Óbidos, Pará, Brazil.

turned over and aerated to prevent deterioration and mold. This process, known as "trenching," is carried out first by the castanheiros, then by the river traders. Up to twenty-five years ago, green, improperly dried Brazil nuts used to be shipped in bulk to foreign ports. This practice occasionally led to mold contamination, which is now avoided by drying the nuts thoroughly in Brazil prior to export. Several Brazilian factories now utilize automatic rotating dryers or other modern drying equipment to dehydrate the unshelled nuts to a moisture content of eleven per cent, and shelled nuts to six per cent. After drying, the unshelled nuts are manually selected to remove moldy, empty, cracked, broken and oily-wet rejects. The nuts are then graded according to the color of their shells, and subjected to quality control before being packed for export in fifty-kilo bags.

The shelling operation of Brazil nuts is easier than in some other hard-shelled nuts, such as the macadamia. The nuts to be shelled are soaked in water for twenty-four hours, boiled for five minutes to soften the shell, and are usually then cracked by hand, for the most part, rather than by machine. The good kernels are dried and graded for quality and size. Shells and spoiled kernels are utilized as fuel to supplement firewood in the power plant, thereby supplying heat for the dryers. Imperfect and broken kernels may also be used for the extraction of Brazil nut oil, an excellent cooking aid. The residue left in the defatted, crushed seeds after extraction of the oil can be employed as animal feed.

Recently exporters in Belém began implementing a new export packaging system for shelled nuts which is designed to provide a higher quality product, and to improve handling and package disposal for importers. After being classified, the nuts are packed in twenty- to fifty-kilogram, laminated, vacuum-sealed bags. Nitrogen is injected into the packaging to retard bacteria and preserve the nuts. The bags are stowed inside corrugated shipping containers for export.

Despite improvement in the Brazilian shelling facilities, the exports of Brazil nuts in shell are still far greater in volume than the shelled. For example, in 1978, 15,472 metric tons of Brazil nuts in shell were exported from Brazil as against only 5,367 tons of the shelled product. However, small shelling factories are active in several small towns along the Amazon river, such as Óbidos in Pará. The United States is the largest importer of Brazil nuts, followed by the United Kingdom, West Germany, Italy, France, Australia and the Netherlands. Brazil nuts in shell are imported into the United States mainly at Mobile, Alabama; shelled nuts are usually shipped to New York.

Although Brazil has the potential to expand Brazil nut production by gathering the crop of innumerable, additional wild trees, it seems more likely that the output will remain in the range of 40,000 to 60,000 tons of in-shell nuts, including exports and internal consumption. Furthermore, large numbers of the wild trees are being felled as a result of the deforestation of the Amazon region.

Brazil nuts are eaten raw, roasted, salted, in ice cream, as well as in bakery and confectionery products. They are an important ingredient in shelled nut mixtures. The nuts possess a high food value, containing approximately 67 per cent digestible fat or oil, 14 per cent protein and 11 per cent carbohydrates in addition to calcium, phosphorous, potassium and Vitamin B.

Since Brazil nuts contain a large percentage of fat, care must be exercised to guard against rancidity. When the nuts are not kept cool, or when they are exposed to air and light, rancidity may occur. Blanching, slicing and chopping tend to stimulate the chemical reaction that causes nuts to turn rancid—so do not plan to keep blanched, sliced or chopped nuts on hand too long. If Brazil nuts (or other nuts) are properly dried and kept in a sealed plastic container or glass jar in a dark, cool place (less than 70 degrees Fahrenheit), they should keep fresh for many months.

A Hint About Shelling Brazil Nuts (V)

Cover unshelled nuts with boiling salted water, allowing 1 tablespoon (15 ml) salt to a quart (1 liter) water. Boil gently 3 minutes. Drain and cool. Crack and quickly remove shells.

Unshelled Brazil nuts may be roasted, too, in a hot oven (400° F/200° C) about 20 minutes. Cool, crack and shell. The nuts come out whole—with the greatest of ease—and with a most delightful toasted flavor.

To Blanch Brazil Nuts (V)

To remove the brown skin, cover 1 pound (450 g) of nuts with 1 quart (1 liter) water. Add 1-1/2 teaspoons (7.5 ml) sodium bicarbonate (baking soda). Simmer 2 minutes. Remove skins while warm.

To Slice Brazil Nuts (V)

Cover with cold water and slowly bring to a boil. Simmer 2 to 3 minutes. The nuts can then be sliced without breaking.

MAIN DISH

Escalloped Crab with Brazil Nuts (V)

Cream Sauce

4 tablespoons (60 ml) butter	2 tablespoons (30 ml) chopped parsley
2 tablespoons (30 ml) flour	1 tablespoon (15 ml) lemon juice
1 cup (250 ml) milk	2 cups (500 ml) crabmeat
1/2 teaspoon (2.5 ml) salt	3/4 cup (175 ml) Brazil nuts, ground
1/2 teaspoon (2.5 ml) paprika	

For cream sauce: In a saucepan, melt butter and stir in flour. Gradually add milk. Cook, stirring, until smooth and thick. Add seasonings and crabmeat. Fill crab or scallop shells (or casserole), sprinkle with Brazil nuts. Bake in moderate oven (350° F/175° C) until golden brown.

Yield: 4 servings

SALAD

Brazilian Potato Salad (V)

6 boiled potatoes, cubed	1/2 tablespoon (7.5 ml) grated onion
1 cooked beet, cubed	Salad dressing
3 small pickles, cut fine	1 cup (250 ml) sliced Brazil nuts
1 stalk celery, chopped fine	1 hard-cooked egg, sliced
Salt, pepper	

Mix potatoes, beet, pickles, celery. Season with salt, pepper and grated onion. Moisten with salad dressing. Add half the sliced Brazil nuts. Chill. Serve on lettuce, garnished with remaining nuts and hard-cooked egg.

Yield: 6 servings

BAKED GOODS

Nut Tropical Cake (VI)

3 cups (750 ml) Brazil nuts (or others), whole	3/4 cup (175 ml) sugar 1/2 teaspoon (2.5 ml) baking powder
1 pound (450 g) pitted dates	1/2 teaspoon (2.5 ml) salt
1 cup (250 ml) candied cherries	3 eggs
3/4 cup (175 ml) sifted all-purpose flour	1 teaspoon (5 ml) vanilla

Put nut meats, dates and cherries into a large bowl. Sift flour, sugar, baking powder and salt over nut meats and fruit. Mix with hands until nut meats and fruit are well coated. In a separate bowl, beat eggs until foamy; add vanilla. Stir into nut-fruit mixture until well mixed. Turn into a greased and waxed-paper-lined pan, 9-1/2 inches × 5-1/2 inches × 2-1/2 inches (23-3/4 × 13-3/4 × 6-1/4 cm). Spread evenly in pan. Bake in slow oven (300° F/150° C) for 1 hour and 45 minutes. Cool completely before cutting. This cake keeps for months.

Yield: 1 cake

Brazil Nut Butterscotch Cookies (V)

1/2 cup (125 ml) butter	1/2 teaspoon (2.5 ml)
1 pound (450 g) brown	salt
sugar	1-1/2 cups (375 ml)
2 eggs, well beaten	chopped Brazil
1-1/4 cup (310 ml) flour	nuts
2 teaspoons (10 ml) bak-	
ing powder	

Melt butter. Add sugar and mix. Add eggs. In a separate bowl, sift flour with baking powder and salt. Add nuts. Stir into sugar and egg mixture. Drop by teaspoonfuls onto a greased cookie sheet. Bake in a slow oven (325° F/165° C) about fifteen minutes. Remove from pan quickly. If cookies harden on the pan, reheat a few minutes.

Yield: About 50 cookies

CANDY

Quick Brazil Nut Fudge (V)

Four 1-ounce squares	1 pound (450 g) sifted
chocolate	confectioners'
2 tablespoons (30 ml)	sugar
butter	1/3 cup (75 ml) milk
1/4 teaspoon (1.5 ml)	1 cup (250 ml) chopped
salt	Brazil nuts
1 teaspoon (5 ml)	Whole Brazil nuts
vanilla	

Melt chocolate and butter over hot water. Stir in salt and vanilla. Stir in sugar alternately with the milk, keeping pan over hot water. Remove from heat and stir in Brazil nuts. Pour fudge in a 7-inch (18-cm) square pan. Garnish with Brazil nuts, cut in halves. Let stand several hours. Cut in squares.

Yield: 49 1-inch (2.5-cm) square pieces

VARIOUS TYPES OF BRAZIL NUT CANDIES

Brazilian Creams (V)

2 cups (500 ml) white sugar	1 teaspoon (5 ml) vanilla
1 cup (250 ml) light brown sugar	1/2 cup (125 ml) chopped Brazil nuts
3/4 cup (175 ml) milk	
2 tablespoons (30 ml) corn syrup	1 cup (250 ml) crystal-lized ginger, finely chopped
2 tablespoons (30 ml) cream	

Put white and brown sugar, milk and corn syrup in saucepan. Stir and melt over low heat, then turn up heat and boil to 238° F (115° C). Remove from fire and cool to about 110° F (45° C). Then add 2 tablespoons (30 ml) cream and the vanilla and beat. Add nuts and ginger and beat again until it begins to hold its shape. Turn into buttered sheet and cut before it is too cold.

Yield: 3 dozen candies

DESSERTS

Bananas with Brazil Nuts (VII)

6 bananas	1 egg white
2 tablespoons (30 ml) lemon juice	1/2 cup (125 ml) heavy cream
1/4 cup (60 ml) peach liqueur	3 tablespoons (45 ml) powdered sugar
1 cup (250 ml) ground Brazil nuts	Berries coated with sugar

Slice bananas, add lemon juice, liqueur and the ground nuts, which have been slightly browned in the oven before grinding. Beat egg white and cream separately, then combine and add powdered sugar. Place the bananas in a pudding dish, cover with the cream mixture and garnish with raspberries or strawberries rolled in powdered sugar. Chill.

Yield: 6 servings

Brazil Nut Torte (VII)

6 eggs separated	1/4 teaspoon (1 ml) salt
1 cup (250 ml) sugar	1/2 pint (250 ml) heavy cream, whipped and sweetened
1/2 pound (225 g) Brazil nuts	
1 teaspoon (5 ml) baking powder	1 can peaches, drained
	Maraschino cherries

Beat egg yolks and add sugar, beating well. Add nuts, baking powder, salt and then fold in stiffly-beaten egg whites. Turn into an oblong baking tin 13 × 9 × 2 inches (33 × 23 × 5 cm) or 2 buttered 9-inch (23-cm) layer cake tins. Bake in preheated 350° F (175° C) oven for 45 to 60 minutes, or until a steel knife blade inserted in the center can be removed clean. When baked, remove from tin and allow to cool. If baked in an oblong tin, cut in half, fill and cover with the whipped cream and on top arrange the peaches garnished with cherries. If layer cake tins are used, join layers with some of the whipped cream mixture, spread the rest on top and garnish with the cherries.

Yield: One torte

CASHEW

CHAPTER THREE

Cashew Nuts

Family: Anacardiaceae

LATIN	*Anacardium occidentale* L.	DUTCH	Kasjoe
SPANISH	Marañón	ITALIAN	Acagiù
FRENCH	Noix d'acajou	PORTUGUESE	Cajù
GERMAN	Elefantenlaus	RUSSIAN	Kashiû Orékh
SWEDISH	Acajou	JAPANESE	Kashu Nattsu
ARABIC	Habb Al-Bilādhir	CHINESE	Yao Kuo

THE CASHEW, *Anacardium occidentale* L., belongs to the Anacardiaceae or cashew family. Other important economic plants of this family are the mango (*Mangifera indica*) and the pistachio nut (*Pistacia vera*). Less popular species of this family include the toxic poison ivy, poison oak and poison sumac.

The English word "cashew" is derived from the Portuguese "cajú," which came previously from the Tupi-Indian "acajú." The Latin American Spanish word for cashew—marañon—presumably originated from Maranhão, Brazil, one of the first regions where cashew was observed by the Spanish.

The cashew tree is a hardy, fast-growing, evergreen perennial with a symmetrical, umbrella-like canopy. Under favorable conditions, it may reach a height of forty to fifty feet. Under less favorable conditions, in the poor soils and marginal locations in which it is usually found, the cashew is much smaller. The stem tends to be gnarled and tortuous and the branches crooked, giving the tree a decidedly unkempt appearance. The lower branches frequently rest on the ground and strike root, thereby enhancing the spreading

form. The leathery, oblong-oval leaves, four to eight inches long and two to three inches in width, are heavily veined. The aromatic five-petaled flowers are yellowish pink and polygamous: The flower cluster is composed of both unisexual and bisexual types. The rough, resinous bark contains an acrid sap.

Cashew trees flourish in the extreme heat of the tropics. During the past four centuries they have been extensively planted in warm regions throughout the world. They are easily cultivated, vigorous, drought-resistant and require little care. The trees may live for thirty or forty years.

North-eastern Brazil, near the equator, is probably the area in which the cashew originated. In 1558, A. Thevet, a French naturalist, visited the territory of Maranhão in northern Brazil and provided the earliest known published illustration of the cashew, showing the natives harvesting cashew "apples" and preparing an astringent juice (see illustration p. 38). Thevet described the tree as follows: "The country from Cape St. Augustine to near Maragnon, dividing the territory of the King of Spain from that of Portugal, is far too good

A VERY EARLY CASHEW ILLUSTRATION

HARVEST OF CASHEWS IN 16TH CENTURY BRAZIL

to belong to the cannibals as it bears fruit in abundance and roots and vegetables together with great numbers of the tree called "aca-jous," which bears fruit as large as your fist and shaped like a goose-egg. Some make from these a beverage, though the fruit itself is scarcely edible, having an unripe flavour. At the base of the fruit hangs a sort of nut, as big as a chestnut and with the shape of a kidney. As to the kernel therein, it is excellent to eat when lightly cooked."

It is likely that Spanish sailors introduced the cashew to Panama and Central America in the sixteenth century, though Carib natives had presumably taken it to the West Indies somewhat earlier.

Portuguese colonists and missionaries had introduced the cashew to their territories in East Africa and Portuguese India (Goa) by 1590. In East Africa the ecological conditions proved to be highly favorable—cashew is growing wild today in Mozambique and Tanzania. Furthermore, Mozambique has become one of the main world exporters of raw cashew nuts.

From Goa, the cashew spread to the Malabar Coast and southwestern India, where it became a very important crop. From there it was carried to the Indian subcontinent and Indonesia by means of bats, birds and hu-

38

SORTING CASHEWS IN MOZAMBIQUE

mans. The cashew is believed to have been brought to the Philippines directly from the New World on the "Manila" galleons that sailed from Mexico.

The cashew is peculiar and versatile: It produces not only an edible nut but also a nutritive, edible "apple" and a valuable nut shell oil.

The highly unusual cashew fruit consists of two distinct parts: The first is the fleshy, pear-shaped stalk, known as the cashew apple, which is juicy, thin-skinned, brilliant yellow, red or scarlet in color, and about two to four and one-half inches in length. It actually looks more like a pear than an apple and in many regions of Brazil the cashew apple is referred to as the "pera." The second is the grayish-brown, kidney-shaped nut, which is about one to one-half inches long. It is attached to the lower end of the apple. The cashew nut is the true fruit, while the cashew apple, about eight to ten times as heavy as the nut, is the swollen stalk, or peduncle, which supports the flower.

The nut shell is smooth, oily and about one-eighth of an inch thick. Its honeycombed, cellular, inner portion contains a toxic, resinous material from which is obtained cashew nut shell liquid, also known as CNSL. The shell encloses a slightly curved, white, finely textured kernel, which is approximately seven-eighths of an inch in length, and is wrapped in a testa or thin brown skin. This is the cashew nut of commerce. The nut shell, with its side indentation pointed upward, looks like a heart. In fact, the generic name *Anacardium* means "shaped like a heart."

Cashew trees start bearing fruit normally in the third or fourth year and, under favorable conditions, reach maximum production in

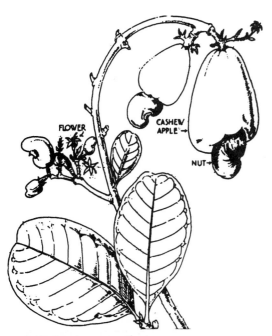

Leaves, flowers and fruits of the cashew (*Anacardium occidentale*). The kidney-shaped nut contains the edible kernel, or cashew of commerce. The fleshy fruit-stalk is known as the "cashew apple."

THE CASHEW NUT

Modeled in glass, in the Ware Collection of Blaschka Glass Models of Plants, popularly called the "Glass Flowers." Botanical Museum of Harvard University, Cambridge, Massachusetts.

CASHEW APPLES AND NUTS HANGING ON MATURE TREE IN INDIA

of apples and nuts from which twenty pounds of unhulled nuts and six pounds of kernels could be obtained. Cashew production in the future may be markedly increased through varietal selection.

Cashew has been called a poor man's crop but a rich man's food. The World Bank has estimated that at least 97% of world cashew production comes from wild growth and small peasant holdings—while at the most 3% is supplied by systematically planned plantations.

The flowering of the cashew tree lasts for two to three months and the fruit matures about two months later. The nut develops first from the cashew flower, while the receptacle or apple swells later between the nut and the stem. After harvesting, the ripe cashew apple will only keep for twenty-four hours, while the nuts may be kept for a year or longer if dried to a moisture content of 8% or less and stored with care. If cashew apple production is desired, the soft fruits should be plucked or cut off the branch before they fall naturally to the ground where they might burst or be badly bruised. On the other hand, if the apples are to be discarded and emphasis is on the harvest of the nuts, the latter are allowed to mature and fall to the ground where they are collected.

The nuts should be dried immediately after harvesting. Sun drying is often carried out on bamboo mats, palm leaves or specially prepared drying floors. The nuts should be constantly turned over with wooden rakes and dried for several days until they rattle in the shell.

Though processing methods have improved considerably during the past fifty years, the nuts still must be roasted in some manner to remove the brown, caustic nut shell liquid (CNSL) which contains the poisonous compounds cardol and anacardic acid. Upon contact with the skin, these toxic inner-shell substances may cause severe allergic reactions such as swelling, blisters and acute dermatitis far more serious than the irritation of poison ivy or poison sumac. Un-

about seven years. Commercial cashew planting is recommended in well-drained friable soils at low elevations in the tropics. The trees require an annual rainfall of 40 to 120 inches, preferably with a pronounced dry season of three or four months. Good drainage is essential, since the cashew tree cannot stand "wet feet." It can also be damaged by frost. In a plantation, the trees are usually planted about thirty-five feet apart, without shade. Propagation is normally by seeds, but seedling cashew trees vary considerably in yield, quality and the form of the fruit produced. Consequently, in recent years more attention has been given to selection of superior varieties or individual trees, and asexual propagation of them through budding, grafting, layering and cuttings. Although yields vary considerably, a fair, average annual yield from a mature cashew tree would be about 100 to 150 pounds

41

CASHEW HARVEST IN NORTHEASTERN BRAZIL

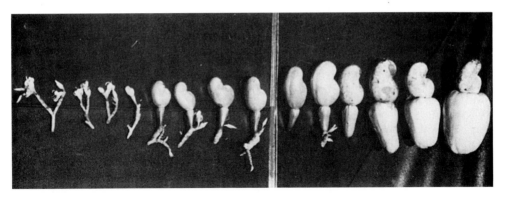

CASHEW DEVELOPMENT

Showing different stages of growth of the cashew from flowering to full development of the apples and nuts.

shelled, unroasted cashew nuts should not be eaten. The virulent compounds in the shell will severely burn the mouth and lips of the unwary individual who attempts to bite into a fresh, green cashew nut.

John Huyghen van Linschoten, a Dutch traveler in India about 1590, was aware of the painful toxicity of the raw cashew nut as he warned Europeans: "When they (the cashew nuts) are raw and unrosted, you must not open them with your mouth for when you touch them with your lips or your tongue, the skin will instantly be bitten off and cause much pain, whereby such as know it are not deceived wherefore you must open their shelles with a knife, or rost [sic] them . . ."

In the traditional manual method, the nuts are roasted in a perforated open pan over a wood fire. Before the roast, the nuts are usually soaked in water to avoid scorching. During roasting, the nuts swell, and the CNSL-containing cells burst, ejecting the resinous liquid which drips through the holes of the pan into the fire. This open-fire roasting is unpleasant and unhealthy for the workers: the spurting oil and smoke are toxic and irritating to the eyes, nose and throat and can cause painful skin rashes. In this type of nut roast, most of the caustic shell liquid is released (and lost), but some remains in the shell. The roasted

nuts are tumbled in ashes or sawdust to absorb the remnants of the irritating CNSL before the sheller handles them.

A more modern method of roasting the nuts and extracting the cashew nut shell liquid is the "hot oil bath." In this mechanized system, introduced in 1935, the nuts are roasted in a bath of hot CNSL. The CNSL-containing cells burst, releasing the liquid into the bath. The excess nut shell liquid overflows, and about 50% of the liquid contained in the nut shells is recovered. Another more efficient solvent extraction process is now available, in which it is possible to extract up to 80% of the CNSL from the shells. However, the solvents are very expensive and the method requires considerable technical expertise.

The most important use for the resinous cashew nut shell liquid is as a friction-modifying material for brake linings of automobiles. Heat is created by friction during the braking action. Cashew resins (CNSL-based) absorb this heat in an efficient manner.

Cashew nut shell liquid is also used in clutch facings, foundry resins, waterproof paints, corrosion resistant varnishes, insulating enamels and special quality lacquers.

In fact, world CNSL production has increased steadily during recent years: about 32,000 tons were produced in 1980 at a price of roughly $1,500 per ton. The principal markets for CNSL are the United States, Great Britain and Japan.

Cashew nut shell liquid, or oil, has been used in tropical medicine in the treatment of scurvy, leprous sores, warts, ringworm, psoriasis, as a gargle for sore throat and to cure cracks in the soles of the feet, among other ailments. In West Africa it is utilized in tattooing. In the West Indies it has been put to cosmetic use in a drastic and hazardous beauty treatment: if applied to the face of a woman who wishes to increase her charms, it will cause such extreme blistering and festering that the facial skin may be peeled off in a few days, giving her a brand-new complexion.

Following the roasting, in the traditional procedure still followed in India, the cashew nuts are shelled manually by women. This is a delicate task requiring dexterity, skill and patience: the women workers squat on the floor and knock on the edges of the nuts gently two or three times with light wooden mallets to crack the shells open without damaging the kernels. Other countries have experienced difficulty in competing with the finger skills and low wages of the Indian workers. During the past fifteen years, however, two large scale, mechanized, cashew-shelling systems have been introduced in the African countries—the Italian Oltremare and the British Sturtevant. In the Oltremare the shell is cut by rotary blades and levered open; in the Sturtevant the shells are shattered against target plates in a centrifugal cracking machine. The use of these mechanized shelling systems is gaining momentum outside of India. The peculiar shape of the cashew nut, however, its varying size, and the brittleness of the kernel combine to make mchanical decortication a troublesome problem.

In India the kernel, after removal from the shell, is dried and its reddish-brown outer coating, the testa, peeled off by gentle rubbing with the fingers. Where the mechanized processes are utilized in Africa, the kernels are mechanically peeled.

The next step after peeling is grading. Final sorting according to quality, size and color is still done manually for the most part, although off-colored kernels can be separated through electronic sorting machines. Grading of the cashew kernels is carried out in accordance with internationally recognized standards based on size and color. For example, typical Indian Government specifications for Whole White Cashew Kernels are as follows: "General characteristics: Cashew kernels shall have been obtained through shelling and peeling cashew nuts (*Anacardium occidentale*); shall have the characteristic shape; shall be white, pale ivory or light ash in colour, reasonably dry, and free from insect damage, damaged kernels and black or brown spots. They shall be completely free from rancid kernels. The kernels shall be completely free from testa."

Other cashew classifications include scorched kernels and dessert kernels (the lowest quality). These types are subsequently divided into whole or broken grades and separated into subgroups according to size.

After grading, the kernels are ready to be packed for export in twenty-five-pound tins from which the air has been extracted and replaced by carbon dioxide. The tins are hermetically sealed to prevent deterioration and insect damage. Two tins form a fifty-pound "case," the common unit of sale in the cashew trade.

Approximately 60% of cashew kernels are consumed as salted nuts; they are also used in bakery products and in confectionery. High-priced cashews represent essentially a luxury product for high income groups. In the snack market, cashews must compete with lower priced peanuts as well as chips, crisps, salted popcorn and other confectionery items.

In a new market, salters usually introduce cashews with other nuts in mixed nut packaging, then sell cashews separately as the consumer gradually acquires a taste for them. In the United States, a proportion of up to sixty percent cashews may be used in mixed nut packs, while in Europe the percentage of cashews in such mixtures may be twenty-five percent or less.

Cashews are more widely used in confec-

SAMPLING IMPORTED CASHEW NUTS

A nut sampler inspecting a cashew shipment at the waterfront in Hoboken, New Jersey. In front of him are the tools of his trade: a hatchet for opening wooden cases, a steel cutter to make a hole in the tin to be sampled, and a scoop.

45

tionery—in nut candies and nut chocolate bars—than in bakery products. The bland cashew is a fitting substitute for higher priced almonds to extend the nut texture. In baking, however, almonds are more suitable for cake decoration than cashews.

The main commercial product of the cashew tree is the nut, including its kernel and nut shell liquid. Unfortunately, about ninety-five percent of the world cashew apple crop—some five million tons—is left to rot under the trees.

Many useful and profitable products can be made from the cashew apple including: fruit juice, fruit paste, candied fruit, syrups, jams, jellies, chutney, pickles, vinegar, wine and liquor. In fact, cashew apple jam was in vogue during the eighteenth century in Europe. In Brazil the cashew apple is more highly regarded than elsewhere. A number of Brazilian factories manufacture cashew apple juice and cashew apple preserves. In some regions of Brazil, cashew apple production has become as important as nut production. Bottles of diluted cashew apple juice known as "cajuina" are especially popular. This beverage, although somewhat acrid and astringent, contains two to three times as much vitamin C as citrus juice. Steaming the cashew apples tends to reduce the astringency. Yellow cashew apples are usually sweeter than red. Fermented cashew apples are utilized in Brazil to prepare a wine resembling Madeira.

In Goa, India, the cashew apple is used to produce a carbonated beverage *cashola*, a low alcoholic drink known as *arrack* and a brandy called *fenni*. This latter word comes from the local Konkini dialect and means "froth." In Tanzania a gin-like liquor called *koniagi* is distilled, while in Mozambique wine is made from cashew apples.

Unfortunately, as noted above, most cashew apples throughout the world are thrown away. If full use could be made of the juicy apple, its potential value might be greater than that of the nut. Since food shortages, even famines, threaten many developing countries, such nutritious fare should not be wasted. One troublesome factor is that the cashew apples are highly perishable, prone to speedy decay and cannot be kept for more than twenty-four hours before fermentation commences. Another obstacle is the taste factor: the unusual, astringent flavor of the cashew apple is not popular outside of Brazil.

Cashew, the most important dessert nut after the almond, has turned out to be a significant gift from the New World to the Old. Although native to Brazil, it has become a valuable commercial crop in distant lands. At the present time, India is the leading world producer of cashew nuts, with a production of 150,000 metric tons during 1979/1980; Mozambique and Tanzania come next with an output of 70,000 metric tons each during the same period, followed by Brazil with 63,000 metric tons. Other important cashew growing countries include: Kenya, Madagascar, Thailand, Malaysia, Indonesia, Nigeria, Senegal, Malawi and Angola.

BODEGAS HISPANO AMERICANAS
VALBOLAN. CIA. LTDA.
QUEZALTENANGO
Grado Max. 15 G.
Añejamiento 1 año
Reg. Sanidad No. A-1704
VINO Marañon
HECHO EN GUATEMALA

CASHEW WINE, MADE FROM THE FERMENTED JUICE OF CASHEW APPLES, IS PRODUCED IN MANY DEVELOPING TROPICAL COUNTRIES

HORS D'OEUVRES

Spiced Indian Cashews (X)

1 tablespoon (15 ml) butter or margarine	1/2 teaspoon (2.5 ml) onion salt
1 cup (250 ml) Indian cashew nuts	1/2 teaspoon (2.5 ml) garlic salt
1 teaspoon (5 ml) celery salt	

Melt butter or margarine in a frying pan. Add nuts and fry until browned. Drain on paper towels. Combine seasoning salts and sprinkle over nuts. Mix lightly.

Yield: One cup (250 ml)

Curried Cashews (IX)

2 tablespoons (30 ml) butter or margarine	1 teaspoon (5 ml) curry powder
1 cup salted cashews	Salt

Melt butter or margarine in a frying pan. Add cashews and curry powder and sauté until lightly browned. Drain on paper towels. Sprinkle with salt to taste.

Yield: One cup (250 ml)

MAIN DISHES

Brown Veal Stew with Cashews (IX)

3 tablespoons (45 ml) butter or margarine	1 celery stalk, chopped
2 pounds (900 g) boneless lean veal, cut into 1-inch (2.5 cm) cubes	1-1/2 cups (375 ml) chopped salted cashews
1 teaspoon (5 ml) salt	2 fresh ripe tomatoes, peeled and chopped*
1/2 teaspoon (2.5 ml) pepper	1-1/2 cups (375 ml) water
1 small bay leaf, crumbled	1 teaspoon (5 ml) flour
1 garlic clove, peeled and crushed	1 teaspoon (5 ml) Worcestershire sauce
1 medium onion, chopped	

*Tip: Two whole canned tomatoes may be substituted for fresh

Melt butter in a deep, heavy skillet. Add veal, salt, pepper, bay leaf, garlic, onion and celery. Cook over moderate heat, stirring frequently, until meat is well browned on all sides. Add cashews, tomatoes and water. Cover loosely and simmer over low heat for 1 hour. Blend flour and Worcestershire sauce; stir into meat mixture. Cook uncovered, stirring occasionally, until thickened. Simmer over lowest heat without stirring for 20 minutes. Serve immediately over rice.

Yield: 6 servings

Indian Cashew Baked Fish Steaks (X)

3 pounds (1-1/3 kg) halibut steaks, cut 1/2-inch (12 mm) thick	1/2 teaspoon (2.5 ml) salt
Salt	1/4 teaspoon (1.5 ml) ground black pepper
3 pats butter or margarine, cut 1/4-inch (6 mm) thick	6 tablespoons (80 m) butter or margarine, melted
3 cups (750 ml) soft bread crumbs	
1/3 cup (75 ml) chopped salted Indian cashew nuts	

Wipe fish with a damp cloth and cut into 6 serving-size pieces. Sprinkle 1/8 (pinch) tsp. salt on both sides of each serving. Arrange fish in a buttered 9 × 9 × 2″ (23 × 23 × 5 cm) baking pan. Top each piece with 1/2 pat of butter or margarine. Combine remaining ingredients and sprinkle 1/2 cup (125 ml) of the mixture over each serving of fish, covering them completely. Bake in a preheated moderate oven (350° F—175° C) 35 minutes or until crumbs are brown.

Yield: 6 servings

47

Shrimp with Cashew Nuts (VIII)

2 tablespoons (30 ml)
  peanut oil
2 pounds (900 g) raw
  shrimp, shelled
  and deveined
1/4 cup (60 ml) finely
  sliced, green
  onions
2 cups (500 ml) or one
  10-ounce/300 g
  package frozen
  peas
1 cup (250 ml) chicken
  bouillon
1/2 cup (125 ml) sliced
  water chestnuts
1 teaspoon (5 ml) salt
1/2 teaspoon (2.5 ml)
  ground ginger
1/4 cup (60 ml) soy
  sauce
4 teaspoons (20 ml)
  cornstarch
1/2 cup (125 ml) dry-
  roasted cashew
  nuts

Heat peanut oil in a skillet. Add shrimp and sliced green onions. Cook, stirring constantly, until shrimp turn pink and onions are tender. Add peas, chicken bouillon, water chestnuts, salt and ginger. Cover; bring to a boil and simmer for 5 minutes or until peas and shrimp are tender. Blend soy sauce and cornstarch. Stir into shrimp mixture and cook until sauce is clear and slightly thickened. Stir in cashew nuts. Serve immediately with hot rice and fried noodles.

Yield: 6 servings

BAKED GOODS

Indian Cashew Chocolate Layer Cake (X)

2 cups (500 ml) sifted
  all-purpose flour
1/2 teaspoon (2.5 ml)
  salt
2 teaspoons (10 ml)
  double-acting bak-
  ing powder
2 teaspoons (10 ml)
  pure vanilla extract
1-1/3 cups (325 ml)
  sugar
2/3 cups (150 ml)
  shortening
3 large eggs
2/3 cups (150 ml) milk
Chocolate Fudge Frost-
  ing (see below)
3/4 cup (175 ml)
  coarsely
  chopped salted or
  unsalted Indian
  cashew nuts
Whole Indian cashew
  nuts

SHRIMP WITH CASHEW
NUTS

Sift together the first 3 ingredients and set aside. Blend vanilla extract and sugar with shortening until mixture is fluffy. Beat in eggs, one at a time. Add flour mixture alternately with milk, beginning and ending with flour. Beat batter 1/2 minute. Turn batter into 2 well-greased, slightly floured, round 9" (23 cm) cake pans. Bake in a pre-heated moderate oven (375° F—190° C) 30 minutes or until a toothpick inserted in the center comes out clean. Cool cakes in pans 10 minutes. Turn out onto wire racks to finish cooling. When cakes are cold, place a layer on a serving plate, spread with Chocolate Fudge Frosting and sprinkle with 1/4 cup (60 ml) chopped Indian cashew nuts. Top with remaining layer and frost top and sides with the rest of the frosting. Sprinkle sides with chopped Indian cashew nuts. Garnish top as desired with whole Indian cashew nuts.

Chocolate Fudge Frosting

1/4 cup (1/2 stick/60 ml) butter or margarine	4 cups (1 l) sifted confectioners' sugar
4 squares (4 oz./120 g) unsweetened chocolate	1/16 teaspoon (pinch) salt
6 to 7 tablespoons (90-105 ml) hot, undiluted evaporated milk or light cream	2 teaspoons (10 ml) pure vanilla extract

Melt butter or margarine and chocolate over hot water. Remove from heat. Add hot milk or cream alternately with sugar, using only enough milk to make a frosting that is smooth and easy to spread. Stir in salt and vanilla extract.

Yield: One 9-inch (23-cm), two-layer cake

Indian Cashew Pie (X)

3 large eggs, beaten	2 tablespoons (30 ml) butter or margarine, melted
1 cup (250 ml) light corn syrup	1 cup (250 ml) chopped, roasted unsalted Indian cashew nuts
1/2 cup (125 ml) sugar	
1 teaspoon (5 ml) pure vanilla extract	
1/4 teaspoon (1 ml) salt	1 tablespoon (15 ml) flour
1/2 teaspoon (2.5 ml) ground cinnamon	Unbaked 9-inch (23 cm) pastry shell
1/4 teaspoon (1 ml) ground nutmeg	

Combine first 7 ingredients. Mix well. Add butter or margarine. Mix Indian cashew nuts with flour and stir into the mixture. Turn into unbaked pastry shell. Bake in a preheated hot oven (400° F/200° C) 15 minutes. Reduce heat to moderate (350° F/175° C), and bake 40 minutes, or until knife inserted in the center comes out clean.

Yield: One 9-inch (23 cm) pie

Indian Cashew Drop Cookies (X)

1 teaspoon (5 ml) pure vanilla extract	1 large egg
1 cup (2 sticks/250 ml/ 60 g) soft butter or margarine	2 cups (500 ml) sifted all-purpose flour
1 cup (250 ml) sugar	About 4 dozen whole Indian cashew nuts
1/2 cup (125 ml) finely chopped salted Indian cashew nuts	

Blend together the first 2 ingredients. Gradually add sugar. Stir in Indian cashew nuts. Beat in egg. Gradually stir in flour. Drop from a teaspoon onto ungreased cookie sheets 2" (5 cm) apart. Top each with an Indian cashew nut. Bake in a preheated moderate oven (375° F–190° C) 7 minutes or until lightly browned around the edges. Cool cookies on wire racks. Store airtight.

Yield: 4 dozen cookies

1 *Castanea.*
Chestnut tree.

CHAPTER FOUR

Chestnuts

Family: Fagaceae

LATIN	*Castanea dentata* (Marsh.) Borkh.	DUTCH	Kastanje
SPANISH	Castaña	ITALIAN	Castagna
FRENCH	Châtaigne	PORTUGUESE	Castanha
GERMAN	Kastanie	RUSSIAN	Kashtán
SWEDISH	Kastanje	JAPANESE	Kuri
ARABIC	Kastaña	CHINESE	Pan Li

THE CHESTNUT, oak and beech belong to the Fagaceae family of cup-bearing trees. The well-known acorn cup may be compared to the chestnut bur, and the acorn itself to the nut of the chestnut. Chestnut leaves resemble beech leaves, but are longer and more sharply-toothed on the margin.

According to the renowned dendrologist Charles Sprague Sargent, the genus *Castanea* (chestnut) existed during the middle Tertiary period (now estimated at about 65 million years ago); at that time *Castanea* was growing in southern Greenland and Alaska where fossils of the leaves and fruits have been found; while in Europe, *Castanea* already existed during the Cretaceous period, some 75 to 100 million years ago.

The American chestnut (*Castanea dentata*) is native to a vast area of the United States east of the Mississippi River. Its natural range once covered more than 200 million acres from the Canadian border to the Gulf of Mexico. In North America, the Indians made good use of the chestnut in pre-Columbian times. The Iroquois from New York called the tree "O-heh-yah-tah," meaning "prickly bur." They ate the nuts raw or pounded, boiled them to make lumps of doughy bread, or cooked them in their corn bread. In 1612, Captain John Smith noted that the Indians in Virginia, after boiling chestnuts for four hours, made "both broath and bread for their chiefe men or at their greatest feasts."

The settlers found in the American chestnut a useful, majestic timber tree commonly reaching a height of 100 to 120 feet and a diameter of up to six feet. The pioneer, when clearing the land, would usually leave a few select chestnut trees standing in his farmstead so his family could gather the nuts in the autumn. Durable, rot-resistant chestnut lumber was utilized for farm fencing, furniture, ship masts, mine props, telephone poles and railroad ties as the country developed. Extracts from the bark and trunk of the chestnut provided a prime source of tannin for the leather industry. It was said that chestnut wood "carried man from cradle to grave, in crib and coffin." The chestnut represented North America's most versatile and valuable tree.

Fresh, sweet chestnuts were prized by man, his domesticated animals and the wildlife of the eastern American forests. In the early fall, farmers fattened their hogs by letting

CHESTNUTTING

An illustration by Winslow Homer. The children are gathering chestnuts in New England about 1870.

AMERICAN CHESTNUT

shadowed it was, when it flower, a bouquet which scented the whole neighborhood, but the squirrels and jays got most of its fruit, the last coming in flocks early in the morning and picking the nuts out of the burs before they fell. I relinquished these trees to them and visited the most distant woods composed wholly of chestnut. These nuts, as far as they went, were a good substitute for bread."

Without warning, disaster struck the American chestnut at the beginning of the twentieth century: a canker-forming bark disease, caused by the fungus *Endothia parasitica*, was introduced to New York City in the 1890s from the Orient with some Asiatic chestnut planting stock. Although Chinese chestnut trees, *C. mollissima*, and the Japanese species, *C. crenata*, were resistant to this destructive bark disease, their American cousin was highly susceptible. The chestnut blight on Ameri-

CHESTNUT TIMBER, NORTH CAROLINA

This photo was taken early in the twentieth century before the magnificent trees were decimated by chestnut blight.

them run loose in the woods to devour chestnut mast. Henry David Thoreau captured the enchanting nostalgia of the chestnut in his book *Walden, or Life in the Woods*, written in 1854:

"When chestnuts were ripe I laid up half a bushel for winter. It was very exciting at that season to roam the then boundless chestnut woods of Lincoln,—they now sleep their long sleeps under the railroad,—with a bag on my shoulder, and a stick to open burs with in my hand, for I did not always wait for the frost, amid the rustling of leaves and the loud reproofs of the red squirrels and the jays, whose half-consumed nuts I sometimes stole, for the burs which they had selected were sure to contain sound ones. Occasionally I climbed and shook the trees. They grew also behind my house, and one large tree which almost over-

53

been unsuccessful. All attempts to put an end to this catastrophic blight have failed. As a result of it, the American chestnut has been eliminated as a commercial species and is no longer a source of market nuts.

Most chestnuts sold in the United States are imported from Italy. The roasted nuts offered for sale on the streets of New York City generally come from Avellino, near Naples; collected from European chestnut trees, *C.*

PARAGON CHESTNUT

can trees was first reported in 1904 at the Bronx Zoological Park. Within fifty years it destroyed virtually all large American chestnuts from Maine to Alabama, making it one of the most damaging diseases in the history of American flora.

The blight fungus is spread by microscopic spores that can be carried by the wind, birds or other animals. A wound parasite, it invades the chestnut tree through wounds or fissures in the bark and continues to grow around the trunks or limbs until it encircles them. The affected parts then die. Sprouts appear and develop into small trees before becoming reinfected, killed and then followed by more sprouts. The roots are not normally infected by the blight. Efforts to develop a blight-resistant American chestnut have so far

FRUITING BODIES (BLISTERS) OF THE CHESTNUT BLIGHT FUNGUS

54

sativa, the nuts are larger but not so sweet and tasty as the defunct American chestnut. Chestnuts have gradually become a minor item in the United States nut trade.

The European chestnut trees have also been attacked by the blight since 1938 and their production is decreasing. Important research experiments initiated in Italy and France are now being carried out by scientists at the Connecticut Agriculture Experiment Station and elsewhere. Individual trees are innoculated with "hypovirulent," virus-carrying strains of the chestnut blight fungus, which convert the killing strains of the blight into non-killing strains. These beneficial virus-carrying strains have been imported to the eastern United States for research which may eventually lead to control of the dreaded chestnut blight.

The poet Robert Frost may have been ac-

curate as well as prophetic in 1930 in his poem *Evil Tendencies Cancel*:

> Will the blight end the chestnut?
> The farmers rather guess not.
> It keeps smoldering at the roots
> and sending up new shoots
> Till another parasite
> Shall come to end the blight.

Henry Wadsworth Longfellow wrote his well-known poem "The Village Blacksmith" in 1839 about a "spreading chestnut tree" which stood at the corner of Brattle and Story Streets in Cambridge, Massachusetts. The tree was chopped down in 1876 in order to widen Brattle Street. Strong evidence confirms that it was not the American chestnut, *Castanea dentata*, but the European horse chestnut tree, *Aesculus hippocastanum*, botanically entirely distinct from and unrelated to

LONGFELLOW'S SPREADING CHESTNUT TREE WAS A HORSE-CHESTNUT

" Under a spreading chestnut tree
The Village smithy stands; "

55

FLOWERS AND LEAVES OF THE AMERICAN CHESTNUT

Leaves, simple, alternate, sharply toothed margins. Flowers, small, yellowish, in long catkins. Petals very small. Fruits in sharp, spiny burs. Usually 3 nuts per bur.

English botanist, John Gerard, explained the origin of the name in 1597: "in English, Horse Chestnut, for that the people of the East countries do with the fruit thereof cure their horses of the cough, shortnesse of breath and such like diseases."

In 1853 the Chinese chestnut, *C. mollissima*, was introduced to the United States. It

FLOWERS AND LEAVES OF THE HORSE CHESTNUT

Leaves, opposite, compound, wavy margins. Flowers, white, much larger than those of the chestnut; in large, open, terminal clusters. Petals white. Fruits covered by a few soft spines. One seed per fruit. The true chestnut, *Castanea dentata*, of the Fagaceae or beech family, is botanically distinct from and not related to the horse chestnut, *Aesculus hippocastanum*, and the red horse chestnut, *A. carnea* (shown in the photo on the right), both of the Hippocastanaceae or horse chestnut family.

the true chestnut. "Under a spreading horse-chestnut tree," however, although scientifically correct, might not have been up to the poet's high rhythmic standards.

The famous, ornamental chestnut trees of Paris, with their showy, pinkish-white flowers and handsome, large foliage are European horse chestnuts, the fruits of which are unpalatable and not fit for human consumption. Oddly enough, horses often refuse to eat horse chestnuts, although horse chestnut meal may be utilized for cattle and sheep. The

56

NUTS OF THREE CHESTNUT SPECIES

Left—Japanese; big, with large basal scar
Center—Chinese; less pointed styler (tip) end, small basal scar
Right—American; typically small nut, attenuated styler end

is resistant but not immune to the chestnut blight fungus. Smaller than the American chestnut, it forms a spreading tree that attains a height of about forty feet. The Chinese chestnut is the most commonly planted orchard species at the present time in the United States. Sturdy and handsome, it is well suited for yard and orchard culture as it begins to bear fruit in five or six years from seed. Chinese chestnuts are sweeter than the imported European, but not so sweet as the American chestnut. Several Chinese cultivars or clones have been selected for abundant production of large nuts, such as the Crane, Nanking and Orrin. There are commercial Chinese chestnut orchards in Maryland and Georgia.

The Japanese chestnut, *C. crenata*, was introduced into the United States in 1876. A variable species, some trees produce huge nuts as large as two inches in diameter and weighing an ounce or more, while others produce small nuts. The Japanese chestnut is not so hardy as the Chinese and is more susceptible to blight. In Japan, this chestnut is used to feed pigs rather than humans. The flavor of the nuts is bitter due to a high tannin content.

Chestnuts are monoecious, which means that male and female flowers are separate, although both occur on the same tree. Chestnuts are also self-sterile, so cross-pollination with pollen from another tree is necessary to produce a good crop of nuts. The male stamen flowers are in long, slender catkin spikes which shed profusely a fine, yellow pollen. The flowers give off a sweet, powerful odor, disagreeable to some people. The pollen is carried by wind or insects to receptive female flowers or immature burs. The burs develop into rough, spiny green envelopes—"involucres"—with a thick velvety lining. In the

57

HAND HARVESTING CHINESE CHESTNUTS IN GEORGIA

Due to problems of diseases, insects, harvesting and marketing, chestnut growing is a
risky business at the present time. There are less than 400 acres of commercial orchards of
Chinese chestnuts in the United States.

true chestnuts (American, European, Chinese
and Japanese) the burs normally contain three
mahogany-brown, closely-packed nuts.

Both Chinese and Japanese chestnuts
have been extensively used in hybridization
through controlled cross-pollination. By
combining the most desirable characteristics
of the different chestnut species, superior
trees may be developed for orchard, ornamental and forest plantings. Four especially
promising hybrid clones which have been selected during recent years for blight resistance, vigor, form and nut bearing, are: Sleep-
ing Giant, Essate-Jap, Clapper and C9.

There are other species of small, hardy
chestnut trees or multi-stemmed shrubs
known as chinkapins (also chinquapins), native to the southeastern United States and the
Ozarks. The chinkapins, *Castanea pumila* and

C. ozarkensis, are distinguished by having only
one nut per bur. They start to bear early—at
an age of two to three years—but are susceptible to the chestnut blight. Their nuts are sweet
and very small—400 to 700 per pound, as
compared to 75 to 160 per pound for the
American chestnut, and 30 to 150 per pound
for the Chinese chestnut. Although chinkapins were prized as human food by the Indians and early American settlers, today they
are consumed for the most part by birds and
wildlife. The little nuts are difficult to shell
and remove from their spiny burs, and are
frequently infested with nut weevils.

Castanea sativa, the European chestnut is
known also as the sweet English chestnut, the
Spanish chestnut and the French chestnut. It
is native to Asia Minor and southern Europe.
The ancient Latin name of the genus, *Casta-*

nea, is said to have been derived either from Kastanea, a city in Pontus, Asia Minor, or from a town of the same name in Thessaly, Greece, where chestnuts were first introduced into Europe. Xenophon, a Greek historian of the fourth century B.C., stated that the children of Persian nobility were fattened on chestnuts. Dioscorides in the first century A.D. called the chestnut the *Sardis nut*, since

THE CHINKAPIN CHESTNUT SHRUBS HAVE ONLY ONE SMALL NUT PER BUR

the best quality nuts were imported to Greece from Sardis in Asia Minor. The Romans took the chestnut to France and Britain. A flour called *polenta*, made of ground chestnuts, provided a staple ration for the Roman legions.

In southern France, Italy, Portugal and Spain the European chestnut has been highly esteemed as food for man and beast for many centuries; in some mountainous regions it is still the staff of life. Chestnut flour, chestnut bread and mashed chestnuts take the place of wheat and potatoes. Roasted or boiled chestnuts are eaten as vegetables or in the form of a thick porridge made of chestnut flour.

In France, selected "marron" chestnuts, larger and sweeter than the ordinary "châtaigne" nut, are preserved in syrup with sugar and spices added to make *marrons glacés* and other delectable French sweetmeats. Chestnuts have long been a favorite ingredient for poultry stuffing. Fritters made from chestnut flour are a popular delicacy.

A sixteenth-century custom in British cookery was to roast chestnuts over a fire, making a slit or puncture in the skin of every nut except one; when that nut popped in an explosive burst, it indicated that the other chestnuts were ready. This practice is reminiscent of Petruchio's speech in Shakespeare's *Taming of the Shrew*, Act I, Scene 2:

And do you tell me of a woman's tongue
That gives not half so great a blow to the ear
As will a Chestnut in a farmer's fire.

THE GREAT CHESTNUT TREE OF MOUNT ETNA *'Castagno de cento cavalli.'*

This huge European chestnut, *Castanea sativa,* measured more than 200 feet in circumference.

Enormous, old chestnut trees are well known throughout southern Europe. The *castagno de cento cavalli* or "chestnut of the hundred horses" near Mount Etna was considered by some writers at the turn of the century to be the largest tree of all Europe. Its trunk measured more than 200 feet in circumference, while its age was estimated at nearly a thousand years.

The European chestnut was introduced to the United States by Thomas Jefferson in 1773. He grafted scions of *C. sativa* onto rootstock of native American chestnut in Monticello, Virginia. In 1802 Irenée Du Pont brought European chestnut seed from France to the Brandywine in Delaware where he grew thousands of seedling trees. In 1850 scions from one of Du Pont's trees were grafted on stocks of the native species to produce a promising chestnut variety known as Darlington. Unfortunately the Darlington va-

riety was wiped out by the chestnut blight many years later, along with other European clones which were fatally susceptible to it.

The chestnut has the lowest fat content of all the main edible nuts with only four to five per cent fat, as compared to sixty-two per cent for the filbert and seventy-one per cent for the pecan. In composition and food value, the chestnut, with a high carbohydrate content of about seventy-eight percent, is more akin to cereal grains, such as wheat, than to nuts with a low carbohydrate content. Examples of the latter include the filbert, with seventeen per cent and pecans, with fifteen per cent carbohydrate content. Since chestnuts are starchy rather than oily, they are readily digestible when roasted or boiled. Chestnuts are also very low in calories: about 1,700 calories per pound, while filberts contain about 2,900 calories and pecans 3,100 calories per pound.

TO SHELL CHESTNUTS (XI)

Pan/Oven Method

Cut a one-half inch (12 mm) gash on flat side of nut and put in a skillet, allowing one-half teaspoon (2.5 ml) of butter to each cup (250 ml) of chestnuts. Shake over heat until butter is melted. Put in oven and let stand five minutes. Remove from oven and with a small knife take off shells. By this method shelling and blanching is accomplished at the same time, as skins adhere to the shells.

Boiled Chestnuts

Place chestnuts in a sauce pan and half cover with water. Boil twenty minutes, empty water and leave chestnuts in the pan to dry off before shelling. By leaving on low heat and drying slightly, the chestnut kernels do not crumble on shelling.

Chestnuts may be stored in jars in refrigerator for later use in other chestnut recipes.

Roasted Chestnuts

After making a cut through the shell near the base to avoid bursting or exploding during roasting, place the prepared nuts in a pan and put in moderate oven (375 F°–190° C). When chestnuts appear about three quarters roasted, remove from oven and place them in the folds of a wool cloth, to keep them soft while cooling down. Chestnuts prepared this way are very tasty.

MAIN DISH

Chestnut Loaf (XII)

2 cups (500 ml) whole wheat bread crumbs	1 cup (250 ml) finely ground carrots
1½ cups (375 ml) ground chestnuts (either raw or cooked)	3 eggs, well beaten
	½ cup (125 ml) cream or vegetable broth
1½ cups (375 ml) minced celery	3 tablespoons (45 ml) minced parsley
	Herb seasoning and salt to taste

Mix all ingredients; place in a well-oiled loaf pan and bake in a moderate oven (350° F/175° C) 45 minutes to 1 hour, or until nicely browned. Serve with mushroom or tomato sauce.

Yield: One loaf

STUFFING

Amish Chestnut Stuffing (XII)

1/2 pound (225 ml) chestnuts	1 teaspoon (5 ml) salt
1/4 cup (60 ml) melted butter	2 teaspoons (10 ml) poultry seasoning
2 cups (500 ml) soft bread crumbs	1 well beaten egg
	1/4 cup (60 ml) chopped celery

Wash chestnuts, make two slits in each shell and bake at 475° F (250° C) for 15 minutes. Shell, boil in water to cover for 20 minutes. Chop fine. Mix with the melted butter, bread crumbs, salt, poultry seasoning, egg and celery. Toss well.

Yield: Enough to stuff a 7- to 8-pound (3 to 3-1/2 kg) bird

DESSERTS

Cold Marron Soufflé (XIII)

1 tablespoon (15 ml) or one package unflavored gelatin	1/4 teaspoon (1 ml) cream of tartar
1-1/4 cup (310 ml) milk	Salt
4 egg yolks, beaten	1/2 cup (125 ml) whipping cream
1 can (8¾ oz-265 g) chestnut spread or Crème de Marrons	3 tablespoons (45 ml) dark rum
5 egg whites	Praline powder (see recipe, page 115)

Sprinkle gelatin into 1/4 cup (60 ml) of milk and stir until dissolved.

Whip egg yolks until thick.

Heat 1 cup (250 ml) milk and pour slowly into beaten yolks. Cook directly over moderate heat, stirring with a wooden spoon, until mixture thickens and will coat the back of a metal spoon. Remove from heat and add chestnut spread, stirring until melted, then add gelatin.

Beat egg whites a little, then add cream of tartar and pinch of salt. Continue beating until they shine and form stiff peaks. Fold into the cooled custard. Set bowl in refrigerator or over ice cubes until it starts to gel. Fold in whipped cream, add rum and pour into a one-quart (one-liter) soufflé dish around which you have tied a paper collar. Soufflé should be a good inch above the one quart dish.

Refrigerate three or four hours or better still, over night. When ready to serve, remove collar and sprinkle sides and top with praline powder.

Yield: 4 or 5 servings

Chestnut Pudding (XII)

1 pound (450 g) chestnuts	1 cup (250 ml) heavy cream
1/2 teaspoon (2.5 ml) vanilla	Juice of 1 orange
2 ounces (60 ml) rum	Currant jelly
1 teaspoon (5 ml) powdered sugar	

Boil chestnuts for 20 or 30 minutes. Peel and remove inner skin, and press through a ricer while still hot. Add vanilla, rum and pow-dered sugar. Mix well and chill. Beat heavy cream until stiff and add gradually the juice of the orange. Now add the puréed chestnuts, and beat all together thoroughly. Put back in refrigerator until cold and serve with a tea-spoon of currant jelly over the top.

Yield: 6 servings

CONFECTIONS

Marron en Chemise (XII)

Peel and skin chestnuts. Boil until tender. Dip in whipped white of egg. Roll in sugar and dry off in slow oven.

Candied Chestnuts (XII)

18 large chestnuts	1/4 cup (60 ml) rum or
2 cups (500 ml) sugar	Maraschino li-
1 cup (250 ml) water	queur (optional)

Shell and peel the chestnuts. Cook in boiling water just until tender. Stick small wooden skewers or cocktail sticks into each chestnut. Heat sugar and water, stirring until dissolved. Add the rum and cook to hard ball stage (270° F/130° C). Dip the chestnuts into the syrup and stand on a cake rack to cool.

Yield: 18 candied chestnuts

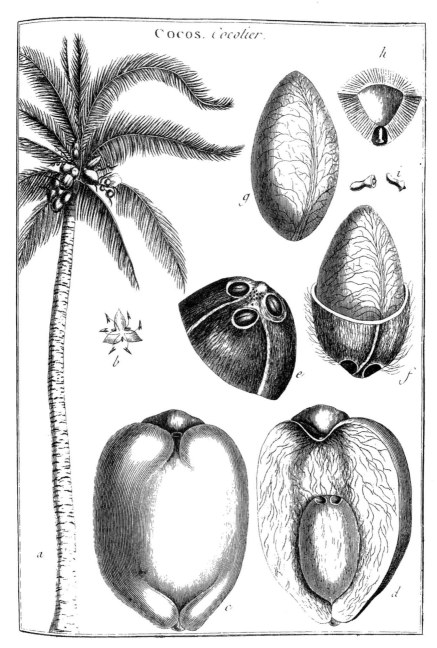

Cocos. *Cocotier*.

THE COCONUT

CHAPTER FIVE

Coconuts

Family: Palmae

LATIN	*Cocos nucifera L.*	DUTCH	Kokosnoot
SPANISH	Coco	ITALIAN	Cocco
FRENCH	Coco	PORTUGUESE	Coco
GERMAN	Kokosnuss	RUSSIAN	Kokós
SWEDISH	Kokosnöt	JAPANESE	Kokonatto
ARABIC	Jauz Al-Hind	CHINESE	Yeh Tzu

THE COCONUT PALM is an alluring symbol of the tropics. Its mention conjures up the image of a picturesque tropical isle—a curving beach lined with tall, stately palm trees leaning gracefully toward the sea. This plant is one of nature's most useful gifts to man, indispensable in the daily existence of millions of the inhabitants of the tropics, where the palm is a primary source of food, drink and shelter. In Sanskrit the coconut palm is called "kalpa vriksha," which means "the tree which provides all the necessities of life."

Every part of the coconut is utilized for some human need: its white nutmeat may be eaten raw, or shredded and dried, in which form it is known as desiccated coconut. A single nut contains as much protein as a quarter pound of beefsteak. The dried meat of the kernels is called copra, and when crushed or "expressed" is the source of coconut oil; its husk yields short, coarse, elastic fibers known as coir, which is widely used to make rope, cables, upholstery and coarse textiles; its large leaves, when interwoven, provide an excellent thatch roofing material for houses and may be fashioned into hats, curtains and baskets; the midribs of the leaves are used for fence posts, brooms, canes, pins and needles; thin strips of the fronds are woven into clothing. The hard, fine-grained coconut shell is a useful domestic utensil—half a shell makes a good cup, while carved shells can become spoons, buttons, ashtrays, saucers or teapots. An excellent charcoal is produced from the shells, employed not only as a cooking fuel but also in the production of gas masks and air filters. In the Far East it is said that there are as many uses for coconuts as there are days in the year. A sugary sap known as *toddy* is obtained by cutting the unopened young flower clusters, known as inflorescenses, to extract a sweet juice which may be consumed fresh, or fermented and distilled to make a strong liquor. The outer part of the trunk of the coconut palm furnishes a construction lumber for houses and furniture, known as "porcupine wood," which has an attractive grain and dark color; it can also be used to build small canoes. The swollen base of the trunk, when hollowed, can be turned into a food storage container or a large Hawaiian hula drum. At the top of the tree, the tender terminal bud (the palm heart), a bundle of tightly packed, cabbage-like, succulent, un-

TUMBLER   SPOON

GOBLET

UTENSILS CARVED FROM THE
COCONUT SHELL

opened leaves, can be used in salads. Extraction of the terminal bud, however, mortally wounds the tree, so the heart of the coconut palm is a rare delicacy. One could live almost endlessly on the coconut's products.

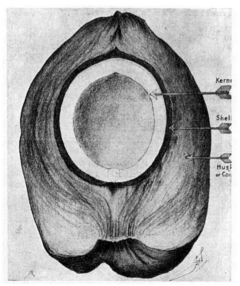

Kern

Shel

Hus
or Co

CROSS SECTION OF COCONUT

The coconut was not known to classical writers. It is first mentioned in 545 A.D. by Cosmos Indicopleustes, an Egyptian monk who visited western India and Ceylon. In his *Topographia Christiana*, Cosmos described it as the "great nut of India." The *Mahavasma*, an ancient chronological history of Ceylon, describes the planting of coconuts in that country in 589 A.D.

An early Chinese travel report, from book 197 of the history of the T'ang dynasty (618-907 A.D.), described the preparation of coconut wine in "Ka-Ling" (Java): "Wine is made out of the flowers of the cocoanut tree; the flowers of this tree are more than three feet long and as large as a man's arm, these are cut and the juice is collected and made into wine, which is sweet and intoxicating." Another Chinese writer in book 222 of the same history observed: "They make wine of the hanging flowers of the cocoapalm (in Java); when they drink of it, they become rapidly drunk."

A remarkable Buddhist temple called Boroboedoer was built of volcanic lava on a hillside in central Java about 900 A.D. Among the ruins of this time-worn shrine there are

ANCIENT INDONESIAN SCULPTURE DEPICTING COCONUTS

Among the ruins of a Buddhist temple called Boroboedoer on a hillside in central Java, dating from about A.D. 900.

numerous, splendid bas-relief carvings, several of which depict the coconut palm. This decorative Indonesian sculpture is undoubtedly one of the oldest known illustrative portrayals of the coconut.

In 1280 Marco Polo described coconut growing in Sumatra, as well as in Madras and Malabar in India, calling it *nux indica*, the Indian nut. The first detailed description of the coconut palm in Western literature was provided by the Italian explorer Lodovico di Varthema in his *Itinerario* in 1510, in which he referred to it as *tenga*.

The generic name "Cocos" and the popular name "coconut" apparently are derived from the Spanish word "coco" meaning "monkey face." Sixteenth-century Spanish and Portuguese explorers gave this name to the coconut because the three scars or markings on the base of the shell resemble a monkey's face—two of the germinating holes representing the eyes, the third the nose. By the end of the sixteenth century the word "coco" became established in the English language. Unfortunately, Samuel Johnson's *Dictionary* of 1755 confused "coco" with "cacao" or "cocoa" (*Theobroma cacao*), a mix-up which has resulted in considerable misunderstanding in scientific, literary and trade circles for over two centuries. The Port of London eventually

THE DUTCH FLEET APPROACHING JACATRA (BATAVIA) JAVA IN FEBRUARY, 1607
Coconut palms may be seen growing along the shore.

68

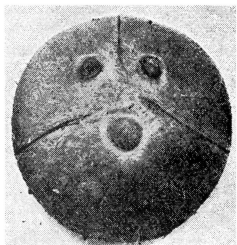

THE ORIGIN OF THE WORD COCONUT

Sixteenth-century Spanish and Portuguese explorers noticed that the three scars on the base of the shell resembled a monkey's face—two of the germinating holes representing the eyes, the third the nose. So they called the nut "coco," which was the Spanish slang word for "monkey face."

had to call the coconut "coker nut" to avoid confusion with cocoa in customs documents.

Although coconut palms tend to lean away from each other in order to get more sunlight when growing close together, they generally grow straight. Those near the shore lean toward the ocean because in that direction there are no other palms to shade them. Atop the unbranching trunk is a radiating crown of thirty or more arching, feather-like leaves measuring up to twenty feet in length. New leaves emerge as spear-like structures from the top-most point of the trunk and slowly unfold and open to take their place in the crown. A normal palm can produce a new leaf every month. After two and one-half to three years the leaf dies and detaches from the tree, leaving behind a distinctive ridged scar which gives the trunk its rough surface. The tough, fibrous, but pliable trunk is capable of bending and is very resistant to strong winds. The coconut is a single-stemmed tree; as in all palms, the sap rises throughout the whole trunk—not through the bark as in most trees. The tall varieties may reach a height of eighty feet or more.

A thick growth of thousands of string-like roots spreads horizontally twenty to thirty feet from the trunk to cover an area greater than the diameter of the crown. Although it has no tap root, the small roots and rootlets are so solidly anchored in the soil that they are seldom uprooted, even during hurricanes. Without such a strong root system, the coconut palm would not be able to lean and grow in such an inclined manner in windy and seaside locations, where it usually leans into the prevailing wind.

At maturity, roughly six to twelve years in tall varieties, the tree begins to produce green inflorescent buds at the leaf base with each new leaf. The developing inflorescence (flower-bearing branch) on its first appearance is two to three feet long, enveloped in a sheath

69

called the spathe. As the bud swells it bursts the sheath, revealing the inflorescence. The flowers are pale and straw-colored. The coconut palm is monoecious, producing both male and female flowers on the same inflorescence. The smaller male flowers are produced on the end of the inflorescence, away from the trunk. The inflorescence can be either self- or cross-pollinated. The tall varieties are nearly always cross-pollinated because the female flowers mature first and are no longer receptive when the male flowers shed their pollen. Although many female flowers are pollinated and set fruit, more than fifty per cent fall during the first two months, leaving a cluster of young coconuts to develop. They look somewhat like large, green acorns at this stage.

After 120 days, the shell becomes filled with a clear, sweet, refreshing liquid called "coconut water," rich in sugar, minerals and vitamins. This liquid is so pure that in extreme emergencies in the Pacific theater during World War II, United States military physicians found that they could drip pure coconut water directly into a patient's veins with satisfactory results if no sterile glucose solution could be obtained. Coconut water is a refreshing drink, popular in producing areas as well as with tourists in the tropics, who sip it directly from the nut through a straw.

As the fruit ripens, this watery juice thickens. After 160 days the nut attains its full size, and the meat (endosperm) begins to form around the inside of the shell as a thin, white, jelly-like layer. The shell begins to harden when the nut is about 220 days old, and full

COCONUT ROOT SYSTEM
Thousands of string-like roots, spreading horizontally are solidly anchored in the soil.

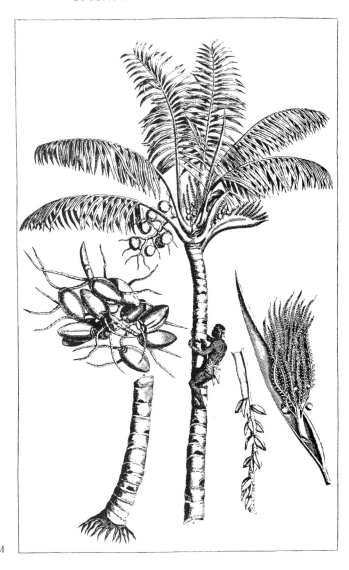

THE COCONUT PALM

maturity is reached at eleven to twelve months when most of the coconut liquid has solidified into nut meat, leaving an air space within the nut. Shaking the coconut to slosh the liquid is a test of its maturity. The average ripe fruit is ovoid, about eight to fifteen inches long, six to eight inches in diameter and weighs around seven to eight pounds. A smooth outside skin covers the thick, fibrous husk. The following figures indicate the approximate percentages of the components of the whole, ripe coconut: shell about 12 per cent; husk about 35 per cent; meat, about 28 per cent; and water, about 25 per cent.

71

Under normal conditions, the nuts will start to fall when fourteen months old. Usually only three to six nuts per inflorescence ever reach maturity, but since each palm carries a dozen or more bunches at a time, all at a different stage of development, mature nuts are borne the year around by a tree which knows no seasons. This habit of continuous flowering, unusual in the plant kingdom, is a very desirable economic and ecological characteristic. Labor for harvesting the crop can be maintained on a permanent basis throughout the year, while nectar is constantly available to bees and other insects.

The coconut belongs to the palm family (Palmae), one of the oldest and most diverse of the plant families. More than 200 genera and over 3,000 species of palms have been described. Palms share a number of botanical characteristics, among them a woody trunk, in many species, perennial growth, leaves which are folded like a fan and the production of a single seed leaf which, along with grasses, lilies and other families classifies them as monocotyledons. All of the other major nut-bearing plants covered in this book have two seed leaves and are consequently classified as dicotyledons, the other major division of the flowering plants.

Cocos nucifera is the Latin name or binomial for the coconut. At one time scientists recognized as many as sixty other species under the genus *Cocos*, but it is now generally accepted that the coconut palm stands by itself and is monotypic—meaning that within the genus *Cocos* only one species, *nucifera*, is recognized. Consequently, every coconut palm in the world is taxonomically the same species, which probably makes it the most abundant single food tree in existence.

Since a number of other palms were once classified as very closely related to the coconut, a plethora of scientific and popular names has confused its history. One example is the double coconut, also known as the Maldive nut or coco de mer, *Lodoicea maldivica*, a huge, fan-leafed palm found only on the Seychelles Islands in the Indian Ocean. This curious, double coconut-like fruit takes its name from the appearance of its massive nut—sometimes attaining a weight of fifty pounds—which resembles two coconuts

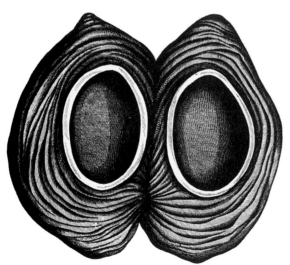

THE CURIOUS DOUBLE COCONUT

Lodoicea maldivica, also known as the Maldive nut or coco de mer. Found only on the Seychelles Islands in the Indian Ocean, this huge nut, sometimes weighing up to 50 pounds, resembles two coconuts joined together—but is not related to the true coconut.

72

joined together, side-to-side; yet it is not related to the coconut. It belongs to the Borassoid group of palms.

Two major classes of coconuts are typically recognized on the basis of stature: tall and dwarf. Most commonly planted for commercial purposes are the tall varieties, which are slow to mature and first flower six to ten years after planting. They produce medium- to large-size nuts and have a productive life of sixty to seventy years. Dwarf varieties probably originated as mutations of tall types. They grow to a height of twenty-five to thirty feet and begin to flower after three years, when only about three feet tall. Their productive life, however, is only about thirty years. Although more difficult to grow, the dwarf varieties are valued because they bear early and are resistant to lethal yellowing disease.

As a result of the world-wide distribution of the coconut in tropical areas throughout the world, a considerable number of named varieties—over eighty, including tall and dwarf—have been described. For the most part, each major coconut-growing region has its own dominant tall variety: for example, Ceylon Tall, Indian Tall, Jamaica Tall, Malayan Tall, Java Tall and Laguna (which is a widely grown tall type in the Philippines). The San Ramon variety in the Philippines produces especially large nuts, while the Macapuno is a tall type, the nuts of which have a jelly-like flesh considered a delicacy, which can be eaten with a spoon. The San Blas from Central America has an unusually high yield of coconut milk. There are also many dwarf varieties: the best known is the Malayan Dwarf. Others include the Dwarf Green and Dwarf Orange from India. The Niu Leka dwarf variety from Fiji produces large nuts, while the Ta-la-roi from Thailand produces very small nuts, some 35,000 being required to make one ton of copra. Only about 3,500 nuts of the San Ramon variety are needed per ton of copra.

The principal coconut-growing regions of the world are located geographically within about twenty-two degrees north and south of the Equator—roughly as far north as Hawaii

and as far south as Madagascar. Its native habitat lies in the humid tropics where it is frequently a pioneer plant on ocean beaches. As a plant capable of "escaping" from cultivation and growing spontaneously, it may be one of the first water-borne plants to arrive and grow on newly elevated land or reefs. Proof of its pioneer role was shown dramatically following the violent volcanic eruption of Krakatau in 1883. All life on the nearby island of Lang (now part of Indonesia) was destroyed by a layer of volcanic ash 100 feet deep. In 1897, however, a scientific team found coconut palms established on the seashore of Lang—proving that they had been growing there for a few years as pioneers, without the aid of man.

Growing naturally along the beach in a narrow band, often only a few feet wide, the coconut habitually borders an island's vegetation. The outermost trees usually lean toward the sea, seeking sun and wind. Away from this coastal fringe the coconut cannot compete successfully with inland vegetation without human assistance, i.e. through intentional planting and clearing of other inland plant life.

As it grows so near the ocean, the coconut may give the impression that it thrives on brackish or salt water. Apart from being able to withstand occasional brief salt water flooding, it needs a regular supply of fresh water to survive—which it derives from a lens of fresh water, which literally floats above the denser salt water, present in the soil under the beach. Originating from inland rainfall, this layer of fresh water furnishes the coconut palm with some of its nutrients, since the sandy beach soils are infertile. It is probable that the ebb and flow of the seashore tides, causing movement of air through the sandy soil, provide the tree with necessary aeration for its roots. Additional nutrients may be supplied by seaweed washed ashore in storms.

Natural dispersal of the coconut palm takes place when ripe nuts drop into the sea from leaning palms, float on ocean currents, and are deposited in new sites. Considerable distances may be traversed, for a ripe coconut can float for three to four months in salt water and still germinate. Cast onto the beach by waves, the palm is able to establish itself and then expand its range along the shore.

Scientists are generally in agreement with respect to the character of the native habitat of the coconut, but not on the particular geographic location where the palm originated. Its exact origin is lost in antiquity because of its wide natural distribution. Theories about the origin of the coconut can be divided conveniently into New World and Old World centers. A New World origin is supported by the historical fact that stands of coconut palms were found on the Pacific Coast of Panama by the first Spanish explorers and by taxonomic affinities between the coconut and various South American palms. Assuming a New World origin, it has been argued that coconuts floated across the Pacific Ocean (like Heyerdahl's *Kon-Tiki* raft to Polynesia in 1947) and thence to the Asian mainland where they spread westward to India and beyond. Opponents of this theory point out that recent plant research casts doubt on the theory of New World origin, and that coconuts were not being used by the natives of Panama when the Spanish arrived in the early sixteenth century. It is not disputed that the stands of coconut palms existed in Panama in pre-Colombian times. But had the coconuts been there before they appeared in Southeast Asia, the inhabitants would undoubtedly have been using co-

conut products at least as much as they were exploited in the Old World.

A much more plausible theory is that the coconut originated in the Old World, probably somewhere in the western Pacific or eastern Indian Ocean. Supporting biological evidence consists of fossilized coconuts found on North Island, New Zealand, dating from the late Tertiary period. In addition, the great number of parasites specific to the coconut which exist in Southeast Asia would seem to indicate that area was their original home. The longer a plant grows in a given area the greater the chances are that it might acquire natural enemies. Cultural and historical evidence is likewise convincing. The occurrence of the coconut in India dates back three thousand years. In the Indo-Pacific region there are countless names for the coconut and its products, deeply imbedded in the native folklore.

If the coconut originated in the Indo-Pacific region, dispersal both east and west can be postulated. Doubtless, many of the Pacific islands received the coconut through human agency, for it was a custom of Polynesian voyagers to carry nuts with them for food and drink and to plant them on new islands.

Study of ocean currents indicates that coconuts could have floated from the South Sea Islands towards South America and that the Pacific Coast of Panama would have been a logical place for them to become established—possibly only a short time before the Spaniards arrived (although no conclusive evidence exists to support this view).

Westward dispersal is evidenced by the many uninhabited islands in the Indian Ocean which already had wild stands of coconut palms when first visited by sixteenth and seventeenth century explorers. The coconut had reached East Africa prior to Vasco da Gama's visit in 1498, for he found it in Mozambique, where it may have been introduced by Arab spice traders. It is generally agreed that the coconut was not to be found in the Atlantic Ocean basin until the Portuguese brought it there after 1500, when they introduced the palm to West Africa and Brazil. In the early sixteenth century, the Spanish carried it to the Caribbean. Through human efforts, the coconut was rapidly disseminated throughout the Caribbean and South America wherever the habitat was suitable, since its products were so highly appreciated. Thus, by means of flotation and later through human assistance, the coconut extended its range until its distribution was pantropical.

When Captain William Bligh was cast adrift from the *Bounty* near Tahiti in an open boat by a mutinous crew, he and his eighteen companions would not have survived their memorable voyage of some 4,000 miles to Timor in the East Indies without the coconut. On May 6, 1789, he noted in his diary: "Our allowance for the day was a quarter of a pint of coconut milk and the (coconut) meat which did not exceed two ounces for every person."

Today the coconut is the most widely cultivated of all palms, grown in more than eighty countries in the tropics. It can be found in most of the islands and coasts of the tropical realm and with some minor extensions into the subtropics, as in the southern tip of Florida. Although some coconuts were growing in Florida in the middle of the nineteenth century, plantings of the palm were given an unexpected boost on January 9, 1878, when the sailing vessel *Providencia*, fully-laden with coconuts from the South Pacific, was shipwrecked on a beach near Lake Worth. By 1900 more than 300,000 coconut palms were growing in Florida, propagated mostly from coconuts imported from Trinidad, but supplemented by coconuts salvaged from the wreckage of the *Providencia*.

As coconuts were brought under more systematic cultivation throughout the tropics, they were moved inland and grown successfully on sites where full sun, good soil drainage and adequate supplies of water were available. Despite the feasibility of this move inland, the coconut is still a coastal tree crop for the most part, due to a large extent to the advantages offered by water transport of nut production.

World production figures provide a picture of where coconuts are most important as a commercial crop. The table below shows that the Indo-Pacific region accounts for about eighty per cent of the world's coconuts. During the past few years, the Philippines and Indonesia have been the leading world coconut producers. Production has declined in India and Sri Lanka, and increased slightly in Malaysia. Mozambique is the largest producer in Africa, while Mexico is foremost in Latin America.

COCONUT PRODUCTION 1981
(metric tons)

Philippines	11,050,000
Indonesia	10,800,000
India	4,500,000
Sri Lanka	1,716,000
Malaysia	1,207,000
All Others	7,392,000
World	36,665,000

SOURCE: *FAO Production Yearbook 1981*.

It is unusual that the presumed home of the coconut is today a major area of production. Most of the world's economic crops, such as rubber, wheat, tobacco, potatoes, sugar cane, coffee, cacao, cinchona bark (quinine), vanilla, peanuts, soybeans, oranges, macadamia nuts and others have become of greatest importance when taken from their native habitat to a new geographic region.

The coconut is propagated only by seed. Unlike the date and some other palms, the co-conut does not produce offshoots at the base of the trunk. Thus asexual or vegetative propagation is extremely difficult at the present time. Each nut contains a single embryo. Germination is slow: about four months are required for the leaf shoot to emerge from the husk. During germination, part of the embryo enlarges within the shell to form the coconut "apple," which persists until root emergence. For small, casual plantings, such as in dooryard gardens, the nuts may be sown directly *in situ*, that is, in the final desired location. Fresh nuts may be planted immediately after harvesting, or stored for a few months in a cool, dry, well-ventilated enclosure. Under plantation conditions, the seed nuts are collected from parent trees exhibiting such desirable characteristics as high nut production, vigorous growth and disease resistance. Sown in specially prepared seedbeds, the nuts are buried in deep, rich, loose soil to about two thirds of their depth. When the young plants are six to twelve months old, they are either transplanted directly to the field, or to a nursery for two to three years more before being set out in final field position.

Since cross-pollination is common in the coconut, consistent results of seed selection are not assured. Because of the great advantage of vegetative propagation (for example, use of grafts or cuttings) over planting of seeds, extensive research is being carried out on asexual propagation techniques. One avenue of research involves tissue culture, whereby plant tissue containing actively dividing cells is grown in a nutrient medium to develop a plantlet which can eventually be transplanted into soil. Encouraging results have been reported. Another research effort is being conducted with reference to the propagation of floral branches, induced to develop shoots which can be separated from the parent plant. Successful progress toward large-scale cultivation via either of these techniques could revolutionize coconut propagation and lead to markedly increased production.

Most coconuts are grown on small hold-

GERMINATING COCONUT

COCONUT PLANTATION
IN THE PHILIPPINES

ings in Southeast Asia. To establish new plantations, large or small, land must be cleared, since the coconut cannot compete successfully with other vegetation. Sites with good soil drainage and annual well-distributed rainfall of 40 to 120 inches are preferable. A mature coconut palm produces on the average of about fifty to seventy nuts per year. Superior trees may yield over 100 nuts, while the record in the Philippines is 470 nuts from one tree. A normal spacing for tall varieties in plantation groves is about twenty-nine feet by twenty-nine feet—sometimes closer—to give a density of fifty to eighty trees per acre. The spacing is designed so that the crowns of the mature palms do not overlap. Annual cash crops such as cassava, sweet potatoes, peanuts, corn or soybeans can be planted between the rows of palms during the first few years in the field. Strict attention must be given to weeding during the first five or six years. Coconut plantations are also utilized as pastures by local populations in some areas. The principal disadvantage of cattle-grazing is

77

HARVESTING COCONUTS WITHOUT CLIMBING THE TREE

Mature bunches are cut down with a curved knife attached to the end of a long bamboo pole.

78

that the ground becomes packed around the trees to such an extent that soil aeration is seriously impeded. Furthermore, the livestock may trample and damage the young trees, and the manure dropped by the animals does not compensate for the loss of nutrients in leaf material which otherwise would be returned to the soil. If cattle are grazed on a coconut plantation, the palms should be at least six to eight years old so that their leaves are out of browsing reach. Sometimes intercropping of bananas or pineapples is employed, and occasionally coconut palms are grown under mixed cultivation with other tree crops such as cacao, cashew or citrus—in which event adequate spacing must be maintained and fertilizer applied to sustain soil fertility. Species of *Indigofera, Crotalaria* and other tall-growing leguminous cover crops which can endure the heavy shade of the coconut palms are useful in preventing erosion, controlling weed growth and improving soils.

Multiple use of the land under coconuts is virtually essential for small holders who need to generate some income and provide foodstuffs for the first eight to ten years before coconut production begins in quantity. On large estates, catch (or supplementary) crops are also utilized to generate income during the early years.

Harvesting coconuts is carried out in different ways, depending upon the size of the grove and the products desired. The simplest method is to wait until the nuts fall to the ground and then gather them up; the coconut is often called "the lazy man's crop." Such is the practice in plantings where the crop is not highly commercialized and the nuts are collected for direct consumption. On commercial plantations, nuts are usually gathered every two months to reduce labor costs. For copra production, which requires fully ripe nuts, free-fall harvesting assures maturity. The disadvantages of this method are that nuts are frequently lost where there is a thick cover crop under the trees and that impact damage to the nuts may occur.

Nuts for copra production may be picked when twelve months old. Picking on low trees is done with a knife or with a long bamboo pole about sixteen feet long, with a curved knife attached to its end. Ripe nuts are selectively cut from the trees and collected from the ground immediately. Occasionally, unripe nuts are harvested by mistake. The dwarf varieties are, of course, the easiest to harvest.

In countries such as India where coir fiber from the husk is also a key product, nuts are picked at about eleven months, when the fiber is of highest quality.

When tall varieties grow to a height beyond the reach of a cutting pole, the trees must be climbed to harvest nuts—an arduous and dangerous undertaking. A number of climbing methods have been developed, but most make use of some type of rope harness which encircles the trunk and permits the climber to move it up and down. Climbing is facilitated by the ridge-like leaf scars on the trunk and is generally done barefoot. When the climber reaches the crown, he grasps leaf stalks for support and cuts loose the ripe nuts. At the same time, he inspects the crown for insect damage so that appropriate control measures can be taken. In addition to the considerable danger of falling from the top of the palm, the climber risks encountering bee or hornet nests, rats and even poisonous snakes which may nest in the crown. Since this work is so exhausting, a climber can harvest only about eighteen trees in a day. Climbing is the most expensive method of harvesting coconuts. In Malaysia, Thailand and Indonesia efforts have been made to reduce harvesting costs by training pig-tailed monkeys to climb the palms and throw down the ripe nuts. The obedient apes, wearing a collar at the end of a long rope, are guided by signals from a keen-eyed handler on the ground.

Copra, derived from the Hindi word "khopra," is dried coconut meat from which coconut oil is expressed; it is the chief commercial product of the palm. To prepare copra, the harvested nuts are first processed to remove the thick, fibrous husk. Ordinarily

HARVESTING OF COCONUTS

A dangerous and exhausting job.

LABOR SAVING

In some regions of Indonesia, Malaysia and Thailand, tame monkeys such as *Pithecus nemestrinus* are trained to climb the coconut palms and loosen the ripe nuts.

this manual task is carried out in the field by impaling the nut on an upright iron spike fixed in the ground and tearing off the husk with three or four vigorous twists. The work is hard, but an experienced worker can de-husk about 2,000 coconuts per day. The husked nuts are transported to the copra processing area where they are split in two by means of a chopping knife or hatchet. In in-dustrialized operations, the released coconut water is collected and made into vinegar. The shell segments with adhering coconut meat are immediately set out to dry in the sun on racks or concrete patios or dried in heated kilns, since any delay results in deterioration. Sun-drying requires sixty to eighty hours of sunshine; the copra is covered at night and during periods of sudden rains. The meat is removed from the shells after two or three days to accelerate the drying process. In kilns, drying can be accomplished in four to five days. About ninety per cent of copra produc-tion comes from small holders, so sun-drying or the use of kilns of limited size is most common.

Drying reduces the moisture content of co-conut meat from fifty to fifty-five per cent down to five to six per cent. Properly cured copra can be stored for extended periods with minimal deterioration or loss from insects or fungi. Before being marketed, copra is graded into about six classes in order of quality, then bagged for export.

Copra comes mainly from the same five

HUSKING THE COCONUT, 1884

A century later, the same method is used to remove husks: the coconut is impaled on a sharp spike set in the ground.

HAULING COCONUTS IN THE PHILIPPINES

The coconuts are transported from the plantation in sleds drawn by carabaos (water buffaloes) to the road where they will be picked up by trucks.

countries which lead in coconut production. The leading copra producer is the Philippines. Coconut planting in that country has a long history: It was mandated by a royal edict of the Spanish court in 1768 which required every adult to plant 18.5 square meters with coconut palms (probably about four to six palms per person).

COPRA PRODUCTION 1981
(metric tons)

Philippines	2,275,000
Indonesia	1,254,000
India	370,000
Malaysia	208,000
Sri Lanka	123,000
All Others	824,000
World	5,054,000

SOURCE: *FAO Production Yearbook 1981*

Copra yields vary considerably depending upon environmental conditions, age of the palms, methods of cultivation and the varieties grown. In tall varieties, about 5,000 nuts will yield one metric ton of copra; among dwarf varieties, from 6,000 to 8,000 nuts are required.

The value of copra is based on its oil content, and with a content of about sixty-five per cent it is one of the richest for vegetable oil extraction. Coconut oil is obtained by direct processing of wet kernels or through crushing of good quality copra. The oil is even more important in the country of origin than in importing nations; about sixty per cent usually goes into domestic use, while the remaining forty per cent is exported. After extraction from copra, coconut oil is refined into a clear liquid which has neither the taste nor the odor of the coconut. It is a fluid in warm tropical climates but at temperatures below 76 degrees Fahrenheit changes to a solid fat with the consistency of butter.

Coconut oil gained international economic stature in the middle of the nineteenth century as an ingredient for soap in Europe. It is one of the finest oils for that purpose; rich in glycerins, it lathers freely in hard or salt water. Following its use in soap-making, coconut oil became a major ingredient in margarine and remained the most important vegetable oil in the world trade, until surpassed by soybean oil about twenty years ago. Coconut oil now constitutes about eleven per cent of the total fats and oils entering world markets; it is one of the most digestible of the vegetable oils, universally popular as an ingredient in cooking and in the preparation of countless tropical dishes. New uses are constantly being discovered for it. The popular cream substitutes for coffee and tea are a good example.

A versatile commodity, coconut oil has many food and non-food uses. In food, in addition to margarine, it is employed in shortening, confectionery, baked products, ice cream, frozen desserts and whip toppings.

" NUT MARGARINE

MADE FROM NUTS AND MILK.

It looks and tastes like FINEST BUTTER."

AN EARLY TWENTIETH-CENTURY CARTOON FEATURING COCONUT OIL AS A SUBSTITUTE FOR ANIMAL FATS

Hindus in India prepare a highly important, vegetarian butter from coconut oil called *ghee*.

Coconut oil's non-food uses include the manufacture of toilet soaps, shaving creams, shampoos, toothpastes and cosmetics such as lipsticks, hair dressings and lotions. The charcoal industry employs it in the production of glycerine, fatty acids, synthetic rubber, plastics and paints; while in pharmaceuticals it is utilized as a solvent for vitamins and hormones, and as an ointment base because of its ready penetration into the skin and water-absorption properties.

According to the United States Department of Agriculture, an estimated 3,017,000 metric tons of coconut oil were produced in the world in 1980, with a market value of between $568 and $836 per metric ton.

After expression of the oil from copra, the remaining residue is a by-product known as coconut cake, copra cake or "poonac," which

when used in limited quantities is a valuable cattle and poultry feed, rich in proteins and fats.

Desiccated coconut is fresh coconut meat which is shredded and dried; it has a moisture content of less than three per cent and an oil content of about sixty-eight per cent. Currently this product is processed to a large extent in the Philippines (for the United States market) and in Sri Lanka (for Europe). Following shelling, the reddish-brown skin is pared off the outside surface of the white meat; the meat is then washed, pasteurized, blanched, shredded, dried and graded into extra fine, fine, medium and coarse qualities. A significant, hygienic pasteurizing process has been developed in the Philippines for desiccated coconut. This product is exported in kraft sacks lined with polyethylene film; it is packaged in fancy cuts—strips, chips, slices and threads—and in recent years has become a fa-

SHELLING COCONUTS IN FACTORY

Cracked shell is pried loose from the nutmeat. A competent worker can shell 1,600 to 1,800 coconuts in 8 hours.

84

PARING COCONUTS

Using a tool similar to a cabbage slicer.

READY FOR THREAD MILL

The coconuts, having been shelled, pared, washed and "capped" are conveyed to thread mills to be shredded.

MILL FOREMAN INSPECTING
FRESHLY SHREDDED COCONUT

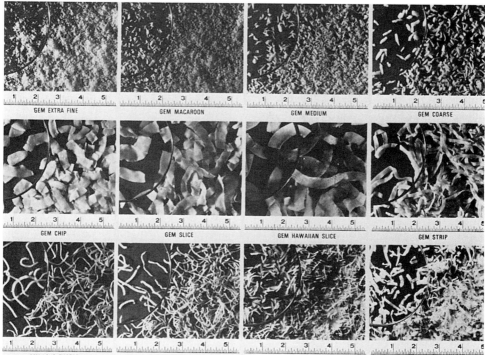

VARIOUS CUTS OF DESICCATED PHILIPPINE COCONUTS

miliar and popular ingredient in the confectionery and baking industries. It may be further processed by sweetening and toasting. At retail, the product is commonly called "shredded coconut" and is sold in plastic bags or cans. Coconut chips, a popular snack food, are sliced strips of desiccated coconut which have been roasted, salted and vacuum-packed in cans. This snack item is popular among tourists in Hawaii and the Caribbean islands.

The adaptability of the coconut is shown in other food products: coconut gelatin, a dessert made of coconut water, sugar, acetic acid and a bacterial pineapple culture; colored coconut, used mainly for topping in confectionery and baking, and prepared by mixing desiccated coconut with a certified food coloring and anhydrous corn sugar; coconut milk, made by squeezing fresh, grated coconut meat through a sieve, often serves as a substitute for cow's milk in Asia where it is fed to infants; coconut cream, a concentrate of coconut milk; coconut spread, a mixture of coconut cream with eggs and sugar; coconut juice, a diluted non-carbonated soft drink, and carbonated coconut soda, both prepared from coconut milk. The juice, milk and cream are consumed at the retail level as the ingredients of the pineapple-coconut-alcoholic beverage known as *piña colada*. Coconut sport or macapuno is an unusual product from a coconut variety in which the ripe fruit contains no water but is filled instead with a thick curd. This delicacy is eaten fresh, or cut into strips and cooked in syrup.

These coconut products, imported for the most part from the Philippines, Thailand, Singapore and Puerto Rico, are processed foods which can be found in jars or cans in food markets in the United States.

Another edible delicacy, well liked in the Far East, is the coconut "apple" which develops in the shell as the nut germinates. A refreshing drink known as coconut lemonade, popular in India, is prepared by boiling coconut water, sugar and lemon juice. Coconut flour, produced from partially defatted edible coconut gratings, is utilized in India and the Philippines in nutrition feeding programs in schools.

Toddy is the sugary sap obtained by tapping the tender, unopened inflorescence of the coconut palm. This sweet liquid can be drunk fresh or boiled down (like maple sap) to make a palm sugar called *jaggery*. Distillation of fermented toddy yields a liquor called *arrack*. Fermentation of toddy (matured by aging in closed casks) also produces coconut vinegar. In India this vinegar is sometimes flavored with spices such as black pepper, nutmeg and cinnamon.

Coir, an important industrial product in India and Sri Lanka, is the stiff, elastic fiber extracted from the husk of the coconut. Its name comes from the Tamil word "kayiru," meaning rope. The short, wiry elastic fibers of the husk are durable and resistant to water. Winning the fiber requires time and much hand labor. The husks must be retted in water for several weeks or longer before the fiber can be extracted. The longest and finest white fiber, obtained from the husks of unripe coconuts, may be spun into yarn for making ropes, cables, twine for lobster pots, rugs and acoustic insulation; a coarser, brown coir produces brush bristles, while the shortest fibers are utilized for stuffing mattresses and upholstery. The husks of approximately 1,000 coconuts are required to produce 180 pounds of coir. Coir dust, a by-product of coir processing, serves as an excellent rooting material and nursery mulch.

Virtually every part of the coconut palm

BEATING COCONUT
FIBERS TO PRODUCE COIR
IN CEYLON, 1884

has some reputed medicinal application. The liquid of the unripe coconut has been prescribed traditionally in India as a medicine to treat fevers, cholera and urinary disorders, as well as an anthelmintic to destroy and expel intestinal worms. Coconut meat is recommended in India as a cure for constipation and to relieve the build-up of gas in the stomach. Coconut oil has been found to soothe and help heal cuts, scratches and burns of the skin, including sunburn. Coconut milk is prescribed in Hindu medicine to help cases of sore throat and to calm stomach ulcers. In the Far East it is believed that ash from burned coconut shells can quell stomach pains; coconut roots may be used as tooth picks.

Because of its multifarious and diversified uses, the coconut palm has been given the names "tree of life" and "tree of heaven" in the Orient. Myth and ritual are involved with the palm in its Indo-Pacific homeland. In New Guinea, a native belief holds that the coconut originated by sprouting from the head of the first man to die. Thousands of miles away in Northern India, the coconut is considered a sacred fruit, linked to prosperity. It is likewise a symbol of fertility: shrines often keep a supply of coconuts to be given by priests to women who wish to conceive.

88

RHINOCEROS BEETLE
(Oryctes rhinoceros)

This dark brown beetle, usually about one and one half inches in length, is probably the most serious pest of the coconut in all coconut growing countries. It bores into the soft tissue of the bud, chews unopened leaves and inflorescences and can cause death in young palms.

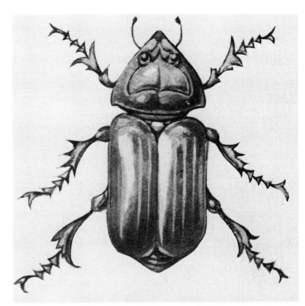

Coconuts themselves have served as primitive money. On the Nicobar Islands in the Indian Ocean, whole coconuts comprised the local currency, and the value of goods was reckoned in coconuts until the early twentieth century. Discs carved from coconut shells formed part of the shell-money strings which served as currency on some islands in the Carolines and in the Bismarck Archipelago in the South Pacific.

The importance of coconuts in human nutrition in the Indo-Pacific region is reflected in the estimated per capita consumption of 140 nuts per year in Sri Lanka; this figure is probably even higher in some Pacific Islands.

Nutritionally, coconut products contain protein, fat and carbohydrates—all three of the major food constituents. Analysis of the products reveals the following percentages:

Probably all plants suffer from insect pests and disease. The coconut palm is no exception. More than 100 species of insects afflict it. The large—up to two inches long—rhinoceros beetle is the most serious, because it penetrates the terminal bud, causing damage to unopened leaves and occasionally death to young palms. This beetle can be controlled by destruction of its breeding sites in decaying vegetable material. Palm weevils are another major pest. They lay eggs in the crown of the tree and the burrowing larvae damage the trunk. Chemical control is usually effective, but in severe infestations the tree must be felled and burned.

A dozen or more serious diseases affect the coconut palm. Of recent prominence in the New World is lethal yellowing disease which first appeared in the Caribbean in 1870,

Product	Water	Protein	Fat	Carbohydrates	Fiber	Minerals
Coconut water	95.4	0.1	0.1	4.0	—	0.4
Coconut meat	36.3	4.5	41.6	13.0	3.6	1.0
Copra	6.8	7.6	63.7	16.1	3.8	2.0
Coconut cake	11.0	19.8	6.0	45.3	12.2	5.7

SOURCE: K.P.V. Menon and K.M. Pandalai. *The Coconut Palm*. Ernakulam, India, 1957.

spread among the islands, and has been devastating coconuts and nearly thirty other species of palms in mainland Florida since it first turned up in Key West in 1955. First symptoms of the disease are dropping of immature nuts and yellowing leaves. Death usually follows in a matter of months. Most of the estimated 500,000 coconut palms in South Florida are the Jamaica Tall variety which is highly susceptible to the disease. The vector has recently been identified as a leaf hopper which transmits the mycoplasma-like organism that causes the disease. Fortunately, dwarf varieties of coconut are resistant to lethal yellowing: Malayan Dwarf and the newly developed Maypan hybrid are being planted to replace the more susceptible tall coconut varieties. At least three-fourths of the tall coconut trees of Jamaica have died due to lethal yellowing. In Florida, widespread injections of oxytetracycline (also known as terramycin in garden shops) have been carried out to control the disease temporarily. These treatments must be repeated at four month intervals. Lethal yellowing, recently reported in the Rio Grande Valley in Texas, looms as a very real threat to Mexico's coconut palms and could spread throughout Latin America. Plant diseases are seldom confined to a limited area despite governmental control programs, and in the years to come there may have to be a wholesale shift to dwarf varieties in the New World.

Planting dwarf varieties leads to earlier production in three or four years, but the nuts are smaller and the trees have a shorter productive life than the tall varieties. Should lethal yellowing reach the Old World, there might be little choice but to shift to dwarf varieties or dwarf hybrids. The brightest hope for coconut growers may be the development of simple and inexpensive vegetative propagation techniques which could be applied to reproduce selected, high-yielding, disease-resistant varieties on a large scale. This could bring about a sharp increase in production and strengthen the competitive position of the coconut in world vegetable oil markets.

Direct competition comes from the oil palm (*Elaeis guineensis*), the highest yielding of any domesticated oil crop per unit area, and from soybeans which are cost-competitive, since they are annual plants and can be cultivated easily by mechanical equipment.

COCONUT PLANTATION
DESTROYED BY LETHAL
YELLOWING DISEASE IN
JAMAICA

The success of the soybean was demonstrated when its oil surpassed coconut oil in 1962 as the major vegetable oil in world trade. Ninety per cent of coconut oil is composed of saturated fatty acids, while soybean oil is unsaturated and, therefore, may be recommended for human consumption over coconut oil, although this is a controversial subject. Coconut oil, however, does enjoy certain competitive advantages: it has highly desirable properties for soap making and it is the most easily digestible of all vegetable oils.

Within producing countries, wide and varied utilization and long-standing cultural traditions assure that coconuts will always be important. Industrialization of coconut products over the past decades has brought about changes. Whereas raw copra used to be the major export, extraction of coconut oil and its export is increasing steadily at the present time. A similar pattern is seen in the shift from exporting coconuts in the shell to exporting desiccated coconut. Both of these changes have benefited the countries of origin by creating additional employment in those tropical, developing areas of the third world.

It is estimated that approximately one billion coconut palms are currently planted throughout the world on some twenty-two million acres. About thirty-three billion coconuts are used annually—roughly eight nuts for every human being. The life cycle of the coconut corresponds curiously to the human: it reaches full bearing at about twelve to fourteen, more or less the time of puberty; produces well until about sixty, when it begins to decline and ultimately dies at about eighty.

MAIN DISHES

Coconut Meat Balls with Piquant Sauce (XIV)

3/4 lb (340 g) lean ground beef	Oil for frying
1/2 teaspoon (2.5 ml) salt	1/4 cup (60 ml) currant jelly
1/8 teaspoon (pinch) black pepper	1 teaspoon (5 ml) dry mustard
2 tablespoons (30 ml) flour	1 teaspoon (5 ml) cider vinegar
1 beaten egg	1/4 cup (60 ml) chopped chutney
1-1/3 cup (325 ml) flake coconut	

Combine the beef, salt and pepper; shape into about 3 dozen 1-inch (2.5 cm) balls. Stir the flour into the beaten egg. Toss the coconut with a pinch of salt on a sheet of waxed paper. Roll the meat balls first in the beaten egg mixture, then in the coconut. Brown meat balls quickly in hot oil in skillet; oil should be one-quarter inch (6 mm) deep. The meat balls may be cooled, then reheated just before serving, or kept warm in a 200° F (95° C) oven while sauce is made.

For sauce: beat jelly until smooth in a small pan; add remaining ingredients and heat through.

Yield: 6 servings

West Indian Pot Roast (XIV)

1 can (3-1/2 oz/100 g) flaked coconut	2 tablespoons (30 ml) fat
3 pounds (1-1/3 kg) beef for pot roast	Salt and pepper
	1 onion, sliced
Flour	1 clove garlic, peeled and minced

Put coconut in bowl and cover with 1-1/4 cups (300 ml) boiling water; let stand until cold. Strain, reserving liquid. Dredge meat with flour and brown on all sides in the fat in heavy kettle or Dutch oven. Pour off fat and put meat on rack in kettle. Season with salt and pepper and add coconut liquid, onion and garlic. Simmer, covered, 3 to 3-1/2 hours, or until tender, adding water if necessary. Remove meat and thicken liquid, if desired.

Yield: 4 servings

SALAD

Chicken Waldorf Salad (XV)

1/4 cup (60 ml) mayonnaise	1/2 cup (125 ml) diced celery
1 teaspoon (5 ml) sugar	1/4 cup (60 ml) flaked coconut, toasted
1/2 teaspoon (2.5 ml) lemon juice	Spinach leaves or salad greens
1 apple	1 small carrot, cut in thin strips
1/2 cup (125 ml) diced cooked chicken	

Combine mayonnaise, sugar and lemon juice in a bowl. Cut half the apple into slices; set aside. Dice remaining apple. Stir diced apple, the chicken, celery and 3 tablespoons (45 ml) of the coconut into mayonnaise mixture. Serve on crisp spinach leaves; garnish with carrot sticks, apple slices and remaining coconut.

Yield: 1-1/2 cups (375 ml) or one entrée serving

BAKED GOODS

Melting Moments (XV)

1 cup (250 ml) unsifted all-purpose flour	1 cup (250 ml) butter or margarine, softened
2 tablespoons (30 ml) cornstarch	1-1/3 cups (325 ml) flaked coconut
1/2 cup (125 ml) unsifted confectioners' sugar	

Mix flour with cornstarch and sugar in a bowl. Blend in butter to form a soft dough. Cover and chill, if necessary, until dough is firm enough to handle. Shape into small balls, about 3/4-inch (18 mm) in diameter. Roll in coconut and place on ungreased baking sheets, about 1-1/2-inches (3.75 cm) apart. Flatten with lightly floured fork, if desired. Bake at 300° F (150° C) for 20 to 25 minutes, or until lightly browned.

Yield: About 3 dozen

Ice Cream Pie (XV)

1 unbaked coconut crust	1 pint *each* pistachio, strawberry and chocolate ice cream

Prepare unbaked coconut crust as directed below. Fill chilled crust with scoops of ice cream. Serve immediately or store in freezer.

For ease in cutting, dip pan briefly into hot water.

Unbaked Coconut Crust

1/4 cup (60 ml) melted butter or margarine	2 cups (500 ml) flaked coconut
4 drops red food coloring (optional)	

Using a fork, gradually stir melted butter or margarine and food coloring into coconut in a bowl; blend thoroughly. Press evenly over bottom and sides of buttered 9-inch (23-cm) pie pan. Chill until firm.

Yield: One 9-inch (23 cm) pie

No-Bake Layered Coconut Bars (XV)

1/2 cup (125 ml) butter or margarine	1-1/2 cups (375 ml) flaked coconut
1 cup (250 ml) firmly packed light brown sugar	27 flaky oblong crackers, broken into squares
1 cup (250 ml) graham cracker crumbs	1 package (4 oz/120 g) sweet chocolate
1/3 cup (75 ml) milk	2 tablespoons (30 ml) butter or margarine
1 teaspoon (5 ml) vanilla	

Combine 1/2 cup (125 ml) butter, the sugar, crumbs and milk in saucepan. Cook and stir over medium heat, until butter is melted and mixture thickens. Remove from heat; stir in vanilla and coconut. Line 9-inch (23 cm) square pan with 9 of the crackers; spread with half the coconut mixture. Add another layer of crackers, pressing down lightly, and top with remaining coconut mixture. Add remaining crackers. Melt chocolate and 2 tablespoons butter in saucepan over very low heat, stirring constantly. Remove from heat, spread over crackers and cool. Cut in bars.

Yield: 18 bars

CONFECTIONS

Crunchy Chocolate-Coconut Balls (XV)

1 package (4 oz/120 g) sweet chocolate	2-1/2 cups (625 ml) flaked coconut
2 tablespoons (30 ml) butter or margarine	1-1/2 cups (375 ml) Grape-Nuts Flakes cereal
1 egg, slightly beaten	
1/2 cup (125 ml) unsifted confectioners' sugar	

Melt chocolate and butter in saucepan over low heat, stirring constantly. Remove from heat; beat in egg and sugar. Add 1-1/2 cups (375 ml) of the coconut and the cereal. Shape into 1-inch (2.5 cm) balls and roll in remaining coconut. Chill until firm. Store in covered container in a cool place.

Yield: About 3 dozen confections

Orange Coconut Balls (XV)

6 tablespoons (90 ml) thawed, frozen concentrated orange juice	1 cup (250 ml) confectioners' sugar
2 tablespoons (30 ml) butter or margarine, melted	2-2/3 cup (650 ml) flaked coconut
2 tablespoons (30 ml) water	2 cups (500 ml) graham cracker crumbs
	1/2 cup (125 ml) finely chopped pecans

Blend orange juice, butter and water into sugar in a bowl. Stir in 1-1/2 cups (375 ml) of the coconut, the crumbs and pecans. Shape into 1-inch (2.5 cm) balls and roll in remaining coconut. Chill for several hours.

Yield: About 3 dozen confections

NO-BAKE LAYERED COCONUT BARS

CRUNCHY CHOCOLATE-COCONUT BALLS

ORANGE COCONUT BALLS

1 *Nux Auellana, ſiue Corylus.*
The Filberd Nut.

CHAPTER SIX

Filberts
(Hazelnuts)

Family: Corylaceae

LATIN	*Corylus avellana* L.	DUTCH	Hazelaar
SPANISH	Avellana	ITALIAN	Nocciola
FRENCH	Noisette	PORTUGUESE	Aveleira
GERMAN	Haselnuss	RUSSIAN	Lesnoi Orekh
SWEDISH	Hasselnöt	JAPANESE	Hashibami
ARABIC	Bunduq	CHINESE	Chên Tzu

THE EUROPEAN FILBERT, *Corylus avellana* L., also known as the hazel and cob nut, is a member of the hazel family (Corylaceae). The genus name *Corylus* comes from the Greek *korys*, which means a helmet or hood, and refers to the shape of the husk which encloses the nut. Traditionally, the smaller, round nuts not entirely covered by the husk were known as hazels or cobs: hazel, from the Anglo-Saxon word *haesel*, or bonnet which the short hazel husk resembled; cob, because these smaller nuts were thought to look like a short, stout English horse called a cob. The larger and longer nuts were known as filberts and they had a tubular husk that completely covered and often extended beyond the end of the oblong nut. For this reason the word filbert is thought by some to have originated from the German *Vollbart*, or full-beard; others claim the name filbert took its origin from St. Philbert, whose feast day is celebrated in England on August 22, about the time the filbert nut matures.

There are two species of *Corylus* indigenous to North America: *C. americana*, the American filbert located primarily in the East; and *C. cornuta*, the beaked filbert, which ranges from the Atlantic to the Pacific. Both are small, hardy, shrubby trees or bushes. Nuts of these American species are small with thick shells and of inferior quality; their primary use is to furnish food for wildlife. In the western United States, *Corylus* nuts are called filberts, while in the East the term hazel is still commonplace. There has been a perplexing confusion for many years among the common names filbert, hazel, cob, cobb and others which have been applied loosely and interchangeably. In 1942 the American Joint Committee on Horticultural Nomenclature decided that the common name filbert should be used for the genus *Corylus*; nevertheless, hazelnut is still the word most commonly used in the international nut trade.

The European filbert is the source of most of the nuts of commerce and has been utilized

95

die Haselnuss (Hazelnut)

cluding Europe, Asia Minor, Asia and North America. The different *Corylus* species have been crossed so extensively and so much hybridization has occurred that husk length by itself is no longer a reliable characteristic for identification.

When the last glacial period in northern Europe ended, the European filbert was one of the first shrub-like trees to move northward as the temperatures moderated. During the Boreal period, which lasted from about 7500 to 5500 B.C., this tree was the dominant form of woody vegetation in the British Isles and some parts of Scandinavia: the number of filbert pollen grains preserved in various peat strata of that era exceeded that of all other trees combined. Since the time when it flourished the filbert has gradually been replaced by other types of vegetation. Be that as it may, this nut has consistently been an important item in the diet of man since prehistoric times, as evidenced by charred fragments of filbert shells found in many Mesolithic and Neolithic sites in Sweden, Denmark and Germany.

In the first century A.D., Pliny mentioned the filbert as a nut which came from Abellina in Asia, allegedly the present valley of Damascus. It was also brought to Greece from Pontus (on the shores of the Black Sea), which led to the name *nux pontica*. The filbert was introduced to Abella, Italy, a town in Campania to the north of Mount Vesuvius, where extensive plantings were established. The specific epithet *avellana* is said to be derived either from the Asian valley or the town of Abella. Apicius, a Roman gourmet and epicure, used the filbert in one of his first-century recipes for home-made sweets and called it *nux abellana*. Pliny observed that "filberts put more fat on the body than one would think at all likely." Dioscorides, the Greek physician, recommended crushed, parched filbert seeds to cure the common cold and persistent coughs; he prescribed ground filbert seeds mixed with bear grease as a cure for baldness. Virgil praised the filbert, stating that it was accorded more honors than the vine, the myrtle and even the bay tree.

as planting stock to develop extensive orchards in Oregon and Washington. The only other species of filbert which produces a nut valuable for human consumption is *C. maxima*, a tall tree indigenous to southern Europe eastward to Turkey. Eight other species of filberts are native to areas which almost encircle the globe in the North Temperate Zone in-

SQUIRRELS AND NUTS

From a painting by Albrecht Dürer, 1512. The nuts are filberts, known in Europe as hazelnuts.

Well-preserved plant remains discovered in 1972 in an archaeological excavation near Pompeii, in a site destroyed by the eruption of Mount Vesuvius in 79 A.D., include some carbonized filbert shells.

The nut-bearing hazel has long been asso-ciated with mystic rites and the occult. In Greek mythology Apollo and Mercury, the two sons of Jupiter, exchanged gifts. Apollo got a tortoise-shell lyre, whose harmony would free the artistic spirit of mankind. Mercury received a winged wand made of hazel

Corylus avellana . L

CARBONIZED FILBERT SHELL

Recovered at Pompeii from site destroyed by the eruption of Mt. Vesuvius in A.D. 79.

wood; its mere touch was supposed to help men express their thoughts through words. The winged hazel rod, entwined with two twisting serpents, became a symbol of communication that is still used.

In ancient Rome, hazel torches were burned during the wedding night as a token of fertility and to ensure a happy marriage. A forked divining rod, made from the Y-shaped branch of a hazel, was looked upon in remote times as a tool for finding buried treasure. During the Dark and Middle Ages the hazel rod was employed to try to detect subterranean streams of water and unseen veins of precious metals. Even today dowsing enthusiasts employ rods made from hazelnut wood.

Hazel nuts were cultivated in England long before Shakespeare's time, both for the nut and the edible oil that was pressed from the kernels. The cracking of the nuts on All Hallow's Eve, accompanied by fortune tell-

FORKED HAZELNUT
BRANCHES HAVE BEEN
USED AS DIVINING RODS
SINCE ANCIENT TIMES

A—Twig. B—Trench.

ing, was a traditional amusement linked with British folklore—October 31 was called "Nutcrack Night."

Shakespeare was familiar with the hazel nut: in *Taming of the Shrew*, Act II, Scene 1, Petruchio, with tongue in cheek, describes the ill-tempered girl:

> *"O sland'rous world! Kate like the hazel-twig*
> *Is straight and slender, and as brown in hue*
> *As hazel-nuts, and sweeter than the kernels."*

The filbert is one of the oldest cultivated plants of Europe, having been grown for many centuries in Turkey, Italy, Spain, France, Germany and England. In 1629 filberts formed part of the selection of seeds sent to the Massachusetts Company. By 1771 filbert plants were being offered for sale in Flushing Landing, Long Island, New York, through William Prince's nursery catalogue. Attempts have been made to establish filbert plantings in the northeastern United States,

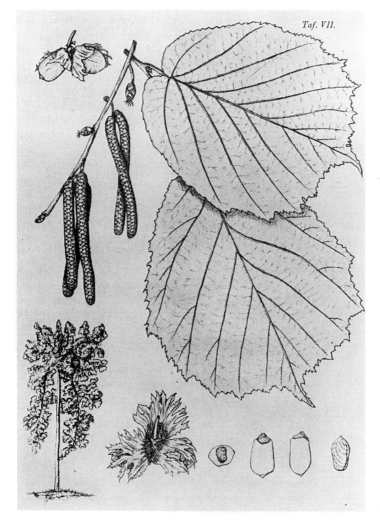

Taf. VII.

HAZELNUT

the Middle West and the South, but for the most part these efforts have been unsuccessful. The causes of failure include a filbert blight, winterkilling of the catkins (pollen-producing organs), winterkilling of the trees themselves and unsuitable soil conditions. In the northeastern United States filberts bloom in the early spring, and their catkins start to develop during the first warm days. If the bloom is followed by some frigid nights, the flowers will be killed and no nuts produced.

Filberts are produced commercially at the present time in only four limited geographical regions of the world, where winters are mild, springs rather warm, late freezes rare and summers cool. In each locale, nearby bodies of water help to moderate the climate. Approximately seventy per cent of the world's filbert production comes from small Turkish farms bordering the southern coast of the Black Sea, another twenty per cent originates in the coastal regions of Italy, seven per cent in Spain's Mediterranean coastal areas, and the remaining three per cent is produced in the coastal valleys of Oregon and Washington in the Pacific Northwest of the United States.

The earliest records of filbert trading are lost in antiquity, but it is known that the nut was exported from regions near the Black Sea before the time of Christ. By the eleventh century, filberts were traded in the markets of Genoa. In 1773 filbert nuts transported to Nijni in Russia were exchanged for leather and velvet. The great International Exhibition in Hyde Park, London, displayed Turkish filberts in 1851.

In the middle of the nineteenth century Turkey started to make serious efforts to increase the production and export of filberts. A Turkish company, formed in 1879, engaged in a thriving export business for several years. In 1903, however, as a result of a military conflict with Crete, several large nut shipments were lost at sea and the firm went bankrupt.

Subsequently Turkish production has gradually increased despite wars, economic depressions and violent changes in government. At the present time, Turkey is the

TURKISH HAND LABOR

Picking filberts is a job for women in Turkey. Mechanical harvesting equipment is not used.

world's leading filbert producer, although its agricultural techniques are still primitive and remarkably different from machine-oriented methods employed in the United States. Instead of being planted in regular rows and trained in single-trunk tree form to permit mechanical cultivation, as in Oregon and Washington, Turkish filberts are multi-trunked shrubs set in rocky, steep hillsides in clumps of four or five bushes in a five-foot circle. The bushes are seedling filberts, mostly of the species *C. avellana*, although much hybridization is believed to have taken place with *C. maxima*. Each bush has several stems about twelve to sixteen feet in height; as the stems grow old in thirty years or so, they are removed to allow younger stems to come into production. In Turkey there are no regular orchard formations, since the bushes are planted in the steep, stony terrain in uneven, haphazard fashion to avoid crags, boulders and other obstacles. Goats and livestock of various kinds are frequently grazed among the filbert bushes to control weeds. In general, the Turkish peasants have allowed nature to take its course—filbert bushes are often the result of chance seedlings taking root. Hand tools and hand labor are used for tilling; there is essentially no mechanization. The nuts are

hand-harvested before the crop drops, instead of being mechanically harvested off the ground as is the practice in the United States' Pacific Northwest. The nuts, still in the husk, are picked from the bushes by women, old men, girls and boys with baskets slung from their sides.

Despite traditional agricultural methods, Turkey has increased its domination of world filbert production during the past few years: of total world production of 410,000 metric tons in 1979, Turkey produced 290,000 tons, while the United States produced only 11,800 tons. In 1966, Turkey produced 190,000 tons and the United States about 11,100 tons. This may be due to a very large increase of filbert acreage planted in Turkey. In Turkey there are roughly 240 filbert bushes per acre; in Oregon and Washington about 108 trees per acre. Although accurate Turkish acreage statistics are not available, if one assumes the average production of filberts in Turkey to be a fair yield of about 1,100 pounds (one-half metric ton) per acre, dry weight with the husks removed, then almost 600,000 acres of filberts are planted in Turkey compared with 24,000 acres in Oregon and Washington.

Once picked in the husk on the Turkish hillsides, the filberts are transported to central

FILBERT PLANTING IN TURKEY

Instead of a single-trunked orchard tree, the Turkish filberts grow in the form of multistemmed shrubs.

SELECTION OF FILBERTS BY HAND LABOR IN TURKEY

locations to be dried in the sun, or, less frequently, in heated buildings. After drying, the husks are removed—some by hand, but most in husking machines. If by hand, the husks are lightly beaten with thin rods or slender shoots taken from the filbert bushes. Turkish shellers crack the shells between revolving millstones or similar equipment set horizontally with clearance adjusted to the size of the nuts. Blowers then clean the nuts to remove the shells. The kernels are screened, graded according to size, sorted and bagged for export.

A Turkish filbert (hazelnut) cooperative called "FKB" (Fiskobirlik) stabilizes the market and the prices paid to farmers, by buying from them. FKB, financed by Turkish government loans at low interest rates, controls the marketing of up to sixty-five per cent of the Turkish filbert crop.

The nuts are classified into trade types according to the region where they were collected. The two main groupings are *Giresun*, the best quality from the Giresun district on the Black Sea; and *Levante* for the rest. The finest Turkish filberts are round ("tombul"), rather than pointed ("sivri"). The round nuts are preferred in shelling since they are less easily damaged during cracking than the pointed types. Europeans prefer shelled filberts over the unshelled; about eighty per cent of Turkish filberts are sold in shelled form for use in the manufacture of candy and bakery products.

An important feature of the Turkish filbert

presumably because of a warmer climate, greater use of fertilizers and more fertile soils. During filbert harvesting in Italy, the bushes are beaten with canes and the nuts picked off the ground.

Italian filbert orchards are expensive. There are numerous instances of absentee ownership, since filberts are a profitable investment for urban professionals and business people. Consequently, tenants often farm the orchards, giving two-thirds of the crop to the owner and keeping one-third for themselves.

In Sicily the filbert plantings are for the most part uncultivated. There are many orchards on the damp, northern slope of Mount Etna. Except for an occasional pruning to collect firewood, the bushes are customarily left to take care of themselves. From time to time weevils wreak serious damage in the Sicilian orchards: they bore small holes in the sides of the young nuts and lay their eggs. Later, maggots are hatched, thereby destroying the value of the filberts for human consumption.

In recent years Italy has produced about 80,000 tons of filberts annually, amounting to roughly one-fifth of total world production. Some popular types or varieties for shelling include the Giffoni from Salerno; the Romana from the Viterbo district and the Round Naples. The San Giovanni and Long Naples are sold usually in the shell. Italy's best customers for the export of filberts are West Germany, France and the United Kingdom. In recent years, the United States has imported virtually no filberts from Italy.

industry is its strict inspection system operated by the government: no lot of filberts may be exported without first being inspected and certified. Currently, Turkey's principal customer, West Germany, buys over fifty per cent of the Turkish filbert exports; the Soviet Union follows as the second largest buyer. The United States' imports of shelled filberts from Turkey have averaged about four thousand tons annually during recent years.

There is very little waste in the Turkish filbert industry. Broken but edible nuts are utilized for extraction of edible filbert oil. Rancid and inferior nuts are made into industrial filbert oil. The combustible trash from the bushes, husks and shells is used for fuel.

Italy's filberts, like those of Turkey, grow for the most part near the sea, in this case the Mediterranean. The industry is located principally in Campania (Naples, Avellino, Salerno) and Sicily. Other filbert plantings exist in the north in the Piedmont region, and Lazio and Viterbo in the vicinity of Rome likewise raise a limited crop.

The Italians space their filbert bushes at more regular planting distances than the Turks, either on a rectangular basis or on contour—though, as is the case in Turkey, the bushes consist usually of several stalks planted in a clump. Yields are higher in Italy

FILBERTS GROWING ON
BRANCH

Most Spanish filbert production comes from the low-lying plains of the northeastern province of Tarragona; other producing regions include the moist hillsides of Barcelona and Oviedo.

The Spanish filbert orchards in Tarragona are usually planted in regular rows, fifteen to twenty-five feet apart, with only one bushy shoot per location, instead of in clumps as in Turkey and Italy. In other parts of Spain, however, clump planting is still common, although there is a trend away from this method. Irrigation is a standard practice in the filbert plantings in Tarragona as well as in other Spanish areas where the soils are poor and rocky. The most popular filbert variety in Spain is the Negreta, a medium-long nut.

Spain figures as the third largest producer of filberts; its annual output is usually about 20,000 tons. France is Spain's foremost export customer, followed by Switzerland. In Spain itself, filberts are a popular nutmeat in the nougat and candy industry.

In traditional Spanish herbal medicine filberts have an unusual application: as a cure for bedwetting, the patient is simply required to eat twelve filbert nuts just before retiring for the night.

105

A VERY OLD FILBERT

One of the oldest filbert trees in Oregon. Planted in 1898, it measures about 27 feet in height, with a spread of about 33 feet. It shows the typical multistemmed character of the filbert.

The cultivated varieties of filberts (C. avellana) were introduced to the West Coast of the United States in 1871 by Felix Gillet, a French barber who established a plant nursery in Nevada City, California. Gillet accurately foresaw that filberts would prosper in the maritime coastal valleys of Oregon and the neighboring state of Washington. The Willamette Valley of Oregon, favored by a moderate climate, produces about ninety-seven per cent of the United States filbert tonnage, the remaining three per cent coming from Washington.

Unlike that of Turkey, the United States filbert industry is mechanized from start to finish—from the time the hole is dug to plant the young tree, to when the nuts are machine-harvested from the ground. Only selected, named cultivars are used: about eighty-five per cent of American filbert production comes from a single cultivar, Barcelona, and five per cent from its pollinizer, Daviana. Both of these cultivars were introduced to the Pacific Northwest by Gillet. In recent years a superior new main crop cultivar named Ennis has been introduced to replace Barcelona—and an exceptional pollinizer Butler, to replace Daviana. Ennis produces very large nuts, over half of which can be sold as "giant" and "jumbo." A premium price is paid for the largest nuts, so size is important in cultivar selection.

Although filberts can be raised from seed, the resulting seedling plants do not come true to type, so asexual propagation through layerage is used in Oregon, since the filbert is difficult to graft. In layerage, year-old stems of the

Barcelona has been the leading filbert cultivar in the Pacific Northwest for the past 50 years and accounts for about 85% of U.S. production.

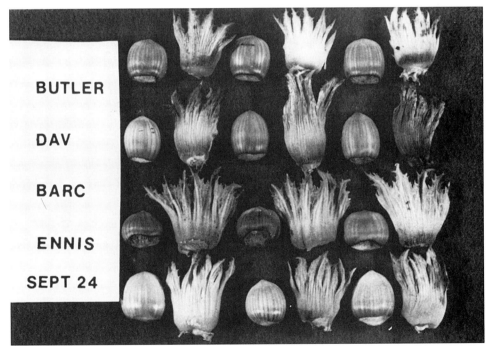

BUTLER

DAV

BARC

ENNIS

SEPT 24

FOUR LEADING FILBERT CULTIVARS IN OREGON

A comparison of nut size and shape as well as husk length and configuration of the Butler, Daviana, Barcelona and Ennis. Pictured just prior to time of nut drop in September, 1979.

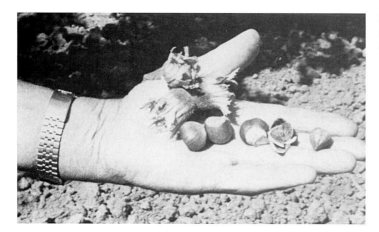

Barcelona variety filberts, showing husks, in-shell nuts, shells and kernels.

desired filbert cultivar are bent into the soil and out again so that the tip is above ground and the U-shaped portion under ground. During the growing season roots are formed on the underground part of the stem. The new layered tree is severed from the parent tree in November and dug in December. Layerage is a slow method of propagation but produces a well-rooted tree large enough for orchard planting.

Various spacings are recommended for commercial filbert orchards, ranging from fifteen feet by fifteen feet to twenty feet by ten feet. To provide uniform pollen distribution

BEGINNING OF NUT DROP

Most filberts in Oregon are harvested following their natural drop to the ground.

within the orchard, pollinizers are planted as every sixth tree in every third row, which amounts to a ratio of one pollinizer to seventeen main crop trees. Filberts are wind pollinated so bees are not required. The orchard should come into commercial production in the sixth year and under favorable conditions may continue to produce for fifty or sixty more years. A good orchard can produce on the average of 2,000 pounds of dry in-shell nuts per acre annually. But it is not uncommon for filberts to produce a heavy crop one year and a light crop the next.

The normal growing pattern of the European filbert, such as Barcelona, is to produce suckers and become a multistemmed shrub. Since the United States growers train their filbert trees to a single trunk to facilitate mechanization of the orchard, the season-long production of suckers is a nuisance. The United States Department of Agriculture has maintained a laboratory in the Pacific Northwest since 1928 to carry out nut research. This laboratory has developed new filbert cultivars and non-suckering rootstocks, and has improved propagation techniques and herbicide evaluation, has developed aids to mechanical harvesting and solved irrigation problems.

During the past decade there has been a shift from cultivating filbert orchards with

HARVESTING FILBERTS IN OREGON (1)

A sweeper goes through the orchard first to windrow the nuts.

HARVESTING FILBERTS IN OREGON (2)

A mechanical harvester straddles the windrow, picks up the nuts, gives them a preliminary cleaning and conveys them to tote bins.

FILBERTS ARE WASHED

Upon arrival at the processing plant the filberts are washed to remove any foreign matter from the outer shell.

FILBERTS IN SHELL

disk and harrow to non-tillage orchard management involving chemical herbicides in the row and mechanical weed control in the aisles. Non-tillage orchard management provides a firmer harvest surface than that obtained by harrowing the ground.

The harvest commences in Oregon towards the end of September or in early October after the filberts drop to the ground. Husk aging and opening can be hastened by spraying the trees thoroughly with ethephon, a plant growth regulator. With good weather and modern harvesting equipment, an experienced crew of five workers can harvest about 200 acres in ten days. Mechanical sweepers sweep the nuts, together with husks, leaves, twigs and other accumulated trash into windrows between the tree rows. The mechanical harvester straddles the windrow and picks up everything in its path, separating the nuts from the rest of the debris. Tote bins are hauled along behind the harvester and catch the nuts following their preliminary cleaning. These same bins are util-

111

ized to convey the nuts to the processor to be washed, cleaned some more and dried to about eight to ten per cent moisture content. The filberts are sold to consumers in the shell, or, in shelled form so the kernels can be used by bakers and salters.

The filberts grown in Oregon and Washington are larger than those produced in the Mediterranean countries. There is a growing export demand for these "giants" and "jumbos," though until now the greatest world demand for kernels was for the smaller sizes. The United States imports about forty-five per cent of the filberts that it consumes annually, so there is room for expansion and a bright future for the Oregon and Washington filbert industries.

RECOMMENDATIONS FOR FILBERT STORAGE (XVI)

Common Storage

1. Dry nuts at 100° F (38° C) to a total moisture content of 7 to 8% for in-shell nuts or 3-1/2 to 4-1/2% for shelled nuts.
2. Use properly sealed plastic bags or glass jars.
3. Store in-shell filberts at not over 70° F (22° C).
4. In-shell nuts dried and stored under the above conditions will keep satisfactorily for about 14 months without serious weight changes or quality deterioration. They will be of substantially better quality than nuts stored under ordinary common storage conditions.

Refrigerated Storage

1. After drying, nuts can be stored at 32-35° F (0°-2° C) for 2 years if packaged in sealed plastic or glass containers if the relative humidity is maintained at 60-65% and the nuts are stored away from odor-producing substances.
2. After storage, allow nuts to warm up in unopened containers to room temperature to avoid drawing of moisture which could cause mold and rancidity.

Freezer Storage

1. Dried nuts can be successfully stored at 27° F (−2.8° C) or lower for 2 years, with or without plastic containers. There is little danger of odor pickup and it is not necessary to control humidity.
2. After storage, allow nuts to warm up in unopened plastic bags, or in well ventilated areas if plastic bags are not used, to prevent mold or rancidity.

PREPARING FILBERTS (XVI)

In using filberts in recipes, the flavor and texture are generally considered best if the nut is slightly toasted first. The skin is thin and not at all bitter. In fact, some experts find the flavor and texture of the filbert skin most desirable.

To Toast and Blanch Filberts

For a rich, toasted flavor spread shelled filberts in a shallow pan and toast in 275 F° (135° C) oven 20 minutes, or until skins crack. Use skinned or unskinned. To remove skins, rub nuts while warm with a rough cloth or between your hands.

To Grind Filberts

Place nuts in a jar of electric blender. Run blender until nuts are finely ground. Or put nuts through food grinder using medium-fine blade. One cup (250 ml) whole filberts yields about 1-1/3 cups (325 ml) ground nuts.

To Chop Filberts

Working with a small handful at a time, place nuts on chopping board and chop with a sharp knife to desired degree of fineness. Or place nuts in a jar of food chopper and chop to desired degree of fineness. Unroasted nuts are easiest to chop. One cup whole nuts yields about 1-1/8 (282 ml) cups coarsely chopped filberts and about 1-1/4 cups (310 ml) finely chopped nuts.

To Slice Filberts

Slicing filberts, like chopping, is easier to do with the unroasted nut. Hold the nut with the slightly flattened end against a cutting surface. Slice with a sharp knife. One cup whole nuts yields about 1-1/2 cups (375 ml) sliced nuts.

VEGETABLE

Frontier Hazelnut-Vegetable Pie (XVI)

1 cup (250 ml) fresh broccoli, chopped	1 cup (250 ml) coarsely chopped hazelnuts
1 cup (250 ml) cauliflower, sliced	1-1/2 cups (375 ml) milk
	1 cup biscuit mix
2 cups (500 ml) fresh spinach, chopped	4 eggs
1 small onion, diced	1 teaspoon (5 ml) garlic salt
1/2 green pepper, diced	1/2 teaspoon (2.5 ml) pepper
1 cup (250 ml) cheddar cheese, grated	

Pre-cook broccoli and cauliflower until almost tender (about 5 minutes). Drain well. Mix broccoli, cauliflower, spinach, onion, green

FRONTIER HAZELNUT-VEGETABLE PIE

pepper and cheese and put into a well-greased 10″ (25 cm) pie plate. Top with hazelnuts. Beat together the milk, biscuit mix, eggs, garlic salt and pepper; pour over hazelnuts and vegetables. Bake at 400° F (200° C) for 35 to 40 minutes; let pie stand 5 minutes before cutting.

Yield: 6 servings

MAIN DISH

Fruit 'N Filbert Pork Chops (XVI)

1 cup (250 ml) chopped onion	1 teaspoon (5 ml) ground cinnamon
2 cups (500 ml) pared and chopped tart apples (3 medium apples)	1/2 teaspoon (2.5 ml) *each* ground ginger, salt and oregano
1 cup (250 ml) chopped dried apricots	Freshly ground pepper
3/4 cup (375 ml) chopped figs (one 1-pound/450-g can, drained)	6 loin pork chops, 1 inch (2.5 cm) thick
	1/2 cup (125 ml) chicken bouillon
3/4 cup (375 ml) toasted* chopped filberts (about 3 ounces/90 grams)	1/4 cup (60 ml) dry white wine
1/3 cup (75 ml) firmly-packed dark brown sugar	2 tablespoons (30 ml) *each* olive oil and soy sauce

Combine onion, apples, apricots, figs, 1/2 cup (125 ml) of the filberts, sugar, and seasonings. Press half the mixture into bottom of shallow baking dish. Brown chops in skillet, using some fat trimmed from edges of chops. Arrange on fruit in pan; cover with remaining fruit mixture. Combine bouillon and wine and pour over top. Cover casserole and bake in 350° F (175° C) (moderate) oven 40 minutes. Remove cover and push fruit from top of chops; brush with a mixture of olive oil and soy sauce. Continue baking, uncovered, for 10 minutes. Brush chops with remaining oil

*Spread filberts in shallow pan and bake in 275°F(135°C) oven 20 minutes, stirring occasionally.

mixture, sprinkle with remaining 1/4 cup (60 ml) filberts and continue cooking for 10 minutes.

Yield: 6 servings

BAKED GOODS

Hazelnut Cake (XVII)

1-3/4 cups (425 ml) sifted, all-purpose flour	1-1/4 cups (310 ml) sugar
2 (10 ml) teaspoons baking powder	3 eggs
	1 cup (250 ml) milk
1/2 teaspoon (2.5 ml) salt	1 cup (250 ml) ground hazelnuts
1/2 cup (125 ml) butter or margarine	

Grease and flour bottom of 9- or 10-inch (23- or 25-cm) tube pan or 9 × 5 × 3-inch (23 × 12.5 × 7.5-cm) loaf pan. Sift flour with baking powder and salt. Cream butter in large mixing bowl. Gradually add sugar; cream at high speed until light and fluffy. At medium speed blend in eggs, one at a time, beating well after each. At low speed add sifted dry ingredients alternately with milk, beginning and ending with dry ingredients. Stir in hazelnuts. Pour batter into pan. Bake at 350° F (175° C) for 45 or 55 minutes, until cake springs back when touched. Cool in pan 15 minutes; turn out and cool completely on wire rack. Sprinkle with sifted confectioner's sugar.

Yield: One 9- or 10-tube cake or one 9-inch loaf

Filbert Pumpkin Spice Cake (XVI)

1 cup (250 ml) chopped filberts, toasted	4 teaspoons (20 ml) baking powder
1/2 cup (125 ml) shortening	1/4 teaspoon (1 ml) baking soda
1 cup (250 ml) sugar	1 teaspoon (5 ml) salt
1 cup (250 ml) brown sugar	1 teaspoon (5 ml) cinnamon
2 eggs, beaten	1/2 teaspoon (2.5 ml) nutmeg
1 cup (250 ml) cooked, mashed pumpkin	1/4 teaspoon (1.5 ml) cloves
3 cups (750 ml) sifted flour	1/2 cup (125 ml) milk

To toast filberts, spread on baking sheet and toast in 275° F (135° C) oven for 20 minutes or until golden. Cream shortening, gradually add sugars. Beat in eggs and pumpkin. Sift together dry ingredients and add alternately with milk to creamed mixture. Fold in filberts. Batter will be heavy. Pour into 3 greased and floured 8-inch (20 cm) layer cake pans. Bake in 350° F (175° C) oven for 30 minutes. Cool 5 minutes in pans; then remove to cooling racks to cool completely. Add toasted chopped filberts to butter icing for frosting, and garnish with sliced filberts.

Yield: One 8-inch, three-layer cake

McKenzie River Hazelnut Pie (XVI)

4 eggs	1 teaspoon (5 ml)
1 cup (250 ml) sugar	vanilla
1/8 teaspoon (1 ml) salt	2 cups (500 ml) roasted
1-1/2 cups (375 ml) dark	filberts, finely
corn syrup	chopped
2 tablespoons (30 ml)	2 unbaked 8″ (20 cm) pie
butter, melted	shells

Preheat oven to 350° F (175° C). Beat eggs until blended but not frothy. Add sugar, salt, corn syrup, melted butter and vanilla; mixing to blend. Stir in nuts. Divide filling between two pie shells, place in oven. Reduce oven heat to 325° F (165° C) and bake 50 to 60 minutes.

Yield: Two 8-inch pies

DESSERT

Filbert Soufflé (XVII)

6 eggs, separated	1/4 teaspoon (1.5 ml)
1 cup (250 ml) sugar	salt
2 teaspoons (10 ml) lem-	1/2 teaspoon (2.5 ml)
on juice	cream of tartar
1/2 pound (225 g) fil-	
berts, ground	

Mix egg yolks and sugar thoroughly; add lemon juice and ground filberts. Add salt and cream of tartar to egg whites and beat until stiff. Carefully fold egg whites into first mixture and bake in a 350° F (175° C) oven in a casserole. Serve with a cream or wine sauce.

Yield: 6 servings

Praline Powder (XVIII)

1-1/2 cups (375 ml)	1-1/4 cups (310 ml)
skinned filberts, al-	granulated sugar
monds or pecans	1 cup (15 ml) water

Spread nuts on a cookie sheet and toast slightly in a 350° F (175° C) oven, stirring several times for ten minutes or so.

Heat sugar in a cast-iron skillet until it comes to a boil, then stir from edges and watch carefully. When it looks clear and thick, add the nuts and stir to coat. Turn the coated nuts out onto an oiled pastry sheet. When cold and like hard nut brittle, break into pieces and place in a food processor. With steel knife, process until a coarse powder is formed.

This will keep for months in a tightly closed jar in the refrigerator or freezer.

Yield: 1-1/2 cups (375 ml)

Fig. 77. — *Macadamia ternifolia.*
Rameau fructifère, demi-grandeur naturelle.

Fig. 78. — *Macadamia ternifolia.*
Fruit, de grandeur naturelle.

Fig. 79. — *Macadamia ternifolia.*
Graine, de grandeur naturelle.

CHAPTER SEVEN

Macadamia Nuts

Family: Proteaceae

LATIN	*Macadamia integrifolia*	DUTCH	Macadamia-Noot
	Maiden and Betche	ITALIAN	Noce di Macadamia
SPANISH	Nuez de Macadamia	PORTUGUESE	Noz di Macadamia
FRENCH	Noix de Macadamia	RUSSIAN	Makadamia Orékh
GERMAN	Macadamianuss	JAPANESE	Makadamia Nattsu
SWEDISH	Macadamianöt	CHINESE	Ao Chow Hu Tao
ARABIC	Jōz Makadamîya		

FOUR THOUSAND YEARS AGO, in the Old World, many important food plants were being cultivated by man, including wheat, rice, barley, onions, tea, apples, olives and almonds. Before the time of Christ, corn, the sweet potato, cacao and kidney beans were under cultivation in the New World. The macadamia nut is a rarity—a "new" crop which was domesticated for the first time in 1858 in Australia. It is the only native Australian plant ever developed as a commercial food crop.

The macadamia is an evergreen tree of the family Proteaceae. It is indigenous to the coastal, subtropical rain forests of southeast Queensland and northern New South Wales in eastern Australia. Before the middle of the nineteenth century, the nut was known only to aboriginal tribes, who since ancient times gathered the nuts each autumn, but in all probability did not cultivate the trees. Heaps of macadamia nut shells were found by the early white settlers in Australia near aboriginal feasting grounds. The seasonal macadamia nut was only a minor food for these aborigines who, depending on their territory, had several different common names for it such

as: *gyndl, kindal kindal, boombera* and *burrawang.*

The edible nuts are produced by two species of the genus *Macadamia: M. integrifolia,* known as the smooth-shell type; and *M. tetraphylla,* commonly referred to as the rough-shell type. Prior to 1956 the former was often called *M. ternifolia* v. *integrifolia;* the latter simply *M. ternifolia.* These designations are no longer used for the edible varieties. *M. ternifolia* now applies to one of the eight other non-commercial or wild species of macadamia which exist: four in Australia, three in New Caledonia and one in Celebes. The kernels of these minor species are for the most part small, bitter and inedible due to the presence of a cyanogenic glucoside.

Both of the edible species of *Macadamia,* if well-grown, may reach a height of sixty feet and a spread of some forty feet. Their glossy, dark green leaves, which resemble holly, make handsome Christmas wreaths.

The *integrifolia* or smooth-shell type has leaves four to twelve inches long which grow in whorls of three, and are usually free from spines; its flowers are creamy white in color.

117

Macadamia integrifolia leaves, flowers and a pollinating bee.

The leaves of the *tetraphylla* or rough-shell type measure from five to twenty inches long and have spines along their entire length. As the name implies, they are usually found in whorls of four. The flowers of *tetraphylla* may be pink or creamy white in color. These two species hybridize when growing in close proximity to each other. Most macadamia trees are self-fruitful (capable of producing self-pollinated fruit), but nut production is higher when two or more cultivars are planted near to each other.

The fruit consists of a fleshy husk which encloses a spherical seed one-half to one and one-quarter inches in diameter with a very hard, durable shell. Inside the shell is the kernel or macadamia nut, whose distinctive flavor has been compared to that of a superfine filbert.

The macadamia tree under favorable conditions begins to produce in six to seven years. It is a long-lived tree which may have a productive life of sixty years or more. In full production, well-grown mature trees may

118

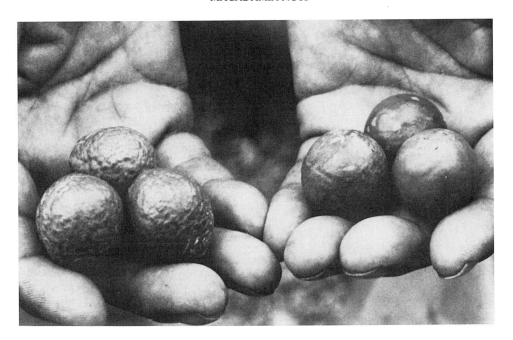

MACADAMIA NUT

In husk, in shell and shelled.

BARON FERDINAND VON MUELLER

First to describe macadamia botanically in 1857.

the time Secretary of the Philosophical Institute of Victoria. Dr. Macadam was born in Glasgow, Scotland in 1827, having come to Australia in 1855 as a lecturer on analytical chemistry, as well as on the adulteration of food, and public health. Tall, endowed with a powerful voice and long red hair, he was reputed to have been a popular and eloquent public speaker. During a rough voyage from Australia to New Zealand in 1865 he fractured his ribs, developed pleurisy, and died at sea at the age of thirty-eight. There is an unconfirmed report from Australia that Dr. John Macadam never saw a macadamia tree nor tasted a macadamia nut. In any event, he was no relation of and had nothing to do with John Loudon McAdam (1756-1836), the British engineer who introduced improved roadways built of crushed stone known as "macadamized" roads.

Although Baron von Mueller was the first to describe macadamia botanically in 1857, a

produce 60 to 150 pounds or more annually of in-shell nuts.

Baron Ferdinand von Mueller has been called Australia's foremost botanist. During the 1850's he travelled incessantly, over 15,000 miles on foot and horseback, methodically collecting 45,000 Australian botanical specimens. In early 1857 von Mueller was in the "bush" near the Pine River in the Moreton Bay District of Queensland, accompanied by Walter Hill, a Scottish botanist and Director of the Botanic Gardens at Brisbane. They discovered an unfamiliar species of tree which did not fit into any previously established genera of the Proteaceae. Consequently von Mueller described it botanically for the first time and named it *Macadamia ternifolia*, in honor of his friend John Macadam, M.D., who was at

JOHN MACADAM (1827-1865)

For whom the macadamia nut was named in 1857.

botanical specimen of it had been collected fourteen years earlier by a German explorer in Australia named Ludwig Leichhardt. A flowering branch of *M. ternifolia*, without fruit, lay overlooked and ignored in the Melbourne National Herbarium until von Mueller himself identified it many years later.

Back at the Botanic Gardens in Brisbane, Walter Hill gave some macadamia nuts in shell to a native assistant to crack with a vice and then plant in a seed bed. It was assumed that the seeds would not germinate unless removed from their hard shells. Since the aborigines had informed Hill that the macadamia nuts were poisonous, he was horrified to find his assistant eating the kernels and proclaiming them delicious! A few days later, when the boy didn't get sick, Hill himself tasted the kernels and was so favorably impressed by their flavor that he became immediately an enthusiastic promoter of macadamia nuts. In 1858 Hill planted what is believed to be the first cultivated macadamia tree on the banks of the Brisbane River in Queensland; it was of the smooth-shell type. This tree is still alive, has a circumference of eight feet at the base and continues to bear nut crops.

Due to Hill's promotional efforts, many individual macadamia trees were planted

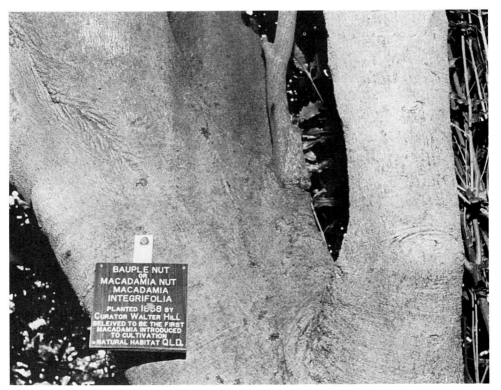

POSSIBLY THE FIRST MACADAMIA TREE EVER PLANTED BY MAN

In 1858, Walter Hill planted this tree near the Brisbane River in Queensland, Australia. It is alive and still produces nuts. So far as is known the aborigines did not cultivate and domesticate macadamia.

121

AN EARLY ILLUSTRATION OF
MACADAMIA

throughout New South Wales during the next few years. The first commercial macadamia orchard was established in Australia about 1888: 250 seedlings of the rough-shell type were planted by Charles Staff on three acres at Rou's Mill near Lismore in New South Wales. This property was purchased in 1896 by the Frederickson family. The orchard is still in reasonably good condition and produces approximately two tons of in-shell nuts annually.

Noting that the white settlers in Australia seemed to like macadamia, the aborigines in New South Wales started to collect more nuts

122

from wild trees during the 1860's and 1870's. King Jacky of the Albert River tribe developed a thriving barter business with macadamia nuts, trading them along with honey to the white settlers in exchange for tobacco and rum. By this time, the macadamia nut had acquired several common names in English and was known as the "Australian nut," the "Queensland nut," the "Bauple nut," the "Bush nut," and the "Australian hazelnut."

The first known introduction of macadamia from Australia into the Hawaiian Islands was made about 1882 by William Her-bert Purvis. He obtained seeds of *M. integrifolia* from the Mt. Bauple region, north of Gympie, Queensland, and subsequently planted several seedling trees at Kukuihaele, on the island of Hawaii. One of these trees is alive and still bearing sizeable crops of medium-sized, smooth-shell nuts at the age of one hundred.

Purvis's seedlings at Kukuihaele were to prove important many years later. Walter Pierre Naquin from Louisiana was the manager of the Honokaa Sugar Company on the big island of Hawaii from 1916 to 1944. Beginning in 1918, he used seed from the original Purvis trees to plant 18,000 macadamia seedlings on Honokaa land as part of a reforestation project. Walter P. Naquin, Jr. has written the following interesting account of his father's efforts as a pioneer in macadamia growing in Hawaii. He also describes his mother's culinary accomplishments in the family kitchen, where meals were secondary to cooking experiments with macadamia. On her home stove she prepared the first marketable chocolate-covered macadamia nuts.

"My father started planting macadamia nut trees in 1918 as a part of a Territory of Hawaii reforestation project. He considered the nut an epicurean delight, and even in those early years, with foresight, planted the trees to an orchard spacing (70 to the acre) so that they could be an alternative to sugar cane.

The macadamia seedlings competed for life at remote locations on the Honokaa Sugar Plantation. They were weeded and constantly fertilized for my father believed in fertilization. It took dedication and a desire to succeed to keep the early orchard financially afloat, because macadamia trees grown from seed are a motley lot and highly variable. Yields varied from nil to excellent. Many of the trees showed poor growth characteristics; some broke off at the trunk during high winds, while others split longitudinally from top to bottom. These were held together with bolts and wire so that they could live long enough to permit yield and nut studies to continue. There were well shaped, good trees which produced nuts with more shell than kernel and some nuts had a bitter el-

WILLIAM HERBERT PURVIS

Introduced the macadamia nut from Australia to Hawaii for the first time about 1882.

ement. The super tree was elusive and seven to ten years in the waiting for a seedling to bear and finally prove its worth.

Nature's knocks, my father's keen eye and hard work on the part of Leon A. Thevenin, Agriculturist for Honokaa Sugar Company (1938-1961) weeded out the unfit and developed an orchard. My father and Thevenin worked well together with mutual admiration and respect to build an orchard up from the original 18,000 to nearly 36,000 trees covering some 500 acres. The early seedlings were top worked with scion material from the better trees and a grafted orchard was developed. Frugality and patience dominated the developmental years.

The beginnings of macadamia nut processing started on the wood-burning kitchen stove of our Kukuihaele home. Here my mother, Ethel Keating Naquin, applied her culinary skills to the hand-cracked kernels which were dried, roasted, fried or deep fat fried to develop a process which was finally translated to the first factory operation.

The family double boiler served to heat the sweet or dark chocolate to make the popular chocolate coated nuts. Whole kernels were dipped into the chocolate with a kitchen fork with the first and third tines removed and then placed on a Duncan Phyfe marble-topped table to cool quickly. Three nuts arranged in a straight line with a chocolate curl on the top to please the eye as well as the taste. The Hilo Drug Company had a tough time keeping this popular item in stock and used to sell the chocolate covered nuts right at the cash register. In the depression years when the factory was started, even the boxes for the chocolate nuts were designed on the sugar plantation and formed by hand to keep people employed and costs down. The first nut factory was established in 1940 across from the Manager's office in Haina. Roasted, salted, vacuum-packed bottles of nuts were produced as well as the popular chocolate coated whole kernels.

At first, the nuts were husked by jacking up the family Buick so that the nuts to be husked could be forced under a spinning rear wheel. Tires are still used today for husking, but without the flurry of nuts and husks into the corner of the garage. Shelled nuts were sun dried, and then roughed up in a hopper to break the ker-

nel loose from the shell. Otto Herrmann, factory engineer for Honokaa Sugar Company, developed three rudimentary cracking devices for the fledgling factory to give the nuts a gentle cracking without damaging the kernels. Subsequently Leon Thevenin researched nut cracking equipment at the University of California at Davis in 1955: pecan cracking machines were reconstructed to accommodate ten size groupings of macadamia nuts. The pilot plant at Haina was replaced in 1958 by a new macadamia nut factory, constructed adjacent to the Honokaa Plantation Store, which is still in operation at the present time.

As a boy I often visited the macadamia nut plantings with my father. Travel was by horseback to inspect closely the extensive plantings. Prominent visitors to the plantation saw the macadamia trees but my father kept his competitive edge at the factory by keeping those operations secret. Everybody tasted my mother's kitchen nuts as it was the custom in those days for visitors to be guests at the Manager's home. Prominent visitors included ship captains who had anchored offshore to receive sugar, and came up the 800 foot cliff in a basket on the wire hoist.''

Another memorable introduction of macadamia from Australia to Hawaii took place in 1892. Robert A. Jordan was the first mate of a sailing vessel which had berthed in Brisbane. A friend gave him half a sugar bag full of smooth-shell nuts which had been collected from wild *M. integrifolia* trees growing near Hotham Creek, Pimpana, about forty miles south of Brisbane. Robert Jordan brought these nuts back to Hawaii to give to his brother E. W. Jordan who lived at Wylie Street, Nuuanu Valley, Honolulu, island of Oahu. Eight seedlings were planted in E. W.'s backyard. Forty years later, during the 1930's, several trees, progeny of the Jordan introduction, were among those selected as potential commercial types when the Hawaii Agricultural Experiment Station of the University of Hawaii, College of Tropical Agriculture, observed and tested some 60,000 macadamia seedlings. The chosen seedlings were grafted to seedling rootstocks and introduced into the plant nursery trade as clonal varieties, destined to play an important role in the development of the macadamia industry in the Hawaiian Islands.

In 1922 Ernest Sheldon Van Tassel organized the Hawaiian Macadamia Nut Company which several years later planted twenty-five acres of macadamia seedlings at Nutridge on the slopes of Mount Tantalus, elevation 900 feet, in back of the city of Honolulu; and 100 acres at Keauhou, elevation 1,800 feet, in North Kona, island of Hawaii. From the agricultural standpoint the latter orchard was more successful than the trial planting near Honolulu.

In 1926 the Legislature of the Territory of Hawaii passed an act exempting from taxation for five years all lands used solely for macadamia nut culture, commencing January 1, 1927. Undoubtedly this legislation greatly stimulated the development of the embryonic macadamia industry.

For many years, because of repeated failures, macadamia acquired the reputation of being impossible to propagate asexually by grafting. In 1926, Ralph H. Moltzau, a young high school student working at the Hawaii Agricultural Experiment Station during his summer vacation, grafted macadamia successfully for the first time. It was found that girdling the branch one month before scion wood was to be taken from it for grafting caused an accumulation of starch in the scion, making it more likely to take when grafted

The following 14 photographs, taken in Guatemala, show how macadamia seed is planted; how grafting of macadamia is carried out by the experienced horticulturist, Jorge Benítez; and how the grafted tree is planted out in the field. The principles that hold for grafting scions of selected types on seedling rootstocks, when asexual propagation is required, apply to macadamia as well as to other nut trees, although propagators may differ in the methods which they prefer to use.

1. PLANTING MACADAMIA SEED IN THE SEEDBED

2. THE SEED GERMINATES IN ABOUT 30 TO 60 DAYS

3. THE YOUNG MACADAMIA PLANT IS TRANSPLANTED TO PLASTIC NURSERY BAG

4. ABOUT 15 MONTHS LATER, THE MACADAMIA ROOTSTOCK IS READY FOR GRAFTING AND IS CUT BACK

5. SCION WOOD OF THE DESIRED VARIETY SHOULD BE OF THE SAME DIAMETER AS THE ROOT-STOCK. THE SCION WOOD IS CUT, LEAVING TWO BUDS, JUST BEFORE GRAFTING

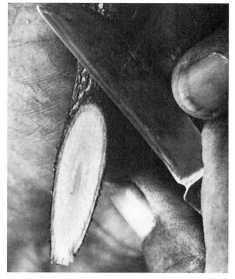

6. A DIAGONAL CUT IS MADE ON THE SCION. A SIMILAR DIAGONAL CUT IS MADE ON THE ROOTSTOCK

7. TO MAKE THE "TOP GRAFT" USED BY BENÍTEZ IN GUATEMALA, SCION AND ROOTSTOCK ARE JOINED, CAMBIUM TO CAMBIUM

8. THE UNION OF THE SCION AND ROOTSTOCK IS BOUND WITH A STRIP OF RUBBER TAPE

9. HOT PARAFFIN WAX IS APPLIED TO THE GRAFT WITH A BRUSH

10. SHOWING A SUCCESSFUL GRAFT 60 DAYS AFTER GRAFTING

127

11. ABOUT 9 MONTHS LATER THE GRAFTED MACADAMIA PLANT IS READY TO BE TRANSPLANTED FROM THE NURSERY TO THE FIELD PLANTING

12. PLANTING IN THE FIELD IN A PREVIOUSLY PREPARED HOLE APPROX. 20″ × 20″ × 24″ DEEP

13. FIELD PLANTING, FILLING THE HOLE WITH SOIL

14. COMPLETING THE FIELD PLANTING, THE SOIL AROUND THE GRAFTED PLANTS IS FIRMLY SETTLED

WILLIAM B. STOREY

Horticulturist who in 1948 introduced the first selected macadamia varieties for propagating clonally in Hawaii. He has also played an important part in the development of macadamia in California in recent years.

onto the rootstock. This was a significant development since it permitted selection of desirable clones for a commercial orchard, instead of growing seedling trees which vary greatly in nut characteristics and nut bearing capacity.

Dr. William B. Storey was a pioneer in this evaluation and selection of macadamia seedlings in Hawaii during the 1940's. Finally, in 1948, after years of field trials, Dr. Storey was able to award varietal status to five selected smooth-shell clones: Pahau, Keauhou, Nuuanu, Kohala, and Kakea. Four of these outstanding cultivars originated from the Mt. Tantalus orchard which had originally been planted with seedlings, descendants of the eight trees in E. W. Jordan's backyard.

One of the most promising macadamia clones in Hawaii today, awarded varietal status in 1971 by Richard A. Hamilton and Masao Nakamura is called Kau, in honor of the Kau district of the island of Hawaii. Dr. Hamilton is a Professor of Horticulture at the University of Hawaii, Hawaii Agricultural Ex-

MASAO NAKAMURA

Has been in charge of the agricultural operations of the macadamia orchards of C. Brewer & Co., Ltd. in Hawaii during the past twenty years. In this photo he is seen with maturing fruits of smooth shell type macadamia of a selected clone of *M. integrifolia*.

ANOTHER GRAFTING METHOD

In many Hawaiian nurseries a "wedge graft" is used for grafting macadamia.

AN EIGHT YEAR OLD GRAFTED MACADAMIA TREE
IN HAWAII

periment Station, who in collaboration with Edward T. Fukunaga, former superintendent of the Kona branch station of the University of Hawaii, has written several important technical articles about macadamia. Mr. Nakamura has been in charge of the macadamia agricultural operations of C. Brewer & Co., Ltd., the largest in Hawaii, for many years. The Kau variety has proved itself to be an excellent cultivar from the standpoint of vigor, wind tolerance, resistance to drought, productivity and kernel quality; the tree is shapely and upright, with strong crotches. Its upright form allows a close spacing in the orchard of about eighteen feet by twenty-five feet between the trees, allowing more trees to be planted per acre. Its in-shell nuts are smooth, medium-brown in color and medium in size. They range from 60 to 70 to the pound, with 36 to 40 per cent kernel and about ninety-eight per cent No. 1 kernels. Its average yield per mature tree of 50 to 100 pounds of in-shell nuts is considered good. The original seedling tree of Kau (Hawaiian Agricultural Experiment Station No. 344) was rediscovered and reselected in 1955 on the slopes of Mt. Tantalus because of its vigor and productivity—another offspring of the significant Jordan introduction of 1892. Other promising Hawaiian macadamia clones at the present time are: Keaau, (No. 660); Mauka, (No. 741); Makai, (No. 800); and Kakea, (No. 508), one of Dr. Storey's original selections of 1948.

In 1948, Castle and Cooke, Ltd. purchased one thousand acres on the slopes of Mauna Loa Volcano at Keaau, near Hilo on the Big Island of Hawaii for planting macadamia with selected commercial varieties. Two thousand adjoining acres were acquired in 1951 to expand the macadamia operation. A macadamia nut processing factory was built in 1965 which produced "Royal Hawaiian" brand macadamia nuts. In 1974, C. Brewer & Co., Ltd., a diversified agribusiness company, purchased these macadamia orchards, including the factory near Hilo, and is now the world's largest grower, processor and marketer of macadamia nuts, macadamia nut brit-

NORFOLK ISLAND PINES
(*Araucaria excelsa*)

Used as windbreaks for macadamia plantings in the orchards at Keaau, near Hilo, Hawaii.

MACADAMIA NUT PRODUCTS

In addition to macadamia nuts, finely ground pieces (right) used in cakes and pastries are produced. Halves and wholes find their way into candies, primarily chocolate-covered confections. Diced nuts (center) may be utilized as garnishes or in ice cream.

131

tle, "bits o' macadamia," butter candy glazed and chocolate covered macadamia nuts, and other macadamia products under the label "MAUNA LOA."

Hawaiian Holiday is another important macadamia company in Hawaii, producing many diversified macadamia products including candies, honeys, jams, jellies and various culinary products especially prepared for kitchen use such as chopped and ground macadamia nuts. Hawaiian Holiday obtains most of its macadamia nuts from independent growers and suppliers in Hawaii.

The following summary, provided by the Hawaiian Agricultural Reporting Service, Honolulu, points out the steady growth of the macadamia industry in Hawaii during the past twenty years. In 1980 about twenty-nine million pounds of in-shell macadamia nuts were produced as compared to less than three million pounds in 1960; the farm price had risen to 70 cents per pound in 1980, from about 18 cents per pound in 1960; acreage in production increased from about 2,000 in 1960 to 10,400 acres in 1980:

The development of a major economic nut crop in Hawaii from a virtually unknown tree within the brief period of half a century has been a remarkable and unprecedented achievement. In the fiftieth state, macadamia nut cultivation has become the third largest agricultural industry after sugar and pineapple. Over ninety per cent of the macadamia nuts marketed throughout the world are produced in the state of Hawaii, where approximately 13,400 acres have been planted with macadamia trees. C. Brewer has the largest plantings, amounting to some 6,100 acres: 2,730 acres at Kau, Hawaii; 2,460 acres at Keaau, near Hilo, Hawaii; and 910 acres on the island of Maui at Wailuka. Mac Farms of Hawaii, Inc., owned by CSR (Colonial Sugar Refiners) of Australia, is another important grower with about 3,250 acres in macadamia at Honomalino, Hawaii. They market their product through the California Almond Growers Exchange under the Blue Diamond label. The Hawaiian production consists entirely of the smooth-shell type macadamia nut.

It is very difficult to obtain accurate figures

MACADAMIA NUTS:
Acreage and Production, State of Hawaii, 1960-80

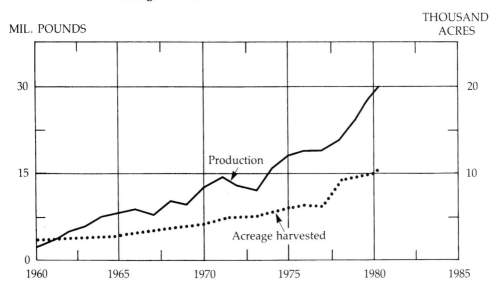

MACADAMIA ORCHARDS AT KAU, HAWAII

with respect to macadamia plantings in other parts of the world. The following data are rough estimates: after Hawaii, the second largest producer is Australia with about 7,000 acres. In 1980, Australia produced 3,300,000 lbs. of nuts, approximately one-ninth of Hawaii's total production. Every year about 1,000 more acres are being planted in Australia. Until 1979 almost all the plantings were in the general area of the native distribution of the macadamia trees, i.e., on the coastal strip approximately 200 miles north and south of Brisbane. New plantings are being developed north of Sydney and on the Atherton Tableland in tropical North Queensland. Apart from a few acres of old tetraphylla and hybrid trees, the Australian industry is based almost entirely on grafted varieties of the integrifolia species. Although demand exceeds supply, small quantities of Australian macadamia

nuts are exported to Japan, England and various European countries.

The Republic of South Africa follows with an estimated 6,000 acres, including smooth-shell and rough-shell; Kenya has about 4,000 acres, mostly rough-shell seedlings; Guatemala has planted about 2,000 acres of grafted, smooth-shell trees; Brazil counts about 1,800 acres, both smooth-shell and rough-shell; Malawi in Africa has about 800 acres; California's plantings amount to an estimated 800 acres, mostly rough-shell; and Costa Rica has approximately 300 acres of grafted, smooth-shell trees. Other countries which have made experimental plantings of macadamia include: New Zealand, Venezuela, Mexico, Zimbabwe, Peru, Indonesia, Tahiti, New Caledonia, El Salvador, Jamaica, Paraguay, Colombia, Western Samoa, Thailand, Taiwan, Fiji, Israel, Tanzania and Ethiopia.

133

MACADAMIA NURSERY IN GUATEMALA
Seedlings of *M. tetraphylla*, rootstock for grafting.

In the continental United States, California is the only state that has been successful in growing macadamia on a scale approaching the commercial. In 1879 Professor C. W. Dwinelle, a lecturer in practical agriculture at the University of California in Berkeley, introduced macadamia to California when he obtained some seeds of *M. integrifolia* from Australia and planted several macadamia seedlings in a garden of economic plants near Strawberry Creek. One of these trees is still alive on the original site. During the ensuing fifty years, several trials were made with the rough-shell type. One of the most noteworthy was made in February 1946, when a planting of 203 selected rough-shell seedlings, known as the Schneider orchard, was established at South Oceanside. Gradual progress in macadamia development has been made in cooperation with the efforts of the California Macadamia Society which now has some 475 members worldwide and about 325 members in the state. The Gold Crown Macadamia Association, which markets the growers' nuts, has also been helpful. Small macadamia plantings of one or two acres are popular with retired people who wish to remain active. To date, there are no large scale, commercial macadamia orchards in California. Although the macadamia industry in Hawaii is based upon clones of the smooth-shell type, and the rough-shell types have all been discarded, the opposite has occurred in California's subtropical climate where *M. tetraphylla* has proved to be more suitable than *M. integrifolia*. Two of the most important cultivars are: Cate, a rough-shell clone which is the most widely utilized in California, comprising over fifty per cent of the state's plantings; and Beaumont, a hybrid clone (*M. integrifolia* x *M. tetraphylla*) which is a good producer and a handsome ornamental tree named in honor of Dr. J.H. Beaumont, a pioneer in macadamia research in Hawaii.

Dr. William B. Storey, who has contributed much to the development of macadamia in California during the past twenty-five years, has made the following pertinent comments about the two main macadamia species:

"There seems to be a contention in some circles, especially in Hawaii, that the nuts of *M. tetraphylla* are inferior in quality to those of *M. integrifolia*. Experience in California and Australia does not support this contention. The quality of nuts from the best tetraphylla-type selections are every bit as good as those from integrifolia-type selections. When I was in Australia in October, 1978, I had ample opportunity to compare dry-roasted samples of both types. All samples were excellent. Admittedly there are differences in the constituents which tend to emphasize the difference in taste, texture and other characteristics between the kernels of the two types, both when raw and when roasted. This is so because first grade integrifolia-type kernels are higher in oil (72% or more) and lower in sugar (about 4%) than tetraphylla-type kernels which are lower in oil (67.5-72.0%) and higher in sugar (6-8%). The former float while the latter sink in pure water (specific gravity 1.000). . ."

Dr. Richard Hamilton, on the other hand, points out that no successful, large scale processing operation based on *M. tetraphylla* (the rough-shell type) has been developed up to the present time. In a recent letter to the author he clarifies this observation:

"Vacuum packed kernels are the major commercial macadamia product, and it is conservatively estimated that more than 98 per cent of the world production of marketable kernels are of *M. integrifolia*. The small amount of *M. tetraphylla* nuts produced are largely from seedling orchards and because of their variability and lower oil content are marketed principally: (1) as dried kernels sold in health stores or dooryard sales; (2) for use in the candy trade; and (3), to produce rootstocks for *M. integrifolia* clones. There are presently no good, commercial tetraphylla clones in existence and until there are, the potential of this species remains theoretical rather than real."

Florida is far behind California in macadamia culture, although it is the only other state in the continental United States with plantings worth mentioning. There are approximately 200 acres planted in Florida, consisting mainly of dooryard, ornamental or experimental trees. To date there are no commercial orchards. Both smooth-shell and rough-shell varieties have been planted during the past thirty years, for the most part along the southeast coast from Miami northwards to Cocoa Beach and on the West Coast between Naples and Clearwater.

The future offers a great potential demand for macadamia. According to a survey made by the Hawaiian Macadamia Nut Producers' Association, only one out of four Americans has ever heard of the macadamia nut and only one in eight has ever tasted it. The macadamia is virtually unknown in the vast, heretofore untapped markets of Europe and in many parts of the Far East, Latin America and Africa. It is a difficult crop to grow, however, which requires considerable capital and patience on the part of the grower since a period of at least ten to twelve years must pass before the original costs of a macadamia orchard can be recovered. Furthermore the areas in the world where the crop can be grown successfully are limited. Although labor in Hawaii at

135

$32.00 per day may be more than ten times as expensive as in many tropical regions of Latin America, Africa and the Orient, significantly higher yields and superior agricultural results to date seem to favor Hawaii. In this respect, Dr. Richard Hamilton has made the following relevant explanation to the author: "To the best of my knowledge, up to now, there are no successful commercial macadamia plantings closer to the equator than fifteen degrees, north or south. These limits are not exact but it is worth noting that unlike coffee, a suitable altitude cannot be substituted for latitude in finding a favorable environment to grow macadamia nuts."

Success of the macadamia orchard depends to a large extent on selection of a suitable site. The tree thrives best without shade, in mild, frost-free, subtropical climates with at least fifty inches of well-distributed rainfall annually. Good drainage and protection from strong winds are most important. In Guatemala in 1978 a promising six-year-old macadamia orchard of some seven hundred acres was virtually destroyed overnight by an unexpected seventy mile per hour wind storm which caused a "blow down" of ninety per cent of the grafted trees.

In Hawaii macadamias grow well from sea level up to elevations of about 2,000 feet. When there is less than fifty inches of rain per year, supplemental irrigation is beneficial. Weed control through the use of approved herbicides is essential. Fertilization is necessary for growth and nut production. Fertilizer should be applied at least three times a year with the amount increasing with the size and productivity of the tree. Macadamias in Hawaii are not affected seriously by diseases and pests, but strict control measures are utilized. Flower racemes are sometimes subject to attack by blight caused by fungi of *Botrytis*; this blight may be controlled by spraying with benomyl. *Phytophthora cinnamomi*, a fungus which causes avocado root-rot, occurs infrequently in commercial macadamia orchards in Hawaii.

All of the commercial macadamia orchards

LAVA SOIL IN HAWAII

Planting a young macadamia tree in field position.

in Hawaii are planted with grafted trees of *M. integrifolia*, the smooth-shell type. A small crop may be expected starting in the fifth year after planting in the field. The trees are normally in the nursery for two years before being moved to final field position. Production increases each year at an accelerated rate until full production is reached in the twelfth to fifteenth year, at which time a yield of 50 to 150 pounds of in-shell nuts per tree may be obtained. In Hawaii various planting distances between the trees in the orchards are used. With standard sized trees, spacings of about twenty-five to thirty-five feet between the rows and eighteen to twenty-five feet be-

This blower unit is used to move leaves from under trees to edges of field. It also moves nuts away from areas close to bases of the trees.

Ramacher sweepers follow the blowers to windrow nuts into a narrow, straight line in the middle of the tree rows.

The ground pick-up unit on the right picks up the nuts windrowed by the sweepers. The nuts are then conveyed to hauling trailers attached to the rear of the harvesters.

MECHANICAL HARVEST IN HAWAII

137

tween the trees in the row are recommended. Closer spacings may require thinning or heavy pruning to avoid excessive crowding of the trees.

Before the nuts drop, the ground should be cleared of weeds, debris, fallen leaves, branches and other obstructions. Since labor is scarce and expensive in Hawaii, various experiments have been made through the years to mechanize the macadamia orchard operations. Large vacuum cleaners were tried, but this method did not work out well as too much dirt and foreign matter were sucked up along with the nuts. Plastic netting supported between the trees to funnel the falling nuts into a collection point was found to be too expensive; furthermore, leaves and branches fell into the nets, causing snarls. Tree shakers have to be used with great care since in nature's plan the nuts fall to the ground when mature. Vigorous shaking of the tree may cause immature, green nuts with unacceptable nutmeats to fall along with the ripe nuts. Currently, in many orchards, where flat surfaces exist, the nuts are picked up off the ground by a Ramacher mechanical harvester which passes up and down the rows. Brushes, similar to rubber fingers, push the nuts onto a conveyor, which deposits them in a bin or trailer. Some hand labor, however, is always necessary. During the harvest season the nuts should be picked up every six to eight weeks to avoid deterioration of the final product.

When the mature macadamia nut falls to the ground, it contains a high percentage of water. This moisture, which may amount to thirty per cent in the husk and ten to twenty-five per cent in the rest of the nut, must be removed as soon as possible to prevent damage by mold. When the nuts arrive at the processing plant, the outer husk is removed by husking machines. There are several commercially available types of equipment which mechanize this husking operation by employing friction as the removal agent. The in-shell nuts are dehydrated in drying ovens to a moisture content of about 1.5 per cent. At the Mauna Loa macadamia nut factory near Hilo,

Hawaii, macadamia nut shells are utilized as fuel for the boiler. Each pound of shells contains approximately 10,000 BTU's; all of the energy required to dry the wet in-shell nuts is generated with this clean-burning, biomass energy.

Following dehydration, the nuts are cracked between stainless steel drums as the kernels are separated from the hard shells by a combination of sieving and air blasting. Kernels are cleaned and sorted to remove damaged nuts and pieces of shell, as they are graded into first quality, second quality and inferior grades. Air flotation may be employed to grade the kernels. Another method of grading involves placing the kernels in water where the first grade kernels, having a higher oil content, and thus a lower specific gravity will float, while poorer kernels will

CULLING MACADAMIA NUTS

Prior to roasting, the kernels are culled in conjunction with electronic color sorters.

CRACKING NUTS MECHANICALLY

In the Mauna Loa macadamia nut factory near Hilo, Hawaii, the macadamia shells are cracked by being squeezed between two counter-rotating steel drums. The spacing between the drums is adjusted according to nut size.

PROCESSING MACADAMIA NUTS

The dried kernels are roasted in refined coconut oil for 12 to 15 minutes at 275 degrees Fahrenheit, then cooled and salted.

sink. Second grade kernels will float on a brine solution of specific gravity 1.025, while still poorer kernels will sink. First grade kernels are processed further for retail sale, while second grade and broken kernels are used for baking and confectionery purposes. In the Hawaiian macadamia industry, the dried kernels are usually roasted in refined coconut oil for twelve to fifteen minutes at 275 degrees Fahrenheit. After roasting, the kernels are drained and cooled, following elimination of excess oil. Most kernels are then lightly salted with finely ground confectionery salt after being coated with coconut oil to ensure adhesion of the salt. An excellent product may also be obtained through dry roasting the kernels in a rotary oven at about 350 degrees Fahrenheit for fifteen to twenty minutes. Kernels to be coated with chocolate or used in confectionery are roasted but not salted.

Kernels which have been roasted and salted are sorted, cooled and vacuum packed in glass jars or tins. First grade, vacuum packed kernels may be stored for up to two years in a cool (60 to 70 degrees Fahrenheit), dry place without serious loss of quality.

Today, the macadamia is considered a gourmet delicacy, ranking with pine nuts and pistachios as one of the world's most expensive nuts.

HORS D'OEUVRE

Macadamia Nut Cheese Ball (XIX)

2 packages (8 ounces/ 225 g each) cream cheese, softened	1/2 cup (125 ml) chopped sweet pickles
1-1/2 cups (375 ml) grated Cheddar cheese	1 teaspoon (5 ml) salt
2 teaspoons (10 ml) minced onion	1/2 cup macadamia nuts, broken into bits

Combine cream cheese, Cheddar cheese, onion, sweet pickles and salt; mix well. Shape into a ball; roll ball in macadamia nuts. Cover and refrigerate several hours or until well chilled. Serve with crackers.

Yield: One cheese ball

MAIN DISHES

Nutted Veal Steaks (XIX)

3 tablespoons (45 ml) butter	1 cup (250 ml) commercial sour cream
4 veal steaks	1/2 cup (125 ml) chopped macadamia nuts or broken macadamia nuts
Freshly ground black pepper and salt	
1/4 cup (60 ml) dry sherry	

Melt butter in a large frying pan, add steaks, and sauté over medium heat until golden brown and tender. Season with pepper and lightly with salt; remove to a warm serving platter; keep warm. Add sherry to pan; cook until slightly reduced. Reduce heat to low. Add sour cream and macadamias and slowly heat through, stirring to blend. Pour sauce over veal.

Yield: 4 servings

Chicken Kiev Macadamia (XIX)

1/2 cup (125 ml) butter, softened	8 split chicken breasts, boned and skinned
1/4 cup (60 ml) minced parsley	1 cup (250 ml) flour
3-1/2 ounces (105 g) macadamia nuts, broken into bits	3 eggs, beaten
	2 cups (500 ml) bread crumbs
	Oil for deep-fat frying

Combine the butter and the parsley; stir in macadamia nuts. Divide the butter mixture into 8 portions and freeze. Place the chicken breasts between layers of plastic bags. Pound them with a rolling pin or other pounder. Place one of the frozen butter pats on the side of the chicken breast that the skin was not on before deboning. Roll chicken; making sure the sides are folded in and that the butter is not sticking out. Refrigerate for 1 hour. Roll each breast in the flour; dip in the eggs and coat with bread crumbs. Heat the oil to 375° F (190°C). Cook for 10 to 12 minutes. Drain on absorbent paper towels.

Yield: 8 servings

LUNCHEON AND SUPPER DISHES

Macadamia Eggs (XIX)

4 large slices natural Swiss cheese	1 tablespoon (15 ml) butter
4 eggs	6 to 8 tablespoons (90-120 ml) heavy (whipping) cream
Salt and pepper	
6 to 8 tablespoons (90-120 ml) finely chopped or broken bits of macadamia nuts	Chopped fresh parsley (optional)

Place cheese over bottom of a buttered shallow baking dish or in four individual ramekins. Gently break an egg onto each slice. Sprinkle with salt, pepper, and macadamias; dot with butter. Pour cream around eggs. Bake in a moderate oven (350° F-180° C) for 12 minutes or until set. Sprinkle lightly with parsley.

Yield: 4 servings

Fettucine with Bits of Macadamia Nuts (XIX)

6 to 8 quarts (6 to 8 liters) water	1/2 cup (125 ml) grated Parmesan cheese
1 pound (450 g) egg noodles	One 3-1/2-ounce (100 g) jar macadamia nut bits
1/2 cup (125 ml) butter	
1/2 cup (125 ml) heavy cream	

Bring water to a boil and cook noodles. Drain. In medium saucepan, melt butter, stir in cream. Remove from heat and stir in Parmesan cheese, reserving a little cheese for the top. Fold in hot cooked noodles and macadamia nuts. Sprinkle with reserved cheese.

Yield: 4 servings

SALAD

Plantation Chicken Salad (XIX)

3 cups (750 ml) cooked white meat of chicken	1-1/2 teaspoons (7.5 ml) salt
1/2 cup (125 ml) orange juice	1/2 cup (125 ml) mayonnaise
2/3 cups (150 ml) finely diced celery	2 large oranges, sectioned
One 3-1/2-ounce (100 g) jar macadamia nut bits	Lettuce leaves

Marinate chicken in orange juice for 20 minutes. Drain. Combine chicken, celery, macadamia nuts, salt, mayonnaise and orange sections; mix gently. Serve on lettuce leaves. Garnish with lychee nuts stuffed with softened cream cheese, cherry tomatoes and more macadamia nuts, if desired.

Yield: 6 servings

Macadamia Nut-Stuffed Mushrooms (XIX)

1/2 pound (225 g) fresh mushrooms	1/4 cup (60 ml) Swiss cheese
1/2 cup (125 ml) butter	1 tablespoon (15 ml) grated Parmesan cheese
1/2 cup (125 ml) thinly sliced green onions	24 to 36 mushroom caps, approximately 2 inches (5 cm) in diameter (in addition to fresh mushrooms above)
1 teaspoon (5 ml) finely chopped parsley	
1 recipe Bechamel Sauce (see below)	
One 3-1/2-ounce (100 g) jar macadamia nut bits	
2 tablespoons (30 ml) bread crumbs	

Finely chop the half pound (225 g) of mushrooms. Place them in a towel and squeeze out the liquid. Heat skillet and add 2 tablespoons (30 ml) of the butter; sauté mushrooms and green onions. Stir in the parsley, Bechamel sauce and 1/2 cup (125 ml) of the macadamia nuts. Cook for about 30 seconds. Remove from heat.

Combine bread crumbs, the remaining macadamia nuts, Swiss cheese, Parmesan cheese and the remaining 2 tablespoons (30ml) of butter and mix with the fingers. Clean mushroom caps and place them in a baking dish. Fill caps with the sauteed mixture. Place a ball of cheese mixture on top of each mushroom. Bake at 375° F (190° C) for ten minutes, or depending on the size of the caps.

Yield: 24 to 36 mushroom caps, stuffed

Bechamel Sauce

3 tablespoons (45 ml) butter
3 tablespoons (45 ml) flour

1 cup (250 ml) milk, scalded

In a heavy saucepan, melt the butter. Add the flour and cook until light and bubbly. Add the hot milk and cook until thickened.

Yield: 1-1/4 cups (310 ml)

DESSERTS

Macadamia Nut Pie (XIX)

3 eggs
2/3 cup (150 ml) sugar
1 cup (250 ml) light corn syrup
1/4 cup (60 ml) melted butter
1 teaspoon (5 ml) vanilla

1 cup (250 ml) chopped macadamia nuts, or 1 cup (250 ml) macadamia nut bits
Unbaked pastry for single-crust 8-inch (20.5 cm) pie

Thoroughly beat together the eggs, sugar, syrup, butter and vanilla. Stir in macadamia nuts. Turn into pastry-lined pie pan. Bake in moderate oven 375° F (190° C) for 40 to 45 minutes, just until filling is set. Cool on a rack.

Serve while slightly warm or when completely cooled, topped, if you wish, with whipped cream that has been lightly sweetened and flavored with vanilla or with rich vanilla ice cream.

Yield: 8 servings

MACADAMIA NUT PIE

Macadamia Nut Cookies (XIX)

2 cups (500 ml) shortening	1 teaspoon (5 ml) salt
1 teaspoon (5 ml) vanilla	1 teaspoon (5 ml) baking soda
3/4 cup (175 ml) brown sugar	7 ounces (210 g) macadamia nuts broken into bits
3/4 cup (175 ml) white sugar	3-1/2 ounces (105 g) whole macadamia nuts
2 eggs	
2-3/4 cups (675 ml) flour	

Combine shortening, vanilla and sugars and beat until creamy. Add eggs and beat well. Combine flour, salt and soda in separate bowl and slowly stir into creamy mixture.

Stir in macadamia nut bits. Place on cookie sheet and press a macadamia nut half on top. Bake at 350° F (175° C) for 10 minutes.

Yield: 5 dozen cookies

Macadamia Creme Chantilly (XIX)

2 cups (500 ml) milk	1 cup (250 ml) whipping cream
1/2 cup (125 ml) sugar	1/2 cup (125 ml) finely chopped macadamia nuts
1-1/2 tablespoons (22.5 ml) unflavored gelatin	
1/2 teaspoon (2.5 ml) salt	1 recipe Macadamia Nut-Orange Sauce (see below)
2 whole eggs	
2 egg yolks	
1/4 cup (60 ml) dark rum or 1-1/2 teaspoons (7.5 ml) rum flavoring	

Scald milk. Combine sugar, gelatin and salt. Beat whole eggs with egg yolks; add sugar mixture. Stir into hot milk. Set in top of double-boiler and cook stirring constantly until mixture thickens slightly and coats spoon. Remove from heat and stir in rum. Chill until mixture begins to thicken, about the consistency of egg white. Whip cream. Fold in whipped cream and macadamia nuts. Chill a few minutes until mixture mounds when dropped from a spoon. Spoon into dessert dishes and chill 1 to 2 hours. Serve topped with Macadamia Nut-Orange Sauce.

Yield: 6 to 8 servings

Macadamia Nut-Orange Sauce

3 well-colored oranges	Pinch of salt
3/4 cup (175 ml) sugar	1/4 cup (60 ml) macadamia nuts, broken in pieces
1/2 cup (125 ml) light corn syrup	
1 tablespoon (15 ml) lemon juice	

With a vegetable peeler, remove only orange portion of peel from oranges. Cut into very thin slivers to make 1/3 cup (75 ml). Squeeze juice from oranges and strain. In a small saucepan combine 1 cup (250 ml) of the orange juice and the peel; simmer 5 minutes. Add the sugar, corn syrup, lemon juice and salt; stir until sugar dissolves. Boil until syrupy, approximately 20 minutes. Cool thoroughly; stir in macadamia nuts.

Yield: 1-1/2 cups (375 ml)

PEANUT (GROUNDNUT)

Arachis hypogaea

CHAPTER EIGHT

Peanuts
(Groundnuts)
Family: Leguminosae

LATIN	*Arachis hypogaea* L.	DUTCH	Aardnoot
SPANISH	Maní	ITALIAN	Arachide
FRENCH	Arachide	PORTUGUESE	Amendoim
GERMAN	Erdnuss	RUSSIAN	Zemlianoí Orékh
SWEDISH	Jordnöt	JAPANESE	Rakkasei
ARABIC	Fūl Sūdāni	CHINESE	Lo Huo Sheng

THE CULTIVATED PEANUT is the hard, ripe, nut-like seed or bean of *Arachis hypogaea* L., an annual herbaceous vine of the pea family (Leguminosae). It is indigenous to South America, having probably originated in Bolivia at the base of the eastern slopes of the Andes. The peanut is thus added to nine other plants of major economic importance which the Americas have contributed to the world's agriculture; namely, corn, cotton, white potato, sweet potato, rubber, common bean, tobacco, cassava and cacao.

The peanut is really a legume, like the pea and bean—not strictly a nut; its name is predicated on the nut-like characteristics of the fruit. Due to popular usage rather than botanical considerations, it is generally considered to be a "nut."

Some forty to seventy other species of *Arachis* occur in Brazil, Paraguay, Argentina and Uruguay, as well as in Bolivia; apart from *A. hypogaea*, only one other species, *A. villosulicarpa*, appears to have been cultivated by abo-rigines for its edible seeds. A wild, perennial species of *Arachis* has become an important ground cover in several towns and cities of Amazonia, such as Leticia in Colombia and Manaus in Brazil, where this prostrate plant forms green lawns that do not require mowing.

There is archaeological evidence that the peanut had already been introduced in pre-Colombian times to the dry, coastal regions of Peru near Trujillo and Ancón some thirty-five centuries ago. Radioactive carbon dating indicates that peanuts were known in Peru at the time of the introduction of ceramic pottery, about 1200 to 1500 B.C. Well-preserved peanut plant remains have been found in Inca mummy bundles and burial sites, often contained in small string bags along with other plant remains including maize, beans, chili peppers and coca. Terra cotta funerary vases, decorated with molded replicas of peanut pods, have been unearthed in several prehistoric, Peruvian coastal cemeteries.

145

Before the time of Columbus, the peanut was unknown in the Old World. It is first mentioned in Spanish chronicles and natural histories of the sixteenth century. In 1535, Captain Gonzalo Fernández de Oviedo y Valdés, appointed historiographer of the New World and governor of Haiti by King Charles V of Spain, wrote in his *Historia General y Natural de las Indias Occidentales:* "Another fruit which the Indians have on Hispaniola is called *maní*. They sow and harvest it. It is a very common crop . . . about the size of a pine nut in the shell. They consider it a healthy food."

Ulrich Schmidt, a German mercenary soldier and historian, participated in the Spanish conquest of Paraguay in 1542 under Álvar Núñez Cabeza de Vaca. He mentioned the peanut as a plant of great importance in the warm lowlands of the Rio de la Plata basin; the Surucusis Indians called it *mandubi* and *mandi.*

Ethnobotanical remains of the cultivated peanut have been found in the Tehuacán Valley, Puebla state, Mexico, dating from approximately 100 B.C. The peanut appears to have been an introduced crop of minor importance in Mexico many centuries before the arrival of Hernán Cortés. It also played a part in Aztec folk medicine. Friar Bernardino de Sahagún made an illustrated, encyclopedic study of the Aztecs in 1566 in which he mentioned the peanut, which was called *tlalcacauatl* in the Nahuatl language (from *tlatle,* meaning earth; and *cacauatl,* meaning cacao seed); i.e., "earth cocoa bean." A peanut paste, not unlike peanut butter, was prepared by the Aztecs as a toothache remedy. The names *cacahuete* and *cacahuate* are commonly used today in Mexico and Central America for the peanut.

Starting in the sixteenth century, two distinct types of peanuts were distributed throughout the world from South America: Portuguese navigators introduced a two-seeded peanut from Brazil to both African coasts and the Malabar coast of southwestern India; the Spanish transported a three-seeded, "hump-backed" type from Peru to the Western Pacific. This peanut was probably taken from Peru to Mexico, then carried across the Pacific Ocean to the Philippine Islands on the Acapulco-Manila galleon line, which had regularly scheduled crossings for

STIRRUP-SPOUTED WATER JAR, DECORATED WITH MOLDED PEANUTS

This pottery vessel dates from around A.D. 500 and was found in a Moche Period cemetery on the arid northern coast of Peru. There, in dry community debris, plant remains survive for thousands of years. In such refuse peanut shells, in association with "Initial Period" ceramics, first appear at about 1500 B.C.

PEANUTS 1658

An early Dutch illustration showing peanuts known as *mundubí* and *mandobí* by Indian tribes in Paraguay and Brazil.

256   **GVLIELMI PISONIS**

Nullius ufus, quantum conftat, folia & caulis; excipiuntur Bulbi, qui more Batatæ pro bono alimento apponuntur.

MVNDVBI & FRVCTVS.

Sícut Mandioca ra-dix aliaque fata menfibus potiffimum æftivis & terris fitien-tibus gaudent; ita alii fructus fubterranei & radices edules humi-da amant loca & tem-pora, inter quæ non folum *Batatas* mox de-fcripta, fed & *Mundubí* & *Mandobí* primatum tenent. Horum prior Lufitanis corrupte *Amenduinas*, Letio *Manobí*. Peruvianis, tefte Monardo *Anchic*, Hifpanis *Ibimani* vocatur.

250 years, from 1565 to 1815. From Manila it found its way to China, Japan, eastern India and the East Indies.

By 1564, the peanut had been established in Senegambia in West Africa, according to a report by Alvares de Almada. The French physician and botanist, Charles de Lécluse (Clusius), who is credited with introducing the potato to Europe, mentioned in 1601 that peanuts were being used as rations for slaves from the Guinea Coast on the slave ships which crossed the Atlantic.

The peanut which the Portuguese took to Africa was quickly adopted. At the time of the American slave trade many African tribes used it as a major food and were accustomed to it. By the end of the seventeenth century, the holds of slave ships were frequently filled with peanuts as the only rations for the trans-atlantic voyage. A small-podded peanut with a spreading, prostrate growth habit was a successful early introduction which was known as African Runner and North Carolina Runner. In 1783, Thomas Jefferson in his "Notes on Virginia" reported that peanuts were being raised in Virginia like garden herbs—for home use only—and were considered to be of little commercial importance.

In 1784, a small-podded, Spanish-type peanut which required a relatively short growing season was introduced into Lisbon, Portugal from the Guarani region of northeast

Argentina, Paraguay and southern Brazil and subsequently taken to Spain and France. A priest named Tabares de Ulloa, who later became bishop of Valencia, is said to have developed the first peanut-shelling machine in about 1805. In Spain the peanut was cultivated both for its oil and for the preparation of chocolate-coated peanuts, a popular confection.

During the early 1800's there was a shortage of edible oils in Europe: starting about 1850, peanuts were imported into Marseilles as oilseeds and soon became an important article of commerce in southern France.

Although the cultivation of the peanut spread rapidly in the tropics—especially in Africa and India—the crop was not limited to tropical regions. Since a period of four to five warm months was sufficient to see it through its life-cycle, successful plantings were carried out in southern Europe, southern Japan, and along the southern Chinese coast. Peanut cul-

tivation now extends throughout all tropical and subtropical parts of the world, chiefly in the range between 38 degrees north and 38 degrees south of the equator.

Before the Civil War, peanuts were known throughout the South as groundnuts, ground peas, monkey nuts, "pindars," "goobers," and "goober peas." The names pindar and goober were African tribal words which slaves remembered. Goober was derived from the Bantu, Central African *nguba*. Dealers in other edible nuts suggested that goobers were lowly food, fit only for poor white trash, slaves and hogs. However, during the military campaigns in eastern Virginia during the Civil War—in regions where the crop was being cultivated—thousands of soldiers from both sides and all parts of the country tasted peanuts for the first time and got to know and appreciate them.

From time to time, peanuts were rations for Confederate troops, which gave rise to the

A VIRGINIA PEANUT FARM IN 1885

Manual labor is accompanied by banjo music.

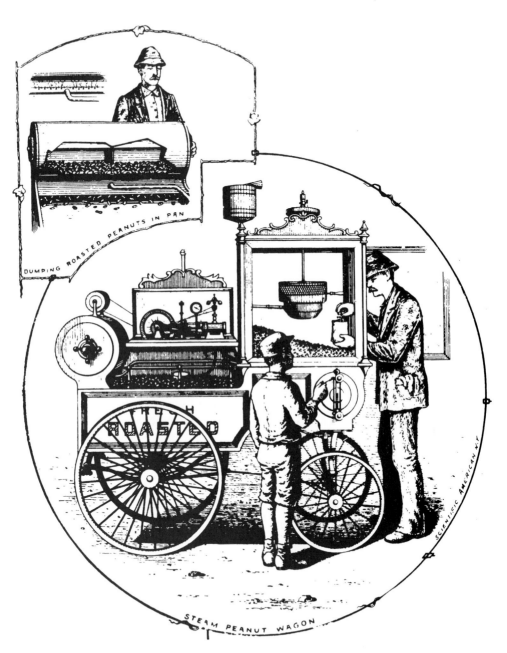

DUMPING ROASTED PEANUTS IN PAN

STEAM PEANUT WAGON

SELLING PEANUTS IN NEW YORK CITY IN THE 1890'S

popular folk song of the day known as "Eating Goober Peas:"

"Sitting by the roadside, on a summer day,
Chatting with my messmates, passing time
away,
Lying in the shadow, underneath the trees,
Goodness how delicious, eating goober peas!
Peas! Peas! Peas! Peas! Eating goober peas!
Goodness how delicious, eating goober peas!"

After Appomattox in 1865, returning soldiers brought back peanuts to places where the nuts had previously been unknown, thus creating a new demand. Within the next five years, peanut production in the United States increased two hundred per cent. Around 1870, the famous showman, Phineas T. Barnum, introduced peanuts to New York City through his circus. By the end of the nineteenth century, peanuts were being eaten

A PEANUT VENDOR ABOUT 1890

as a snack throughout the country, sold fresh-roasted by street vendors as well as at baseball games and circuses, as circus wagons rolled into towns from Maine to California. Peanuts were consumed in the cheap seats of theater balconies, which became known as "peanut galleries."

Peanut planting in the United States received a tremendous boost in about 1900 when equipment was invented which enabled farmers mechanically to plant, cultivate, harvest and pick the nuts from the plants, as well as to shell and clean the kernels. At the same time, progress was made in plant selection to increase yields. A few years later, mechanical improvements were made in roasting, blanching and salting peanuts, and in the preparation of peanut butter. Marketing techniques progressed as automatic packaging machines were developed. Modern technology pointed out the nutritional value of peanuts while home economists discovered hundreds of new ways to utilize peanuts in a wide assortment of foods.

About 1920 farmers in the southern states were forced to find another cash crop to take the place of cotton: the boll weevil, a grayish, long-snouted beetle that infested and destroyed cotton bolls, had ravaged cotton to such an extent in many regions that the crop was no longer profitable. Peanuts were found to be an ideal substitute: they grew well on cotton land, while labor, cropping systems and oil mills could readily be converted from cotton to peanuts. Many southern farmers harvested and dried peanuts on the vines, then fed them during the winter to farm animals. Cows consumed the hay and peanut meal, while hogs devoured greedily or "hogged off" the peanuts left in the fields following the harvest. It was discovered, however, that pigs which were fed only peanuts produced soft pork. While the loins and hams were a delicacy, the packers and merchants had problems with other portions of the hog as sides of bacon and shoulders from peanut-fed hogs tended to be flabby with little eye appeal. (Since corn is now cheaper to produce

150

Born a slave during the Civil War, George Washington Carver (1864-1943) rose to fame as a botanist, scientist and pioneer in peanut research. Called the "The Peanut Wizard," he discovered over 300 uses for peanuts, peanut shells and peanut foliage. Carver also carried out important experimental work in sweet potatoes, pecans, soybeans and other agricultural products.

and easier to store than peanuts, it has largely replaced them as hog feed, although there is a good demand for peanut meal, fortified with amino acids, as a high-protein feed.)

George Washington Carver (1864-1943), an American botanist, was a pioneer in peanut research. Born a slave on a Missouri farm, he worked his way through school and college, earning a master's degree in agriculture from Iowa Agricultural College (later Iowa State), where he became the first black faculty member. In 1896 he accepted Booker T. Washington's invitation to come to Tuskegee Institute as head of the new Department of Agriculture at an annual salary of $1,000. For forty-seven years, Carver taught, wrote and worked in his Tuskegee laboratory

where he developed over 300 products from peanuts, peanut shells and peanut foliage, ranging from cheese and mayonnaise to shaving cream, soaps, dyes, wallboard and plastics. He was able to serve an entire dinner in which all food was made from peanuts, including soup, meat, vegetables, milk, ice cream and coffee. He taught negroes in the South how to increase their peanut production and grow better peanuts, while he encouraged farmers to plant hardy peanuts instead of cotton, a crop which inevitably caused soil exhaustion and was increasingly becoming prey to the boll weevil. Carver also carried out important experimental work in sweet potatoes, pecans, soybeans and cow peas. This extraordinary scientist refused to allow any of his discoveries to be patented, since he wanted them to be available for the widest possible use.

During the 1930's, Carver spent much of his time exploring the curative value of massage with peanut oil in the treatment of various afflictions, including muscle damage from poliomyletis. Although he denied he had found a "cure" for polio, thousands flocked to Tuskegee for therapeutic peanut oil massage; many believed themselves helped by the treatment although it was never endorsed by the American Medical Association.

Another important individual in the development of the peanut industry in the United States was Amedeo Obici (1876-1947), known as the "Peanut King." Born near

MR. PEANUT
®

In 1916, Obici sponsored a contest, offering a prize for the best peanut symbol. A 14-year-old schoolboy in Suffolk, Virginia, submitted the winning drawing. After a commercial artist added the cane, hat and monocle, "Mr. Peanut," the well-known trademark of the Planters Company, was born.

AMEDEO OBICI, 1876-1947

Founder of the Planters Company, Obici was known as the "Peanut King."

Venice, Italy, he arrived in Brooklyn in 1888 as a twelve-year-old immigrant. He soon got a job as a bell boy in a hotel in Scranton, Pennsylvania, at one dollar a week. He moved to nearby Wilkes-Barre where he peddled fruit and peanuts. In a few years, he opened up his own fruit stand and conceived the idea of selling salted, roasted peanuts. At the time, peanuts were usually bought in the shell and if the buyer wanted any seasoning, he did it himself after removing the shell. Obici's peanuts met with immediate success. In 1906, abandoning the fruit business, he went into partnership with his future brother-in-law, Mario Peruzzi; they rented a small factory and installed two large peanut roasters. The name "Planters" sounded dignified and important, so the business was called "Planters Peanut Company." The factory's peanut production was delivered to stores by a horse and cart. Two years later, chocolate was added to the line, so the firm was enlarged and incorporated as "Planters Nut and Chocolate Company." Peanuts were combined with chocolate and syrups to produce tasteful, flavored confections. The company prospered and expanded as emphasis was placed on good quality, brand name, creation of consumer demand and repeat business. By 1910, salted peanuts and packaged peanut confections were sold in glassine, "see-through" bags. Two years later, Obici decided to establish the company's own processing plant for raw peanuts in Suffolk, Virginia, near where peanuts were grown. The Planters Suffolk factory opened in 1913; by 1927 Planters had become an industrial giant, which eventually would own thirty-six buildings in Suffolk and factories in San Francisco and Toronto.

In 1916, Obici sponsored a contest and offered a prize for the best peanut symbol. A 14-year-old Suffolk schoolboy submitted the winning drawing—a humanized peanut. "Mr. Peanut" was born after a commercial artist added the cane, hat and monocle to the peanut figure. Soon the familiar Planters displays featuring "Mr. Peanut" were launched in highly successful national advertising throughout the country.

In 1930, Obici initiated a promotional campaign to increase the consumption of edible peanut oil, which also proved to be auspicious. During the Great Depression, he popularized a "Nickel Lunch" featuring peanuts. Cellophane replaced glassine in 1932 as the primary material for the five-cent peanut packages and automatic machinery was installed a few years later at Suffolk for forming, filling and packaging peanut products.

PLANTERS SALESMAN'S CAR, 1927

Amedeo Obici continued as the company's president until his death in 1947. His friend and partner, Mario Peruzzi, succeeded him. Planters had become the largest and most diversified peanut-processing corporation in the world. In 1960, the Planters Company became the property of Standard Brands, Inc., now known as Nabisco Brands, Inc.

Peanut production increased rapidly in the United States during and after World War I, to such an extent that in 1934 the government initiated controls of prices, production and acreage. During World War II these controls were lifted so that increased peanut production would be available to meet the intensified demand for fats and oils as a result of curtailment of importation of coconut oil from Asia. Government controls were reestablished in 1949 and have been in effect ever since. For many years, United States peanut plantings were held by legislation to 1,600,000 to 1,700,000 acres under govern-

ment acreage/poundage quotas. The Agriculture and Food Act of 1981 (Peanut Provisions, Title VII), however, instead of acreage limitations, established national poundage quotas at 1,200,000 tons for 1982 to be reduced gradually to 1,100,000 tons by 1985, although additional quantities of peanuts may be grown for crushing stock or for export. A new adjustable price support system was established; the minimum support rate for 1982 crop peanuts was 27.5 cents per pound, farmers stock basis. The national average price support is to be determined annually, based on the national average of peanut production costs. The farm value of United States peanuts is about 800 million dollars annually, while the total crop amounts to about four billion pounds. Eight states grow ninety-nine per cent of the peanuts: Georgia, which produces approximately forty per cent is the leader, followed by Alabama, North Carolina, Texas, Virginia, Oklahoma, Florida and South Carolina. About sixty per cent of United States produc-

EARLY DEVELOPMENT

The buds are peanuts starting to form on a farm in Georgia.

THREE COMMON PEANUT TYPES

Left to right: fruits and seeds
of Virginia, Spanish and
Valencia peanuts.

tion comes from the Southeast, while the Southwest accounts for approximately twenty per cent and the Virginia-Carolina region about twenty per cent.

Three main types of peanuts are grown in the United States: Virginias and Runners, which have red skins; and Spanish, with tan skins. These varieties usually contain two kernels in each shell. The Virginia kernels, grown mostly in the Virginia-Carolina region, are the largest and, when shelled, are in demand as cocktail nuts and salted peanuts. The medium-sized Runners and small Spanish peanuts are utilized in the manufacture of peanut candies, peanut butter and peanut oil. The Southeast grows mainly Runners, while the Southwest produces roughly two-thirds Spanish and one-third Runners. A small amount of another type of peanut called Valencia, in demand for roasting in the shell, is produced in New Mexico; it has a long shell which contains three or four small, sweet kernels. The relative popularity of these various types has changed over time and today the Runner dominates, accounting for seventy-

two per cent of total production; Virginias follow with some sixteen per cent, Spanish about eleven per cent and Valencias only 0.6 per cent. Runners are now the leading type due to the introduction in the 1970's of a new, superior Runner variety known as the Florunner, which has been responsible for spectacular increases in peanut yields.

In the United States, peanuts are raised for the most part on relatively small plots of 50 to 150 acres. Although the area planted with peanuts has remained about the same for the past twenty years, the development of higher yielding varieties, such as the Florunner, combined with improved planting and harvesting techniques and better utilization of fertilizers, insecticides and fungicides have increased yields substantially to about 2,600 pounds per acre in a normal year—roughly double the average yields of 1960. Even though all commercial peanut production is grown from seed, peanuts can also be propagated asexually from cuttings, a technique which may in the long run facilitate selection of new, superior varieties through plant

155

PEANUT PLANT

breeding. Desirable characteristics include: adaptation to the local environment; early maturation; resistance to drought, diseases and pests; good shelling percentage; high oil and protein content and suitability for mechanical harvest. Following thousands of crosses, selections are thoroughly tested by experiment stations of the United States Department of Agriculture before being released for planting, harvesting and further testing prior to being distributed as certified varieties.

India is by far the world's largest producer of peanuts, followed by mainland China. India and China together produce over fifty per cent of the world's peanuts. The United States follows in third place, despite much higher yields per acre—about triple the average in India. Other major peanut-producing countries include Senegal, Sudan, Brazil, Argentina, South Africa, Malawi and Nigeria. India grows about eighteen million acres of peanuts, to produce some six million metric tons annually on a shelled basis; because of dependence on peanuts as a source of protein food and vegetable oil, India is not usually a large exporter. China, on approximately six million acres, produces approximately 2.8 million metric tons. The crop in the United States amounts to about 1.8 million metric tons on roughly 1.7 million acres, and this country has recently become the world's largest exporter of peanuts. Other important exporting countries are Sudan, South Africa, Argentina and China. Major importers include Western Europe, Japan and Canada.

Peanut cultivation in China, which proba-

PLANTING PEANUT SEED IN SOUTHERN INDIA

In the United States, peanuts are planted, harvested and processed with specialized machinery. In many other countries, including India, hand labor is usually employed rather than machines. Nevertheless, India is the world's foremost producer of peanuts.

bly began in the seventeenth century, dramatically increased after 1889. In that year, an American Presbyterian missionary took with him to Shantung four pounds of peanuts which he distributed to two Chinese converts for planting. The plantings were highly successful: one proselyte ate his entire crop, however, while the other saved his harvested seed for further propagation and distribution to neighboring farmers. Following this modest plant introduction, the peanut was widely grown in Shantung province which, in the course of time, has become one of the principal peanut-producing regions of the world.

In 1946 the British Government decided to carry out a huge peanut-growing project of over three million acres in East Africa, in order to alleviate the world's chronic shortage of fats. It was known as the "groundnut scheme." Extensive sunflower plantings were also planned. It was estimated that at least 800,000 tons of peanuts would be produced annually, using mechanical production methods for the most part. Unfortunately this

PEANUT PLANTING IN RAJKOT, WESTERN INDIA

157

bold, ambitious enterprise turned out to be a total fiasco and had to be abandoned several years later at a loss of over 36,000,000 British pounds. In West Africa there is a droll witticism which covers foreign business failures known as "WAWA"—West Africa Wins Again—only too familiar to veteran observers of that region. This time, since the collapse of Her Majesty's agronomics took place on the other side of Africa, the epigram "EAWA" might well have been appropriate. The heavy, stubborn bush in Kongwa, central Tanganyika, proved to be unyielding and unmanageable—impossible to clear on schedule. Bureaucratic errors, drought, plant disease and breakdown of equipment added to production woes. The main reason for failure of the groundnut scheme, however, was planting too much of the acreage on hard clay soil which, when cleared, baked as hard as cement when strong sun followed rain. Since the peanut will not ripen unless the fertilized ovary is pushed underground, thousands of acres were found to be useless for the crop. It was discovered belatedly that the peanut is not a plant which lends itself readily to mass production on vast acreages in remote areas. This agricultural disaster pointed out the problems involved when attempting to bring about abrupt change through a "crash program" without sufficient experimentation in less developed, tropical areas of the third world. A similar lesson has been learned recently in the Amazon from the difficulty of settling land adjacent to the Trans Amazon highway due to the failure of planned rice harvests.

The peanut is an annual that is propagated by seed. It grows best in a warm climate with a yearly rainfall of twenty-five to fifty inches. Absence of frost is essential. From planting to harvest time takes about four to five months, depending on the variety. The Spanish types mature approximately 120 days after planting, while Virginia and Runner types require about 140 days. The seeds are usually planted in April or May. It is an unusual plant because of its flowering and fruiting habit. The yellow inflorescences are borne from the axils of the leaves. After fertilization above the ground, the young fruit begins to develop at the end of a pointed stalk-like structure known as the "peg." Unlike most floral structures the peg is positively geotropic, that is it gradually curves over until it faces downward, towards the soil. At the same time, the cells at the tip of the young fruit quickly become woody and push aside the flower remains so that they

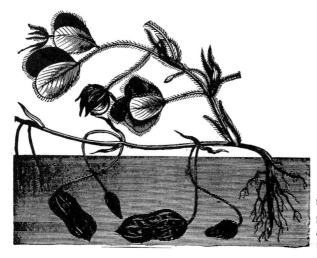

SPREADING "RUNNER" TYPE PEANUT

Showing how the minute pods from above-ground flowers are forced into the soil to grow and ripen.

form a protective cup by the time the peg reaches the soil surface. The peg continues to grow downward with amazing force while it manages to bury the young fruit two or three inches deep in the soil to mature. Unless the peg is able to penetrate the ground no pod will be formed. In many parts of the world, the peanut is quite logically called a groundnut, since it plants its own seeds and thus protects the developing fruit. The specific name, *hypogaea*, comes from the Greek word meaning "growing beneath the ground." An underground legume, the peanut plant is a nitrogen-fixer in that the soil where it is planted is enriched by bacteria-containing nodules formed on its roots, which transform nitrogen from the air into soluble nitrates. Nevertheless, peanut monoculture exerts a serious drain on the fertility of the soil, severely depleting it of calcium and potassium. Peanut yields are highest when the crop occupies the land not more than once every three years.

There are erect, upright, "bunch" types, such as Virginia Bunch and Spanish, which develop like bushes and reach a height of eighteen inches. Valencias are coarse with heavy reddish stems, and large foliage. They sometimes grow up to four feet high. Other types, known as "runners," grow in the form of prostrate vines, like Runner and Virginia Runner, which spread low along the ground. A cluster of twenty-five to fifty peanuts normally grows on each vine, underground.

The peanuts have to be dug out of the soil during the harvest, like a root crop, so a light, friable sandy soil is preferred. It should be free of weeds, and well-fertilized. A light soil also helps the seeds to bury themselves in the ground. Good drainage is vital, since the crop cannot withstand being waterlogged. In many developing countries, peanuts are still sown and dug up by hand, while in the United States they are generally planted and harvested with special equipment in a highly mechanized operation.

Peanut growers in this country normally plant certified seed of good quality which has been treated with fungicides to prevent seedling disease. The seeds are planted by machine-drill approximately two inches deep, at intervals of four to six inches, in rows about three feet apart—about 60,000 to 80,000 per acre. (Hand planting rates, applied in many other parts of the world, are much lower.) Virtually all acreage is treated with herbicides for weed control before planting, as well as in postemergence applications. Provided the soil temperature is warm (about 68 degrees Fahrenheit) and there is sufficient moisture, the seeds will germinate and in approximately two weeks the first leaflets will appear. Several months later, when the vines have a slightly yellowish appearance, it will be time for the harvest. Pods are checked frequently to determine the optimum picking time: the harvest should commence when approximately seventy per cent of the nuts per plant are mature. The farmer will drive his digger up and down the rows, loosening the plants in the soil as it cuts the tap roots four to six inches below the ground. Just behind the digger, a shaker lifts the plants, gently shakes the loose soil from the cluster of peanuts, and lays the plants in windrows with the peanuts on top.

The peanut crop is very unpredictable in its response to fertilizers, which should be applied with caution. Attention must be given to control various diseases including *Cercospora* leaf spot which may cause defoliation, and *Sclerotium* white mold which weakens the plants. Sanitation, rotation and the application of selected systemic fungicides are recommended. Troublesome peanut pests include the velvet bean caterpillar and lesser cornstalk borer in the United States, the *Sphenoptera* beetle in India, and numerous thrips, leaf hoppers, aphids, mites, worms, caterpillars and miscellaneous insects which damage the crop throughout the world. Satisfactory control through insecticides and nematicides presently exists for the common peanut pests.

Freshly-harvested peanuts contain twenty-five to fifty per cent moisture content,

MECHANIZED HARVEST

This inverted harvester turns peanuts up toward the sun and away from the soil. The peanuts are usually dried in the field for a few days and then artificially dried in bins or wagons.

which must be reduced to ten per cent or less to avoid spoilage. The peanuts are usually left out in the field to dry for two to three days, on top of the windrows. The farmer then drives his combine over the windrows, lifting the plants. The peanuts are separated from the vines and blown into a hopper, while the vines are left in the field to be gathered as feed for farm animals, or are plowed under. The peanuts are dumped into drying wagons to be dried through forced hot air; then they are usually taken to buying stations to be inspected, sampled, and graded by the Federal State Inspection Service to determine their value, following which they are stored.

At the buying station, the inspectors check the peanuts for size and moisture content and try to be sure a mold is not present which might contain aflatoxin, a carcinogen which has been known to cause fatalities in turkeys in Great Britain, although there is no direct evidence concerning its effect on humans. Aflatoxin is the term applied to the toxic metabolites produced by some strains of the fungus, *Aspergillus flavus*, a pathogen which may grow on numerous commodities in various parts of the world, including peanuts. Aflatoxin-contaminated peanuts are inedible, and their use is limited to the production of peanut oil. Careful disease, nematode and soil insect control and proper drying after the harvest minimize the risk of aflatoxin.

160

About ten per cent of the United States peanut crop is sold in the shell—mostly large Virginia types and small Valencias. The remainder is shelled, after having been thoroughly cleaned of dirt, bits of vine, rocks and other refuse. During shelling, the peanuts rub against each other in drums until the shells split open and the kernels fall out. The kernels are graded, sized and packed in bags, ready to be sold, usually to a processor who will then market them to the public. About half of the total United States consumption of peanuts is in edible products; approximately one fourth are exported, mainly to Canada, Western Europe and Japan; the remaining one fourth are crushed for oil and meal, employed for feed and seed, or lost on the farm.

Kernels are normally graded into sizes based on the counts per ounce. Kernels which count 60 to 80 per ounce, such as the Spanish types, are considered small; 40 to 60, like the United States Runners, are medium; and 30 to 40, like Virginia types, are graded as large.

In the United States, the major use of domestic peanuts is in peanut butter, followed by salted shelled peanuts, peanut candy, roasted-in-shell peanuts and peanut butter sandwiches. Little peanut butter is consumed in other countries. It is believed that a physician in St. Louis invented peanut butter about 1890 as a health food. During the same period, Dr. John H. Kellogg, famous for breakfast cereals, prescribed peanut butter as nourishment for his patients at Battle Creek Sanitarium in Michigan. Peanuts are said to contain fiber or roughage of value in assisting

DRYING PEANUTS IN ALABAMA

Two huge burners, fired by butane gas, create hot air which is forced through pipes to the trailers which are filled with peanuts.

the digestive system to regulate itself; they have a slightly acid effect upon digestion. Peanuts are acceptable in most diabetic diets.

By law, any product in the United States labeled "peanut butter" must consist of at least ninety per cent peanuts. The remaining ten per cent usually contains salt, a sweetener, and an emulsifier or hardened vegetable oil which prevents the peanut oil from separating and rising to the top. No artificial sweeteners, chemical preservatives, natural or artificial coloring additives are allowed. Over eighty-five per cent of the peanuts used in making peanut butter are of the Runners variety. About 700 million pounds of peanut butter are produced annually in the United States.

To prepare peanut butter, the raw, shelled peanuts are roasted, cooled and blanched, i.e. the skins are rubbed off. The heart or germ is also removed. The blanched kernels are cleaned, blended and ground, to produce a smooth, even-textured butter. During grinding, the peanuts are heated to about 170 degrees Fahrenheit while emulsifiers are added; the product is cooled to 120 degrees or lower while the emulsifiers are crystalized, trapping the peanut oil.

To prepare chunky peanut butter, the manufacturer will add bits of coarsely ground or broken peanuts to the finely ground product. High-quality peanut butter, packed in hermetically-sealed containers, will retain its flavor and creamy texture for many months.

Nut processors produce roasted, shelled peanuts which are known as "salters." Small, Spanish-type peanuts are usually roasted with their skins on; other types may be roasted with their skins on or off. Snack peanuts are shelled, blanched, roasted and salted. The two basic methods of roasting are oil roasting and dry roasting. Oil-roasted peanuts are deep-fried in hot oil for about five minutes; following draining, the slightly cooled kernels are evenly salted. Dry-roasted peanuts are cooked in high temperature ovens by dry, forced hot air, without the use of oils and sugar. The kernels, which have a dull, non-greasy, gray appearance, are often coated with a mixture of selected spices. They are a popular snack at cocktail parties.

Partially defatted peanuts are prepared from blanched, whole peanuts which have had over fifty per cent of their oil removed by means of a hydraulic press. After being soaked in brine to restore them to their natural size and shape, they are deep-fat-fried. They contain about one-third less calories than regular peanuts, and can be molded and flavored to resemble other edible nuts such as almonds and pecans. Many years ago, before the advent of strict regulations pertaining to the adulteration of foodstuffs, ground, pressed, peanuts, shaped like coffee beans, were frequently sold as "Austrian coffee," although the resultant beverage was reputed to be virtually tasteless.

Many different types of candies contain peanuts: candy bars may combine them (whole, chopped, or in the form of peanut butter) with various mixtures of chocolate, caramel, nougat, marshmallows, other nuts and dried fruits. Peanut brittle and chocolate-covered peanuts are traditional favorites. It is estimated that over sixty per cent of the nuts utilized in candies in the United States are peanuts.

Other snack items making use of high protein peanuts include roasted-in-shell peanuts and peanut butter sandwiches. Roasted-in-shell peanuts, commonly called "ball park" peanuts, are sold by vendors at all types of sporting events as well as out on the street. They are also available at grocery stores. Peanut butter sandwiches may be purchased through vending machines and at grocery outlets. The sandwiches consist of two small crackers with a layer of peanut butter in between. The crackers may be plain or contain cheese, ham, chili or other flavors.

Since the middle of the nineteenth century, peanut oil has been an important ingredient in French, Italian and Oriental cuisines. It was first produced commercially in the United States in 1934 by the Planters Company, making use of a process Amedeo Obici had observed in France. Most countries grow peanuts primarily for peanut oil; in the United States, on the other hand, only about fifteen per cent of the crop is dedicated to oil production.

There is considerable variation in the oil content of different peanut varieties. The small-podded Spanish may contain a high oil content of about fifty per cent, which makes this type ideal for crushing for oil; larger-podded varieties, such as Virginia Bunch, generally have a lower oil content of only

PEANUT PLANTS, PEANUTS, PEANUT TARTS

thirty-five per cent, but are more readily digestible and appropriate for use in snacks or as candy nuts.

Approximately three-fourths of the peanut oil produced in the United States is devoted to cooking and salad oil; about twenty per cent is exported, while the remainder is used in the manufacture of margarine and shortening.

Peanuts are chopped and cooked by steam before the peanut oil is either extracted by solvents or squeezed out mechanically by being crushed by a screw press. The crude oil is filtered and refined, heated under vacuum and blown by superheated steam to produce a clear, amber-colored, edible oil with a slightly nutty taste. Peanut oil has a high smoke point; it can be heated to 450 degrees Fahrenheit (hotter than most other cooking oils) before it smokes. It also does not transfer flavors, so it can be used over and over again to prepare different foods. Due to the presence of natural antioxidants, peanut oil has good resistance to rancidity. It contains approximately eighty-one per cent unsaturated fats, twenty-eight per cent of which are polyunsaturated.

In many countries the best grades of peanut oil are used in the manufacture of margarine and other edible fats, or blended with olive oil for use as a salad oil. Peanut oil is an effective preservative agent in the canning of fish. The poorer grades are employed in soap making, in the manufacture of lubricants, as a constituent of illuminants and for oiling wood.

Peanut flour is becoming more popular as a highly digestible protein extender in bakery and confectionery products, especially for diet-conscious consumers. During processing, a high proportion of the oil and calories is removed, leaving a flour product that contains about sixty per cent protein and less than one per cent fat.

Peanut meal is a by-product of peanuts processed for oil. This residual cake is an important, concentrated, high protein livestock feed. Peanut hulls, a by-product of shelling peanuts serve as a roughage filler in livestock feed. The hulls may be processed as "fireplace logs" and are also found in many industrial products including abrasives, sound-insulating material and wall boards.

Peanuts, ever since their introduction to Africa and the Far East, have been greatly prized by the inhabitants of those areas for their high food value, pleasing taste and easy cultivation. They continue to play an important role in the diet of millions of people of the third world who cannot afford animal fats and proteins from other sources. "Groundnut chop" is a famous, native dish in West Africa. It is an elaborate chicken stew to which roasted peanut meal and piquant seasonings have been added. In India, peanuts are a common ingredient in soups, stews and curries. Vast quantities of peanut oil are employed in India in the manufacture of vegetable ghee. The nuts themselves, coated with sugar, are widely consumed in sweetmeats. As a special Indian delicacy, peanuts are allowed to germinate, and then seasoned with spices before being eaten. A popular dish in Indonesia known as "onchom" consists of a paste made of fried, round, partially fermented peanut kernels.

Peanuts contain about twenty-six per cent protein—higher than dairy products, eggs, fish and many cuts of meat. According to the National Peanut Council, a glass of milk and two peanut butter sandwiches provide eighty-three per cent of a growing child's daily need for protein. The total food energy in one pound of peanut butter equals two and one-quarter pounds of steak, a gallon of milk or thirty-two eggs. Peanuts contain many of the essential B vitamins including thiamin, riboflavin and niacin, as well as appreciable amounts of calcium, phosphorous, potassium, iron and magnesium—including a balanced share of calories, but no cholesterol.

Sales of peanuts and peanut products through vending machines are expected to increase since Americans are consuming more and more food away from home. Improvements have been made in packaging and the use of cellophane lamination to preserve freshness and make snacks more attractive.

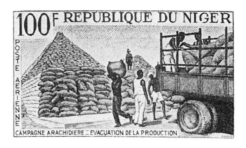

During the past thirty years, the per capita consumption of edible peanuts in the United States has risen from 6.4 pounds in 1950 to 9.5 pounds in 1979. It is expected that this trend will continue.

PREPARING PEANUTS

Dry-Roasting (XXI)

Spread raw peanuts in one layer in a shallow baking pan.

Heat in a slow oven at 300° F (150° C) for 30 to 45 minutes, depending on how brown you want them.

Stir peanuts often as they heat. Check on brownness from time to time by removing the skins from a few of the peanuts. Serve warm.

If you like peanuts salted, add 1 teaspoon (5 ml) butter or margarine to each cup (250 ml) of peanuts immediately after removing from oven. Stir until peanuts are evenly coated and sprinkle with salt.

Homemade Peanut Butter (XXI)

1 cup (250 ml) freshly roasted peanuts	1/2 teaspoon (2.5 ml) salt
3 tablespoons (46 ml) peanut oil	

In the container of a blender, put peanuts and 1-1/2 tablespoons (23 ml) peanut oil.

If you prefer salted peanut butter, add salt.

Blend briefly, turn blender off and use rubber spatula to push down whole peanuts which rise to top.

While alternating the blender and the use of spatula, gradually add another 1-1/2 table-spoons (23 ml) of peanut oil (or enough to make the peanut butter the desired consistency).

Note: Blending the peanuts will transform the peanuts' red skins into tiny red flecks in the finished peanut butter.

Deep-Frying (XXI)

Put peanuts into a colander or frying basket. Submerge in peanut oil preheated to 350° F (175° C) and fry for 2 minutes.

Drain on paper towels. Sprinkle with salt. Serve warm.

For an unusual snack, add 1/4 teaspoon (1 ml) garlic powder or chili powder for each cup peanuts. Mix thoroughly, and serve warm.

HORS D'OEUVRES

Peanut Chicken Pick-Me-Ups (XX)

2-1/2 cups (625 ml) ground cooked chicken	3/4 cup (175 ml) low-sodium mayon-naise
1/2 cup (125 ml) grated carrots	1-1/2 cups (375 ml) ground, dry-roasted, unsalted peanuts
1/2 cup (125 ml) minced fresh parsley	
1/2 cup (125 ml) finely chopped onion	1/4 cup (60 ml) unsalted margarine, melted

Toss together chicken, carrots, parsley and onion. Add mayonnaise, mix well. Roll into 1-inch (2.5 cm) balls. Roll each ball in peanuts. Dip one side of ball in margarine and place on ungreased baking sheets, margarine side up.

Bake at 400° F (200° C) for 15 minutes, or until golden. Cool 5 minutes before serving.

Yield: About 36 1-inch (2.5 cm) pieces

Peanut Butter Pâté (XXII)

1/2 cup (125 ml) chopped fresh or canned mush-rooms	4 tablespoons (60 ml) creamy peanut butter
2 tablespoons (30 ml) butter or margarine	2 slices of bacon
2 tablespoons (30 ml) lemon juice	3 green onions, finely chopped
1 package (8 ounces/225 g) cream cheese, softened	Assorted crackers

Cook and stir mushrooms in butter 5 minutes; stir in lemon juice. Remove from heat. Beat cream cheese and peanut butter until fluffy. Stir in mushrooms and cover. Refrigerate at least 1 hour. Fry bacon until crisp; drain and crumble. Shape cream cheese mixture into a ball. Roll ball in bacon and onions; cover. Refrigerate until serving time. Serve with crackers.

Yield: about 35 canapés.

SOUP

Georgia Peanut Soup (XX)

1/4 cup (60 ml)
 margarine
1/4 cup (60 ml) finely
 chopped onion
1/4 cup (60 ml) finely
 chopped celery
1 cup (250 ml) creamy
 peanut butter
1 tablespoon (15 ml)
 flour
4 cups (1 liter) beef
 bouillon
2 teaspoons (10 ml) lem-
 on juice
1/2 cup (125 ml)
 chopped cocktail
 peanuts

In a large heavy saucepan, melt margarine.
Add onion and celery; sauté until tender. Stir
in peanut butter and flour; blend well. Gradually stir in beef bouillon and lemon juice until
smooth. Cook over medium heat for 20 minutes, stirring occasionally. To serve, garnish
with chopped cocktail peanuts.

Yield: 6 to 8 servings

GEORGIA PEANUT SOUP

MAIN DISHES

Nutted Sweet and Sour Pork (XX)

2 tablespoons (30 ml)
 peanut oil
2 pounds (900 g) boned
 pork loin, cut in
 strips
2 medium green pep-
 pers, cut in 1-inch
 (2.5-cm) squares
1/2 cup (125 ml) sliced
 green onions
1 can (1 pound/450 g)
 apricot halves
1/2 cup (125 ml) cocktail
 peanuts
1/3 cup (75 ml) vinegar
1/4 cup (60 ml) soy
 sauce
1 large clove garlic,
 peeled and minced
1/4 teaspoon (pinch)
 ground ginger
2 tablespoons (30 ml)
 cornstarch
1/4 cup (60 ml) water
4 cups (1 liter) hot
 cooked rice
1/2 cup (125 ml)
 chopped cocktail
 peanuts

Heat oil in skillet. Add meat; brown. Add
green pepper and green onion; cook several
minutes.

Drain apricots; reserve fruit. Add liquid to
meat with peanuts, vinegar, soy sauce, garlic
and ginger. Cover; cook over low heat 45 minutes, or until pork is tender. Stir occasionally. Blend together cornstarch and water. Stir
into sauce. Cook, stirring until thickened.
Add apricots; heat.

Combine rice and chopped peanuts. Serve
pork over rice.

Yield: 8 servings

Chicken Curry with Peanuts (XX)

1/3 cup (75 ml)
 margarine
1/4 cup (60 ml) chopped
 onion
2 cloves garlic, peeled
 and finely chopped
1/4 cup (60 ml) unsifted
 flour
1-1/2 teaspoons (7.5 ml)
 curry powder
1 teaspoon (5 ml) salt
1/4 teaspoon (1 ml)
 pepper
2 cups (500 ml) chicken
 bouillon
1 cup (250 ml) unpeeled
 apple slices
3 cups (750 ml) cubed
 cooked chicken
2 cups (500 ml) hot
 cooked rice
1 cup (250 ml) chopped,
 dry-roasted pea-
 nuts
1/2 cup (125 ml)
 chopped green
 pepper
1/2 cup (125 ml) toasted
 flaked coconut
1/4 cup (60 ml) chutney

Melt margarine in a heavy saucepan over low heat. Sauté onion and garlic until tender, about 10 minutes. Blend in flour, curry powder, salt and pepper. Cook over low heat, stirring occasionally, until mixture is thick and bubbly. Gradually stir chicken bouillon into flour mixture. When thick and smooth, add apple slices. Cook 5 minutes over medium heat. Add chicken and cook 5 minutes longer.

Serve over hot cooked rice with chopped, dry-roasted peanuts, green pepper, coconut and chutney as accompaniments.

Yield: 6 servings

Hawaiian Shrimp (XX)

1 pound (450 g) large shrimp, peeled and deveined	3/4 cup (175 ml) milk
	1-1/2 cups (375 ml) very finely chopped, dry-roasted peanuts
1 cup (250 ml) unsifted flour	
1 egg	Peanut oil

Slit each shrimp down the back without separating the halves; press flat, like a butterfly. Combine flour, egg and milk; heat well. Dip shrimp in batter, then in chopped peanuts. Fry in deep hot 375° F (190° C) oil for 5 to 8 minutes.

Yield: About 30 shrimp

LUNCHEON AND SUPPER DISHES

Peanut Seafood Salad (XXIII)

3 cups (750 ml) cooked, chilled rice	1 cup (250 ml) chopped, roasted peanuts
1 large can tuna (may also use shrimp or crabmeat)	1/4 cup (60 ml) lemon juice
	1/4 cup (60 ml) chopped bell pepper
2 hard-cooked eggs, chopped or sliced	
2 large tomatoes, cut in wedges	

In a large salad bowl, place rice, tuna, chopped eggs, tomatoes, peanuts and lemon juice. Toss thoroughly. You may serve it on a lettuce leaf and garnish with bell pepper rings. It may be served plain or with a special French Dressing.

French Dressing

1/2 cup (125 ml) peanut oil	1/2 teaspoon (2.5 ml) salt
1/4 cup (60 ml) white vinegar	1/4 teaspoon (1 ml) oregano
1 clove garlic, peeled and crushed	

Place all ingredients in screw top container and shake vigorously. Allow to stand about 15 minutes before using. Remember to keep dressing at room temperature.

Yield: 6 servings

Perfect Peanut Quiche (XXII)

One 9-inch (23-cm) unbaked pie shell	2 tablespoons (30 ml) chopped, green onion
1 cup (250 ml) shredded Swiss cheese	1/4 teaspoon (pinch) salt
4 eggs, slightly beaten	Dash of cayenne
1-3/4 cups (425 ml) light cream or half-and-half	1 can (6-1/2 ounces/ 195 g) peanuts

Sprinkle cheese in pastry-lined 9-inch (23 cm) pie plate or quiche pan. Combine eggs, cream, onion, salt and cayenne. Stir in peanuts. Pour mixture over cheese in pan. Bake in preheated 375° F (190° C) oven 45-50 minutes or until just set. Let stand 10 minutes before cutting. Top with onion brushes.

Yield: 6 servings

VEGETABLES

Creamed Onions and Peanuts (XX)

2 tablespoons (30 ml) margarine	1 cup (250 ml) milk
2 tablespoons (30 ml) flour	3 cups (750 ml) small white onions, cooked
1/4 teaspoon (1 ml) salt	1/4 cup (60 ml) chopped cocktail peanuts
1/8 teaspoon (pinch) pepper	

Melt margarine over low heat in a saucepan. Gradually blend in flour, salt and pepper. Stir in milk and continue stirring until mixture thickens. Add onions and simmer another 10 minutes. Before serving, add chopped peanuts.

Yield: 4 to 6 servings

BAKED GOODS

Dixie Peanut Pie (XXIII)

1/4 cup (60 ml) peanut butter	3/4 teaspoon (4 ml) maple extract
1 cup (250 ml) dark corn syrup	2/3 cup (150 ml) coarsely chopped roasted peanuts
1/2 cup (125 ml) sugar	
2 eggs	One 9-inch (23-cm) pie shell
3 tablespoons (45 ml) butter or margarine	

Combine the peanut butter, corn syrup, sugar, eggs and butter. Stir in the maple extract and coarsely chopped peanuts. Pour mixture into an unbaked pastry shell. Bake at 325° F (165° C) for 55 minutes, or until golden brown.

Yield: One 9-inch (23-cm) pie

Nut-Topped Rhubarb Squares (XX)

1 package (16 ounces/450 g) frozen rhubarb	1/2 cup (125 ml) unsifted flour
6 tablespoons (90 ml) water	3/4 cup (175 ml) chopped, dry-roasted, unsalted peanuts
1/2 cup (125 ml) sugar	
2 tablespoons (30 ml) cornstarch	1/4 cup (60 ml) wheat germ
1/4 cup (60 ml) unsalted margarine	1/4 teaspoon (1 ml) vanilla extract
2 tablespoons (30 ml) honey	
1 cup (250 ml) old-fashioned oats, uncooked	

In a medium saucepan combine rhubarb and 4 tablespoons (60 ml) water. Place over medium heat and bring to a boil; reduce heat and simmer 5 minutes, breaking up rhubarb. Stir in sugar and simmer 10 minutes. Combine cornstarch and remaining 2 tablespoons (30 ml) water until smooth; mix into rhubarb and cook over medium heat stirring constantly, until thickened and clear. Remove from heat and cool.

In a small saucepan combine margarine and honey; cook over low heat until margarine is melted.

In a bowl mix oats, flour, 1/2 cup (125 ml) peanuts and wheat germ. Stir in honey mixture and vanilla. Press into bottom of a greased 9 × 9 × 2-inch (23 × 23 × 5-cm) pan.

Bake at 375° F (190° C) for 10 to 15 minutes, until lightly browned at edges. Remove from oven and spread rhubarb mixture over top; sprinkle with remaining peanuts. Bake 10 minutes longer. Remove from oven and cool in pan on wire rack. Cut into squares to serve.

Yield: 16 servings

Peanut Yummy Caramel Bars (XXIII)

32 caramels or 1 cup (250 ml) caramel syrup	1 cup (250 ml) old-fashioned oats, uncooked
1/3 cup (75 ml) light cream or evaporated milk	3/4 cup (175 ml) butter or margarine
1 cup (250 ml) all-purpose, sifted flour	One 6-ounce (180-g) package semisweet chocolate pieces
1/2 teaspoon (2.5 ml) baking soda	3/4 cup (175 ml) chopped peanuts
1/4 teaspoon (1 ml) salt	
3/4 cup (175 ml) dark brown sugar, firmly packed	

Melt caramels and cream in top of double boiler over hot (not boiling) water. Set aside. Sift flour, baking soda and salt together into a large mixing bowl. Stir in brown sugar and oats. Using a pastry blender, cut in butter until mixture looks like coarse crumbs. Turn half of the oat mixture into an 11 × 7 × 1-1/2-inch (27.5 × 17.5 × 3.75-cm) greased baking pan and press evenly with chocolate pieces and nuts. Spread this with caramel mixture. Sprinkle remaining oat mixture evenly over the caramels. Bake in a preheated 350° F (175° C) oven for 20 minutes or until lightly browned. Cool for approximately 30 minutes on wire rack. Chill in refrigerator until caramel layer is set. Cut into bars. Store in an airtight container.

Yield: 24 bars

Groundnut Bread (XX)

2-1/2 cups (625 ml) warm water (105°-115° F/ 41°-47° C)	1 cup (250 ml) crunchy peanut butter
2 packages or cakes yeast, active dry or compressed	1/4 cup (1/2 stick/60 ml) margarine, softened
1 tablespoon (15 ml) salt	1 egg white
1 tablespoon (15 ml) margarine, melted	1 tablespoon (15 ml) cold water
7 cups (1-3/4 liter) unsifted flour	1/4 cup (60 ml) chopped cocktail peanuts

Measure warm water into a large warm mixing bowl. Sprinkle or crumble in yeast; stir until dissolved. Add salt and melted margarine. Add flour and stir until well blended (dough will be sticky). Place in greased bowl, turning to grease top. Cover; let rise in warm place, free from draft, until doubled in bulk, about 1 hour.

Turn dough out onto lightly floured board. Divide into 2 equal portions. Roll half of dough into an oblong, 15 × 10 inches (37.5 × 25 cm). Combine peanut butter and softened margarine. Cover dough with half of mixture. Then, beginning at wide side of dough, roll up tightly toward you. Taper ends and seal edges by pinching together. Starting at one end, coil roll of dough on a greased baking sheet. Repeat for other half of dough. Cover, let rise in a warm place, free from draft, until doubled in bulk, about 1 hour.

With sharp knife score tops of loaves, criss crossing top three times in each direction.

Bake in hot oven, 450° F (235° C) 25 minutes. Remove from oven and brush with egg white mixed with cold water. Sprinkle with chopped peanuts. Return to oven, bake 5 minutes longer.

Yield: 2 round loaves

CANDY

Peanut Brittle (XX)

Aluminum foil	1 cup (250 ml) dry-roasted peanuts
1 cup (250 ml) sugar	1/8 teaspoon (pinch) baking soda
1/2 cup (125 ml) water	
1/4 cup (60 ml) light corn syrup	
1/2 teaspoon (2.5 ml) margarine	

Line a large electric skillet with aluminum foil.

Combine sugar, water, corn syrup and margarine in skillet. Set temperature gauge at 375° F (190° C). Cook, stirring occasionally until syrup turns golden brown. Stir in peanuts. Continue stirring until mixture turns medium brown. Add soda; stir vigorously. Remove foil containing candy from skillet and let cool. Break brittle into pieces.

Yield: 1 pound (450 g)

169

CLUSTER OF PECANS

CHAPTER NINE

Pecans

Family: Juglandaceae

LATIN	*Carya illinoinensis* (Wangenh.) K. Koch	Syn.	*Carya pecan*
SPANISH	Pacana	DUTCH	Pecan-Noot
FRENCH	Pacane	ITALIAN	Noce di Pecan
GERMAN	Pekannuss	PORTUGUESE	Noz-Pecã
SWEDISH	Pecannöt	RUSSIAN	Pekán
ARABIC	Jōz Amîrki	JAPANESE	Piikan
		CHINESE	Mei Chow Hu Tao

THE PECAN, *Carya illinoinensis*, is undoubtedly the most important nut tree native to North America. Although named for its northernmost natural habitat, it is actually indigenous to a wide geographical area, including Texas, Oklahoma, Louisiana, Mississippi, Arkansas, Missouri, Kansas, Kentucky, Tennessee, Illinois, Indiana, Nebraska, Iowa and Mexico as far south as Oaxaca.

For North American Indian tribes in the south central region of the United States, especially in the Mississippi Valley, the pecan served as a dietary staple long before the arrival of Europeans. Later they traded pecans to the settlers for furs, trinkets and tobacco. Before the early sixteenth century, no European had ever seen a pecan nut.

Lope de Oviedo, member of a Spanish expedition to the New World in 1533, described pecans growing near the Guadalupe River in Texas: "There were many nuts on the banks of this river which the Indians ate in their season, coming from twenty to thirty leagues about. These nuts were much smaller than the Spanish . . . walnuts."

Alvar Núñez Cabeza de Vaca, a Spanish colonial official and explorer, was treasurer of the ill-fated Nárvaez expedition to the Gulf Coast of North America in 1528. When all the Spanish ships were wrecked during a violent storm in the Gulf of Mexico, Cabeza de Vaca and three other survivors were captured by Indians on an island near the Texas coast and imprisoned for several years. During his miserable captivity, he noted that for two months of the year his Indian captors lived on nothing but pecans ("nogales") when they habitually visited the so-called "river of nuts," which was the Guadalupe.

In 1729, Jean Penicaut, carpenter on a French ship, reported that the Indians at the village of Natchez on the Mississippi river had three different kinds of walnut trees, one of which produced excellent, edible nuts as small as a man's thumb. They were called "pacanes." The French in Louisiana adopted this name for the pecan.

The Algonquin Indian word "paccan" included also walnuts and hickories—referring to nuts so hard they had to be cracked with a

171

PECAN NUTS

stone. In other related dialects, the Crees called the nuts "pakan;" and for the Abnaki the name was "pagann." These highly nutritional nuts were stored by Indian tribes along the Mississippi for use during the winter. A creamy liquid called *powcohicoria* or "hickory milk" was prepared by the Algonquins: paccan kernels were pounded into small pieces, cast into boiling water, strained and stirred. This rich, nutty concoction was added to broth to thicken it, and to corn cakes and hominy as a seasoning; it was sometimes fermented to produce an intoxicating liquor that was consumed at tribal feasts.

The pecan was formerly known botanically as *Hicoria pecan*—the Latin name of the genus *Hicoria* having been derived from powcohicoria. In recent years, however, *Carya*, instead of *Hicoria* has been accepted as the generic name for the pecan. Walnuts, hickory nuts and pecans belong to the Juglandaceae family.

Towards the end of the French and Indian Wars, in about 1760, fur traders introduced the pecan from the territory of the Illinois Indians to the Atlantic seaboard. Thus it became known as the "Illinois" nut. John Bartram, a renowned Philadelphia botanist, made the first recorded shipment of pecans abroad. In 1761, he sent a package of seeds to a friend, Peter Collinson, in London. By 1772, William Prince, a New York nurseryman, was raising and selling pecan seedlings.

George Washington was fond of pecans and frequently carried them in his pockets. In 1774 he planted several young pecan seedlings at Mount Vernon which lived to a great age. Thomas Jefferson started growing pecan trees at Monticello in 1779. He wrote to a friend: "I am going to procure me two or three hundred paccan-nuts from the western country. The paccan-nut is . . . the Illinois nut. The former is the vulgar name south of the Potomac." Both Washington and

THE PECAN

Formerly known as *Hicoria pecan* and *Carya pecan;* now classified as *Carya illinoinensis.*

Jefferson are said to have esteemed the pecan as a handsome ornamental tree for gardens in the United States.

An important historical event took place in the pecan industry in 1847: Antoine, a slave gardener on Oak Alley plantation in southern Louisiana, succeeded in topworking sixteen native pecan trees—a technique which involved cutting back numerous pecan seedlings and grafting scions of a selected parent tree on the young sprouts. This discovery was a significant milestone in asexual propagation of the pecan: Antoine's selection was given the name Centennial in 1876 in commemoration of the hundredth anniversary of the United States, and over the years became a popular variety. Since 1848, more than 500 other pecan cultivars have been named.

173

CENTENNIAL, THE OLDEST PECAN CULTIVAR

First propagated asexually in 1847 by Antoine, a Louisiana slave gardner.

Union soldiers, returning north in 1865 after the Civil War, brought pecans with them and helped to increase the nut's popularity.

Texas was blessed with more native pecan trees than any other state: possibly as many as seventy-five million growing wild, mostly near the state's many watercourses. The pecan is the official state tree of Texas. Some loyal Texans claim in fact that the tree should have been named *Carya texana*. In 1880, F. A. Swinden of Brownwood, Texas, planted 400 acres of pecan seedlings—the first commercial pecan orchard. The early pecan orchards were invariably planted with seedling trees, since grafted or budded varieties were scarce or virtually unknown. In 1882, a commercial nursery in New Orleans established a new trend when it offered budded and grafted pecan trees for sale, including the Centennial variety, at the price of $2.50 per tree.

During the late 1880's, E. E. Risien of San Saba County, Texas, carried on the important task started by Antoine some forty years earlier, of topworking native pecan trees. Risien noticed that pecan seedlings did not reproduce true to type, so he selected superior parent trees for asexual propagation by budding or grafting, rather than attempting to propagate them by planting their seed. The Western Schley, has been and continues to be a most important cultivar in the Southwest; it was selected and developed originally in Risien's nursery.

On March 2, 1906, Governor James Stephen Hogg of Texas provided further impetus to pecan growing, on his death bed, when he declared: "I want no monument of stone or marble, but plant at my head a pecan tree and at my feet an old-fashioned walnut . . . and when these trees shall bear, let the pecans and walnuts be given out among the plain people of Texas so that they may plant them and make Texas a land of trees."

Between 1900 and 1925, numerous real estate projects which featured pecan trees were developed in the southeastern states. Exaggerated "get rich quick" claims were put forth

PECAN GROVE IN TEXAS

The cattle should be removed six weeks prior to harvest; if not, they may destroy large
quantities of pecan nuts which are far more expensive than cattle feed.

about making easy money through pecan
growing. Hundreds of thousands of acres
were planted, mostly with Stuart variety pecans, in Georgia, Alabama, Mississippi and
northern Florida by so-called pecan orchard
development companies—whose main objec-
tive was to produce quick profits, rather than
cultivate nuts, by selling sections of the "orchards." Land was divided into five and ten
acre plots, to be unloaded onto the unsuspecting public at high prices. Many of these operations were honest and did help to expand a
struggling, new industry. Unfortunately,
hundreds of gullible investors were fleeced by
other unscrupulous operators and suffered
disappointing losses when promises of in-

stant wealth failed to come true. One problem
was the long time required—ten to twelve
years—for Stuart pecans to enter into production. Instead of getting rich in retirement from
the sale of nuts from their own pecan trees,
numerous investors went broke, especially
during the depression years of the 1930's.
During the 1960's, thousands of acres of these
Stuart pecans were rehabilitated, heavily fertilized, and brought back into production.

During the early nineteenth century, appreciable progress toward increasing production was made by topworking native pecan
seedlings with new, standard varieties in Texas, Oklahoma and Louisiana. H. A. Halbert of
Coleman, Texas, was a pioneer in this type of

175

STUART VARIETY PECANS IN SUMMER
BEFORE SHUCK SPLIT, BACONTON,
GEORGIA

LARGE PECAN ORCHARD NEAR LAS CRUCES, NEW MEXICO

propagation: he traveled extensively throughout Texas for forty years as a specialist in topworking. Halbert died in 1926, at the age of 77, when he fell from a pecan tree that he was budding.

It took about four centuries for the pecan to become an important crop in the United States: it reached a commercial scale in 1920 and has increased steadily ever since. The average, annual pecan production is now over 200 million pounds, although there is considerable variation from year to year. The pecan industry, like the macadamia nut, has largely developed during the twentieth century. Pecan and macadamia nut producers have something else in common: they are both involved in long term projects which require considerable capital investment over a period of many years before any profits can be expected.

Most edible tree nuts are essentially one-state crops: almonds, pistachios and walnuts are produced in California; filberts in Oregon and macadamia nuts in Hawaii. The pecan, on the other hand, is a multi-state crop, stretching across the country from the Southeast to the Southwest throughout some twenty states.

The states where pecans are grown today may be divided geographically into three regions: the Southeast, including Georgia, parts of North and South Carolina, Florida, Alabama, Mississippi and Louisiana; the southwestern states of Texas, New Mexico, Arizona and southern Oklahoma; and the North, including northern Oklahoma, Kansas, Illinois, Missouri, Iowa, Kentucky, Tennessee and Indiana. Pecans grow further north, however, than they will produce satisfactory crops. Some trial plantings (about 1,500 acres) have also been made in California.

The most important producing regions are the Southeast and the Southwest. Among the states, Georgia is usually the largest producer, followed by Texas, Alabama, New Mexico and Louisiana. The largest pecan orchard of some 6,000 acres is located near Tucson, Arizona; another large orchard of about 4,000 acres has been established near Las Cruces, New Mexico.

Total United States drought-stricken production in 1980 amounted to 183.5 million pounds of pecans—considerably less than usual since the average of the three previous crops was approximately 232 million pounds and the estimated production for 1981 was 328 million pounds. During 1980, 105 million pounds of pecans were produced in Georgia; the average price to the producer was about 78 cents per pound.

The following report of the United States Department of Agriculture summarizes utilized pecan production in the United States during 1978, 1979 and 1980:

UTILIZED PECAN PRODUCTION 1,000 POUNDS

	1978	1979	1980
Alabama	22,000	4,000	20,000
Arkansas	3,200	1,500	900
Florida	4,200	2,600	6,000
Georgia	135,000	65,000	105,000
Louisiana	9,000	16,000	14,000
Mississippi	10,000	2,500	4,500
New Mexico	15,000	14,700	14,700
North Carolina	4,000	1,300	1,700
Oklahoma	15,500	10,000	3,500
South Carolina	6,000	2,000	2,200
Texas	26,000	91,000	11,000
Total United States Production	249,900	210,600	183,500

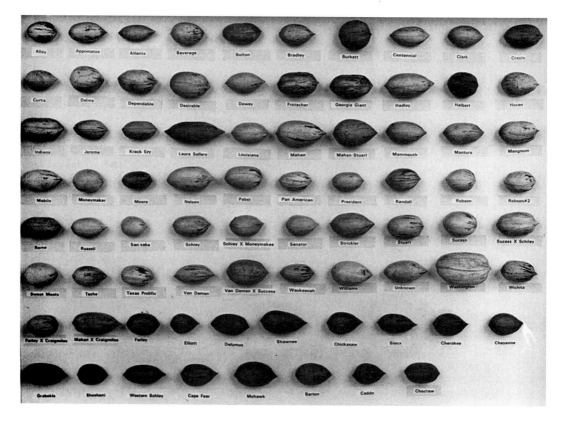

Showing 78 of the more than 500 cultivars (varieties) of pecans which have been propagated. The names of most were taken from the name of the man who discovered the native tree, or the location where it was found. Selections were mainly from non-irrigated lands of Louisiana and Mississippi during the period 1910 to 1925. During the past 30 years, many cultivars have resulted from crosses made in Texas and elsewhere, selected specifically for dense planting under irrigated conditions and given Indian tribal names, including: Caddo, Cheyenne, Cherokee, Chicksaw, Choctaw, Creole, Grabokis, Mohawk, Shawnee, Wichita, etc.

In the Southeast, more than eighty per cent of pecan production comes from improved varieties. In the Southwest, most nuts are still produced from seedling trees, although there has been a recent trend toward selected varieties. Overall, about half of the pecans of commerce are still native, while the remaining production originates from standard varieties or cultivars developed during the past fifty years. Pecans of these improved varieties are generally larger than seedling nuts, have thinner shells and nutmeats that are somewhat darker in color, especially late in the harvest season. Different varieties of pecan produce nuts which vary in size from less than one-quarter to more than one inch in diameter, from one-quarter to two inches in length, and which yield from roughly 40 to over 200 nuts per pound. Each variety tends to have its own unique shell shape, shell color and texture, nutmeat color and oil content—which may range from less than fifty per cent to more than seventy-five per cent, with varying degrees of unsaturation. Most pecan oil is unsaturated, which may be a desirable attribute in view of medical reports which suggest a possible relationship between saturated fats and circulatory disorders in humans. Pecan varieties with plump, well-filled kernels usually have a high oil content with a low degree of unsaturation.

The trend for the future will undoubtedly be less production of native seedling pecan nuts, with greater emphasis on orchards planted with selected cultivars developed through hybridization programs carried out in cooperation with the United States Department of Agriculture and state and local experiment stations.

Outside of the United States, pecans have been planted in Mexico, Australia, Brazil, South Africa, Israel and a few other countries. Since the pecan is indigenous to Mexico, plantings in that country have been made for over a hundred years, principally in the states of Nuevo León, Coahuila, Chihuahua and Durango. The Mexican producing areas are located mostly in semi-arid regions where commercial orchards require irrigation from rivers, lakes and wells. In recent years, Mexican production has been increased by top-working native pecan trees and by new plantings of commercial varieties introduced from the United States, including the varieties known as Western Schley and Wichita.

Since 1968, substantial acreage has been planted with pecans in the northwestern plains of New South Wales, Australia, by a subsidiary of Stahmann Farms, Inc., a company which owns a large pecan orchard near Las Cruces, New Mexico. New orchards of budded Western Schley and Wichita trees have been established in over 1,800 acres of Australian land, levelled for irrigation, in a mechanized operation which has been highly successful. Following preliminary processing

in Australia, the pecans are shipped to Las Cruces for final processing and marketing.

The only truly commercial nut among the hickories is the pecan. Other hickories, such as the shagbark and the shellbark, bear edible nuts, but the trees grow very slowly and their nuts have such poor cracking quality they have little economic importance. Pecans and hickories, when cross pollinated, produce vigorous natural hybrids known as "hicans," which tend to be poor nut producers but make desirable ornamental shade trees and have potential as dwarfing rootstocks.

The pecan, although it resembles the walnut, is more elongated, has a smoother shell

WORLD'S LARGEST PECAN TREE

In Natchez Trace State Park, Henderson County, Tennessee. Vital statistics: 110 feet tall, 68 inches in diameter, with a limb spread of 130 feet.

PECAN

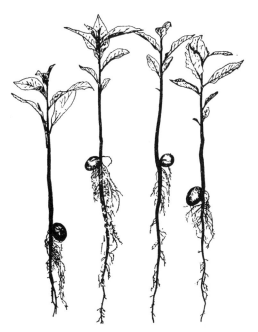

YOUNG PECAN SEEDLINGS

grayish in color. The leaves consist of some eleven to fifteen leaflets, sharp-pointed and serrated, bright green on the upper surface, lighter-hued on the lower surface, and quite smooth when mature. Because the wood is brittle, the trees may easily be damaged by strong winds or by rough treatment during harvesting. The tap-root may penetrate to a depth of thirty feet, but most of the roots occur at about four feet deep and may spread to twice the span of the crown.

The pecan tree is monoecious: that is, the male (staminate) and female (pistillate) flowers occur separately on the same tree. The male, pollen-bearing flowers are in slender catkins, while the female, fruit-bearing flow-

and a higher proportion of kernel in its shell. In the pecan, the partitions which separate the two halves of the kernel are thinner than in the walnut. When mature, the husk of the pecan, unlike that of the walnut, splits open into four segments.

The pecan is a large, stately deciduous tree. Under favorable circumstances it may grow to over 100 feet in height, with a trunk diameter of six feet and a limb spread of some 100 feet. Pecan trees are very long-lived; some native trees in the Southeast are known to be over a thousand years old. To succeed, the pecan needs a deep, well-drained soil, freedom from drought and adequate rainfall. Irrigation is essential if rainfall is lacking. Although the pecan needs a frost-free growing season of 140 to 210 days, a cool period is also required for good nut production, since the trees should be subjected to a chilling interval to break dormancy. Different varieties have somewhat dissimilar climatic requirements.

The bark of the pecan is rough, broken and

A HEAVY LOAD OF CATKINS (MALE FLOWERS) INSURES GOOD POLLINATION

181

ers grow in small, erect clusters. The pecan is seldom self-pollinated and usually requires pollination from another tree before fertilization takes place so that nuts may be formed. The fruit is a drupe, one and one-half to three inches in length. The oblong nut is smooth, thin-shelled and pointed.

Pecan trees are perennial in growth and production: they begin to bear nuts in about six to ten years, and continue to produce for many years, sometimes for as long as two centuries. For income tax depreciation purposes, the Internal Revenue Service usually considers the life of the pecan tree to be fifty years. Under favorable growing conditions, trees of good cultivars may be expected to bear approximately 20 to 60 pounds of in-shell nuts at the age of eight to ten years; 70 to 100 pounds when 11 to 15 years old; and 100 to 150 pounds when they reach 16 years or more

INLAY BARK GRAFT

Inserting a scion of an improved pecan cultivar onto the stock of a native tree.

of age. Very high yields of as much as 800 pounds per tree have been reported from exceptional individual trees growing under unusually favorable conditions, but such yields are unlikely to be attained through normal, commercial cultivation practice.

The pecan is difficult to propagate; patch budding and inlay bark grafting require considerable skill. The varieties known as Riverside and Apache are often used as rootstocks in the West, while Curtis is a popular rootstock in the East. When establishing a new pecan orchard, budded or grafted trees known as "budlings," with one-year old scions and three-year old stocks, are generally transplanted.

For many years, the commonly accepted practice was to plant the trees at a rather wide spacing of a minimum of 60 feet by 70 feet, up to 100 feet by 100 feet. It was assumed that the orchard would not reach the productive or "break even" stage until the eleventh or twelfth year. Recently, however, the trend is toward higher density planting, using selected cultivars which start producing earlier—in about the fifth or sixth year in the field. Instead of the old, standard varieties such as Stuart, Success and Schley, precocious new cultivars like Cheyenne and Wichita are being planted at closer intervals. The Texas Agricultural Extension Service recommends, as the most practical planting system, a spacing of thirty-five feet by thirty-five feet, or thirty-five trees per acre, to be thinned out to wider spacings after fifteen to twenty years. The traditional, very wide spacing of 100 feet by 100 feet accommodated only four trees per acre. The high density concept is more commonly accepted in the irrigated growing acres of the southwestern states of Texas, New Mexico and Arizona than in the Southeast. Although high density plantings must eventually be thinned out, much higher returns per acre may be obtained in the early years. Intensive orchard management in the form of constant pruning and tree training of the precocious cultivars should be carried out when the trees are grown this way.

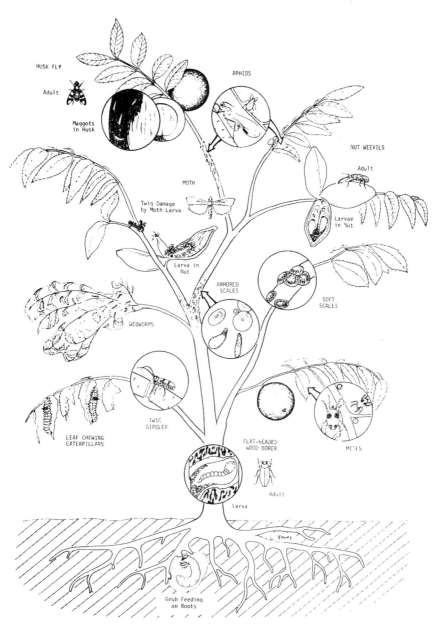

PEST INSECTS WHICH ATTACK AND DAMAGE NUT TREES

In some years, up to 50 percent of the total nut crop in the United States is lost because of insects and mites. Growers should consult local Extension Service specialists to find out the proper chemical control measures to use.

183

Appropriate fertilization with nitrogen is important to increase yields in the orchard. Constant attention should also be given to the control of weeds, diseases, insects and other pests. Trees weakened by disease or insect infestation not only have lower yields, but produce poorly filled nuts with damaged kernels. More than 180 insect and mite species have been found on pecans and about 40 have the potential to harm the nuts. The rapid growth of the pecan industry has brought about new problems in pest control. Due to the trend away from native stands, where every tree is genetically different, towards orchards of uniform varieties, the damage caused is more severe. The pests multiply rapidly because large acreages of pecan provide a favorable environment and an abundance of food. Pest species that were not common in the past have moved to pecans from hickories and other host plants. Insects which damage pecan foliage and fruit, and which should be controlled by approved insecticides, include: hickory shuckworm, pecan nut casebearer, pecan weevil, stink and plant bugs, spittlebugs, aphids and leafminers. Some of the most common plant diseases are pecan scab, powdery mildew and pink mold. If ignored, these pernicious blights may cause premature nut drop and destroy the quality of the nutmeats. Scab, caused by the fungus *Fusicladium effusum*, which invades the young, rapidly growing shoots and leaves, and later the developing nuts, is the most destructive pecan disease. To check it, regular spraying with fungicides is essential.

ORCHARD SPRAYING

A large air-mist sprayer, capable of spraying 100 feet into the air, is spraying a dilute solution of zinc, fungicide and insecticide at the rate of 400 gallons per acre. The 15-year-old pecan trees, located in the Brison orchard at Texas A & M, are planted at a spacing of 50 feet by 50 feet.

Rosette or zinc deficiency of pecan is a problem throughout the pecan belt. Typical symptoms are small, bronzed, crinkled leaves and short, zinc-deficient shoots known as rosettes in the affected trees. Since leaves are known to influence both the current season's and the following year's crops, the leaves must be adequately nourished. Control measures for rosette have included foliar sprays for trees growing in alkaline soils of the West and soil application for trees planted in the acid soils of the Southeast.

In addition to precocious and persistent nut bearing, other desirable characteristics of new cultivars being developed in the pecan breeding work of the United States Depart-

HARVESTING PECANS IN THE EARLY TWENTIETH CENTURY

A PRODUCTIVE VARIETY

The Caddo cultivar starts to produce at an early age, has good foliage, is resistant to scab disease and is an excellent shelling pecan.

ment of Agriculture include disease and insect resistance, vigorous growth, more branching to insure higher yields, wide-angled branches, adequate foliage, early nut maturity, easy-opening shucks and bright, easy to shell kernels with wide grooves.

The high cost and low availability of labor have brought about changes in harvesting techniques. Years ago, pecan nuts were allowed to drop from the trees and were harvested by hand from the ground. Hand harvesting practices have gradually been replaced by mechanical systems, including tree shakers, nut sweepers, vacuum harvesters, conveyors and trash separators. Nuts can now be mechanically shaken from the tree in fifteen seconds, picked from the ground, cracked and shelled, virtually untouched by the human hand.

Pecans harvested mechanically by tree shakers have a higher moisture content than

185

TREE SHAKER

Firmly grasps the trunk, without injuring it; then shakes down the pecans.

PECAN HARVESTER

Follows the windrower, sweeping up nuts, leaves and twigs.

nuts which drop naturally to the ground. The kernel moisture content must be reduced as soon as possible to 4.5 per cent to obtain high-quality pecan products. Drying is essential to prevent mold and discoloration of the kernels. During the drying process, adequate circulation of air is important: warm, dry air (not over 100 degrees Fahrenheit or sixty percent relative humidity) is blown through the nuts for nine to seventeen hours. Once dried, nuts should be refrigerated at 32 degrees Fahrenheit and the humidity should be maintained at sixty-five per cent during storage in order to maintain high product quality of the pecans for up to one year. For longer periods of storage, freezing will provide adequate quality protection. At the present time, most pecans which are to be shelled are stored under refrigeration directly from the orchard and then shelled just prior to marketing. The unbroken shell of the pecan meanwhile protects the nutmeats from contamination, discoloration, insect and mold damage.

Since the early 1920's, mechanical equipment has been developed and improved to size, crack, shell, grade, dry and package pecans. A steady increase has taken place in the proportion of pecans shelled prior to marketing; this now amounts to about 85 per cent of the total crop. The remaining 15 per cent of the nuts are sold in the shell.

The percentage of kernel in the pecan varies widely, depending on variety and other factors: it may range from 30 to 60 per cent. Although shelling greatly reduces the amount of inedible product to be marketed, it also shortens storage life significantly; once shelled, the nuts become more susceptible to damage by insects, oxidation, mold and bacterial contamination. Packing the shelled pecans under vacuum or with nitrogen helps to extend storage life.

Pecan shelling plants are located throughout the important production areas of the Southeast and Southwest, as well as in Chicago and several other cities. When local

THE "MOON" PECANS

NASA in Houston prepared "Desirable" pecans from Texas A & M orchards for the various Apollo flight crews. They were used as snacks on the moon flights by the astronauts. The pecan is ideal for this purpose since it only contains three to four per cent water, will freeze down to 170 degrees below zero Centigrade and thaw without ill effects. It is completely digestible, even in the raw state.

supplies are adequate, the southeastern shelling plants will shell nuts of improved varieties, while the southwestern plants will shell native seedling pecans. It is often necessary, however, for shellers to buy pecans from other geographical regions in order to operate efficiently.

Prior to shelling, "pops" (nuts with empty, shriveled kernels), trash and other foreign matter are removed. The nuts are sized over screens and conditioned by being soaked in tanks of warm water or steamed. This moistening process makes the kernels less brittle and less likely to break during cracking and shelling. For optimum results, the shells should shatter easily, while the kernels should be pliable and limp. The United States Food and Drug Administration requires that sufficient heat be applied during the conditioning process to destroy coliforms of *Escherichia coli* and other bacteria, accomplished usually by dipping the in-shell nuts in near boiling water for a few minutes to destroy any such organisms which might be present. Cracking is accomplished by applying force to the ends of the nuts, one at a time. After being cracked, the pecans go into a sheller where the shell and middle partition are removed by specialized equipment making use of centrifugal force, shaking and other means, following which the kernels are screened and separated into various sizes of halves and pieces. These nutmeats are dried by forced currents of warm air and then cooled rapidly to prevent quality deterioration. Defective kernels and foreign matter are removed by electronic sorters or by hand picking before the kernels are packaged into as many as thirty-eight different sizes of halves and pieces.

Shelled pecans are sold for the most part to bakeries (thirty-six per cent) and to confectioners (twenty per cent); lesser quantities are marketed to retailers, grocery-wholesalers and dairies for ice cream production as well as to other outlets.

There are six United States grades for shelled pecans: U.S. No. 1 halves; U.S. No. 1 halves and pieces; U.S. Commercial halves; U.S. No. 1 pieces; U.S. Commercial pieces; and Unclassified. The U.S. No. 1 halves consist of pecan half-kernels which are well dried, cleaned and free from pieces of shell and center wall, foreign material, chipped halves, broken kernels, particles of dust, noticeable shriveling, rancidity, mold, decay and insect injury; and also free from damage caused by leanness, hollowness and discoloration. Pecan halves in any lot should be fairly uniform in size and color. There are specified tolerances based on weight for the various grades.

Shelled pecan halves are graded as: Mammoths (250 halves per pound or less), and then, in gradually reduced sizes, including Junior Mammoth, Jumbo, Extra Large, Large, Medium, Small, down to Midget (751 halves or more per pound). The seed coat color of pecan kernels is described as Golden, Light Brown, Medium Brown, Dark Brown and Dark Amber. When more than twenty-five per cent of the surface is dark brown, the kernel is classified as Dark Amber and considered to be "damaged."

The demand for in-shell pecans has been declining in recent years in favor of shelled nutmeats. In-shell pecans have traditionally been bleached or washed in wet sand to remove black streaks and other blemishes—and then waxed, polished and dyed. Polished, dyed pecans, packed in window-type cartons, are still quite a popular item for export to Europe.

During shelling, the kernels are sometimes bruised; this causes an oily film to migrate from the nutmeats which can cause rancidity unless adequate care is taken. Pecans are high in oil content and have volatile flavors; they may also have biochemically active substances. Therefore, they must be carefully packaged or refrigerated to protect the kernels from high humidity, insects, rodents, molds, foreign flavors, light and air. Corrugated, grease-proof cartons are widely used for packaging pecans for bulk handling and retail distribution. Glass jars and flexible bags of cellophane, polyethylene, saran and aluminum are employed for consumer packages. Toasted pecans and pecan pieces do not keep as well as raw pecans, which can be stored for prolonged periods in vacuumized tin cans or glass jars.

There is a large demand for pecans in bakery products such as fruit cakes, pies, cookies, cake fillings and nut bread. Pecan pieces add flavor, color and consistency to many baked goods. Although pecan butter is a desirable flavor ingredient for milkshakes and numerous other food products, it is not widely acceptable as a sandwich spread because of its strong, rather bitter, characteristic taste. Pecans are popular in confectionery products, including pralines, pecan brittle, chocolate-covered pecan halves, pecan candies and fudge as well as in pecan ice cream.

Pecan shells, a by-product of the shelling operation, are useful in many ways: as "gravel" for driveways and walks, as fuel for steam boilers and as a mulch for ornamental plants. Reduced to flour, they are employed to clean parts of airplane engines of unwanted grease, as an ingredient in rug cleaners and to provide filler for insecticides, fertilizers, veneer wood and polyesters.

In the timber market, pecan is an excellent hardwood: pecan veneer and lumber are in demand for decorative paneling, fine furniture and attractive flooring.

The versatile pecan is growing in popularity as an ornamental tree for planting near homes, where it can provide beauty and shade as well as edible nuts. Some compact cultivars, such as Cheyenne, are appropriate for planting if the space is limited. Other varieties, more upright or spreading, can be selected according to landscape requirements.

HORS D'OEUVRES AND CANAPES

Pecan Cheese Crackers (XXIX)

1 pound (450 g) sharp cheddar cheese, grated	Several dashes cayenne pepper
2 sticks (1/2 pound/225 g) butter or margarine	3 cups (750 ml) sifted flour
	1 cup (250 ml) chopped pecans

Combine cheese and butter, cream thoroughly. Add cayenne pepper to taste. Add flour and mix thoroughly (the mixture will be very stiff). Shape into rolls and refrigerate overnight. Slice 1/4-inch (6 mm) thick and bake in 350° F (175° C) oven for 12 to 15 minutes. Do not brown. Can be frozen before or after baking and used as desired.

Yield: About 60 crackers

Cheesy Corn Spread (XXVIII)

3/4 pound (338 g) sharp cheddar cheese	1/4 cup (60 ml) finely-chopped pecans
1/2 cup (125 ml) sour cream	One 12-ounce (360 g) can whole kernel corn with sweet peppers, drained
1/2 cup (125 ml) mayonnaise or salad dressing	
1/2 teaspoon (2.5 ml) salt	

Shred cheese; mash to a smooth consistency using a fork or spoon. Blend in sour cream, mayonnaise or salad dressing and salt. Stir in chopped pecans and drained canned corn with sweet peppers. Chill thoroughly. Serve with crisp crackers.

Yield: About 2-1/2 cups (625 ml) spread

Cream Cheese Christmas Tree (XXV)

One 16-ounce (450 g) package cream cheese	2 tablespoons (30 ml) chopped green pepper
6 ounces (180 g) blue cheese	2 tablespoons (30 ml) chopped pimiento
1/2 teaspoon (2.5 ml) garlic salt	Pecan halves

Blend cheeses. Stir in garlic salt, green pepper and pimiento. Place mixture on sheet of aluminum foil and flatten to 3/4 inch (18 mm) thickness; cut in shape of tree. Move tree, on foil, to serving platter and trim away foil even with tree shape. Arrange pecan halves in rows across surface. At serving time, arrange parsley or endive around edge of tree. Serve with assorted crackers.

Yield: 15 to 20 servings

CREAM CHEESE
CHRISTMAS TREE

MAIN DISHES

Pecan Stuffed Peppers (XXVII)

6 green peppers	
1-1/2 cups (375 ml) cooked rice	2 pounds (900 g) ground beef
1-1/2 cups (375 ml) chopped pecans	1-1/2 tablespoons (23 ml) minced onion
1-1/2 teaspoons (7.5 ml) salt	3 tablespoons (45 ml) celery, chopped fine
3/4 cup (175 ml) tomato juice	3/4 cup (175 ml) water or 3/4 cup (175 ml) tomato juice
3 tablespoons (45 ml) shortening	

Boil green peppers, which have been seeded and cored, until just tender enough to prick with a fork. Drain and keep warm. Make stuffing by combining rice, pecans, salt, and tomato juice. Sauté in shortening, beef, onion and celery.

Mix meat mixture with rice mixture, stirring thoroughly, but without handling too much. Stuff peppers and place in greased baking pan. Either 3/4 cup (175 ml) water or 3/4 cup (175 ml) tomato juice may be poured into pan around peppers. Bake for 1/2 hour and serve with sauce.

Yield: 6 peppers

Pecan Chicken Roll (XXX)

1/2 cup (125 ml) finely chopped fresh mushrooms	5 ounces (150 g) sharp natural cheddar cheese, shredded (1-1/4 cups/310 ml)
2 tablespoons (30 ml) butter or margarine	6 or 7 boned, whole chicken breasts
2 tablespoons (30 ml) all-purpose flour	All-purpose flour
1/2 cup (125 ml) light cream	2 slightly beaten eggs
1/4 teaspoon (1 ml) salt	3/4 cup (175 ml) fine dry bread crumbs
Dash cayenne pepper	3/4 cup (175 ml) finely chopped pecans
1/4 cup (60 ml) chopped pecans	

Cook mushrooms in butter about 5 minutes. Blend in flour, stir in cream. Add seasonings and 1/4 cup pecans; cook and stir until mixture is very thick. Stir in cheese; cook over very low heat, stirring, until cheese melts. Turn into pie plates. Cover, chill 1 hour. Cut firm cheese mixture into 6 or 7 pieces; shape into short sticks.

Remove skin from chicken breasts. Place each piece, boned side up, between clear plastic wrap, overlapping meat where split. Pound out from the center with a wooden mallet to form cutlets not quite 1/4 inch (6 mm) thick. Peel off wrap. Sprinkle meat with salt. Place cheese stick on each piece. Tucking in sides, roll as for jelly roll. Press to seal well. Dust rolls with flour, dip in egg, then crumbs and chopped pecans. Cover and chill thoroughly, at least 1 hour.

An hour before serving, fry rolls in deep, hot fat 375° F (190° C) for 5 minutes, or until golden brown. Drain on paper towels. Bake in shallow baking dish at 325° F (165° C) for 30 to 45 minutes.

Yield: 6 or 7 servings

LUNCHEON AND SUPPER DISHES

Chicken Pecan Salad Sandwich (XXV)

1 cup (250 ml) cooked chicken, diced	1/4 cup (60 ml) chopped pecans
1/4 cup (60 ml) chopped celery	One 2-ounce jar (60 g) chopped pimiento
1/4 cup (60 ml) fresh or canned, sliced mushrooms	1/4 cup (60 ml) mayonnaise

Combine all ingredients and mix well. Spread four slices of bread or English muffins with butter or margarine or mayonnaise. Place lettuce and tomato slices on bread and top with filling. Serve open-face style, hot or cold.

Yield: 4 servings

Chilled Macaroni Pecan Salad (XXV)

One 16-ounce package (450 g) macaroni	1/2 cup (125 ml) chopped green pepper
1/4 cup (60 ml) vinegar	2/3 cup (175 ml) chopped pecans
1/2 cup (125 ml) salad oil	1/2 cup (125 ml) grated sharp cheddar cheese
1/4 teaspoon (1 ml) paprika	
2 teaspoons (10 ml) salt	
1/4 cup (60 ml) chopped green onion	

Cook macaroni according to package direction. Drain under cool water and chill. Combine vinegar, oil, paprika, and salt. Add macaroni and toss. Chill 1 hour. Add green onion, green pepper, and pecans. Mix in grated cheese. Chill before serving. Bacon, ham, tuna or chicken could be added to salad.

Yield: 6 to 8 servings

Chicken Pecan Quiche (XXV)

One 9-inch (23-cm) pie shell, baked and cooled	1 tablespoon (15 ml) flour
1 cup (250 ml) cooked chicken, finely chopped	1/2 cup (125 ml) chopped pecans
	2 eggs, beaten
1 cup (250 ml) grated Swiss cheese	1 cup (250 ml) milk
1/4 cup (60 ml) chopped onion	1/2 teaspoon (2.5 ml) brown mustard (hot)

Mix chicken, Swiss cheese, onion, flour and 1/4 cup (60 ml) of pecans. Sprinkle into cooled crust. Mix eggs, milk and mustard and pour over chicken mixture. Top with remaining 1/4 cup (60 ml) pecans. Bake at 325° F (165° C) for 50 minutes.

Yield: 6 servings

VEGETABLES

Apple Pecan-Stuffed Squash (XXV)

2 medium acorn squash	1/2 teaspoon (2.5 ml) salt
1/2 cup (125 mil) butter or margarine	2 teaspoons (10 ml) lemon juice
2 cups (500 ml) apples, finely chopped	1 cup (250 ml) pecans, chopped
1 teaspoon (5 ml) cinnamon	Generous dash nutmeg

Cut squash in half crosswise and remove seeds. Bake, cut side down, in shallow pan at 350° F (175° C) for 45 minutes. Remove cooked squash from shells and mix with butter or margarine, apple, cinnamon, salt, lemon juice and pecans, reserving 1/4 cup (60 ml) pecans for topping. Spoon into shells and top with nutmeg and remaining pecans. Bake at 350° F (175° C) for 10 minutes.

Yield: 4 servings

BAKED GOODS

Praline Pecan Loaf (XXIV)

2 tablespoons (30 ml) butter or margarine, melted	1 cup (250 ml) pecan halves, toasted in oven
3/4 cup (175 ml) brown sugar	2 tablespoons (30 ml) honey
1 teaspoon (5 ml) cinnamon	2 tablespoons (30 ml) water

Spread margarine or butter on bottom of 9 × 5 × 3-inch (23 × 12.5 × 7.5-cm) loaf pan. Sprinkle with brown sugar and cinnamon. Spread pecan halves over mixture. Combine honey and water and drizzle over pecans. Set aside.

Streusel

1/2 cup (125 ml) chopped pecans	1/2 cup (125 ml) flour
3 tablespoons (45 ml) melted butter or margarine	1/2 cup (125 ml) brown sugar
	1/2 teaspoon (2.5 ml) cinnamon

Mix into crumbly mixture. Set aside.

Loaf

1 package dry yeast
1/4 cup (60 ml) warm
   water
2-1/4 cups (560 ml)
   sifted flour
2 tablespoons (30 ml)
   granulated sugar
1-1/4 teaspoons (6 ml)
   cinnamon

2 teaspoons (10 ml) bak-
   ing powder
1/2 teaspoon (2.5 ml)
   salt
1/3 cup (75 ml) butter or
   margarine
1/3 cup (75 ml) milk,
   scalded and cooled
1 egg, beaten

Dissolve yeast in warm water. Set aside. Sift flour, sugar, cinnamon, baking powder, salt together into mixing bowl; cut in butter or margarine until mixture resembles fine crumbs. Combine yeast with milk, beaten egg and stir into bowl and beat well. Knead about 5 minutes on floured surface until dough is no longer sticky. Roll out to 15 × 10-inch (37-1/2 × 2.5-cm) rectangle. Sprinkle with streusel mixture, and roll up from short side (like a jel-ly roll). Cut into three equal pieces and place in loaf pan, (cut sides up), press lightly. Cover with oiled plastic wrap and let rise in warm place 1-1/2 to 2 hours or until even with top of pan. Bake in preheated 350° F (175° C) oven on middle rack about 30 minutes. Remove from pan onto rack to cool.

Yield: 8 to 10 servings

Pecan Spice Cake (XXVII)

2 cups (500 ml) sifted
   cake flour
1/2 teaspoon (2.5 ml)
   salt
1 teaspoon (5 ml) bak-
   ing powder
1/2 teaspoon (2.5 ml)
   baking soda
1/8 teaspoon (large
   pinch) ginger
1 teaspoon (5 ml)
   cinnamon
1/2 teaspoon (2.5 ml)
   nutmeg

1/2 teaspoon (2.5 ml)
   allspice
1 cup (250 ml) brown
   sugar
1/2 cup (125 ml)
   shortening
3/4 cup (175 ml)
   buttermilk
2 eggs
1/2 cup (125 ml)
   chopped pecans

Have all ingredients at room temperature. Sift flour, salt, baking powder, soda, and spices together into mixing bowl. Add sugar, short-

ening, and buttermilk. Beat 200 strokes (or 2 minutes in electric mixer at low speed), scrap-ing the bowl frequently. Add eggs and beat 100 strokes (or 1 minute). Add pecans and beat 100 strokes (or 1 minute).

Pour into 2 greased 8-inch (20 cm) cake pans and bake in a moderate oven 350° F (175° C) for 30 minutes. Remove from pans. When cool, ice with Orange Pecan Frosting. (See fol-lowing recipe for frosting.)

Yield: Two 8-inch (20-cm) layers

Orange Pecan Frosting

1/4 cup (60 ml) butter
2 cups (500 ml) confec-
   tioners' sugar
1 egg yolk, beaten
2 tablespoons (30 ml)
   orange juice

1-1/2 teaspoons (7.5 ml)
   orange rind, grated
1/2 cup (125 ml)
   chopped pecans

Cream butter. Gradually add 1 cup of the sug-ar while beating constantly. Add remaining sugar alternately with egg yolk which has been beaten and blended with orange juice and rind. Spread on cooled cake. Sprinkle pe-cans on top of cake.

Yield: Enough for two 8-inch (20-cm) layers

Texas Pecan Pie (XXIV)

Crust

1-1/3 cups (325 ml) all-
   purpose flour
1/2 teaspoon (2.5 ml)
   salt

2/3 cup (150 ml)
   shortening
3 tablespoons (45 ml)
   water

Mix flour and salt together; add shortening and cut into flour with fork or pastry blender. Add water and mix gently with fork in stirring motion. Gather pastry into a ball and place in 9-inch (23-cm) pie tin. With tips of fingers, spread pastry along bottom and sides of pie tin, shaping a high, fluted edge.

Filling

1-1/2 cups (375 ml) dark brown sugar, firmly packed	2 eggs
1/2 cup (125 ml) granulated sugar	1/2 cup (125 ml) evaporated milk
1/4 cup (60 ml) water	1-1/2 cups (375 ml) pecan halves
2 tablespoons (30 ml) all-purpose flour	3/4 teaspoon (4 ml) vanilla
1/2 teaspoon (2.5 ml) salt	

Combine first five ingredients in small bowl and mix well. Beat in eggs, one at a time. Add evaporated milk and mix well. Stir in pecan halves and vanilla. Mix well and turn into unbaked 9-inch (23-cm) pie shell. Cook in preheated 400° F (200° C) oven for 10 minutes. Reduce heat to 350° F (175° C) and cook an additional 35 to 40 minutes, until filling is puffed in center and is well browned. Let pie cool before cutting.

Yield: One 9-inch (23 cm) pie

Lemon Pecan Loaf (XXV)

1/2 cup (125 ml) vegetable shortening	1/2 teaspoon (2.5 ml) grated lemon rind
1 cup (250 ml) honey	1/2 cup (125 ml) chopped pecans
2 eggs, beaten	1/4 cup (60 ml) honey
1/4 cup (60 ml) milk	Juice of one lemon
3/4 cup (175 ml) whole wheat flour	
1 teaspoon (5 ml) baking powder	

Mix shortening and honey. Add eggs. Add milk alternately with mixture of flour and baking powder. Stir in lemon rind and pecans. Bake in 9 × 5 × 3-inch (23 × 12.5 × 7.5 cm) greased pan at 350° F (175° C) for 45 minutes to one hour. Cool 10 minutes before poking holes in top and pouring mixture of lemon juice and honey over top of loaf.

Yield: One loaf

DESSERT

Pecan Snowballs with Praline Sauce (XXVII)

1 quart (1 liter) vanilla ice cream	1 cup (250 ml) toasted pecans

Sauce

2 cups (500 ml) light cream or half-and-half	3 tablespoons (45 ml) honey
1/4 cup (60 ml) butter	1-1/2 cups (675 ml) light brown sugar

Scoop 6 large balls of ice cream. Roll balls in toasted pecans and place in freezer to harden.

To make sauce, combine ingredients in heavy saucepan; cook over very low heat, stirring constantly, until mixture is smooth and has thickened slightly, about 5 to 10 minutes. Cool, stirring frequently. Serve with Pecan Snowballs.

Yield: 6 servings

CANDY

Pecan Toffee (XXIX)

1 cup (250 ml) butter (do not use substitute)	3 squares semi-sweet chocolate
1 cup (250 ml) sugar	1 cup (250 ml) coarsely broken pecans
1/4 cup (60 ml) water	
1/2 teaspoon (2.5 ml) salt	

Combine butter, sugar, water and salt in heavy saucepan. Cook, stirring constantly, to hard crack stage 300° F (150° C), watching carefully. Immediately pour into ungreased 13 × 9-inch (33 × 23-cm) pan. Cool until hard.

Melt chocolate over hot, not boiling, water. Spread on toffee, sprinkle with nuts and press them down into chocolate. Let chocolate set 2 or 3 hours. Break into bite-sized pieces.

Yield: 1 pound (450 g) toffee

Pralines (XXVIII)

Colonial Pralines

3 cups (750 ml) brown sugar, firmly packed
1 cup (250 ml) granulated sugar
3/4 cup (175 ml) water
2 cups (500 ml) pecans

Combine sugars and water in saucepan. Cook mixture until it reaches 238° F (115° C) or forms a soft ball in cold water. Remove from heat, add pecans. Return to heat and bring again to a boil. Remove from heat and stir until syrup becomes slightly cloudy. (Mixture will be thin.) Pour large spoonfuls of mixture on waxed paper to form pralines.

Yield: 25 pralines

Creole Pralines (XXVIII)

1 cup (250 ml) light brown sugar
1 cup (250 ml) granulated sugar
5 tablespoons (75 ml) water
1 tablespoon (15 ml) butter
1/2 pound (225 g) chopped pecans

Combine sugar, water and butter. When mixture begins to boil rapidly, add pecans. Stir constantly until mixture forms large bubbles. When mixture forms hard ball when dropped into cold water, drop by teaspoonfuls onto well-buttered platter.

Yield: 25 small pralines

Pistacia vera

CHAPTER TEN

Pistachio Nuts

Family: Anacardiaceae

LATIN	*Pistacia vera* L.	DUTCH	Pistache
SPANISH	Pistacho	ITALIAN	Pistacchio
FRENCH	Pistache	PORTUGUESE	Pistácia
GERMAN	Pistazie	RUSSIAN	Fistáshka
SWEDISH	Pistasch	JAPANESE	Pisutasho
ARABIC	Fustuq	CHINESE	Hu Chen Tzu

In 1965 archaeological excavations were carried out in Beidha, a very early Neolithic settlement in the Hashemite Kingdom of Jordan, north of Petra, which flourished about nine thousand years ago. One of the ancient dwellings excavated had evidently been destroyed by a very fierce fire which baked and solidified masses of clay, mortar and plaster from the roof and mud-brick walls, thus supplying a magnificent series of well-preserved plant impressions. On the floor, in perfect condition, was found a heap of carbonized pistachio nuts, which may have originally weighed some forty pounds. The nuts had apparently been in a large basket. The radiocarbon date of these carbonized pistachio nuts at Beidha, calculated by the Copenhagen Radiocarbon Laboratory, is 6760 B.C.—unquestionably one of the earliest, authentic historical records of any edible nut.

Another archaeological investigation in southeastern Turkey at Cayönii Tapesi has revealed pistachio and almond kernels which date from about 7000 B.C., according to preliminary analyses of substantial botanical remains.

In the book of Genesis the sons of Jacob carried "nuts" with them to Egypt when they went to beg for food supplies from their brother Joseph, whom they had previously sold into captivity. It is believed that these nuts were pistachios, *Pistacia vera*.

The Queen of Sheba was especially fond of pistachio nuts and is said to have monopolized the limited pistachio output of Assyria for herself and her court favorites. This demand for pistachios by people with sophisticated taste is still prevalent in some countries of the Middle East and the Orient where the nut is consumed for the most part by the well-to-do classes. In Syria, it forms an important ingredient of wedding feasts. Following a social call in Syria, the departing guest is frequently given a small bag of pistachio nuts as a gesture of good will.

Although the pistachio tree has been known throughout recorded history, its place of origin is uncertain. It is probably native to

197

ANCIENT PISTACHIO NUTS

Found in 1965, during archeological excavations in Beidha (Jordan). The radiocarbon date
of these pistachios is 6760 B.C., unquestionably one of the earliest authentic records of any
edible nut.

western Asia and Asia Minor, but is found
growing wild eastward as far as Pakistan and
India. According to Pliny, the pistachio was
introduced to Italy from Syria during the
reign of Tiberius, early in the first century
A.D. Subsequently its cultivation spread to
other Mediterranean countries.

The nuts from wild pistachio trees in
rocky, hilly regions of northern Iran and Afghanistan are generally much smaller than
those of the cultivated varieties and possess
an unusual terebinthine or turpentine-like flavor which appeals to the nomadic tribes who
inhabit that remote, inhospitable area. For
many centuries these nomads have quarreled
and fought among themselves over the right
to collect the tiny pistachio kernels which
have traditionally formed an important part
of their migratory diet during the winter
months when food is scarce. Historically, the
wild pistachio has been to the Asian nomad
what the pine nut once was to the Indian in
the American Southwest.

The pistachio belongs to the family Anacardiaceae, of which the cashew, mango, sumac and poison oak are also members. There
are about a dozen species of *Pistacia*, most of
which exude turpentine or mastic and a few of
which produce small nuts. Only *P. vera*, however, yields the acceptable, larger edible nuts
of commerce. The nuts of *P. vera* were known
in Persia as *pisteh*, from which the name pistachio is derived. *P. lentiscus*, the "mastic tree,"
one of the other *Pistacia* species, has been cultivated since ancient times in Greece and the
Greek island of Chios as a source of mastic,
one of the oldest known high-grade resins.
Mastic has long been popular in the Orient as
a soft and ductile chewing gum, and in Turkey as an ingredient of a popular liqueur. It is
mainly utilized today in the manufacture of
transparent varnishes. Another *Pistacia, P.
terebinthus*, is the terebinth tree of the Bible,
whose spreading branches used to provide
shelter for nomadic wanderers of the patriar-
chal age as well as venerable shade for burial

198

Piſtacia. Welſch Pimpernüßlin.

PISTACHIOS, 1679

selected cultivars of the more important pistachio nut of commerce, *P. vera*.

Pistacia vera L. is a deciduous tree which grows slowly to a height and spread of twenty-five to thirty feet. It can survive under dry, adverse conditions in poor, stony terrain where for most of the year there may be no rainfall. It can grow quite well on steep, rocky slopes suitable only for goats; it can endure drought but not "wet feet," so well-drained soil is important. It thrives in areas which have winters cool enough to break bud dormancy and hot, long summers—the latter being essential for proper ripening of the nuts. The tree is resistant to cold and wind but cannot tolerate excessive dampness and high humidity. It flourishes in some regions of Iran where temperatures may vary from over 110 degrees Fahrenheit in the summer to 15 degrees Fahrenheit during the winter months. In the future, the pistachio nut tree could play an important role in the development of some arid regions throughout the third world

Pistacia vera

grounds. *Pistachio terebinthus* was later called the "turpentine tree" of Cyprus: numerous slight incisions in its trunk caused it to ooze a superior thick turpentine which habitually sold for a higher price than common turpentine from the Scotch Pine. An excellent, edible oil is produced in the Middle East from the very small, crushed nuts of *P. terebinthus* and *P. atlantica*. This latter *Pistacia*, also known as the "Mt. Atlas mastic tree," is the source of a timber with a brown heartwood resembling walnut. Seedlings of these latter two species serve as rootstocks for budding and grafting

THE NUTS ARE BORNE ON
THE FEMALE PISTACHIO
TREES IN CLUSTERS
SOMEWHAT LIKE GRAPES

where low rainfall precludes the successful growing of almost any other commercial crop.

Sometimes known as the "pistache," the pistachio differs from other popular dessert nuts in the characteristic green of its kernel. This coloration, which varies from yellowish through various shades of green, is not limited to the surface but extends throughout the kernel. In general, the deeper the shade of green, the more the nuts are esteemed. The fruits grow in clusters resembling grapes. Although popularly known as a nut, the fruit of the pistachio is classified botanically as a drupe, the edible portion of which is the seed. This oblong kernel about one inch in length and one-half inch in diameter, is protected somewhat from dust, dirt and other impurities by a thin, ivory-colored, bony shell. When conditions are favorable, the shells split longitudinally along their sutures prior to harvest and have the apearance of a laughing face. In Iran this is called "pistehkhandan," the "laughing pistachio." It is a desirable characteristic since the nuts are usually marketed in-shell, and when the shell is split, the kernel can be more readily extracted with the

fingers. If unfavorable weather and other adverse conditions prevail during nut growth and development, the shells do not split open. A sorrowful, time-honored expression of the Turkish growers covers this unfortunate turn of events: "Too bad, our pistachios are not laughing." The unsplit nuts are not popular with the consumer and sell for a lower price.

The world's major pistachio producing areas are Iran, Turkey and the San Joaquin Valley of California. Other countries which produce and export pistachio nuts include: Syria, Afghanistan, Italy, India, Greece, Pakistan and Tunisia.

Pistachios have been produced for many centuries in the Middle East and central Asia, the production coming for the most part from wild or semi-wild trees. Since 1900, when it became evident that promising export markets existed in the United States and in Europe, more attention has been given to the selection of superior varieties and development of formal, cultivated pistachio orchards, especially in Iran and Turkey. In Afghanistan, however, small nuts of a desirable green color

200

MATURE PISTACHIO FRUIT

From left to right: nut with hull; hull removed, showing split shell; two halves of shell; kernel.

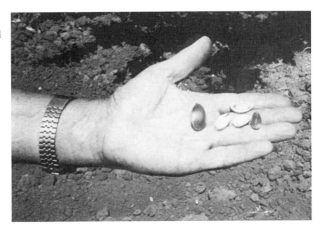

are still harvested from wild pistachio trees rather than from orchard plantings. Unfortunately, many wild pistachio populations in central Asia, the Middle East and the Mediterranean basin have been wiped out by forest clearance, destructive grazing by goats and charcoal production (pistachio wood yields a high-quality charcoal).

The main producing area in Iran is Kerman, located in the arid southeastern part of the country. Large scale pistachio plantings have also been established in Sirjan, Rafsanjan, Damghan and Ghazirn. Several excellent Iranian pistachio cultivars have been developed in recent years including Momtaz, Owhadi, Agah and Kalehghouchi. The latter is the largest and highest priced variety, but the lowest in yield. Iran was the top supplier of

PISTACHIOS ARE HARVESTED IN TURKEY BY HAND LABOR

pistachios to the United States market in 1979 with twenty million pounds. Following the seizure of the American hostages and the subsequent cutoff of all imports from Iran, the total of Iranian pistachios imported in 1980 fell to less than one million pounds. The recent political turmoil in Iran has disrupted the pistachio trade and forced up prices.

Turkey, traditionally the other large supplier of foreign pistachios to the United States, has selected and developed some promising cultivars in recent years including Uzun and Kirmizi. Most of the Turkish production comes from the dry, barren foothills of western and southeastern Turkey, principally from the regions of Gaziantep and Urfa.

Foreign methods of harvesting pistachios are primitive: women do most of the work. In Iran the ripened nuts with their pulpy, reddish hulls are picked by hand or knocked off the trees with poles onto burlap spread on the ground. Some are hulled as soon as possible following the harvest, but the major portion is dried in the hull for hulling at a convenient time later. At that time, the nuts are soaked in

CRACKING PISTACHIO SHELLS BY HAND IN IRAN   water, enabling easy hull removal when

DRYING PISTACHIOS IN THE SUN IN IRAN

squeezed between the fingers. Some mechanical hulling is employed but most nuts are hulled by hand. The nuts are then usually spread out in the sun to dry on stone, concrete or earth floors. These crude harvesting and hulling methods result in nuts with stained and blemished shells which, unless camouflaged, appear unappetizing. United States importers employ a non-toxic, red vegetable dye, approved by the Food and Drug Administration, to give the nuts visual appeal. The red color serves another purpose as well, since it appeals to consumers who are used to it and even demand it. Some imported pistachios are coated with a thin layer of cornstarch and salt. In California, however, pistachios are mechanically hulled and dried within twenty-four hours of harvesting, and, as a rule, most are not colored but instead left in their unblemished, natural state.

Considerable controversy exists in the United States concerning the relative merits of home-grown, as opposed to imported, pistachios. The American importers of Iranian and Turkish pistachios describe the California counterparts as beautiful but tasteless. The California producers, on the other hand, claim their pistachios taste about the same as the imported nuts but are larger, fresher and easier to open.

The pistachio tree was first introduced into the United States in 1854 by the Commissioner of Patents, Charles Mason, who distributed seed for experimental plantings in California, Texas and some southern states. In 1875 a few small pistachio trees, imported from France, were planted in Sonoma, California.

During the 1880's imported pistachios were popular among American immigrants from the Middle East and were found in ethnic food shops, especially in New York City. In the 1920's and 1930's the colorful red- and white-coated nuts became available to the general public in the United States—a dozen for a nickel—through vending machines, strategically placed in subway stations, bars, diners, restaurants and on other public premises. These small-bulk nut-vending machines ac-counted for most pistachio nut sales at that time.

In the early 1900's, the United States Department of Agriculture assembled a collection of *Pistacia* species and pistachio nut varieties at the Plant Introduction Station in Chico, California. In 1929 a U.S.D.A. plant explorer, W. E. Whitehouse, visited Iran and Turkestan to study pistachio culture. He brought back seed selected from some ninety different sources, including a cultivar subsequently named Kerman, from the district of that name in Iran. This proved to be a most important plant introduction since virtually all pistachios produced now in California are of the Kerman variety. Whitehouse, in cooperation with Lloyd Joley, a government botanist at Chico, following numerous painstaking trials, selected and developed this Kerman cultivar which possesses the desirable characteristics of large nut size and a high percentage of split shells.

California is the only state which produces pistachios on a commercial scale: most production comes from the San Joaquin and Sacramento Valleys, although some small acreage has been planted in the California desert near Barstow and Mojave, as well as in other parts of the state. Trial plantings have also been made in Arizona and New Mexico.

At the present time approximately 39,000 acres have been planted with pistachios in California: about 28,000 acres have already entered into production and the balance will start to produce within the next few years. The production of pistachio nuts in California has increased notably during recent years, as illustrated by the following data:

Year	Total production, pounds	Average price to growers per pound
1977	4,500,000	$1.04
1978	2,500,000	$1.24
1979	17,200,000	$1.60
1980	26,200,000	$2.05
1981	14,500,000	$1.36
1982	43,200,000	$1.40

By 1985, the California Pistachio Association estimates that California will produce 45,000,000 pounds of pistachios; and by 1990, some 80,000,000 pounds.

The 1980 Californian production of 26,900,000 pounds consisted of 18,600,000 pounds of marketable in-shell pistachios (of which nearly one-third was exported to Europe, the Middle East, Canada and Mexico); and 8,300,000 pounds of unsplit and second quality nuts for shelling. The California Pistachio Association, founded in 1972 and located in Fresno, represents most of the California pistachio acreage. During 1981 a Pistachio Commission, approved by the Californian growers, was established in order to promote sales and assist in the marketing of pistachio nuts.

A pistachio boom in California in 1928 failed in the 1930's because American growers dependent on hand labor (comparatively expensive despite the depression), could not compete with cheap foreign labor in growing, harvesting and processing the nuts. Times have changed: although foreign pistachio picking and processing in the Middle East and elsewhere abroad still depends almost entirely on hand labor, the Californian industry has become thoroughly mechanized.

The pistachio is usually propagated in California by budding or grafting selected scions of *P. vera* onto seedling rootstocks of *P. atlantica*, *P. terebinthus* and *P. integerrima*. These rootstock species are used because of their vigor and resistance to nematodes and soil borne fungi.

The pistachio is dioecious: male and female flowers are borne on separate trees. Wind carries the pollen from the male to the female flowers, both of which are small and have no petals. In California, the Kerman is the most common female cultivar, while Peters is a prolific pollen producer. One male Peters tree is usually adequate to pollinate eight or ten female Kerman trees. The male trees are placed in the orchard to take advantage of prevailing winds.

The orchard should be established in deep, friable, well-drained soils to obtain maximum growth and productivity. The young pistachio trees are generally set out at a spacing of eleven to fifteen feet between trees in the row and twenty-two to thirty feet between rows, depending upon soil conditions. Years later, when the trees start to crowd each other, every other tree in the row may be removed to leave the remaining trees on a square.

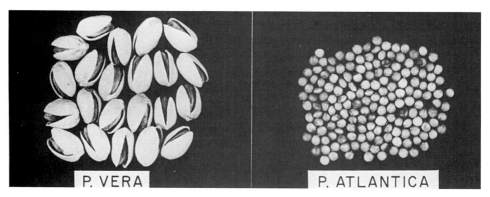

NUT COMPARISON OF TWO PISTACHIO SPECIES

Relative size of *P. vera* and *P. atlantica* nuts. *P. vera* yields the edible nut of commerce. *P. atlantica* is used in California as rootstock for budding or grafting scions of Kerman, a cultivar of *P. vera*.

FEMALE AND MALE PISTACHIO
INFLORESCENCES

Left, female flowers of "Kerman," the most
important California cultivar; right,
inflorescences of the "Peters" cultivar, a
predominant male pollinator.

Pruning is important during the early years of an orchard. High-headed trees permit easy maintenance with mechanical orchard equipment; strong crotches should be developed to withstand the stress later on of power-driven shakers during the harvest.

The most serious plant disease impairing the growth of pistachio trees in California is Verticillium wilt, a soil-borne fungus which causes branches to die back; it can quickly kill trees of varying age. Cotton is a host plant for this fungus, so land previously planted to cotton is not considered suitable for a new pistachio orchard and should be avoided unless the soil is fumigated prior to planting. In established orchards a grass cover crop tends to minimize Verticillium damage. *P. integerrima* has been found recently to be resistant to this disease. Trees killed by Verticillium are being replaced with those having *P. integerrima* roots, which are also used for most new plantings.

Pistachio trees begin production in about six or seven years, but full bearing is not attained until the fifteenth to twentieth year when fifty pounds of dry, hulled nuts may be produced per tree. The trees, however, tend toward biennial bearing, producing a heavy crop one year followed by little or none the next. Under favorable conditions, pistachio trees live and produce for centuries: in the Kerman region of Iran a 700-year-old tree is still standing.

A VERY OLD PISTACHIO TREE

Near Kerman, Iran. Approximately 700 years old.

Although the pistachio tree will grow and produce some nuts under adverse conditions, it gives highest yields, of course, when the agricultural environment is optimum. Its response to proper irrigation and fertilizer application in California has been like that of other fruit and nut trees.

The nuts hang well under normal conditions and they may be left on the tree until most are ripe. A single shaking will then bring down the bulk of the matured nuts. Some pistachios, particularly those on trees just starting to bear, are harvested in California by shaking the nuts from the trees onto canvas, but most are harvested mechanically by conventional prune- or soft fruit-type harvesting equipment made up of two separate, self-propelled units. The shaker, with a catching frame, and another catching frame with a conveyor belt are positioned simultaneously on either side of the tree. The shaker mechanism causes the nuts to fall into the canvas

apron of the catching frame where they roll onto a conveyor belt which carries them past a primary cleaner and deleafer and then dumps them into movable bins to be hauled to the processing plant. Two skilled machine operators can harvest about one acre of pistachio trees per hour.

A problem of especial concern to the grower of the Kerman cultivar is the production of "blanks." Within a few days after flowering and pollination the young nuts commence rapid growth, forming a full-sized but empty shell in a few weeks. The ovules or kernels then expand gradually to fill the empty shells. However, in some years as many as twenty-five per cent of the Kerman kernels fail to develop, so the shells remain empty and are known as blanks. Fortunately, blanks are harder to shake loose and about three-quarters of them remain on the tree during the boom-shaking phase of the mechanical harvest.

BOOM SHAKING OF PISTACHIOS ONTO CANVAS IN CALIFORNIA

FRUIT HARVESTERS SHAKE NUTS FROM TREES

At the rate of about two trees per minute, the machines harvest the nuts, remove twigs and leaves and load the nuts into boxes. Within a few hours the nuts must be hulled and cleaned to produce natural undyed California pistachios.

Following harvest, the nuts must be hulled and dried within twenty-four hours to maintain their high quality and unblemished appearance. Basically, three types of machines have proved satisfactory for dehulling pistachios. Abrasive vegetable peeling machines produce an attractive product but are limited to a batch of nuts at a time, generally no more than fifty to sixty pounds. These small machines are not adaptable to dehulling the large volumes of pistachios that are being produced currently in California. Modified walnut dehulling machines with rubber-coated discs, designed for continuous operation, work satisfactorily on pistachios. The bulk of the crop, however, is hulled in machines consisting of two parallel rubberized belts rotating in the same direction, one faster than the other. The nuts are fed continuously between the adjustable belts and emerge without hulls at the other end in float/sink

separators where they are washed and separated from stray blanks and immature nuts. The latter will float, while the preferred, mature, filled nuts will sink.

The nuts are dried with forced air at 150 to 160 degrees Fahrenheit. The moisture content which was as high as forty-five per cent in the freshly harvested nuts is reduced to five per cent in about ten hours. "Electric eye" sorters may be employed to remove blemished nuts, which can be dyed red or white and sold as dyed nuts, or shelled to be sold in the form of nut meats. The good quality splits are graded to four sizes, roasted, salted and packaged. About ninety per cent of California pistachios reach the consumer roasted and salted in their shells for consumption in the popular "snack" trade. Shelled pistachios are utilized commercially in confectionery, ice cream, candies, sausages, bakery goods and flavoring for puddings.

207

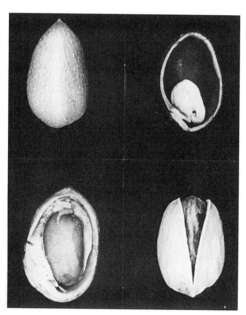

DEVELOPMENT OF KERMAN PISTACHIO IN CALIFORNIA

Top left: external appearance during middle of May.

Top right: hull and shell reach ultimate size in the middle of May and enclose a curved stalk that supports an immature seed at its apex.

Bottom left: developing seed has about filled the locule (cavity) by the middle of August.

Bottom right: hull has been removed and split shell contains the kernel.

Pistachios vary considerably in size as expressed by the number of nuts per ounce. Iranian pistachios range from eighteen to forty nuts per ounce, while the California nuts are generally larger—sometimes as few as fourteen to the ounce. The pistachio kernel is so small and expensive, however, it is generally not included in salted mixes with other larger tree nuts.

Pistachio nuts are rich in oil, with an average oil content of about fifty-five per cent. Because of the high price of the nuts, pistachio oil is not produced commercially.

In marketing tree nuts, the product is generally sold "in-shell" or "shelled." Pistachios and filberts are usually sold in-shell to the retail trade, while almonds and pecans are typically sold shelled to the industrial trade, i.e. salters, confectioners, bakers and ice cream manufacturers. The pistachio is unique in the nut trade due to its semi-split shell which enables the processor to roast and salt the kernel without removing the shell and which at the same time serves as a convenient form of packaging provided by nature.

The single item vending machines of the 1930's have given way to multiple-choice machines which are capable of vending and dispensing almost any kind of food product which can be packaged within the required size dimensions—including snack nuts such as "Vend pack" almonds, peanuts and pistachios. Furthermore, the pistachio mail order business is growing.

Today, about thirty million pounds of in-shell pistachio nuts are consumed annually in the United States. It is expected that with ever increasing California production and additional promotion, the United States market should grow to at least fifty million pounds per year within the next decade. Tenneco West, through television promotion of Sun Giant nuts, has played a leading role in developing the market for California pistachios.

HORS D'OEUVRE

Duck Pâté (XXXII)

One 4-pound (1-3/4-kg) duckling, cut in quarters, fat and skin removed (reserve uncooked liver)

1 clove garlic, peeled and crushed

1 bay leaf

1/2 teaspoon (2.5 ml) dried thyme

1/2 teaspoon (2.5 ml) allspice

1 egg

2 tablespoons (30 ml) flour

1 package unflavored gelatin

1 tablesoon (15 ml) Cognac or sherry

1/2 pound (225 g) hot sausage meat

1 tablespoon (15 ml) grated orange peel

1/4 cup (60 ml) pistachios

In water, simmer duck with garlic, bay leaf, thyme and allspice until meat is tender. Reserve cooking broth.

In a blender, combine egg, flour, gelatin, Cognac or sherry, reserved liver and a little hot duck broth. Chop duck meat; mix with sausage, orange peel and liver mixture. Add pistachios and pack firmly in glass or pottery loaf pan. Bake in a pre-heated, 350° F (175° C) oven for 1 hour. Cool, then refrigerate. When cold, slice and serve with sweet pickles.

Yield: 1 loaf of pâté

MAIN DISHES

Pork Roast with Apple Pistachio Dressing (XXXII)

4 pounds (1-3/4 kg) boneless loin of pork	1 cup (250 ml) dry white wine
2 teaspoons (10 ml) salt	3 tart apples, peeled, cored and diced
1 teaspoon (5 ml) pepper	5 cups (1-1/4 liter) dried bread cubes
1 teaspoon (5 ml) powdered ginger	4 eggs
1 cup (250 ml) finely chopped onion	1 cup (250 ml) milk
	3/4 cup (175 ml) pistachio nuts

Remove pork from refrigerator one hour before roasting. Trim the loin of excess fat and rub surface with salt, pepper and ginger.

Place in a shallow roasting pan which will hold the roast with no more than three to four inches (7.5 to 10 cm) of space between the roast and the sides. Don't use a rack.

Roast for 25 minutes at 450° F (235° C). Add onions and roast five to 10 additional minutes, until onions are lightly browned.

Add wine, diced apple and bread cubes to the onions in the pan and roast for 25 minutes, stirring occasionally.

Beat eggs and milk together and stir into mixture in roasting pan. Stir in nuts. Roast for additional 25 minutes or until pork is done.

Yield: 6 servings

Chicken with Tangerines (XXXII)

2 large onions, sliced	4 tablespoons (60 ml) lemon juice
4 tablespoons (60 ml) butter	1/2 pound (225 g) carrots, peeled and thinly sliced
1 stewing chicken	
1 teaspoon (5 ml) saffron	1/2 cup (125 ml) candied orange or tangerine peel
1 can beef or chicken bouillon	
1/4 cup (60 ml) water	1 tablespoon (15 ml) flour
1 to 2 teaspoons (5 to 10 ml) salt	3 tangerines, peeled
1/4 teaspoon (1 ml) pepper	4 tablespoons (60 ml) slivered pistachios

Sauté onions in butter until golden brown. Add chicken, whole or cut up; sauté until golden brown on all sides. Stir in saffron; add bouillon, water, salt, pepper and lemon juice. Cover and simmer over low heat 1 hour.

Add carrots and candied citrus peel. Continue simmering until peel is tender. Thicken sauce with flour, using a wire whisk to prevent lumps. Separate and peel tangerine segments; add to chicken. Sprinkle with pistachios and serve with rice.

Yield: 6 servings.

LUNCHEON AND SUPPER DISHES

Chicken and Rice with Pistachios (XXXI)

4 cups (1 liter) cooked rice	1/2 cup (125 ml) shelled pistachios, coarsely chopped
2 cups (500 ml) chopped cooked chicken	
1/2 cup (125 ml) mayonnaise	1/2 teaspoon (2.5 ml) crushed dill seed
1 teaspoon (5 ml) lemon juice	1 teaspoon (5 ml) salt
1/4 cup (60 ml) snipped green onion tops	1/2 teaspoon (2.5 ml) pepper

Cook rice and rinse. Combine with remaining ingredients and toss well. Chill before serving.

Yield: 8 servings

Pistachio and Spinach Quiche (XXXII)

One 10-inch (25-cm) unbaked pie shell
6 eggs
1 cup (250 ml) ricotta cheese
2 cups (500 ml) whipping cream
1 cup (250 ml) grated Swiss cheese
2 tablespoons (30 ml) grated Parmesan cheese
1-1/2 cups (375 ml) chopped, cooked spinach, loosely packed
1/2 cup (125 ml) shelled, chopped pistachio nuts
2 teaspoons (10 ml) salt
1-1/2 teaspoons (7.5 ml) chopped fresh dill or 1 teaspoon (5 ml) dried dill
1/2 teaspoon (2.5 ml) white pepper
1/2 teaspoon (2.5 ml) sugar
Grated Swiss and Cheddar cheese, about one cup (250 ml) for topping
Paprika, optional

Preheat oven to 400° F (200° C). To prevent shrinking, prick sides of pie shell with fork. Bake seven minutes and remove from oven. Reduce temperature to 350° F (175° C).

In large mixing bowl combine ingredients, except cheese topping, in order given. Mix well after each addition. Pour into partially baked pie shell and bake 45 to 55 minutes or until firm. Top with grated cheeses and sprinkle with paprika. Return to oven until cheese melts.

Yield: 1 quiche

Ham and Pistachio Mousse (XXXI)

1 envelope plain gelatin
1/2 cup (60 ml) cold water
2 tablespoons (30 ml) cider vinegar
2 cups (500 ml) finely cubed cooked ham
1 cup (250 ml) finely diced celery
2 tablespoons (30 ml) dill pickle, chopped
1/2 cup (125 ml) coarsely chopped, shelled, red pistachios
2 tablespoons (30 ml) sugar
1/2 cup (125 ml) whipped cream, whipped
1 teaspoon (5 ml) dry mustard

Soften gelatin in water and vinegar. Place over boiling water to dissolve. Remove from heat. Stir in ham, celery, pickle, pistachios and sugar. Whip cream with mustard and fold into ham mixture. Turn into a mold and chill until set. Unmold and serve with horseradish sauce.

Horseradish Sauce

Combine 3 tablespoons (45 ml) well drained horseradish, 1/2 teaspoon (2.5 ml) salt and 1/2 cup (125 ml) whipped cream, whipped.

Yield: 6 to 8 servings

DESSERT

Pistachio Ice Cream (XXXII)

1 cup (250 ml) shelled pistachios, preferably unsalted
4 cups (1 liter) milk
1 cup (250 ml) heavy cream
1-1/2 cups (375 ml) sugar
10 egg yolks
1 tablespoon (15 ml) almond extract
5 drops pure vegetable green food coloring

Unless they are blanched, drop the pistachios into boiling water and simmer about two minutes or until outer coating can be removed easily with the fingers. Drain and remove the outer coating. Put the pistachios in a small skillet and cook over low heat, shaking the skillet continuously, until the nuts are lightly toasted. Set aside.

Combine the milk and cream in a saucepan and bring just to the boil.

Place the sugar and egg yolks in a mixing bowl and beat with a whisk to the ribbon state—that is, until thick and pale yellow in color and, when the beater is lifted, the mixture falls back on itself in a ribbon.

Pour a cup or so of the combined hot milk and cream into the egg mixture, beating rapidly with the whisk. Scrape out the entire contents of the bowl into the saucepan containing the hot milk mixture.

Using a wooden spoon, cook the sauce over low heat, stirring this way and all over the bottom of the saucepan, taking care that the sauce does not stick. Also, be cautious that the sauce does not curdle. Cook only until the mixture coats the bottom of the spoon like very thick cream. Do not at any point boil the sauce, or it will curdle. Add the almond extract and food coloring.

Immediately strain the sauce into a mixing bowl. Let stand until cool. Chill thoroughly in the refrigerator or freezer without freezing.

Pour the custard into the canister of a hand-cranked or electric ice-cream machine and freeze according to the manufacturer's instructions. When the ice cream is partly frozen, add the pistachios and continue freezing.

Yield: About one and one-half to two quarts (1-1/2 to 2 liters)

CONFECTIONS

Pistachio Nougat (XXXI)

Marshmallow Cream Stock

3/4 cup (175 ml) sugar	1/2 cup (125 ml) water
3/4 cup (175 ml) light corn syrup	2 egg whites
	1/8 teaspoon (dash) salt

Stir together sugar, corn syrup and water in a pan. Cook to 238° F (115° C). In a mixing bowl, beat egg whites with salt. Whip to short stiff peaks. In a thin, steady stream, gradually pour hot syrup into beaten egg whites until whites are stiff and glossy.

Candy Syrup

2 cups (500 ml) sugar	2 tablespoons (30 ml) vanilla
2 cups (500 ml) light corn syrup	1/4 teaspoon (1 ml) almond extract
2 cups (500 ml) water	1 cup (250 ml) pistachio meats, diced small
1/2 cup (125 ml) butter	
1/2 teaspoon (2.5 ml) salt	

In a heavy 3-quart (3-liter) pan, stir together sugar, light corn syrup and water. Cook to 272° F (135° C). Remove from heat and pour in marshmallow cream stock. Let stand 5 minutes without stirring. Add butter, salt, vanilla and almond extract. Beat until well blended. Stir in nuts. Pour into well buttered 8- or 9-inch (20.5-or 23-cm) square pan. Set on rack

to cool about 3 hours. Loosen sides and remove from pan. Cut into squares and wrap immediately in wax paper.

Yield: about 70 nougats

Halva (from Iran) (XXXII)

1/3 cup (75 ml) butter	3 tablespoons (45 ml) rosewater
1/4 cup (60 ml) corn oil	1 tablespoon (15 ml) slivered almonds
1 cup (250 ml) flour	
1/3 cup (75 ml) sugar	
1/4 teaspoon (1 ml) saffron	1 tablespoon (15 ml) pistachio nuts

Mix butter and oil in a saucepan on medium heat until butter melts. Add the flour and stir until the mixture is light brown. Remove from heat.

Combine sugar, saffron and rosewater, and bring to a boil for two minutes.

Combine the sugar mixture and the butter mixture and mix well. Heat on low heat about 3 minutes. Remove from heat and serve cold, topped with almonds and pistachios.

Yield: 6 servings

BAKED GOODS

Glazed Pistachio Rum Cake (XXXII)

1 cup (250 ml) margarine or butter	1/2 teaspoon (2.5 ml) *each* baking soda, baking powder, cinnamon and ground cloves
1 cup (250 ml) firmly-packed brown sugar	
1 cup (250 ml) granulated sugar	1/4 teaspoon (1 ml) salt
2 teaspoons (10 ml) grated lemon rind	3/4 cup (175 ml) buttermilk
4 eggs	1/2 cup (125 ml) rum
3 cups (750 ml) regular all-purpose flour	1/2 cup (125 ml) shelled pistachios, chopped

Glaze

2 tablespoons (30 ml) margarine or butter	1/2 cup (125 ml) shelled pistachios, chopped
1/4 cup (60 ml) rum	
2 cups (500 ml) sifted powdered sugar	

GLAZED PISTACHIO RUM CAKE

Measure the 1 cup (250 ml) margarine, the brown sugar, granulated sugar and lemon rind into large mixing bowl. Beat until smooth and creamy. Add eggs, one at a time, beating well after each addition. In small mixing bowl, stir together flour, baking soda, baking powder, salt, cinnamon and cloves. Add flour mixture and buttermilk, alternately, to the butter mixture. Stir in rum and the chopped pistachios. Pour batter into well greased 10-inch (25 cm) tube or bundt pan. Bake in 325° F (165° C) oven for 50 minutes or until wooden pick inserted near center comes out clean. Cool on wire rack 10 minutes. Turn out of pan.

To prepare glaze, melt the 2 tablespoons (30 ml) margarine in small saucepan. Remove from heat. Stir in rum and powdered sugar. Mix well. Stir in pistachios. Drizzle over top of warm cake.

Yield: 12 servings

Pistachio Refrigerator Cookies (XXXII)

2 cups (500 ml) all-purpose flour	1 teaspoon (5 ml) vanilla
1-1/2 teaspoons (7.5 ml) baking powder	1/2 teaspoon (2.5 ml) almond extract
1/2 teaspoon (2.5 ml) salt	1/8 teaspoon (pinch) green food color
2/3 cup (150 ml) butter	1/2 cup (125 ml) pistachio meats, small diced
1 cup (250 ml) sugar	
1 egg	

212

Combine flour, baking powder and salt in a mixing bowl. Sift together and set aside. In another large bowl cream butter, sugar, egg, vanilla and almond extract until mixture is light and fluffy. Add the green color and pistachio meats to about one cup (250 ml) of the dough mixture. Form the green dough into a roll and chill. Form the white dough into a rectangle 10 × 4 inches (25 × 10 cm) and chill. When dough firms, wrap white dough around green dough. Slice cookies 1/8-inch (3 mm) thick. Place on ungreased cookie sheet about 3 inches (7.5 cm) apart. Bake at 375° F (190° C) for 8 to 10 minutes. Dough may be rolled in chocolate or multi-colored nonpareils before slicing and baking.

Yield: about 50 cookies

Salted Pistachio Cookies (XXXI)

1/4 cup (60 ml) shortening	1-1/2 cups (375 ml) all-purpose flour
1/4 cup (60 ml) butter or margarine	1/4 teaspoon (1 ml) soda
3/4 cup (175 ml) brown sugar	1/2 teaspoon (2.5 ml) salt
1 egg	1 cup shelled pistachios, red or natural
1 teaspoon (5 ml) vanilla	

Preheat oven to 375° F (190° C). Mix shortening, butter, brown sugar, egg and vanilla. Measure flour and mix with soda and salt; stir into butter mixture. Coarsely chop pistachio meats and mix into dough. Drop by spoonfuls 2 inches (5 cm) apart onto lightly greased baking sheet. Bake 10 to 12 minutes, or until lightly browned.

Yield: 3 dozen cookies

Pistachio Yogurt Pie (XXXII)

1 prepared baked pie shell	1 cup lemon flavored yogurt
1 pkg pistachio/almond flavored pudding	1 cup (250 ml) milk
1 pkg dry whip topping mix	1/2 cup (125 ml) pistachio meats, small diced
1 cup plain yogurt	Whipped cream

Prepare pie shell as desired. Set aside. In a large mixing bowl combine pistachio/almond pudding mix and whip topping mix. Add cold milk and beat until mixture is thick and of pudding texture. Stir in plain yogurt and lemon yogurt and pistachio meats. Pour into prepared pie shell. Top with sweetened whipped cream. Chill before serving.

Yield: 1 pie

1 *Flos Solis maior.*
The greater Sun-floure.

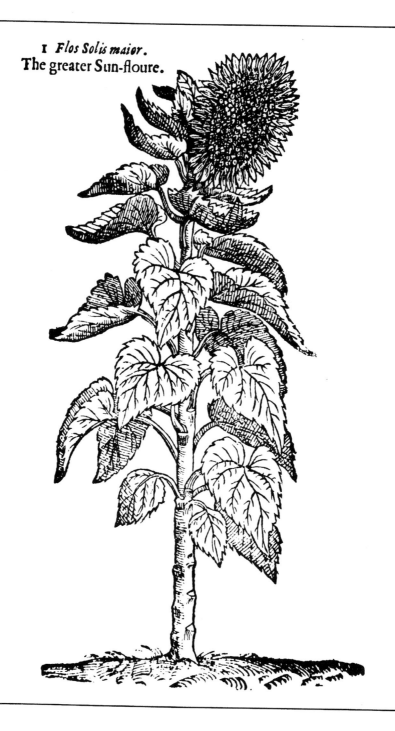

CHAPTER ELEVEN

Sunflower Seeds
Family: Compositae

LATIN	*Helianthus annuus* L.	DUTCH	Zonnebloem-Zaad
SPANISH	Semillas de Girasol	ITALIAN	Semi de Girasole
FRENCH	Graines de Tournesol	PORTUGUESE	Sementes de Girassol
GERMAN	Sonnenblumesamen	RUSSIAN	Sémechki
SWEDISH	Solrosfrö	JAPANESE	Himawari No Tane
ARABIC	Habb' Abād Ash-Shams	CHINESE	Kuei Huo Tzu

"Ah sunflower! weary of time,
Who countest the steps of the sun,
Seeking after that sweet golden clime,
Where the traveller's journey is done;"

(From *Songs of Experience*,
by William Blake, 1794)

AMONG THE WILDFLOWERS of North America, the common sunflower, *Helianthus annuus*, ranks as one of the most familiar. Its brilliant yellow color, large flower head and tall stature make it stand out wherever it grows. The sunflower's botanical name, given to it by the great Swedish naturalist Carolus Linnaeus in the eighteenth century, is truly descriptive of the plant: *Helianthus*, the genus name, comes

Facing page: This same botanical print first appeared in Europe in 1568 in the herbal of the Belgian, Robert Dodoens, who erroneously called the plant *Chrysanthemum peruvianum*. The sunflower originated in North America; there is no evidence that it was cultivated in Peru until recent times. The illustration was reproduced in John Gerarde's *Herball* of 1636.

from the Greek words *helios*, meaning "sun," and *anthos*, meaning "flower;" the species name, *annuus*, is derived from the Latin word for "annual."

The common sunflower is an annual plant which grows to a height of three to twelve feet, and has either a single unbranched or a branched stem, fibrous in structure and covered with rough hair. The plant bears heart-shaped, serrated leaves, often covered with soft hairs. Anchoring the plant in the soil is a root system made up of a deeply penetrating taproot—up to nine feet long—and a network of shallow lateral roots extending in all directions. In the unbranched forms, a massive, single flower head is produced which may measure up to thirty inches in diameter, although heads one foot across are more common. If the plant is branched, a smaller flower head will develop at the end of each branch.

The sunflower head is usually composed of a hundred or more small flowers, closely packed together somewhat like the honeycomb of the bee. The conspicuous outer fringe of yellow ray flowers apparently functions only to attract insects, since these ray flowers themselves are infertile. The tiny, dark-red or

215

SUNFLOWER HEIGHT

Although sunflowers have been known to reach 18 feet in height, the modern trend is to produce shorter plants spaced closer together in the field.

LARGE SUNFLOWER HEADS

Sunflower heads one foot across are common; the record is about two and one-half feet.

FLOWERING OF THE SUNFLOWER

The sunflower head consists of several hundred small disc flowers which flower over a 5 to 7 day period of time, starting at the outside and finishing at the center. The head in this photo has been in bloom for about 4 days; the small, sunken area in the center has not yet started to flower.

yellow disk flowers, or disk florets, which cover the center of the head, are fertile and produce the sunflower fruits or matured ovaries technically known as achenes. The achene consists of one seed, or kernel, whose thin, outer hull does not burst when ripe.

Facing east at sunrise, the sunflower's head follows the sun across the sky to face west at sunset. This heliotropic movement, called nutation, results from a bending of the stem toward the sunlight; there is asymmetric growth on the shaded side, causing the inflorescence, or flowers, to be in a position facing toward the sun. Growth is equalized during the night, the stem slowly straightens out and by dawn is facing east again. On a cloudy, overcast day, the sunflower remains facing eastward, awaiting the next clear sunrise. The leaves are also heliotropic and may trigger the light-seeking response; if they are removed, the sunflower's head no longer follows the sun. Once the ray flowers are fully developed, the heliotropic movement ceases and most heads remain facing eastward. The sunflower usually reaches maturity three to four months after the emergence of the seedling. As the seeds develop, the heads begin to droop with the added weight and at maturity face nearly downward.

There are some fifty species of the genus *Helianthus,* including annual and perennial types, all of which are native to North America. The annual sunflowers are most common in the western United States, while the perennials are more abundant in the eastern states. The so-called Jerusalem artichoke, *Helianthus tuberosus,* is a perennial grown both as an ornamental plant and for its fleshy, edible underground tubers whose flavor is said to resemble that of the true or globe artichoke, *Cynara scolymus,* which also belongs to the composite family. The edible portion of the globe artichoke is found aboveground in the modified, fleshy leaves which surround its flowers. Among the sunflower species, only the common sunflower and the Jerusalem artichoke are cultivated food plants, while many others are prized as ornamentals.

A number of the species crossbreed in nature to produce natural hybrids, the occurrence of which has caused perplexing difficulties for botanists attempting to classify and describe each individual sunflower species. Compounding the botanist's problem is the fact that extreme variability may occur even within many species. Some other notable species include: *H. argophyllus,* the ornamental silver-leaf sunflower, native to coastal Texas;

217

H. debilis subsp. *debilis*, another ornamental known as the beach sunflower, a prostrate form of the species found along the Atlantic coast of Florida; *H. debilis* subsp. *cucum-*

HELIANTHUS TUBEROSUS.

THE JERUSALEM ARTICHOKE, A PERENNIAL SUNFLOWER

A food plant, domesticated by the American Indian. The flavor of its fleshy tubers is said to resemble that of the artichoke.

erifolius, cucumber-leaf sunflower, a widely propagated annual which looks like a black-eyed susan; *H. petiolaris,* the prairie sunflower, found often as a weed in sandy locations; *H. bolanderi,* the native California sunflower, which is also weed-like; and *H. giganteus,* the giant sunflower, a perennial four to twelve feet tall with several rough, hairy stems. The common sunflower hybridizes freely with the cucumber-leaf, the silver-leaf, the native California and the prairie sunflowers. The Mexican "sunflower," *Tithonia rotundifolia,* a striking garden ornamental from Mexico and Central America with orange ray flowers, is not a true sunflower although it is sometimes confused with the sunflower species.

The sunflower probably originated somewhere in the southwestern part of the land now occupied by the continental United States, in a region including Colorado, New Mexico, Arizona and southern California. Archaeological explorations have come upon wild sunflower remains in Colorado and New Mexico. The American Indian was the first to utilize the sunflower, which was unknown to Europeans until the sixteenth century. Evidence of its cultivation dates from as early as 900 B.C. In a period far back in time, some Indian tribes recognized the value of and cultivated the single-stemmed sunflower, whose

218

SUNFLOWERS IN INDIAN VILLAGE

In this late sixteenth-century engraving of *The Towne of Secota*, an Indian village in North
Carolina, sunflower plants may be seen at point E.

219

head and seeds were larger than the branched-stem, ornamental type. Samuel de Champlain observed cultivated sunflowers in eastern Canada in 1615. Further west, other Indians did not cultivate the plant but gathered its wild seeds for food much as their ancestors had done. The North American explorers Lewis and Clark found this to be the case in 1804-1806 among the Shoshonis in the Lemhi River region of Idaho and Wyoming, whose custom was to roast the seeds and then grind them into a fine flour to make cakes and mush. Dried and then milled, wild sunflower seeds were an important source of food for the Pah-Utes and Gosuite Indians of Utah. Sunflower cakes were taken along as rations on war forays by the Apaches in New Mexico.

The sunflower also played an important role in Indian tribal medicine: the Zuñis of New Mexico valued it as a cure for rattlesnake bites; among the Dakotas, an infusion of boiled sunflower heads was considered to be a remedy for pulmonary afflictions and was employed to soothe chest pains; and the Cochitis smeared the sticky juice of freshly crushed sunflower stems on wounds to avoid infection.

The Cheyenne and Hopi Indians made use of wild sunflowers by wearing them in their hair at ceremonies. Seed oil was utilized by the Iroquoian tribes as a hairdressing for feasts. Sometimes magical or religious significance was attributed to the sunflower: the Onondago tribe of New York incorporated it into their creation myths. The sunflower was also the source of a yellow dye. The Hopi cultivated a distinctive type of sunflower with a purple seed hull which yielded a striking purple dye when boiled in water—effective for ceremonial body painting as well as for coloring textiles and baskets.

The sunflower was significant in the Indian hunting calendar. When the plants were tall and in full bloom, the buffalo were said to be fat, with plenty of good meat.

In northern Mexico, the sunflower was referred to in sixteenth century Spanish writings as *tornasol*, while its native Nahuatl name

was *chimalacatl*. Today it is sometimes called *maiz de Tejas*, which may be construed to mean that the sunflower was probably introduced to Mexico from the north in exchange for such items as corn, beans and squash.

Peru was first believed to be the original home of the common sunflower, an erroneous notion which may be attributed to the writings of a prominent Belgian herbalist named Rembert Dodoens; he called the plant *Crysanthemum peruvianum* in 1568. This error was subsequently repeated in numerous European botanical works. The confusion may have originated in 1532 when Francisco Pizarro and his conquistadors, upon invading Peru, found Inca priestesses wearing gold emblems on their breasts which resembled the sunflower. Those glittering adornments, however, were in all probability a representation of the sun god worshipped by the Incas. There is no evidence that the sunflower was cultivated in Peru nor anywhere else in South America until recent times.

The common sunflower and the Jerusalem artichoke enjoy the distinction of being the only important food plants domesticated by the North American Indian. Domesticated plants exhibit characteristics which distinguish them from their wild ancestors: the common sunflower is single-headed and has larger seeds than wild plants, while the Jerusalem artichoke has an underground, tuberous stem which is larger than its undomesticated progenitor.

Sunflowers belong to the Compositae or composite family, the second largest of the flowering plants; it is outranked in size only by the orchid family. Despite its large size, the Compositae has supplied only a few other cultivated plants: most noteworthy are safflower, lettuce, globe artichoke, tarragon spice and chicory; ornamental plants belonging to the composite family include chrysanthemum, dahlia, marigold and zinnia. This family has also produced some obnoxious weeds including goldenrod, dandelion and ragweed.

The common sunflower species can be

SUNFLOWER HEAD SIZE INCREASES WITH DOMESTICATION

Lower left, the small, wild sunflower; upper left, the somewhat larger weed sunflower; on the right, the large, domesticated sunflower.

The Sunflower. Charles B. Heiser, Jr. Copyright 1976 by the University of Oklahoma Press.

subdivided into three varieties: the wild, the weed and the cultivated. The wild form is found growing extensively in the western United States; it measures three to five feet in height, is branched with several small heads, scanty ray flowers and produces very small seeds. The weed sunflower is taller, branched, has larger flower heads, more numerous ray flowers and its seeds are somewhat larger than those of the wild; it grows commonly in the midwestern United States in sites such as vacant lots, railroad yards and along roadsides. The cultivated variety is unbranched and usually has only a single, massive flower head with numerous ray flowers; it produces the largest seeds.

The actual domestication process was probably initiated when Indian groups in the western United States began collecting wild sunflower seed for food. Many of these tribes never practiced agriculture, depending instead on wild plants, hunting and fishing for their sustenance. The seed gatherers presumably selected plants bearing the largest seeds to maximize their labor. Since the sunflower bears in late summer, sizable quantities were most likely collected both for immediate food use and for storage during the winter. In their migratory movements, these western Indian peoples, carried supplies of sunflower seed and would lose small quantities of the seed at different campsites. In this way, sunflower was introduced to new locations and gradually became a camp-following weed, incorporated into the cultural practices of a number of Indian tribes.

As utilization and appreciation of the sunflower spread among Indian groups, it is postulated that seed was carried eastward into the midwestern United States. Charles B.

221

Heiser, Jr. of Indiana University, a world authority on the sunflower, suggests that domestication occurred in that region during the first millenium B.C. In bringing the sunflower to cultivation, the Indians probably selected the largest seeds for planting, thereby favoring the evolution of plants producing large seeds, such as the single-headed sunflowers. Thus the selection for large seeds and the single-headed character seem to have gone hand-in-hand and gradually given rise to the domesticated sunflower. Archaeological evidence from a number of sites in the midwestern United States appears to support this hypothesis, since it shows that Indians some fifteen hundred years ago were growing sunflower plants roughly equal in size to those now being cultivated.

During the domestication process, the sunflower lost its ability to propagate itself and survive without human assistance. This phenomenon apparently took place because any seed that had reached maturity and beyond in the flower head was gathered for utilization and planting. Over a number of generations, selection favored this seed-holding characteristic until the cultivated sunflower no longer dropped seed to assure a succeeding population the following year. Several important food plants have been modified in this manner, including corn.

The Indian tribes of the Midwest—there may have been several involved in independent domestications—who modified weed sunflower and transformed it into the cultivated sunflower with a single head and large seeds, seem to have been interested mainly in the food value of the seed. At the time domestication occurred, about the ninth century B.C., these tribes were probably cultivating

ANCIENT SUNFLOWER HEADS IN KENTUCKY

Remains of sunflower heads found in the Newt Kash Hollow Shelter archaeological site.

COMPARISON OF ANCIENT AND MODERN SUNFLOWERS

On the left, achenes (dried fruits) from the Cramer village archaeological excavation in
Ohio; on the right, achenes of a modern, cultivated variety.

squash, but corn and beans had not yet been introduced from Mexico. In the early centuries of its cultivation, the sunflower may have been a more important crop than it was later, after corn had become widely grown. This may explain why Europeans did not find the sunflower being grown anywhere in North America as a major crop, although it was being cultivated as a minor crop from southern Canada to northern Mexico.

In the sixteenth century, the Spanish introduced the sunflower from Mexico to Europe. Subsequently, the English and French, from their respective New World territories, also made introductions of the plant. For more than two centuries the sunflower was of little importance in Europe. Its reputed medicinal properties aroused some interest, but it was admired for the most part as a curious and ornamental garden flower. As it spread eastward along the trade routes to Italy, Egypt, India, Russia and China, experiments were made to test various parts of the plant. Seed oil was expressed and the seed itself was eaten, but sunflower did not catch on as a food source; seed was roasted and ground as a coffee substitute, immature flower heads were boiled and eaten as a vegetable said to resemble the artichoke in flavor, dried leaves were tried as a tobacco; a silky fiber was extracted from the stalk and blotting paper was produced from the seed hulls. None of these uses, however, developed beyond the experimental stage.

As the sunflower spread abroad, so did its use as a medicinal plant—at least on a limited scale. In Turkey and Persia, a tincture prepared from the seed, when mixed with wine, was thought to be effective in place of quinine for the treatment of intermittent fevers; in China, the seeds were administered as a cure for dysentery; in Brazil, an infusion of the leaves was employed in the treatment of asthma; in Cuba, a decoction, extracted by boiling the flowers in water, was prescribed for the common cold. In many countries, sunflower

223

seeds were found to possess diuretic and expectorant properties, helpful in treating coughs, colds and various pulmonary ailments.

An historical quirk in Russia is credited with the first large-scale adoption of sunflower as a food and edible oil. In the early nineteenth century, the Holy Orthodox Church of Russia decreed very strict dietary regulations during Lent and the forty days preceding Christmas: nearly all foods rich in oil were proscribed by name and forbidden. Since sunflower had only recently been introduced to the country and was virtually unknown, it was not on the prohibited list. The people eagerly adopted it as a food and source of oil, all the while complying with Church regulations. Sunflower became extremely popular. Seed oil was extracted on a commercial scale, while seedcake became an important poultry feed. The stage was set for rapid expansion of sunflower growing; by the middle of the nineteenth century, mills in the Voronezh region were producing 2,000 metric tons of seed oil per year. Migrating peasants spread the crop to Kuban and the Ukraine. At the turn of the century, sunflower had become a major Russian agricultural product. Russia took the lead as the world's leading sunflower-growing country and has held that position ever since.

Paralleling the development in Russia, the sunflower became prominent in the eastern European countries of Romania and Hungary. During the present century, expansion has spread to Turkey, Yugoslavia and Spain, which are now important producers. Like many other world crops, sunflower did not achieve initial commercial importance in its own native area.

Direct food utilization of sunflower seed became widespread in Russia and eastern Europe. Roasted, whole sunflower seed is a popular snack item in the Soviet Union, much as the United States public enjoys roasted and salted peanuts in the shell at a baseball game. A Russian, skilled in the art of eating sunflower seed, is said to be able to put the unhulled seed in one side of his mouth, remove the kernel, eat it, and eject the hulls from the other side of his mouth on a nonstop basis.

Once the sunflower achieved major crop status in Russia, improved varieties developed there were reintroduced to the New World during the 1880's. Immigrants who came from Russia to the United States and Canada brought sunflower seed with them. However, despite the success of sunflower for food and oil in Russia, it was used in North America principally for silage. As a silage crop, the entire plant is utilized; it is highly productive and nutritionally comparable to corn silage.

Although wild sunflowers are abundant in Kansas, the cultivation of sunflower has never been significant in that state. Nevertheless, in 1903 the sunflower was designated as the official state flower and floral emblem of Kansas, which is now known as "The Sunflower State." Furthermore, legislation has recently been proposed to the Congress in Washington which would designate the sunflower as the official flower of the United States; however, passage of this motion is uncertain.

During World War II, sunflower became a more important oilseed crop in Canada and in the United States, based upon introductions of new, improved varieties with higher oil

224

content that had been developed in the Soviet Union. In South America, Argentina began to cultivate sunflower early in this century, and here again the original impetus came from Russian immigrants who were familiar with the crop and appreciative of its food and oil uses. Sunflower became a major crop in the Argentine during the Spanish Civil War in the late 1930's when supplies of olive oil from Spain were cut off. For many years, until recently surpassed by the United States, Argentina was the second largest world producer of sunflower seed, following Russia.

The cultivated sunflower has been the principal source of edible vegetable oil in Russia and eastern Europe for the past fifty years. It is one of the four most important annual world crops grown for its edible oil, along with the soybean (*Glycine max*); the peanut (*Arachis hypogaea*); and rapeseed (*Brassica napus*). There is also a considerable demand for sunflower seed in other than edible oil markets: some seed is hulled and the kernels are consumed as confectionery "nuts" in the snack trade. Larger seeds are roasted whole, like peanuts and vast quantities of smaller, whole seed are utilized as rations for birds and small animals.

In North America, sunflower growing is

concentrated in the northern Great Plains region, including North Dakota, Minnesota, South Dakota and the adjoining province of Manitoba where the bulk of Canadian production is concentrated. Texas, California and a few other states also grow sunflower. North American production is primarily for oilseed and secondarily for non-oilseed purposes.

A recent survey status of world sunflower seed production is shown by country in the following table:

SUNFLOWER SEED PRODUCTION 1979
(metric tons)

U.S.S.R.	5,370,000
United States	3,488,000
Argentina	1,430,000
Romania	889,000
Turkey	590,000
Yugoslavia	522,000
Spain	500,000
All Others	2,417,000
WORLD	15,206,000

SOURCE: *FAO Production Yearbook 1979*

These data include combined production for oilseed and non-oilseed purposes. The percentages represented by the two types are not published on a world basis, but in the United States in 1977, about ninety per cent of the sunflower seed was produced for oil and the remainder for direct human consumption and birdseed. As indicated in the tabulation, the U.S.S.R. in 1979 still held first place in world sunflower seed production, accounting for about thirty-five per cent of the total. Ranking second, the United States contributed some twenty-three per cent, followed by Argentina with about nine per cent. Thus in 1979, two-thirds of all sunflower seed production was concentrated in just three countries.

Sunflower is an annual crop, propagated from seed. Two distinct types are grown commercially: oilseed and non-oilseed. The oilseed varieties, grown as a source of vegetable oil and high-protein meal, have small black seeds, about 3/8 of an inch long, with a thin hull which adheres to the kernel, and an oil

225

TWO MAIN TYPES OF SUNFLOWER SEED
Left, *confectionery*; right, *oilseed*.

content of roughly forty per cent. The non-oilseed or confectionery varieties, used for human food and birdfeed, have larger seeds, approximately five-eighths of an inch in length, with striped, black and white or black and light gray coloration and a relatively thick hull which remains free of the kernel and is easily removed. The oil content is about twenty-seven per cent.

Major advances have been made in plant breeding of sunflowers to develop high-yielding, disease-resistant varieties. Much of this work has been carried out in the Soviet Union. In 1940, the average oil content of most commercial oilseeds was about thirty-three per cent; in recent years, strains with an oil content of approximately fifty per cent have been developed in Russia.

Commercial growers must purchase hybrid seed of improved varieties for planting from seed companies to assure maximum yield and the crop uniformity that is so critical in mechanized agriculture. Field standards for producing this certified seed require that the plants be grown in isolation at least one-half mile from other wild or cultivated sunflowers. The distance functions as a buffer to

minimize the risk of insects bringing in unwanted pollen. Minnesota, North Dakota and California are major United States sources of certified sunflower seed.

In sunflower breeding, scientists have an invaluable asset in wild sunflower species, which are resistant to insects and disease and provide an excellent source of breeding material for exploiting the genetic variability of the plant. Sunflower displays great promise for potential plant improvement to make it a more productive annual crop. It is also playing a role in gene splicing. In 1981 it was reported that genetic engineers had developed a technique for transplanting a gene from the seed of a French bean into a sunflower cell. Eventually, it is possible that this experimental technology could lead to the development of a high-protein, hybrid "sunbean" plant.

For maximum productivity, the sunflower—oilseed or non-oilseed—requires a certain set of environmental conditions. The plants perform well in temperate zones with sunny climates. Sunflower requires open sunlight, but is tolerant of both cold and hot temperatures. Latitude, through its influence on

226

temperature, has a significant effect on the chemical characteristics of seed oil. Sunflower grown north of the thirty-ninth parallel in North America has a higher polyunsaturated fatty acid content in its seed oil than those grown further south. Cooler temperatures during seed development account for the difference. Sunflower is more resistant to drought and frost than either corn or soybeans, and does not require soils of high fertility like wheat or corn to produce satisfactory yields. In general, sunflower requires a 120-day frost-free period to mature; some early cultivars have been developed which mature in 90 days, and other late-maturing varieties need 140 to 160 days to mature. Due to their size and weight, sunflower heads are particularly susceptible to damage from hailstorms.

Planting practices followed by sunflower growers are much the same as those employed for corn. Seedbed preparation should insure that the field to be planted is free of weeds, which can be a serious problem for the sunflower. Fertilizer application is carried out in advance, or with seed at the time of planting. A wide range of planting dates is possible, since in most areas the growing season is longer than needed. In the northern Great Plains, sunflower is planted in May. For oilseed varieties, higher yields and higher oil percentages in the seed may be obtained through early planting.

Sunflower is a row crop, and seed is planted at a depth of one to two inches. Spacing of twenty to forty inches between the rows is typical, while plants are spaced six to eighteen inches apart in the rows. The two kinds of sunflower are grown in similar fashion except for the spacing of the plants. Larger seeds are produced at wider spacings, so confectionery varieties are planted at a population of between 14,000 and 18,000 plants per acre. The oilseed varieties are planted closer together, with a density of 15,000 to 25,000 plants per acre. A premium is paid for large seeds of the confectionery type.

Yield losses due to weed growth in the sunflower fields can be avoided if the weeds are destroyed within three weeks of sunflower seedling emergence. Weed control by herbicides, combined with mechanical control, is most common in North America. After about a month, the sunflower plants compete successfully with most weeds.

Commercial farmers usually do not grow

BEES PLAY AN IMPORTANT ROLE IN POLLINATION OF SUNFLOWERS

sunflowers in successive years on the same field for two main reasons: first, crop rotation is important in order to control serious disease losses in sunflower; second, sunflower crop residue amounts to only about one-half that contributed by a field of corn and so soil fertility declines rapidly under continuous sunflower cultivation. Three or four years between sunflower crops is recommended in North America. Corn and small grains such as wheat are often planted to separate sunflower crops in a rotation, since the former do not support pathogens which cause sunflower diseases.

As sunflower production is dependent on insect pollination, cultivation practices which might adversely affect insect populations should be avoided. Bees are the most effective pollinators, so bee colonies are frequently placed in the fields. This practice increases sunflower yields and at the same time produces sunflower honey, a valuable commodity.

A major reason for the initial success of the sunflower as a commercial crop in Russia was that it did not suffer from the same magnitude of insect and disease problems encountered by the plant in its native North American habitat. When the sunflower was reintroduced to North America in the late nineteenth century as an improved crop, insect populations and plant diseases which plague wild sunflowers eagerly moved into cultivated fields. In recent years, however, significant progress has been

BIRDS ARE A TROUBLESOME PEST, FREQUENTLY DAMAGING SUNFLOWER CROPS

made in the Northern Great Plains to limit sunflower losses due to diseases, insects and even birds. The most serious diseases are caused by fungi including Verticillium wilt (leaf mottle), downy mildew, rust and stem and head rots. Fungicidal protection is not usually economical, but varieties or hybrids have been developed which are resistant to most but not all plant diseases. Potentially damaging insects such as the sunflower moth, cutworm, sunflower midge, long-horned beetle and seed and stem weevil may be controlled by approved insecticides, but considerable care must be taken to protect the pollinators and their bee hives. Fall tillage, weed control and a minimum of three-year rotations between plantings of cultivated sun-flower have helped to check insect infestations.

Since sunflower is grown for birdfeed—a "caviar" so to speak for birds—it is not surprising that they constitute a major pest. Blackbirds, in particular, eat large amounts of seed in maturing fields, while other birds feed on the seed at earlier stages of development. The seeds are exposed and the large sunflower head serves as an ideal perch during feeding. Due to an unfortunate biological circumstance, the sunflower crop of North America growers matures at the precise time when food demands of bird populations are at their peak because the young have been added to the flocks. Noise-making devices, scarecrows, fright owls and aluminum strips that

MECHANIZED SUNFLOWER HARVEST

At maturity, most sunflower heads permanently face east.

glisten in sunlight are somewhat successful in frightening away birds if they are put into operation before major bird feeding begins. Careful selection of planting sites can also reduce bird damage: sunflower fields should not be planted near roosting places for blackbirds, such as marshes or sloughs. It is likewise recommended that crop lands of other earlier crops, which have already been harvested, should not be tilled or plowed until after the sunflower harvest, since they provide a feeding ground for birds and relieve pressure of the sunflower crop as a food source.

When sunflower plants reach maturity, most flower heads permanently face east while their backs change color from green to yellow. In higher latitudes, a killing frost will hasten the drying of the head; elsewhere, a chemical desiccant may be sprayed so that the head, stalk and leaves will dry more rapidly and thus permit an earlier harvest. Dry and brittle flower heads are most effectively harvested by combines, originally designed for wheat or soybeans, but adapted for sunflower harvest through the addition of large, metal trays to catch the seed shaken loose from the heads before the stalks are guided into the cutting blades to be severed. Formerly, sunflower heads were manually harvested, allowed to dry, and then threshed.

Early harvesting may reduce seed loss and lessen bird damage, but results in seed with excessive moisture content. Artificial drying prior to storage is required to reduce the moisture content to below 12 per cent if the unhulled seeds are to be stored temporarily, and to less than 9.5 per cent in the case of longer storage. The latter percentage effectively retards growth of molds and other microflora.

In the United States, average yields of sunflower seed range from about 900 to 1,200 pounds per acre. Higher yields for oilseed va-

AERIAL SPRAYING TO SPEED UP HARVEST

When the backs of the sunflower heads have turned from green to yellow and crop moisture is 35 per cent or less, some farmers spray a desiccant such as Paraquat by means of aircraft to accelerate drying and hasten the harvest—thus reducing bird damage and shatter losses in the fields.

rieties are sometimes obtained because of greater use of hybrids, closer planting densities and improvement in breeding disease-resistant types. One hundred pounds of dry, mature, oilseed sunflower seeds will yield approximately forty pounds of oil, thirty-five pounds of meal and twenty to twenty-five pounds of hulls.

Oilseed and non-oilseed varieties have very similar seed characteristics, though they differ in seed size and oil content. Oilseed may be hulled or not prior to processing; the quality and quantity of oil production are not affected, although hulling does reduce the fiber content of sunflower meal. The major commercial use of sunflower seed oil, or "sunoil," is in food products, including salad oil, cooking oil, margarine and shortening. Sunoil, high in polyunsaturated fatty acids and low in saturated acids, contains no cholesterol; it ranks as the second most important vegetable oil in the world, after soybean oil. It usually costs about 10 per cent more than oil made from soybeans or corn, but contains about 68 per cent polyunsaturated fats compared to approximately 60 per cent for soybean oil and 54 per cent for corn oil. Increasing consumer consciousness about health has helped the growing sunoil market. Sunoil also has a wide range of potential industrial utilization, but its high value for food use and its limited supply have not encouraged such diversified usage. It may be employed, for example, in the manufacture of paints, varnishes and plastics. It will work as a satisfactory fuel in diesel engines, provided the diesel fuel is mixed with 25 to 50 per cent sunoil.

Sunflower meal, the by-product of crushing the seed for oil extraction, is used in animal feed for livestock, poultry and swine; with a protein content of 38 to 40 per cent, it is a valuable protein supplement for cattle and sheep. In France it is one of the most important feeds for commercial rabbit production.

Research is being carried out to expand the food use of sunflower meal for humans, employing meal made from dehulled, defatted, ground and refined sunflower kernels; this cream-colored sun meal is bland in flavor and highly nutritious. When refined into flour to fortify wheat flour, it can be utilized in baked products where color is not a major concern. The development of sun meal for human consumption, however, has been hampered due to the presence of a phenol compound in the sunflower seed which, while non toxic, gives the meal an undesirable green tint. This has not prevented sun meal from being used as feed for poultry and cattle.

Hulling oilseed and non-oilseed sunflower yields hull material as a by-product. In the United States, most sunflower hulls are ground and added as a coarse roughage component or bulk for mixing with livestock feed. In other countries, the hulls are normally employed as a fuel to generate steam in processing plants. The hulls can also be utilized in the production of fireplace logs and fiberboard.

Although seed size is largely immaterial for oilseeds, it is an important factor in the non-oilseed or confectionery sunflower crop. After harvesting and drying, the seeds are cleaned and graded into three sizes: large, medium and small. The separation is effected by means of sieves. The largest size, i.e. those seeds which normally pass over a twenty/sixty-four-inch round-hole sieve, are referred to as "in-shell" seeds. This classification represents about fifteen to twenty-five per cent of the confectionery crop; the unhulled seeds are sold to nut processors to be salted, roasted in the hull and packaged for the snack trade. For salting, the whole seeds are soaked in salt brine, boiled for a few minutes and dried. Salted, whole seeds may be given a different flavor if fried in edible oil. Large, uniform seeds, unblemished by insect, fungal or weather damage bring the highest prices for cocktail and snack food. Hull appearance is important: the ideal hull is smooth, loose, with bright, white stripes on a black background.

Medium-sized or "hulling" seed accounts for some forty to sixty per cent of the non-

CONFECTIONERY SUNFLOWER SEEDS

oilseed crop. Following hulling, cleaning and sorting, the kernels are utilized by nutmeat processors for the snack trade and as nut substitutes in baked products and candies. A "new" product of interest is sunflower butter, or "sunbutter," which has been advertised recently as an alternative to higher-priced peanut butter. In point of fact, the Havasupai Indians of Arizona for many centuries have prepared sunflower seed butter by parching and grinding the seeds and adding water.

In the United States, raw sunflower kernels are a crunchy health-food item, consumed alone or in mixture with other nuts and dried fruits. They provide a tasty addition to salads, mixed in or sprinkled on top. Roasted kernels are vacuum packed in cans or glass containers, or packaged in cellophane and marketed as a cocktail or snack food. As a substitute for other nuts, they are a popular ingredient in candies, cakes, cookies, muffins and ice cream toppings.

The smallest size seeds constitute the re-

maining fifteen to twenty per cent of the non-oilseed crop. Like the largest seeds, the smallest are usually not hulled. Their major market is for birdfeed, either pure or in blends with large grains (corn) or small grains (wheat, oats, millet and sorghum). The small seed is suitable for caged birds; canaries and parrots are fond of it. It is also appropriate for outdoor feeding of wild birds, such as cardinals, chickadees, finches and bluejays. Seed-eating pets, like hamsters and squirrels, have a liking for it.

Non-oilseed sunflower, although only a small, specialized market in comparison with oilseed sunflower, is nevertheless constantly growing in size and importance due to the increasing demand for sunflower seed in the health-food, confectionery and snack trade. In the United States, it is estimated that about half of the non-oilseed production is for human consumption and the remainder for bird and pet food.

Non-oilseed sunflower plays a minor role

232

in foreign trade; it is for the most part produced and consumed domestically. This is in sharp contrast to sunflower oilseed, sunoil and sun meal, which are important commodities in international trade. European consumers generally prefer sunoil over other vegetable oils except for olive oil, which is much higher priced. The United States exports most of its oilseed crop to Europe as whole seed rather than sunoil, because the European Economic Community levies an import duty on vegetable oil, but not on whole oilseed. In 1981, approximately 1,800,000 metric tons of sunflower seed were produced in the United States—1,500,000 tons of which were exported.

During the ten year period from 1967 to 1976, non-oilseed sunflower prices averaged $171 per metric ton as compared to $162 per metric ton for oilseed. Higher prices for non-oilseed sunflower are often required to offset lower yields per acre due to wider spacings and sparser planting densities.

The sunflower has gradually acquired status as a farm commodity. There is now a National Sunflower Association in Bismarck,

North Dakota. Futures contracts in sunflowers are traded on the Minneapolis Grain Exchange.

Sunflower seeds are a bargain, in comparison with other edible nuts in retail markets in the United States. In mid-1981, hulled, raw sunflower kernels ranged in price from $2.00 to $2.25 per pound; sunflower seed, roasted and salted in the shell, carried a retail price of about $1.50 per pound. Dry-roasted sunflower seeds are being marketed by the Planters Division of Nabisco Brands, Inc. as "sunflower nuts." Sunflower seeds, although composed of a rich, oily kernel surrounded by a brittle shell, have not generally been regarded as edible nuts in the past; they are gradually acquiring "nut" status, especially at cocktail and snack time.

High in protein content and in concentrated sources of many nutrients, edible nuts including sunflower kernels may be recommended as meat substitutes. When compared to other popular nuts in the following table, sunflower kernels rate high in nutritional aspects but low in sodium content, calories and fats—excellent ratings on the whole:

NUTRIENT CONTENT OF 1/4 POUND SUNFLOWER KERNELS AND SELECTED NUTS

Nutrient	Sunflower kernels Amount	Rank	Walnuts Amount	Rank	Almonds Amount	Rank	Peanuts Amount	Rank	Pecans Amount	Rank
Protein, gm	27.2	2	16.8	4	21.1	3	29.7	1	10.4	5
Fat, gm	53.3	5	72.6	2	61.5	3	55.2	4	80.8	1
Calories	635	5	738	2	678	3	664	4	829	1
Minerals										
Calcium, mg	136	2	112	3	265	1	82	5	88	4
Phosphorus, mg	949	1	431	4	572	2	462	3	328	5
Iron, mg	8.0	1	3.5	3	5.3	2	2.5	5	2.7	4
Sodium, mg	34.0	1	2.3	4	4.5	3	5.8	2	trace	5
Potassium, mg	1,043	1	510	5	877	2	795	3	684	4
Vitamins										
A (IU)	57	2	35	3	—	—	—	—	148	1
Thiamin, mg	2.25	1	.37	3	.27	5	.36	4	.98	2
Riboflavin, mg	.26	2	.15	5	1.05	1	.15	3	.15	4
Niacin, mg	6.18	2	1.05	4	3.98	3	19.4	1	1.03	5

SOURCE: *Sunflower Production and Marketing*, Extension Bulletin 25. North Dakota State University. July, 1978.

In 1970, only a few thousand acres were planted with sunflowers in the United States, compared to about four million acres at the present time. There should be further growth ahead for the sunflower industry. If the demand continues to rise for a highly unsaturated vegetable oil as part of human diet, sunoil should be the most desirable and economical product available.

The increased interest in natural health-foods bodes well for future sunflower seed usage. Most snack foods contribute little to diet except calories. Raw or roasted sunflower kernels are nutritious and relatively inexpensive; in the growing snack market they are distributed through nut counters in food stores, vending machines and snack racks—both in-shell and shelled. Because of its high protein content, sunflower meal has been recommended as a major ingredient in concentrated food for human consumption in less developed countries of the third world.

ROASTED SUNFLOWER KERNELS (XXXIII)

1 cup (250 ml) hulled sunflower kernels*	1 teaspoon (5 ml) melted sunflower margarine (optional)
Salt to taste	

*To prepare kernels, cover unshelled seeds with salted water (2 quarts/2 liters water and 1/4 to 1/2 cup/60 to 125 ml salt). Bring to a boil and simmer 2 hours. Drain on absorbent paper towel. Shell. Unshelled seeds may be roasted. Pre-soak overnight in salted water. Drain. Follow recipe for roasting kernels.

Place kernels in a single layer in a shallow pan. Bake at 300° F (150° C), stirring occasionally. Remove from oven and add margarine, if desired. Stir to coat. Spread on absorbent paper towel. Salt.

Variation

1 cup (250 ml) hulled sunflower kernels*	Salt to taste
1/4 cup (60 ml) sunflower oil	

Deep-fry at 360° F (184° C) until golden brown. Skim off kernels and drain on absorbent paper towel. Salt. Store in tightly covered container.

Yield: 1 cup (250 ml)

HORS D'OEUVRE

Mushroom-Sunflower Appetizer (XXXIII)

2-1/2 pounds (1-1/4 kg) fresh mushrooms, chopped fine	1 cup (250 ml) milk
	1/4 teaspoon (1 ml) salt
	Dash paprika
2 tablespoons (30 ml) sunflower margarine	Dash nutmeg
	1/4 cup (60 ml) chopped, toasted, unsalted sunflower kernels
3 tablespoons (45 ml) sunflower oil	
3 tablespoons (45 ml) whole wheat flour	24 toasted whole wheat bread rounds
1/4 cup (60 ml) non-fat dry milk	

Sauté minced mushrooms in margarine. Prepare cream sauce by heating the oil, then blend in the flour, stir in dry milk and milk, cooking until mixture thickens. Add seasonings and cool. Pour cream sauce over mushrooms, add sunflower kernels and stir. Place mixture in serving bowl and circle edges with bread rounds.

Yield: 24 servings

LUNCHEON AND SUPPER DISHES

Nutty Chicken (XXXV)

One 3 to 3-1/2 pound (1-1/3 to 1-1/2-kg) broiler-fryer, cut up
Salt
1 cup (250 ml) biscuit mix
3/4 cup (175 ml) water
2/3 cup (150 ml) chopped salted, roasted sunflower nuts
Vegetable oil for frying

Lightly salt chicken pieces. Combine biscuit mix, water and nuts. Dip chicken in batter. Fry in 2 inches (5 cm) of hot oil in skillet until golden. Place chicken in shallow baking dish; bake at 350° F (175° C) for 1 hour or until fork tender.

Yield: 4 servings

Olive Lambwiches Greco (XXXIII and XXXVI)

1 pound (450 g) ground lamb
1 cup (250 ml) chopped ripe olives
1 cup (250 ml) chopped onion
1 teaspoon (5 ml) garlic salt
1 teaspoon (5 ml) crushed rosemary leaves
Four 6-inch (15-cm) pita breads
2 ounces (60 g) feta cheese*, crumbled
1 tomato, sliced
2 ounces (60 g) sunflower sprouts

Brown lamb, crumbled, until fully cooked. Drain. Add olives, onion, garlic salt and rosemary leaves. Stir well to blend ingredients. Cover and cook over low heat. Mixture should be fairly dry. Keep hot.

Cut pita breads into halves. Open gently to form pockets. Spoon 2 ounces (60 ml) lamb mixture into each pocket. Top with cheese, 1 teaspoon (5 ml) for each half. Place 2 tomato slices and 1/4 ounce (7 g) sprouts in each pocket. Serve immediately.

Yield: 4 servings

*You may substitute Edam, bleu cheese, mozzarella or string cheese.

VEGETABLE

Pioneer Brown Rice Dish (XXXIII)

1 cup (250 ml) uncooked brown rice
2 cups (500 ml) chicken broth
1/2 teaspoon (2.5 ml) kelp (optional)
1 teaspoon (5 ml) salt
1/2 cup (125 ml) chopped onion
1 cup (250 ml) chopped celery
1-1/2 tablespoons (22.5 ml) sunflower oil
1/2 cup (125 ml) chopped, toasted, salted sunflower kernels

Combine rice, broth and seasonings; heat to a boil, stirring once. Reduce heat and simmer covered for 35 minutes or until tender. Cook onions and celery in oil until tender. Add onions, celery and sunflower kernels to rice.

Yield: 6 servings

SALAD

Sunflower Potato Salad (XXXIV)

6 cups (1-1/2 liters) potatoes, cooked, peeled and cubed (6 medium)
1 cup (250 ml) chopped onion (1 medium)
3/4 cup (175 ml) chopped celery (1 stalk)
1-1/2 cups (375 ml) sliced fresh mushrooms
8 slices bacon, fried crisp and crumbled, or 1/3 cup (75 ml) imitation bacon bits
1/3 cup (75 ml) mayonnaise or salad dressing
1 teaspoon (5 ml) prepared mustard
3 hard-cooked eggs, diced
1 teaspoon (5 ml) salt
1/4 teaspoon (1 ml) pepper
1/4 cup (60 ml) sunflower nuts

In large bowl combine first ten ingredients. Toss gently until well mixed. Refrigerate. Just before serving, toss with sunflower nuts.

Yield: 6 servings

235

Graham Cracker Bars (XXXIII and XXXVI)

3/4 cup (175 ml) sun-
flower margarine
1/2 cup (125 ml) milk
1 cup (250 ml) sugar
1 egg, slightly beaten
1 cup (250 ml) crushed
graham crackers
1 cup (250 ml) flaked
coconut

1 cup (250 ml) whole
sunflower kernels
20 whole graham crack-
ers (approx.)
Powdered sugar
frosting

Combine margarine, milk, sugar and egg in a saucepan and bring to a boil. Remove from heat. Stir in crushed graham crackers, coconut and sunflower kernels. Line a 9-inch (23-cm) square pan with whole graham crackers. Spread warm mixture over crackers, and cover the mixture with another layer of whole graham crackers. Top with a slightly thin powdered sugar frosting. Cook before cutting.

Yield: Forty 1 × 2-inch (2.5 × 5-cm) bars

Sunflower Meal Cookies (XXXVI)

1 cup (250 ml) sunflow-
er kernels, ground
fine in food
processor or
blender
1/2 cup (125 ml) white
sugar
1/2 cup (125 ml) brown
sugar
1/2 cup (125 ml) sun-
flower margarine

1 egg
1/2 teaspoon (2.5 ml)
vanilla
1-1/4 to 1-1/2 cups (310
to 375 ml) all-
purpose flour
3/4 teaspoon (4 ml) soda
1/4 teaspoon (1 ml) salt

Mix first six ingredients until creamy. Add remaining ingredients, a little flour at a time—until the dough is thick enough to form into 1-inch (2.5-cm) balls. Shape into 30 balls and place on ungreased cookie sheet. Press down with fork. Bake in 375° F (190° C) oven for about 10 minutes.

Yield: 2-1/2 dozen cookies

Bonzaville Sunflower Pie (XXXIII)

3 eggs
1/2 cup (125 ml) firmly
packed brown
sugar
1/4 cup (60 ml) granula-
ted sugar
1/4 teaspoon (1 ml) salt
1/2 cup (125 ml) light
corn syrup
1/2 cup (125 ml) dark
corn syrup
3 tablespoons (45 ml)
melted sunflower
margarine, cooled

1 teaspoon (5 ml)
vanilla
1 cup (250 ml) roasted,
salted sunflower
kernels
1 unbaked 9-inch
(23-cm) pie crust
1/4 cup (60 ml) chopped
sunflower kernels

Set oven to 350° F (175° C). Beat eggs until blended, but not frothy. Combine sugars, salt, syrups, margarine and vanilla; stir into eggs. Spread sunflower kernels on the bottom of the pie shell; pour mixture over. Top with chopped sunflower kernels. Reduce oven heat to 325° F (165° C) and bake 50 to 60 minutes, or until knife inserted in center comes out clean.

Yield: One 9-inch (23 cm) pie

Variations

For the syrups, substitute 3/4 cup (175 ml) white syrup and 1 tablespoon (15 ml) molasses, or use either all dark or all light syrup.

Sunflower Bread (XXXIII)

3-1/2 to 4 cups (875 ml to
1 liter) all-purpose
flour
1 package active dry
yeast
3 tablespoons (45 ml)
sugar
1-1/2 teaspoons (7.5 ml)
salt
1/2 cup (125 ml) milk

2 tablespoons (30 ml)
sunflower marga-
rine
1 egg
1 tablespoon (15 ml)
grated orange peel
1/2 cup (125 ml) orange
juice
2/3 cup (150 ml) sun-
flower kernels

In bowl combine 1-1/2 cups (375 ml) flour, yeast, sugar and salt. Heat milk and margarine to 115° F (47° C). Add to flour mixture. Add egg, orange peel and juice. Beat at low speed 1-1/2 minutes; beat at high speed 3 minutes. Stir in sunflower kernels by hand and add enough flour to make soft dough. Knead 10 to 12 minutes; let rise until doubled. Punch down and let rest 5 minutes. Shape into loaf and place in greased 8-1/2 × 4-1/2 × 2-1/2-inch (21 × 11 × 6-cm) loaf pan. Cover and let rise until doubled in bulk. Bake at 375° F (190° C) for 40 minutes. Remove from pan immediately and brush top with butter.

Yield: One loaf

CANDY AND CONFECTION

Sunflower Bark (XXXIII and XXXVI)

1 pound (450 g) white chocolate	3/4 cup (175 ml) sunflower kernels

Melt white chocolate according to package directions or in your microwave. When completely melted, remove from heat and stir in sunflower kernels. Mix well and spread on waxed paper to desired thickness. Cool at room temperature.

Yield: 1 pound (450 g)

Sunflower Brittle (XXXIII)

1-1/2 cups (375 ml) sugar	1 teaspoon (5 ml) soda
1 teaspoon (5 ml) lemon juice	1 teaspoon (5 ml) vanilla
1 cup (250 ml) light corn syrup	2 cups (500 ml) roasted sunflower kernels
3 tablespoons (45 ml) sunflower margarine	1/4 teaspoon (1 ml) salt (omit if kernels are salted)

Combine sugar, lemon juice and syrup in two-quart (2 liter) pan. Cook uncovered at high temperature, stirring occasionally during first five minutes of cooking. When temperature of mixture reads 290° to 295° F (144° to 147° C) (hard-crack stage) on candy thermometer, remove from heat and add margarine, soda, vanilla, sunflower kernels and salt. Stir. Pour onto greased jelly-roll pan. Cool until brittle can be handled. Pull to paper thinness. Break into pieces.

Nux Iuglans.
The Walnut tree.

CHAPTER TWELVE

Walnuts

Family: Juglandaceae

LATIN	*Juglans regia* L.	DUTCH	Walnoot
SPANISH	Nogal	ITALIAN	Noce
FRENCH	Noyer	PORTUGUESE	Nogueira
GERMAN	Walnuss	RUSSIAN	Gretskiĭ Orékh
SWEDISH	Valnöt	JAPANESE	Kurumi
ARABIC	Jōz	CHINESE	Ho Tao

A spaniel, a woman, and a walnut tree
The more they're beaten, the better still they be.

Old English proverb

TIMES HAVE CHANGED. Today, the chauvinistic jingle above strikes a discordant note. Years ago, it was believed that beating walnut branches with light poles during the harvest encouraged the development of fruiting buds, which would cause increased nut production in the following year. Experiments at the University of California at Davis have shown that this ancient belief was erroneous. In any event, the rhyme is of historical interest.

There are about fifteen species of Juglans, the walnut genus. Belonging to the walnut family, the Juglandaceae, they are indigenous to east Asia, southeastern Europe and North and South America. All walnuts are edible, but *J. regia*, known as the Persian or English walnut, is probably the most delicious and certainly the most important. It is believed to be native to a vast region including Turkey, Iran, Iraq, Afghanistan, southern Russia and northern India. In prehistoric times, walnuts were most likely collected from wild trees for food, a process that lasted for millenia. Starting with the caveman, knowledge was gained gradually about walnuts, and preference was undoubtedly given to nuts with the largest and sweetest kernels, with thin shells which were easier to crack.

With the advent of the domestication of annual grains, seeds of selected walnuts were presumably planted in or near villages. Cultivation of trees from selected seed, away from wild populations, would have afforded the opportunity for natural cross-pollination to occur and even larger and better quality nuts to be produced, which in turn could be used for propagation. Generation after generation, this selection process created a domesticated form of walnuts discernably different from the wild types. It has been conjectured that this process occurred originally in or near Persia, many thousands of years ago, and that the larger, sweeter nuts, with kernels easy to crack open, were harvested from selected trees and carried by ranging herdsmen both eastward and westward where they were subsequently cultivated. Walnuts have been found in prehistoric deposits dating from the

239

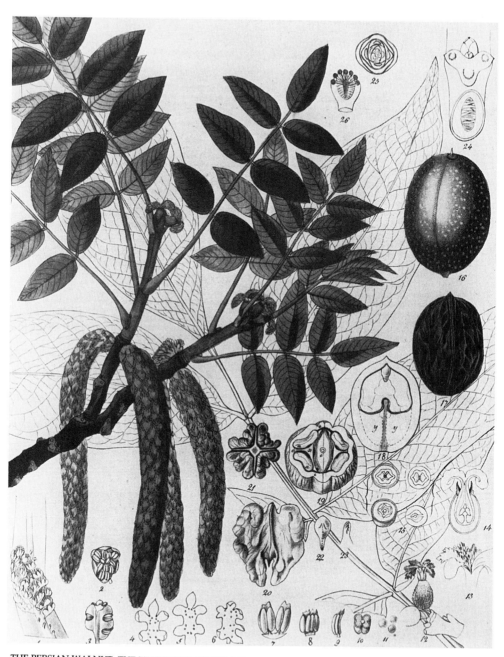

THE PERSIAN WALNUT, THE EDIBLE NUT OF COMMERCE

PETRIFIED WALNUTS, BREAD AND GRAINS

Destroyed by the volcanic eruption of Mount Vesuvius in A.D. 79. Preserved at the National Museum, Naples.

Iron Age in Europe. Persian walnuts were introduced to Greece and gradually moved east across Asia to China, where the walnut is mentioned in the earliest Chinese written records. From Greece the walnut was taken west to Italy.

Walnuts, prevalent in Palestine and Lebanon, were well-known in Biblical times. They were mentioned in *Song of Solomon* 6:11: "I went down into the garden of nuts (walnuts) to see the fruits of the valley . . ." King Solomon's nut garden of approximately 940 B.C., is said to have been located at Etham, about six miles from Jerusalem. No trace of it remains today.

The generic term *Juglans* is a contraction of the Latin *Jovis glans*, nut of Jupiter, or nut of "the Gods." The specific epithet *regia* means "royal" and in the first century A.D., the Roman scholar, Pliny, stated that the walnut had been sent to Greece from Persia "by the kings;" the best quality walnut was known as "Persian and royal." At that time, the walnut was considered to be superior to other common nuts such as acorns, beechnuts and chestnuts. Remains of husked, well-pre-

served, unbroken walnuts have been found in the ruins of Pompeii, recovered from a site destroyed by Mount Vesuvius in 79 A.D.

The Romans extended the cultivation of the walnut northward through France, or an-

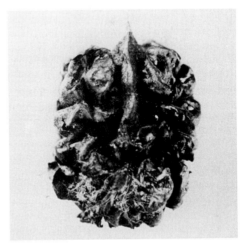

PERSIAN WALNUT KERNEL, A.D. 79

Recovered at Herculaneum, from a site destroyed by Mount Vesuvius.

241

cient Gaul. Thus when the nut eventually reached England, the name "Gaul nut" may have been corrupted to "walnut" by English-speaking people; or possibly the "wal" of walnut is derived from the Anglo-Saxon word "wealh," meaning foreign or alien.

In England the walnut never became profitable for nut production, although the tree has traditionally been popular as an ornamental and for its exceptional hardwood. Superior walnut varieties from warmer climates are unsuitable for Britain since they break into growth prematurely in the early spring; the young growth and flowers are subsequently destroyed by spring frosts, year after year.

The Greeks called the walnut *caryon*, from the word *kara*, meaning head, due to the resemblance of the shell and kernel of the walnut to the human skull and brain. Following the Doctrine of Signatures in the sixteenth and seventeenth centuries, various plants in medieval Europe and England were employed in herbal medicine as specific cures due to a fancied resemblance of the shape of a root, leaf or fruit to a particular part of the human body. Thus the walnut was the perfect "signature" of the human head, while its kernel bore an uncanny likeness to the brain. Therefore, the ground, outer husk of the walnut was prescribed to cure a head wound and eating the walnut was recommended for the mentally ill. William Cole, a famous English herbalist, stated in his work *Adam in Eden* (1657): "If the wall-nut Kernel be bruised, and moystned with the quintessence of Wine and laid upon the Crown of the Head, it comforts the brain and head mightily."

Many legends and superstitions have been associated with the walnut. The Greeks and Romans regarded it as a symbol of fecundity. It was customary at Roman weddings for the bridegroom to toss handfuls of walnuts—much as we now throw rice—to be scrambled for by young boys. By flinging the nuts away, the bridegroom showed he was mature and had finally laid aside childish amusements. In China, where the cricket has traditionally been considered a creature of good omen,

WALNUTS 1553

musically-trained, singing crickets were carried about in intricately carved walnut shells.

In the Middle Ages, it was believed in Europe that evil spirits lurked in walnut branches; thus the walnuts themselves were thought to be useful in warding off lightning, fevers, witchcraft, the evil eye and epileptic fits. This superstition may have originated when it was noted that many other plants withered and died if planted near walnut trees, a phenomenon Pliny had mentioned many centuries earlier. In recent years, Pliny's observation has been substantiated: a toxic substance called *juglone* has been isolated from roots of trees of the walnut family and apparently does cause wilting in some sensitive plants, but not in all plants, when their roots come into contact with walnut roots.

By the end of the sixteenth century, the walnut was familiar in England. Shakespeare referred to it in *Taming of the Shrew*, Act IV, Scene 3, when Petruchio exclaims:

"Why, 'tis a cockle or a Walnut-shell,
A knack, a toy, a trick, a baby's cap."

In days gone by, walnuts were employed for medicinal purposes. An infusion of powdered walnut leaves (supposed to have an astringent quality) was once used both internally and externally to treat swollen glands, shingles and sores. Walnut oil was prescribed for colic and to soothe the intestines. The juice of green walnut husks, diluted in warm water, was recommended as a gargle and also to stop diarrhea. On the other hand, a green walnut, boiled in sugar, was said to relieve constipation. Powdered walnut bark was prescribed to treat ringworm.

In West Germany today, a tea made of walnut leaves, to be taken daily for two to six months, is prescribed in herbal medicine for growing children as a treatment for the chronic running nose as well as to alleviate skin problems such as adolescent acne and eczema.

In southern Europe, especially in France, walnut oil has long been a popular cooking oil, frequently substituted for olive oil. Walnut meal, left over after expression of the oil, has traditionally been a thickening agent for both savory and sweet dishes.

The walnut has been introduced to a broad range of temperate climates extending across the Northern Hemisphere, and to a limited extent in the Southern Hemisphere, most notably in Australia and New Zealand. This broad dispersal has led to the development of numerous walnut varieties, suited to the different ecological conditions in each location.

Throughout a long history of cultivation, the walnut has been highly esteemed as a superior dessert nut which requires neither roasting nor salting to enhance its flavor. Walnuts were blanched, pulverized and soaked in water to provide walnut milk, a nourishing substitute for dairy milk in European households until the end of the eighteenth century. The Chinese, too, have an ancient custom of making walnut milk. In China, walnuts were thought to be strength-building as a food, as well as possessing medicinal properties.

The green, immature walnut, including the husk, is edible. In England, young walnuts are traditional delicacies when pickled. While still green, they are gathered in June or July, then soaked in salt and water for about ten days before being placed in vinegar. Green walnuts can also be made into walnut marmalade, added to jams, or preserved

A LONDON STREET SCENE

An early 19th century print by Thomas Rowlandson. Pickled walnuts are a traditional British delicacy. Gathered while still green in June or July, the immature walnuts are soaked in salt and water for about ten days before being placed in vinegar.

whole in syrup. A nut brandy can be prepared from green walnuts.

Artists, including the great Venetian masters, have made use of walnut oil: walnut oil dries in a slow manner which allows the oil painter considerable flexibility in blending colors.

Like the maple, the walnut tree can be tapped in spring for the rising sweet sap and the liquid boiled down into sugar—a procedure widespread among the Tartars of eastern Asia.

As a dye source, the walnut has a long history. The green hulls contain a yellowish dye, while a brownish colorant is yielded by the mature husks. When boiled, walnut roots yield a darker pigment which has traditionally been utilized by gypsies and theatrical performers to stain their skin a deep brown.

A distinction should be made between commercial walnut growing for nut production, on the one hand, and the cultivation of the tree as an ornamental or for timber on the other. Nut-producing trees should have large crowns and considerable branching to develop abundant fruiting wood, while timber trees should have narrow crowns and long, straight trunks. Dispersed as it was across Europe and eastward toward Asia, the walnut tree was found to be tolerant of a wide range of temperatures when planted for ornamental or timber purposes; in cooler climates, however, nut production was minimal or nil. In northern Europe, for example, the Persian walnut will grow to a fair size, but it ripens nuts only when above average winter temperatures are experienced.

Walnut has traditionally been a preferred wood for making furniture. This use dates back to the beginning of the Christian era. Strabo, a first-century Greek geographer, recorded that royal walnut wood was highly appreciated by wealthy Romans, many of whom possessed fine walnut tables. During the Middle Ages, it was known as Circassian walnut, and was the major commercial hardwood of Europe. It became the principal furniture wood of England in the late seventeenth century, during the reign of William and Mary. The succeeding period of the monarchy of Queen Anne has been called the "Age of Walnut," due to the popularity of the wood.

Since English trading ships transported walnuts from the Mediterranean countries to markets all over the world, the Persian walnut came to be known as the English walnut. Thus in the United States, where it was first brought to New England by the early settlers and then later to California in the eighteenth century by Spanish missionaries, it was generally known as the English walnut—a misnomer analogous to those used for the "Irish" potato (originally from Peru), and the "Bermuda" onion (of Asian origin).

The eastern black walnut, *J. nigra*, is native to the deciduous forests of the eastern United States and Canada. It is the largest of the native species of North America, reaching a height of up to 150 feet. It bears dark-colored, edible nuts within a thick, hard, black shell, smaller in size, more circular in outer shape and with a somewhat stronger flavor than that of the Persian walnut. Its high-quality wood has long been prized for furniture, cabinet making and gunstocks. Black walnut is, in fact, the most valuable hardwood in the United States. Fantastic prices have been paid for black walnut trees, up to $30,000 for a

Juglans regia L. Arrë

SHQIPERIA 20q

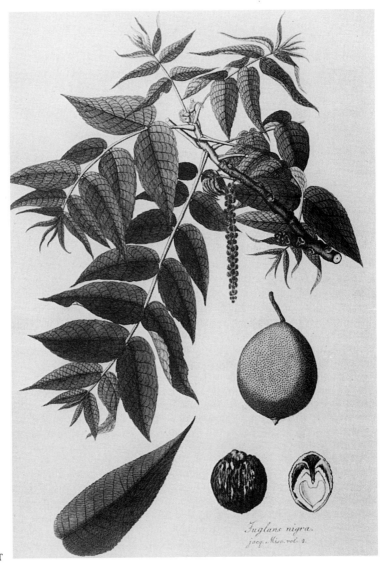

Juglans nigra.
jacq. Misc. vol. 2.

BLACK WALNUT

single tree with an especially long, clear bole! Black walnut wood for rifle stocks became a strategic material early in this century. Kaiser Wilhelm II is reported to have purchased large quantities of it to stockpile for the German infantry, several years before the outbreak of World War I.

There is a brisk demand for black walnuts—especially during the Thanksgiving and Christmas holidays—for use in candies, cakes and ice cream. The nuts are scarce and expensive—the average wholesale price in 1982 was about $3.25 per pound, compared to $2.40 for Persian walnuts.

Juglans nigra. BLACK WALNUTS.

Approximately ninety-nine per cent of the eastern black walnut crop comes from wild tree plantings in Missouri, Kentucky, Tennessee, Arkansas and West Virginia. There is also a limited production of California black walnuts (*J. hindsii*). A black walnut shelling industry is located mainly in Missouri and Arkansas. It is not feasible to harvest the wild black walnut crop mechanically. Yields are low, and the shell-out percentage of kernels is very low indeed, only about eight per cent. Thus, despite their distinctive, delicious flavor, economic factors up to the present time have prevented black walnuts from being as profitable a nut crop as California Persian walnuts, almonds and pistachios. There are a few small, commercial black walnut farms in Missouri and Indiana. Research is being carried out in Missouri by the Hammons Products Company and the University of Missouri, to develop plantings of selected varieties of black walnut on a commercial basis. The annual black walnut crop in the United States is small—about 20,000 tons in shell, as compared to over 200,000 tons for California Persian walnuts.

In addition to the eastern black walnut, there are five other walnut species native to North America: the butternut or white walnut, *J. cinerea*, of the eastern United States; the northern California black walnut, *J. hindsii*, mentioned above, which is of importance mainly as a vigorous, disease-resistant rootstock widely utilized in California for grafting selected cultivars of the Persian walnut; and three other minor species, *J. microcarpa*, *J. major* and *J. californica*, whose very small nuts are prized for the most part by wildlife. Foreign walnuts worthy of mention include *J. ailanthifolia* var. cordiformis, the "heartnut" of Japan, which produces heart-shaped edible nuts; the Manchurian walnut, *J. mandshurica*, a handsome ornamental tree, and the Andean walnut, *J. neotropica*. The walnut family (Juglandaceae) includes other edible nuts treated elsewhere in this book such as the pecan, the pignut and other hickories.

The Persian walnut, *J. regia*, is a large,

246

MALE WALNUT FLOWERS

The yellow catkins, usually 4 to 6 inches long, bear numerous staminate flowers; when the catkins turn black, they shed as many as 2 million pollen grains per catkin.

shapely, round-headed, deciduous tree which under favorable conditions grows to a height of about 100 feet. It has a clear, straight trunk and silvery-gray bark. The feathery leaves are six to twelve inches long, divided into leaflets three to six inches in length. Male and female flowers are borne separately on the same tree. The male flowers, borne on pale-yellow catkins, may not open at the same time as the female flowers which can prove to

FEMALE WALNUT FLOWERS

The rather inconspicuous pistillate flowers are shown in a receptive stage.

Juglans regia.
THE PERSIAN WALNUT.

be a drawback in isolated trees, since the female flowers may receive no pollen, the ovules will not be fertilized and thus no nuts will form. When other walnut trees are in the vicinity, fertilization takes place readily; different varieties and species of walnut hybridize freely. The fruits are ovoid, green, leathery, aromatic and occur in groups of one to three. The hull encloses the familiar, tan-colored walnut; the smooth, large nuts of the Persian walnut separate readily from the hulls at maturity. In the cultivated varieties, the shells are thin and easily broken. The kernel consists of two identical lobes, united at the apex; the ivory-colored nut meat is protected by a thin, light-brown testa. The hulls fall away from the shells more readily in the Persian walnut than in the black walnut. The kernel of the Persian walnut is likewise easier to withdraw from the shell intact than that of the black walnut, which has a thicker endocarp. The inner shell of the black walnut is harder to crack without damaging the kernels, so black walnuts are generally sold already shelled.

In California, Persian walnuts were first grown in the eighteenth century by Franciscan fathers in the early Spanish missions. These so-called "mission walnuts" were small and hard-shelled. The trees flourished, however, and soon nut production was up to the standards of the Mediterranean region, which was not surprising since the climates were quite similar. For satisfactory nut production, Persian walnuts require deep, well-drained, fertile soils.

A further distinction should be drawn regarding commercial walnut growing throughout the world, because two distinct types exist. In countries such as Turkey and Greece, there is no specialized walnut acreage and production originates from trees in scattered plantings. Under such conditions, most of the crop is consumed by the farmers themselves or is sold in local markets. By contrast, walnut growing in the United States (California), Italy (Piedmont region and the area near Naples) and France (the Bordeaux and Grenoble regions) is systematically organized in orchards. Production is fully commercialized and a portion enters world markets.

A recent survey of world walnut production is shown by country in the following table. The totals include both informal and formal production:

WALNUT PRODUCTION 1979
(metric tons, in-shell weight)

United States	185,972
Turkey	135,000
China	118,000
Soviet Union	55,000
Greece	52,500
Italy	49,000
France	41,500
Romania	41,000
All Others	174,842
WORLD	852,814

SOURCE: *FAO Production Yearbook 1979.*

For many years, the United States has been the leading world producer. California accounts for nealy 100 per cent of the United States total. The outlook for the 1980's is for California's walnut crops to exceed regularly 200,000 tons—and possibly to reach 250,000 tons per year. At the present time, there are over 200,000 acres planted with walnuts in California. Oregon has a smaller production, but orchards in that state suffered from a severe hurricane in 1962 and a damaging early freeze in 1972.

Modern commercial Persian walnut orchards are the result of a long and painstaking history of improvements in its culture, especially with regard to propagation. Many years ago, the trees were grown from seed, and some gradual betterment of quality and yields was achieved through the planting of selected seed from superior trees. Due to cross-pollination, however, seed propagation was not an effective method of crop improvement.

The French are credited with initiating modern, improved cultivation techniques in the eighteenth century through the development of new walnut varieties that were vegetatively propagated. Some French cultivars, such as the Franquette, date back over 200 years. During the past century, more and more selected cultivars of Persian walnuts have been propagated asexually, instead of by seed. Since walnut cuttings do not root well, it was necessary to resort to budding or grafting of scion wood chosen from superior trees. Within respective walnut-growing areas, it has been possible to develop new varieties especially suited to local conditions of climate and soils.

California walnut production is primarily concentrated in the San Joaquin and Sacramento Valleys. Only a few commercial walnut orchards remain in southern California, which at one time was the state's most important area of production. Development of modern walnut orchards in California commenced in the 1870's from seeds planted near Santa Barbara by Joseph Sexton, from which the Placentia variety originated. Several superior French varieties, including Franquette and Mayette were imported from France and planted in central and northern California a few years later by Felix Gillet. Current improved cultivars are descendents of these imported French varieties.

About 1936, the center of walnut production in California gradually shifted northward toward Stockton—the geographic center of the walnut producing areas—about seventy-five miles east of San Francisco. The major share of California walnut production is handled at the present time by Diamond Walnut Growers, Inc., the world's largest walnut processor—a federated Cooperative which markets its products through the Sun Diamond Growers of California. This cooperative has a membership of about 2,600 grower-members.

Hartley has become the most extensively planted walnut variety in California, especially suitable for the in-shell trade. Most walnuts

HARVESTING WALNUTS IN CALIFORNIA WITH BAMBOO POLES IN 1915
It took many hours of back-breaking work to gather a few sacks of walnuts.

in the growing foreign market are sold in-shell. The domestic market in the United States, however, shows an increasing preference for packaged walnut kernels. Important in-shell varieties, in addition to Hartley, include Serr, Franquette, Eureka, Payne, Ashley and Vina, which combine high kernel yield and superior quality. A well-filled walnut shell yields a higher kernel percentage, but the kernel should not be so tight in the shell that it is hard to extract and would tend to break in the cracking machine. So a superior walnut should be well filled, but have adequate space between shell and kernel.

Considerable experimental work was required to find an appropriate rootstock. Success was achieved with the northern California black walnut, *J. hindsii*, which gave good growth and was resistant to oak root fungus, although somewhat susceptible to crown rot. Recently, another desirable rootstock has been developed known as the Paradox hy-

brid, the result of natural hybridization between the northern California black walnut and some Persian walnut trees which were being grown in close proximity.

Budding and grafting of Persian walnut scions onto other rootstock is done either in the nursery, or the rootstock is transplanted into the field; then, when it is two to four years old, it is cut back and the scion wood is grafted onto the rootstock trunk.

A significant amount of breeding to improve walnuts has been carried out in California, and more than one hundred named varieties have been grown in the state. The University of California at Davis has been carrying on a breeding program since 1948 and continues to release new varieties, from time to time, after they have been thoroughly tested. In California, all orchards are now planted with named varieties.

Mature walnut trees require a spacing of at least 50 feet in each direction to obtain maximum yields. Most recent plantings in California are 30 feet by 30 feet, or closer. The trees are gradually thinned to a wider spacing as they develop to maturity. Depending upon the variety grown, harvestable crops are produced at age five to eight years; therefore, when closer planting is employed, the walnut grower may obtain five to six years of production from the excess trees before their removal. Cover crops may be grown in the orchards and plowed under in the spring to improve the condition of the soil. Young trees are trained to form five or six main scaffold branches and thereafter are pruned by thinning out and removing weak and crowded branches. Other cultural practices involve weed control, fertilizer application and replacement of dead trees to maintain fields at their maximum density. In most areas in California, walnuts are grown under irrigation. It is difficult to obtain accurate information on the useful life of walnut orchards. Some reports mention trees 50, 75 or even 100 years old which continue to bear good crops.

Persian walnuts are mature when the hull can easily be separated from the shell. Normally, the hull opens while still attached to the tree, and the nut falls to the ground. But wind may bring down the hull and nut together. In California, the walnut harvesting season extends from early September to late November; exact dates vary in relationship to the variety grown and the local climatic conditions. Areas beneath the trees must be kept clear to facilitate the nut harvest.

Harvesting commences when about eighty per cent of the nuts can be removed from the trees; it may all be done at one time, or over a period of several days. Mechanical or hand shaking of the branches speeds the nut fall. Mechanical shaking has largely replaced hand shaking; a one-man-operated tree shaker is used by a skilled operator who must be careful not to bruise or injure the trees, or their roots. Most walnuts are harvested mechanically because of high labor costs. Nuts are mechanically windrowed and collected by a mechanical picker which separates out leaves and trash. Since all the nuts have not separated naturally from their hulls, the harvested crop is a mixture of hulled and unhulled walnuts. Machines hull and wash the walnuts brought in from the orchards. To prevent deterioration, the walnuts must be thoroughly dried as soon as possible by mechanical dehydrators—a notable improvement over the traditional sun-drying methods carried out years ago.

Data on yields of walnuts per acre are not widely available, in part because of the informal cultivation practices of many producing countries. National world statistics sel-

THE PERSIAN WALNUT IS READY FOR HARVEST WHEN THE HULL SEPARATES FROM THE SHELL

WINDROWING WALNUTS

A sweep machine clears the nuts away from the trees as it forms windrows.

dom include the areas cultivated as part of the published data, providing only production figures. In California, many orchards produce two to three tons per acre, but the average is approximately one ton per acre. Considerable variation exists from orchard to orchard throughout the state. Specialized walnut production in Italy is reportedly about one ton per acre on the average. The average yield per acre in other walnut-producing countries is undoubtedly considerably lower.

Walnut growing is not without its biological problems. More than thirty different pests and diseases affect walnuts in California alone. Pests of the nuts include the navel orange worm, whose larvae enter the nut when the hull splits and begin feeding. Chemical control is not effective, but if ripe nuts are harvested early, hulled and dried immediately, infestation can be reduced. Another pest is the coddling moth, which lays eggs on the developing nuts and the larvae feed on the kernel. Approved pesticides are effective if sprayed at the peak of moth flight activity.

Spider mites and the walnut aphid feed on the leaves. Introduction of the wasp parasite, *Trioxys pallidus*, has proved to be an effective aphid control.

Another serious threat to walnut plantings in California is "blackline" disease, a fatal ailment caused by cherry leaf roll virus which is spread by contaminated walnut pollen grains. In infected trees, a black line appears at the point of the graft union around the trunk; the trees are then removed to reduce further spread. Efforts are being made to develop resistant varieties.

Several bacterial diseases also affect walnuts. Walnut blight attacks flowers and developing nuts and is controlled with copper sprays. Walnut canker disease attacks the cambium layer of the tree, between the bark and the heartwood. Crown gall is a bacterial disease affecting the roots; greater care in planting and cultivation can prevent the cuts and abrasions which allow the bacterium to enter.

Following the harvest, walnuts in

252

WALNUT SAMPLING

At a Research Laboratory in California, in-the-shell walnuts undergo a continuous sampling during the packing operation to be sure that all quality specifications are met.

California are dried to a moisture content of eight per cent maximum to prevent darkening of the kernels, retard mold development and permit efficient shell bleaching. They are separated into three categories, depending on how they will be marketed: in the shell, as kernels, or as by-products.

The cooperative walnut growers are paid a special premium for those walnuts suited for in-shell package sales. In-shell walnuts are placed in steel tanks and fumigated with methyl bromide gas for about four hours to destroy any insects which may be present. Sorting is followed by bleaching, which is accomplished by washing the walnuts for two to three minutes in a dilute sodium hypochlorite solution, similar to a weak household bleach. This is not harmful, since the weak bleach solution does not penetrate the shell. The walnuts are rinsed and rubbed to obtain a uniform tan color. After bleaching, the nuts are dried and sampled to determine their quality. The walnuts are then ready for bulk shipment to retail outlets, or to be packaged into four size specifications: Jumbo, Large, Medium and Baby. Each size is automatically packaged in clear, one-and two-pound film bags. "Culls" are walnuts that are shelled because of defects that exclude them from in-shell packaging. About thirty per cent of California's walnut crop is sold in-shell.

The remaining seventy per cent of the crop—known as "cracking stock"—is shelled. The cracking stock is first graded and separated into six sizes to obtain the highest possible percentage of unbroken kernels. After cracking, the kernels are conveyed to air-separators to remove shell and fiber material, then sorted by electronic, color-sorting machines which separate dark walnuts from light. The shells and fiber material are sent to the oil mill. The shelled walnuts are packaged in vacuum cans, clear, film bags of various sizes, or bulk cartons.

To preserve freshness in the clear, film bags, the walnut kernels are treated with an

WALNUTS PASS THROUGH DRUM GRADERS

They are mechanically sorted into jumbo, large, medium and baby sizes at the Sun-Diamond processing plant in Stockton, California.

WALNUT CRACKING MACHINE

About 30 per cent of the annual California walnut crop at Sun-Diamond is sold in the shell. The remaining 70 per cent is machine cracked to produce shelled walnuts. The giant walnut crackers delicately crack the shells without damaging the tender kernels inside.

254

antioxidant, approved by the United States Food and Drug Administration, which is odorless, colorless and tasteless. It takes about two and one-half pounds of walnuts to obtain one pound of kernels.

Shelled walnuts are ordered in large quantities by commercial producers of food products. The Diamond Walnut Growers produce well over a hundred special cuts and combinations of shelled walnut kernels, in different color grades, for various commercial clients such as bakeries, candy companies, and producers of ice creams, frozen foods, packaged cake and cookie mixes and others.

The shelling operation does not remove all of the kernel from the shell. The remaining small kernel particles are recovered by a wet separation process and mechanical grinding device, and either go into bulk packaging for commercial use or are combined with other oil-bearing materials and selected plant residue to be reduced to a mash for pressing. This mash is subjected to tremendous pressure to extract the walnut oil; a cake is formed of the remaining material. The walnut oil is filtered and utilized in the paint industry. The cake, left over after the extraction of the oil, is reduced to a meal, valuable for dairy feed.

As the largest producer of walnuts, the United States has also become the leading supplier to a growing world market. About ninety per cent of the exports are in-shell, and the balance in the form of shelled nuts. Between August 1, 1979, to July 31, 1980, exports totalled 34,569 and 3,878 metric tons, respectively. West Germany and Spain imported most of the in-shell nuts, while the largest buyers of shelled walnuts were West Germany, the United Kingdom, Australia, Spain, the Netherlands, Israel and Japan.

In-shell walnut prices were $819 per short ton, in 1979, giving a value to the United States crop of about 170 million dollars. During the holiday season of 1981, in-shell walnuts sold at a retail price of approximately $1.80 per pound, roughly the same price as almonds, Brazil nuts and filberts.

Although the United States is the world's leading walnut producer, at least two gourmet items apparently are not produced domestically on a commercial scale. Walnut oil for salads and cooking is imported from France and retails for 60 cents per fluid ounce. Pickled green walnuts are an imported British product sold at $4.75 per 10-ounce jar. Both are small volume, specialty items not easily found in retail stores.

Major improvements in plant breeding, vegetative propagation and cultivation practices have been made. Research is continuing in these areas and further progress can be expected. Breeding efforts will be facilitated by the gene pool represented by the numerous species of *Juglans*. Many of the cultivation and harvesting techniques which have been mechanized in California could be applied in other major areas of production. United States exports of walnuts are showing signifi-

WALNUT PROCESSING IN CALIFORNIA

In-the-shell walnuts are inspected on a moving conveyor belt.

In many countries of the world, walnut cultivation and processing are performed by hand labor, as in the past.

cant increases, but this country can expect greater competition in the future from China and India, where the walnut industry is being expanded.

The considerable volume of shells created by the shelling of walnuts is utilized in a variety of products. It is used as a filler for exterior plywood glue, plastics, hard rubber products, asphalt roofing material, fire brick, tiles, and stuffing in toys. Shells are converted into dust for insecticides and are used as an abrasive for cleaning jet aircraft engines. A non-polluting, cogeneration system has recently been developed for processing plants to make use of energy derived from burning walnut shells which, in turn, produces steam that drives a turbine to generate electricity.

Nutritional studies have pointed out that walnuts are rich in food value. Along with the macadamia and pecan, the Persian walnut belongs to the group of nuts that are considered high in fat content. They provide energy, essential vitamins and minerals and due to their fat content, satisfy the appetite. The walnut contains a high proportion of unsaturated fatty acids, a factor which many believe to be important in certain types of diets. Although research on this controversial subject is incomplete, it has been found that dietary sources of unsaturated fats may help reduce blood cholesterol levels.

From the standpoint of calories, walnuts are neither among the lowest nor the highest of energy-producing foods. Eight to fifteen walnut halves, depending on the size of the kernels, contain 98 calories. United States Department of Agriculture Bulletin No. 302 reports that walnuts are a good source of iron and Vitamin B, also rich in phosphorous.

Walnuts are said to be the American homemaker's favorite ingredient nut—their most popular use being in cookies, but consumed as well in cakes, pies, sugar- and honey-sweetened confections, fruitcakes and combinations including chocolate. Their crunchy texture combines well with many other foods. Baklava, a popular dessert of Mediterranean origin, combines walnuts and honey. Shelled walnuts, served plain or toasted, make tempting between-meal snacks, and may be served with cocktails.

Currently, health-conscious people are including more natural foods, such as walnuts, in their diets. "Hiker's Hash," for example, combines diced dried fruits, coconut, sesame and sunflower seeds, and toasted walnuts.

HORS D'OEUVRES AND CANAPES

Mushrooms Stuffed with Butter and Walnuts (XXXVIII)

32 fresh whole mushrooms, veils unbroken	1/2 clove garlic, peeled and chopped or crushed
1/2 cup (125 ml) butter	2-1/2 tablespoons (40 ml) chopped fresh parsley
2 tablespoons (30 ml) chopped walnuts	
4 green onions, finely chopped	Salt and pepper to taste

Wash and dry mushrooms: remove stems. Lay caps upside down in well-buttered baking dish. In small skillet melt 2 tablespoons (30 ml) butter: add mushroom stems and sauté lightly. In small bowl combine stems, remaining butter, walnuts, onion, garlic, parsley, salt and pepper; mix thoroughly. Fill each cap with a rounded teaspoon (5 ml) of butter mixture. Heat broiler. Broil mushrooms for 3 to 5 minutes until bubbly. Serve immediately.

Yield: 32 mushrooms

SOUP

Cucumber Soup with Walnuts (XXXVIII)

1 clove garlic, peeled	1 tablespoon (15 ml) lemon juice
1/2 teaspoon (2.5 ml) salt	Freshly ground black pepper
2 tablespoons (30 ml) olive oil	1/2 cup (125 ml) chopped walnuts
2 cups (500 ml) plain yogurt	Ice water
1 cup (250 ml) seeded, finely chopped, cucumber (1 medium)	Minced fresh parsley
	1 cup (250 ml) finely cracked ice

Crush garlic with salt in a 2-quart (2-liter) bowl. Add olive oil and blend. Add yogurt and stir until smooth. Add cucumber, lemon juice, pepper to taste and nuts. Blend. Stir in enough ice water to make 4 to 5 cups (1 to 1-1/4 liter) soup. Divide among 6 soup bowls. Sprinkle with minced parsley. Add a little cracked ice to each just before serving.

Yield: 6 servings

MAIN COURSE

Chicken with Walnuts (XXXIX)

1 teaspoon (5 ml) salt	3 tablespoons (45 ml) peanut oil
1 teaspoon (5 ml) sugar	
1/2 teaspoon (2.5 ml) ground ginger	1 cup (250 ml) walnuts
3 tablespoons (45 ml) soy sauce	1 can (8 ounces/240 grams) bamboo shoots, drained
2 cloves garlic, peeled and minced	1 tablespoon (15 ml) cornstarch
2 large chicken breasts, boned, skinned and cut into bitesized pieces	1 cup (250 ml) water
	Hot cooked rice

Combine salt, sugar, ginger, soy sauce and garlic in a bowl. Mix in chicken. Let stand 20 minutes, stirring occasionally.

Heat oil in a stainless steel skillet over high heat. Add walnuts. Stir-fry 1 minute. Remove walnuts from skillet with slotted spoon: set aside.

257

Add marinated chicken mixture to the hot oil in skillet. Cook 5 minutes, stirring constantly. Mix in bamboo shoots. Blend cornstarch and water; add to skillet. Cook, stirring until sauce is thickened and clear. Stir in prepared walnuts. Serve with rice.

Yield: 3 or 4 servings

Calcutta Turkey Salad (XXXVIII)

2 cups (500 ml) cooked, diced turkey	1/2 cup (125 ml) blue cheese dressing
One 11-ounce (330-g) can mandarin orange segments, drained (1-1/3 cups/325 ml)	1 teaspoon (5 ml) curry powder Lettuce Shredded coconut
1/2 cup (125 ml) diced green pepper	Chopped walnuts Crisply cooked bacon, crumbled
1/2 cup (125 ml) sliced celery	Chopped, hard-cooked eggs

Combine first 6 ingredients, toss lightly. Chill. Serve in lettuce-lined salad bowl. Surround with bowls of coconut, walnuts, bacon and chopped egg for guests to make their own additions.

Yield: 4 to 6 servings

VEGETABLE

Fan Tan Potatoes with Walnuts (XXXIX)

6 medium baking potatoes	2/3 cup (150 ml) walnuts
Cold water	1/2 cup (125 ml) freshly grated Parmesan cheese
6 tablespoons (90 ml) margarine, melted	

Peel potatoes and place in cold water. Place one potato at a time on a wooden spoon large enough to cradle it. Slice down at 1/8-inch (3-mm) intervals across the potato. (The curved bowl of the spoon will prevent the knife from slicing completely through the potato.) Return potatoes to cold water.

When ready to roast, dry potatoes and place them in a 9-inch (23-cm) square baking

dish. Brush with 2 tablespoons (30 ml) margarine. Bake at 425° F (220° C) for 1 hour, brushing with an additional 2 tablespoons (30 ml) margarine after 30 minutes.

Chop walnuts and combine with remaining 2 tablespoons (30 ml) margarine. Mix in Parmesan cheese. Spoon mixture onto roasted potatoes. Return potatoes to oven and bake until cheese melts, about 5 minutes.

Yield: 6 servings

Kataife (XXXVII)

12 shredded wheat biscuits	3/4 cup (175 ml) melted butter
2 cups (500 ml) chopped walnuts	2 cups (500 ml) honey syrup (see below)
1-1/2 teaspoons (7.5 ml) cinnamon	

Split shredded wheat biscuits and line a greased baking pan with the bottom halves. Mix nut meats and cinnamon, and sprinkle half of the mixture over the shredded wheat. Pour 1 tablespoon (15 ml) of butter on each. Place top half of shredded wheat biscuits on the bottom half and sprinkle the remainder of the nut-cinnamon mixture over each top. Pour butter on each and bake at 300° F (150° C) for 45 minutes. While still hot from the oven, pour the honey syrup slowly over the tops until all has been absorbed. Cool and separate each shredded wheat biscuit.

Syrup

2 cups (500 ml) sugar	2 cups (500 ml) water
1 cup (250 ml) honey	Juice of 1/2 lemon

Mix all ingredients and simmer 10 minutes.

Yield: 12 servings

Dried Apple Black Walnut Pudding (XXXVII)

1 cup (250 ml) dried apples
1 cup (250 ml) dark molasses
1 teaspoon (5 ml) cinnamon
1/2 teaspoon (2.5 ml) ground cloves
3 tablespoons (45 ml) butter
1 egg, well beaten
1-1/4 cups (310 ml) flour
1 teaspoon (5 ml) baking soda
1/2 cup (125 ml) chopped black walnuts

Soak apples overnight in enough water to cover. Cut apples in bite size pieces when softened. In large saucepan add chopped apples, molasses, spices and whatever moisture is left from soaking apples. Place over medium heat and bring to a boil. Add butter and mix thoroughly. Remove from heat and add beaten egg and flour mixed with soda. Add walnuts. Pour mixture into buttered baking dish. Bake at 325° F (165° C) for 45 minutes. Serve warm with a rum pudding sauce.

Yield: 4-6 servings

BAKED GOODS

Chocolate Nut Wafers (XXXVIII)

1 cup (250 ml) sugar
3/4 cup (175 ml) butter or margarine
2 squares (2 ounces/60 g) unsweetened chocolate, melted, or 2 envelopes premelted chocolate
1 teaspoon (5 ml) vanilla
1 egg
2-1/4 cups (560 ml) all-purpose or unbleached flour
1/4 teaspoon (1 ml) soda
1/4 teaspoon (1 ml) salt
1/4 teaspoon (1 ml) cinnamon
1/2 cup (125 ml) chopped walnuts

In large bowl, combine first 5 ingredients; blend well. Stir in flour, soda, salt, cinnamon and nuts. Divide dough in half; place each half on waxed paper and shape into a roll 2 inches (5 cm) in diameter. Wrap and chill 3 to 4 hours until firm. Heat oven to 400 ° F (200° C). Cut dough into 1/8-inch slices. Place 1 inch apart on ungreased cookie sheets. Bake 6 to 8 minutes until lightly browned; do not overbake.

Yield: 5 to 6 dozen cookies

Walnut Linzer Balls (XL)

1-1/2 cups (375 ml) walnuts
1/2 cup (125 ml) butter
1/2 cup (125 ml) granulated sugar
1 egg, separated
3/4 teaspoon (4 ml) grated lemon peel
1 cup (250 ml) sifted all-purpose flour
1/4 teaspoon (1 ml) salt
1/4 teaspoon (1 ml) cinnamon
1/8 teaspoon (dash) cloves
1/2 cup (125 ml) apricot or seedless raspberry jam

Grate one cup (250 ml) walnuts, using a Mouli grater, or put 1/4 cup (60 ml) at a time into blender and blend very fine. Chop remaining 1/2 cup (125 ml) walnuts fine. Cream butter, sugar, egg yolk and lemon peel together. Resift flour with salt and spices. Blend into creamed mixture, add grated walnuts and mix well. Chill dough 1/2 hour or longer, for easier handling. Shape into small balls. Beat egg white lightly. Dip balls in egg white, then roll in chopped walnuts. Place on greased baking sheet and make an indentation in top of each. Fill with jam. Bake at 350° F (175° C) about 18 minutes. Remove to wire racks to cool.

Yield: About 3 dozen balls

Walnut Marmalade Bread (XL)

2 cups (500 ml) sifted all-purpose flour
2-1/2 teaspoons (12.5 ml) baking powder
1/2 teaspoon (2.5 ml) baking soda
1-1/2 teaspoons (7.5 ml) salt
1/2 teaspoon (2.5 ml) nutmeg
1 cup (250 ml) stirred whole wheat flour
1 tablespoon (15 ml) cooking oil
1/4 cup (60 ml) granulated sugar
1 large egg
3/4 cup (175 ml) orange marmalade
1 cup (250 ml) orange juice
1 cup (250 ml) chopped walnuts
1/2 cup (125 ml) flaked coconut

In a large bowl, resift all-purpose flour with baking powder, soda, salt and nutmeg. Stir in whole wheat flour. In a separate bowl, beat together well the oil, sugar and egg. Blend in marmalade and orange juice; add all at once to dry mixture, along with walnuts and coconut, mixing just until flour is moistened. Turn into a well-greased 9 × 5-inch (23 × 12.5-cm) loaf pan. Bake below oven center at 350° F (175° C) for 65 to 70 minutes, until loaf tests done. Let stand 10 minutes; turn out onto a wire rack to cool completely.

Yield: 1 loaf

Shape variations
9-inch (23-cm) tube pan: Bake at 350° F (180° C) about 45 minutes.

3-inch (7.5-cm) muffins: Divide batter among 12 muffin cups; bake at 400° F (200° C) about 20 minutes. Turn out immediately.

6 × 3-inch (15 × 7.5-cm) loaf pans: Divide batter among 3 pans and bake at 350° F (175° C) for about 40 to 45 minutes.

Raspberry Walnut Torte (XXXVIII)

Torte

1 cup (250 ml) all-purpose or unbleached flour	3/4 cup (175 ml) chopped walnuts
1/3 cup (75 ml) powdered sugar	1 cup (250 ml) sugar
1/3 cup (75 ml) butter or margarine, softened	1/4 cup (60 ml) flour
	1/2 teaspoon (2.5 ml) baking powder
	1/4 teaspoon (2.5 ml) salt
2 packages (10 oz/300 g each) frozen raspberries, thawed	1 teaspoon (5 ml) vanilla
	2 eggs

Raspberry Sauce

1/2 cup (125 ml) sugar	1/2 cup (125 ml) water
2 tablespoons (30 ml) cornstarch	1 tablespoon (15 ml) lemon juice
1 cup (250 ml) reserved raspberry syrup	

Heat oven to 350° F (175° C). In small bowl, combine first three torte ingredients; blend well. Press into bottom of ungreased 8- or 9-inch (20- or 23-cm) square pan. Bake for 15 minutes. Cool.

Drain raspberries, reserve liquid for sauce. Spread berries over crust; sprinkle with walnuts. In bowl, combine remaining torte ingredients; mix at low speed until well blended. Pour over walnuts. Bake at 350° F (175° C) for 35 to 40 minutes, until golden brown. Cool, cut into squares. Serve with whipped cream and Raspberry Sauce.

Raspberry Sauce

In small saucepan, combine all ingredients except lemon juice. Cook, stirring constantly, until mixture thickens and comes to a boil. Stir in lemon juice. Cool.

Yield: 9 servings

Speedy Lady Baltimore Cake (XL)

1 package (18-1/2-ounce/555 g) white cake mix	1 teaspoon (5 ml) vanilla

Speedy Lady Baltimore Frosting

1/3 cup (75 ml) *each* chopped raisins and dates	1/2 teaspoon (2.5 ml) vanilla
2/3 cup (150 ml) finely chopped walnuts	1/4 teaspoon (1 ml) lemon flavoring
2 tablespoons (30 ml) brandy or orange juice	Walnut halves for decorating
2 packages (7.2 ounces/216 g each) fluffy white frosting mix, divided	

Prepare white cake mix as package directs, adding 1 teaspoon (5 ml) vanilla. Pour batter into 3 greased and floured, 8-inch (20-cm) layer cake pans. Bake at 350° F (175° C) for 20 minutes. Cool layers on wire racks. Put together with Speedy Lady Baltimore Frosting.

Speedy Lady Baltimore Frosting: Combine raisins, dates, walnuts and brandy and let soak. Mix frosting as package directs; add vanilla and lemon flavoring. Add fruit-walnut mixture to 1/3 of the frosting; leave remaining plain. Put layers together with the fruited Speedy Lady Baltimore Frosting. Spread plain frosting over sides and top of cake. Decorate with walnut halves.

Yield: 10 to 12 servings

LADY BALTIMORE CAKE

Walnut Pumpkin Chiffon Pie (XI)

1-1/2 cups (375 ml) finely chopped or ground walnuts
3 tablespoons (45 ml) granulated sugar
2 tablespoons (30 ml) soft butter
1 envelope unflavored gelatin
1/4 cup (60 ml) cold water
3 eggs, separated
1/2 cup (125 ml) milk
3/4 cup (175 ml) brown sugar, packed
1/2 teaspoon (2.5 ml) salt
1-1/2 teaspoons (7.5 ml) pumpkin pie spice
1 cup (250 ml) canned pumpkin
1/4 teaspoon (1 ml) cream of tartar
1/3 cup (75 ml) granulated sugar
Whipped cream
California walnut halves and large pieces for decorating.

Combine chopped or ground walnuts with 3 tablespoons (45 ml) sugar and butter. Pat over bottom and sides of a 9-inch (23-cm) pie pan to form crust. Bake at 350° F (175° C) 10 to 12 minutes, until lightly browned. Cool, then chill. Soften gelatin in water. Beat egg yolks with milk; beat in brown sugar, salt and spice. Add gelatin and pumpkin. Cook and stir over moderate heat (or in top of double boiler over hot water) until filling thickens and gelatin dissolves, about 10 minutes. Remove from heat and cool. When mixture begins to gel, beat egg whites to soft peaks with cream of tartar. Gradually beat in the 1/3 cup (75 ml) sugar to make meringue. Fold into pumpkin mixture and turn into baked, chilled walnut crust. Chill 3 or 4 hours or longer, until firm. Decorate with additional whipped cream and walnuts.

Yield: 6 servings

CANDY AND CONFECTIONS

Walnut Creams (XXXVII)

1-1/2 cups (375 ml) granulated sugar
1-1/2 cups (375 ml) brown sugar
1/8 teaspoon (dash) salt
1 cup (250 ml) milk
4 tablespoons (60 ml) butter
1 cup (250 ml) walnuts, chopped
1 teaspoon (5 ml) vanilla
1/2 teaspoon (2.5 ml) almond extract

Put the sugar, salt and milk in a saucepan and stir until the sugar is dissolved. Boil until soft ball, 238° F (115° C). Add the butter. Let stand until lukewarm and then beat vigorously. When it begins to get creamy, add the walnuts, vanilla and almond extract. Pour into a greased pan. Cool.

Yield: about 40 creams

262

Thirty Other Edible Nuts

Acorns

ACORNS were an important food for prehistoric man before formal crops began to be cultivated, when he depended on wild, edible plants for nourishment. As civilization advanced the utilization of acorns for human nutrition gradually decreased. What in early ages might have made a feast for a king is no longer in demand.

The term "acorn" refers in a general sense to the nut of any oak tree. All true oaks belong to the genus *Quercus* (Latin for "oak tree") and are placed in the beech family along with the chestnut and beechnut. The oak genus is native to the temperate regions of the Northern Hemisphere and to high altitudes in the tropics. Worldwide, more than 450 species of oak are known, some sixty of which occur in North America. Edible, sweet acorns are found in Europe, Asia and North America. *Quercus alba*, the white oak, a noble, deciduous tree of the northern United States, produces the most popular acorns. In North America nature has been bountiful: without costly planting and cultivation, the annual nut crop from oaks is larger than that of all other tree nut crops combined, despite the fact that oaks are not cultivated as a tree crop in the United States. Compared with coniferous species, oaks are too slow-growing to be an economic timber crop. Acorns are scarcely utilized commercially at the present time in this country, although they are traditionally sought after by wildlife and livestock.

The oak is mentioned frequently in the Bible. The oak in Genesis (35:4 and 8) is thought to have been the holm oak, *Quercus ilex;* other species of oak are prevalent in the mountainous regions of Syria, Lebanon and Palestine. Most modern authorities believe it was an oak on which Absalom caught his hair and was hanged. The oak has played a prominent role in religion and mythology as a symbol of strength and sturdiness. Merlin, the medieval

ACORNS AND DRAGONFLY, 1585

265

magician, carried out his enchantments under an oak. The Druids performed mystic ceremonies beneath oaks; their diet consisted mainly of acorns and berries. According to Greek mythology, oak roots extended all the way down to Hades, and Christian lore held that its branches were uplifted in prayer to heaven; it became the tree of Mary, mother of Jesus. Joan of Arc was accused of worshipping a bewitched oak.

Many Greek and Latin writers, as early as Theophrastus in the third century B.C., and including Pliny, Virgil and Ovid, referred to acorns as wholesome fare. In Pliny's day, the oak symbolized bravery and a crown of oak leaves was a glorious reward for outstanding military valor. In the United States Army today the Oak Leaf cluster is bestowed as an additional honor on those already decorated for exceptional service.

When properly prepared, acorns of most oaks are edible, although some are much more palatable than others. Acorns were the staff of life for many North American Indians, who gathered them for food to prepare their daily mush and bread. They used both sweet and bitter types. The latter were not consumed directly, but were ground and then leached or soaked in water before being eaten. The astringent characteristics of bitter acorns are caused by tannin, a substance readily soluble in water, which in most cases can be leached out to leave a sweeter, nut-flavored product. Sweet acorns, such as those from the white oak, were eaten raw or roasted, or were ground into a meal and formed into dark brown cakes for baking in crude ovens. Sometimes acorn meal was mixed with corn meal to make biscuits, or to thicken venison stew. Fresh nuts were boiled

WHITE OAK (*Quercus alba*)

266

ACORNS (*Quercus alba*)

to obtain acorn oil for cooking, or for use as a liniment; the boiling process yielded an oil that was skimmed off. In the autumn, the Indians gathered large quantities of acorns and spread them in the sun to dry before storing them for winter food. Some tribes built thatched, cone-shaped granaries for storage, several feet wide at the base and raised off the ground on platforms supported by wooden poles; others prepared holes in the ground to shelter the harvest. In either case, protected from rain and rodents, the acorns kept very well. It is said that the Indians devised their granary construction techniques from observing how squirrels hoarded their nuts. In December 1620, the Pilgrims in Massachusetts came upon baskets of roasted acorns, hidden in the ground by Indians. The New England settlers prepared a palatable dish of boiled sweet acorns, whose flavor was supposed to compare favorably with that of the European chestnut. During the Civil War, when coffee was unavailable, a tolerable substitute beverage was obtained through roasting and cracking white oak acorns.

The oaks may be conveniently divided into white oak (*Quercus alba*) and black oak (*Q. velutina*) groups. Species of the white oaks are the most widely distributed and best known, ranging all around the Northern Hemisphere. These majestic trees reach heights of 80 to 120 feet, with sturdy trunks three to five feet in diameter, stout, wide-spreading branches, and stately, rounded crowns. Their bark is light gray, rough and often deeply furrowed, while the black oak bark is usually blackish. The light brown, oblong-ovoid acorns of the white oak, with their familiar, bowl-like cup, are about three-fourths of an inch long; they mature in one year, fall to the ground and germinate soon thereafter. The white oak leaves in the East have rounded lobes without bristles, while leaves of the black oak group possess bristles or pin-point tips. In general, white oak acorns are sweeter than those of the black oak group, whose very bitter acorns contain more tannin. The white oak grows slowly and may attain an age of 500 years or more. Yields of acorns vary with region and site; annual production may vary from a few pounds to several hundred pounds per tree. The state tree of Maryland, the white oak, is generally considered to be the most valuable hardwood species in the

United States; the wood is strong, durable, light brown in color and an excellent timber for furniture, flooring and cooperage. White oak barrels are universally employed for aging whiskey and rum. In the early history of America oak wood played an important role—it was utilized to construct block houses, forts, cabins, bridges, tools and countless necessities of daily living.

The high nutritional value of acorns makes them an excellent animal feed, especially for hogs, which are often turned loose to devour the nuts from beneath the trees. Frontier farmers in America took advantage of this food resource, and the practice has persisted in some southern states. Hogs which eat mostly acorns produce a softer, less-desirable flesh than that of corn-fed animals. The meat of the former is not acceptable for sale to consumers. Thus if acorn meal is utilized to feed livestock, it should form only a portion of their total rations. Both sweet and bitter acorns are suitable for feed, since animals can tolerate limited amounts of tannin present in the bitter types. Some cautions must be used since an excessive diet of bitter acorns might lead to livestock poisoning.

As a producer of forage, the oak genus has received more attention in many European countries than in the United States. The best known European acorns are produced by the evergreen oak, *Quercus ilex*, which occurs in southern Europe and North Africa. In Spain and Portugal, selected varieties of this oak produce edible acorns quite similar to chestnuts in food value and taste. Like the chestnut, the acorns are starchy—not rich, oily nuts such as the walnut and pecan. Cervantes mentions these fine acorns, known as "bellotas," in *Don Quixote*. Extensive stands of bellota oak occur in Spain and Portugal, intermixed with the cork oak, *Q. suber*. These valuable forests produce timber, cork and via the use of acorns in feed, pork. Single, well-developed bellota oaks are said to yield enough acorns for 100 pounds of pork. Portuguese hogs often double or triple their weight in three months, well-fattened in an orgy of

WHITE OAK
Quercus alba
USA 15c

devouring bellota acorns while lolling about in open pasturage beneath the trees. To obtain the highest production of acorns and cork, the forests are thinned from time to time. Cork bark is stripped every ten to twelve years. Very little expense is required to maintain these precious woodlands, which are looked upon as an ideal form of absentee ownership by numerous Portuguese and Spanish landowners.

The flavor of the acorn is controversial. Some consider it to be rough and disagreeable; others claim that fresh, sweet acorns, roasted and salted, provide a good snack food, tasting like a cross between sunflower seeds and popcorn. Acorns are rich in starch and nutritious. The edible portion of fresh acorns consists of: carbohydrates (50.4%); water (34.7%); fat (4.7%); protein (4.4%); crude fiber (4.2%); and ash (1.6%). A pound of acorns yields 1,265 calories.

In Great Britain, the acorns of the common English oak, *Quercus robur*, have long been an important foodstuff for livestock, but usually are too astringent for human consumption, except in times of famine. A few Asian species yield edible acorns, including *Q. cuspidata* and *Q. glabra* in Japan, and *Q. cornea* in China. For the most part, however, acorns throughout the world constitute a valuable feed for hogs, goats, and wildlife, including squirrels, raccoons, deer, wild duck, wild turkeys and other undomesticated creatures.

At present, most of the acorn crop in the

United States comes from wild seedling trees, unimproved by selection, breeding and grafting. Various federal and state forestry agencies have distributed millions of oak seedlings during recent years, but these have been planted mainly for timber, wildlife and landscaping. If acorns were to be adapted for animal feed on a larger scale, it seems likely that natural stands of oaks would be brought under technical management to increase acorn yields. This development, in turn, could lead to selection of superior, sweet acorn varieties possessing desirable charac-teristics of taste, rapid growth, precocious bearing and higher yields. There is a vast potential for improvement in the neglected acorn, similar to advancements made in the almond, Persian walnut, pecan, macadamia nut and other orchard crops, although many years of selection and plant breeding would be required to obtain notable results. Some day, in the distant future, sweet acorns and acorn meal might be restored to the American diet, as well as made available to others around the world who suffer from chronic hunger.

Almondettes

THE ALMONDETTE is an important article of commerce in central India, where it is known as "chironji" and is commonly used as a substitute for the almond. The tree bearing these nuts, *Buchanania lanzan*, belongs to the cashew family (Anacardiaceae). Native to southern Asia, and prevalent in India and Malaysia, it grows best in the deciduous forests of hot, dry regions, at elevations of up to 3,000 feet. The almondette tree is medium-sized, growing to about fifty feet in height, and bearing black, single-seeded fruits measuring

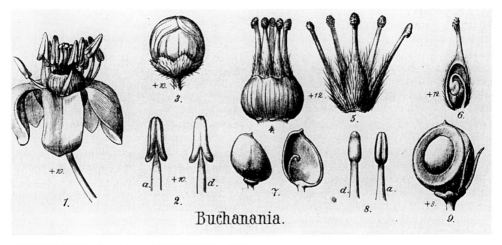

ALMONDETTE (*Buchanania lanzan*) BUCHANANIA SEED

269

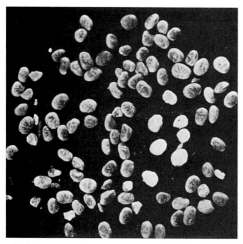

ALMONDETTES (BUCHANANIA SEEDS)

and since early times have been prized as a sweetmeat when cooked. The delicious flavor of the almondette may be compared to a combination of almond and pistachio. Virtually unknown in the United States, the almondette is quite popular in England. The dried fruits with the kernel intact are pounded, dried and baked in India to prepare a native bread. Rich in oil and protein, these nutritious nuts are composed of oil (51.8%); protein (12.1%); starch (21.6%) and sugars (5%). The light yellow, wholesome oil has a pleasant aroma and is a satisfactory substitute for either almond or olive oil.

A few other uses of the tree are reported: the bark and the fruits yield a natural varnish; the bark can be employed in tanning and the leaves as fodder; the tree itself serves the purpose of retarding erosion on steep slopes in its native habitat. Although no formal cultivation of almondette trees has been carried out up to the present time, a potential demand appears to exist for this tasty but little-known edible nut.

about one-half inch in diameter. The pear-shaped kernels, which are often mottled, are about one-quarter of an inch long.

In India the nuts are eaten raw or roasted,

Beechnuts

ANOTHER EDIBLE NUT belonging to the beech family, along with the acorn, is the American beech, *Fagus grandifolia*. The generic name Fagus is derived from the Greek word *phagein*, meaning "to eat," referring to the edible character of the nut. As a fattening feed for hogs and poultry, the history of the beechnut antedates the Christian era in Europe. Pliny and Virgil, moreover, extolled its virtues as a food for humans. The beech has been intimately associated with books and writing since early times. Before books were written, messages were indelibly scratched on the smooth, light-gray surface of the bark of the European

beech, *F. sylvatica*, or on beechen boards. The word "beech" comes from *bōece*, the Anglo-Saxon name for the tree, which eventually became *Buch* in German, and *book* in English. As a monumental tree, the beech has no rival: for many centuries its bark has served as a convenient place to register challenges to the enemy, epitaphs, and most frequently the initials of loved ones.

American beech trees are native to the eastern half of the United States, the same range as the white oak. But in contrast to the many species of oak, North America has only a single species of beech. In addition to the

270

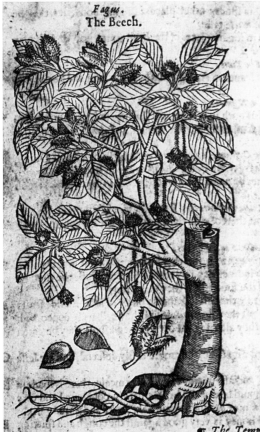

Fagus.
The Beech.

¶ *The Names.*

The tree is called in Greeke, ὀξύα: in Latine, *Fagus* : in high Dutch,**Buchbaum**,or
Buch:in low Dutch,**Bukenboom** : in Italian, *Faggi* : in Spanish, *Haia*, *Faia*, and *Fax* :
in French, *Fau*,or *Hestre*:in English, Beech
tree, Beech-mast,and Buck-mast.

The fruit is called in Latine, *Nuces Fagi*:
in Greeke, βάλανοι ὀξύα: in low Dutch,**Bue-**
ken nootkengs:in French, *Faine*:in English,
Beech-mast. *Dioscorides* reckons the Beech
among the Acorne trees,and yet is the mast
nothing at all like to an Acorne. Of *Theo-*
phrastus it is called *Oxya*:of *Gaza*, *Scisina*.

Pliny also makes mention of this tree,but
vnder the name of *Ostrya*(if so be in stead of
Ostrya we must not reade *Oxya*)*lib*.13.*ca*.21.
It brings forth,(saith he, meaning Greece)
the tree *Ostrys*, which they likewise call *O-*
strya, growing alone among watery stones,
like to the Ash tree in barke and boughes,
with leaues like those of the Peare tree,but
somwhat longer and thicker,and with wrinkled cuts which run quite through, with a
seed like in colour to a Chestnut, and not
to barley:the wood is hard and firme,which
being brought into the house there follows
hard trauell of child, and miserable deaths,
as it is reported ; and therefore it is to be
forborne, and not vsed as fire wood, if *Pli-*
nies copies be not corrupted.

¶ *The Temperature.*
The leaues of Beech do coole: the kernell of the Nut is somewhat moist.

European beech, from which our cultivated purple and copper beeches are descended, there are six Asiatic species. The American beech is a medium-sized tree, reaching a height of sixty to eighty feet, with a diameter of two to three feet. Slow-growing, it may live 400 years or more. This deciduous tree has a rounded crown, and oval, pointed leaves, three to six inches long, which resemble the chestnut. The beech bears fruit in the form of woody burs which enclose two to three small, triangular nuts about three-eighths to one-half inch across. The burs open and the nuts ripen and fall to the ground in October; a few seeds, not consumed by squirrels, birds, wildlife or humans, germinate and possess enough vitality to establish themselves even in the deep shade of the forest.

Beechnuts gathered from the wild may be eaten fresh, dried or roasted; they usually have a sweet taste, although the flavor may vary from tree to tree. Unless properly dried, fresh nuts will deteriorate within a few weeks. The shells can be removed readily with the fingernails. The beechnut was one of the favorite foodstuffs of the North American Indians. Flour can be prepared by mashing the nutmeats, allowing the resultant paste to content is 19.4 per cent, carbohydrates 20.3 per cent, and its energy value 2,576 calories per pound. In Germany, the oil of the European beechnut has been utilized as a salad oil and as a substitute for butter. In France, roasted and ground beechnuts have occasionally served as a substitute for coffee. During times of famine in Scandinavia, beechwood sawdust was boiled in water, baked and mixed with flour to make bread.

The beech has been neglected as a source of edible nuts. Little effort has been made to cultivate, select, propagate and improve fruiting varieties. This indifference may be due to the small size of the nuts, the frequency of unfilled nuts, the irregular bearing habit of the trees and the difficulty of harvesting the nut crop. At the present time, the only economic product of the beech in the United States is its wood; generally dark to reddish-brown, strong, heavy and hard, it makes excellent furniture, flooring and other miscellaneous articles such as clothespins. Given the other competing wild and cultivated edible nuts available in North America, the beechnut appears to have a limited potential for food or feed. The most significant value of the beech, in the long run, may be in landscaping, where it is in demand as a noble, symmetrical, nut-bearing tree—ornamental and attractive at every season for park planting.

BEECHNUT LEAF, BUR AND NUT

dry out, then grinding it. Beechnut meal can be used to make bread or biscuits, while the expanding, elongated, pointed beech buds may be eaten in the spring.

Although similar to the chestnut in flavor, the beechnut is much richer in fat content (fifty per cent) as compared to about four per cent for the chestnut. The beechnut protein

BEECHNUTS

272

Betel Nuts

THE BETEL NUT, or areca nut, is the seed of a palm of the same name (*Areca catechu*), belonging to the palm family. It is a single-stemmed, slender, graceful tree which grows up to 100 feet in height, with a crown of feather-like, pinnate leaves four to six feet in length. Annually, the tree bears two to six bunches of conical fruits, each one about the size of a hen's egg, which ripen to an orange-yellow color. Although the original habitat of this palm is uncertain, since it has never been found in the wild, it is sometimes considered to be indigenous to Malaysia. Its nearest relatives are native to southeastern Asia. The betel palm was domesticated probably in that region, taken westward to India over two thousand years ago, spread eastward through the Pacific islands at an early time and reached eastern Africa before 1500.

The hard seed or kernel of the betel, miscalled a "nut," is a masticatory; it is not swallowed but is chewed in much the same way as plug tobacco. The chewer of the betel nut derives a mild narcotic effect from it. Betel ranks as one of the world's major stimulants. It is estimated that at least ten per cent of the human race indulges in the habit of betel nut chewing—some 400 million people from India and southeast Asia to the central Pacific islands, East Africa, the Philippines and southeastern China. On a global basis, it is more popular than chewing gum. Where and when betel nut chewing began is unknown, but references to it can be found as early as 1000 B.C. in China, and the beginning of the Christian era in India. Marco Polo repeatedly mentioned it. Over its long history in India, where it is known as *pan*, the betel palm has come to be considered a sacred plant. The leaves and nuts play a role in the Brahman religion, and the tree has been compared to an arrow shot into the ground by God from the heavens above. It has also achieved social significance in that guests to a Hindu home are offered the betel nut as a sign of welcome.

Preparation of betel for chewing com-

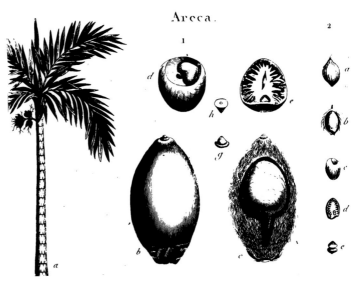

Areca.

BETEL NUT (*Areca catechu*)

273

BETEL NUTS

mences with the harvest of partially ripened fruits, which are boiled and then dried in the sun. Although betel may be chewed alone, more commonly a few thin slices of the kernel are made into a quid, smeared with a dab of fine, slaked lime and wrapped in a fresh leaf of the perennial, climbing betel pepper vine, *Piper betle*, to add piquancy. This quid is chewed slowly, usually after meals as a breath sweetener, and spit out when the flavor is gone. On ceremonial occasions, the quid may be flavored with spices such as cloves or cardamom, or sometimes tobacco. Betel chewing stimulates a copious flow of red sali-

va which is constantly expectorated; the scarlet-splashed pavements of Calcutta are notorious. Chewing betel is said to produce mild stimulation—a feeling of well-being—and to dull the appetite. It causes the lips, tongue and teeth to become brown, and eventually black. The habit of betel chewing has taken an extremely strong hold on the people who are prone to it, addicting rich and poor, young and old, men and women.

The betel nut contains various alkaloids, the most important of which is the narcotic, arecoline (about 0.1 per cent). Raw nuts are astringent, containing about 21 to 30 per cent

SELLING BETELNUT QUID, WRAPPED IN BETEL LEAF, INDIA

A betelnut salesman. By an artist in Benares, circa 1815-20.

274

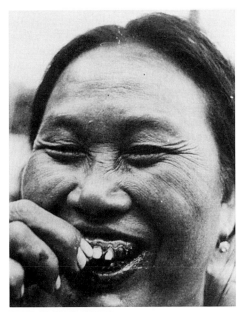

to three years old, the palms begin to bear when seven to ten years of age. They reach maximum annual yield levels of some 200 to 250 nuts per palm when fifteen years old and have a useful life of fifty to sixty years. Betel palms are usually cultivated as a plantation crop, whose requirements are quite similar to those of the coconut palm. India is by far the world's leading betel nut producer.

In India and elsewhere in Asia, competition for agricultural lands to grow food crops for export has placed negative pressure on betel nut production. Likewise, the practice of betel chewing is supposed to be declining gradually because of its unsanitary nature and the health risks already referred to. Nevertheless, the betel nut is so deeply rooted in the culture of India and other Asian countries it seems likely it will continue to be chewed for many years to come.

BETEL-STAINED TEETH

23 years of betel-nut chewing in Bangkok have turned this woman's teeth black, and the inside of her mouth brown. Betel-stained teeth, formerly considered as beautiful as "dark sapphires," are no longer regarded as symbols of beauty.

tannin; cured nuts 8 to 15 per cent. No food value is derived from betel nut chewing, and the high tannin content is a health hazard. Recent investigations have shown a notable incidence of mouth, throat and esophageal cancer among overindulgent chewers. In addition to being a masticatory, however, the betel nut has various medicinal uses in India. Ground into a powder, it is employed as a dentifrice and carminative agent; it is also prescribed to treat dysentery, roundworms and tapeworms. In Madras, fishermen "medicate" octopus bites by chewing betel and spitting on their wounds.

Betel palm cultivation has remained for the most part in its historic region: India, Sri Lanka, Malaysia, Indonesia and Polynesia. Commonly propagated by seed in nurseries and transplanted to field position when two

CLUSTER OF BETEL NUT FRUITS

Breadnuts

TWO RELATED TREES produce nuts or seeds which are designated as breadnuts: the breadnut (*Brosimum alicastrum*), and the seeded variety of the breadfruit (*Artocarpus altilis*); both are members of the Moraceae or mulberry family. Despite their familial affinity, their native habitats are widely separated. The breadnut is native to southern Mexico, Central America and the Caribbean, while the breadfruit comes from the Pacific islands. The seeds of both trees are quite similar in texture and taste.

Breadnut trees are evergreen and large, up to 120 feet in height, with trunks up to three feet or more in diameter. The species is adaptable; although it grows usually in areas with a pronounced dry season, it can also thrive under more humid conditions. The ripe fruits are yellow, about one inch in diameter, and contain a single seed or breadnut about the size of a small chestnut. During the dry season, branches are cut from the trees to permit livestock to browse on the leaves and young shoots.

In Mexico and Central America, the Spanish name for the breadnut tree is *ramón*, which comes from the verb *ramonear*, meaning to forage or browse. Groves of large breadnut trees known as *ramonales* are regarded as superior pastures in southern Mexico and Central America; cattle and hogs greedily devour the fallen leaves and nuts, especially in arid regions where the nutritious, evergreen leaves—which contain an average of ten percent crude protein on a dry weight basis—may furnish the only fresh forage available during the dry season. The Maya word for the breadnut tree is *ox,* a name given also to stocks of shelled maize kernels; the tree is found in abundance among the ancient Maya ruins in Yucatan in Mexico, and Tikal in northern Guatemala. It has been suggested that chicle and breadnut trees may have been largely responsible for the Maya archaeological discoveries since 1890. Chicle gum provided the incentive to explore and cut trails through virgin forests, while the foliage of the breadnut trees foddered at first the mules of the *chicleros,* then later those of the archaeologists. The ancient Mayas had no livestock, but it is believed that they gathered and stored breadnuts in their subterranean storehouses, since the nuts were an important alternative food when the yield of other crops was poor.

Brosimum alacastrum. BREADNUT.

"Brosime Comestible."

276

BREADNUTS

The scanty pulp of the breadnut fruit is edible, and the seeds themselves are nutritive; their crude protein content of 12.8 per cent is higher than that of corn and compares favorably with wheat. When the seeds are boiled, their flavor is somewhat like that of potatoes. The Mayas ate the breadnuts raw, or dried them, then ground them into a *masa* to mix with corn to make *tortillas*. A Maya dessert was prepared by combining ground breadnut seeds with honey. It should be pointed out, however, that breadnuts are not so popular today as they were during the period of the ancient Mayas; they are a specialty item, rather than a subsistence food. The nuts are not usually collected for human consumption. There seems to be a sociological stigma associated with eating them, possibly because the crop is so well known as a forage for cattle.

At the present time, in southern Mexico an extract is made of the fruits of *B. alicastrum* which is claimed to be an effective galactagogue, to stimulate lactation—the flow of milk in postpartum women, as well as in livestock. A tonic is prepared from the bark to treat asthma and chest pains. The latex, which is abundant in the trunk, is mixed with chicle or drunk like cow's milk.

Ground breadnut seeds may be added to cold milk and sugar to make a nutritious and tasty milk shake. The seeds, when roasted, develop a nutty-cacao flavor; a beverage somewhat similar to coffee can be prepared

BREADFRUIT (*Artocarpus utilis*)

277

by grinding the roasted seeds and steeping them in boiling water.

The wood is light in color and rather soft, used primarily to make inexpensive furniture, packing crates, beehives and tool handles, as well as for firewood.

The breadnut tree is a potentially valuable natural resource of the Western Hemisphere. It could play an important role in the future by helping to solve the problems of diminishing supplies of food for humans, and even forage for cattle. Mature Mexican breadnut trees reportedly yield up to 125 pounds of dried nuts per year, with little or no cultivation. If, in time, a satisfactory market could be developed in the United States and elsewhere for this little-known, minor nut, substantial supplies could be made available from southern Mexico, Central America and the Caribbean region. Further research is needed in the selection of high-yielding, tastier breadnut varieties to establish formal plantations, and also in the improvement of the present, primitive seed-processing techniques.

The seeded breadfruit, native of the hot, moist Pacific islands, and regarded for years as a romantic symbol of abundance and easy living in the South Sea Islands, is now grown throughout the tropics of the world. It is a handsome, fast-growing tropical tree which attains a height of sixty feet or more, with very large, thick, shiny and deeply-cut leaves. The normally spherical fruit, pea-green in color, is eight to ten inches long by about four inches in diameter. The pulp of the breadfruit, rather than the seeds, forms an important part of the diet of the natives of numerous islands of the East. The best varieties are seedless; the seeding types contain many elongated, brownish seeds imbedded in the pulp, which, in either case, is a solid white, fibrous, fleshy mass which becomes yellowish when fully ripe. The pulp is usually not eaten raw. It may be sliced and roasted; or baked whole, in which case it takes on the consistency of bread, which accounts for the popular name. The breadfruit is deeply rooted in the folklore of Polynesia, where it is a traditional, staple foodstuff. Breadfruit seeds are edible, but are of minor importance compared to the pulp. The seeds are usually boiled, roasted or fried before being eaten; their mild flavor is reminiscent of chestnuts.

Towards the end of the eighteenth century, after its use was reported by Captain Cook, the British Government considered it vital to introduce the breadfruit from Polynesia to their colonies in the West Indies. The purpose of the dramatic, ill-fated voyage of Captain William Bligh in 1789 on the "Bounty" was to bring a thousand young breadfruit plants, suitably packed in tubs and

NUTS OF SEEDED
BREADFRUIT FROM
MONTSERRAT, LEEWARD
ISLANDS

278

pots, from Tahiti to Jamaica and St. Vincent. Following the famous mutiny, Bligh and eighteen loyal companions managed to survive a long ordeal at sea, after being set adrift in an open lifeboat in the Pacific. Undaunted by the failure of his first attempt, Bligh took charge of a second expedition of the Royal Navy to the Pacific, and in January, 1793, successfully introduced 1,200 seedless breadfruit plants to the island of St. Vincent (where one of the original trees still exists). The French had already introduced seeds of the seeded breadfruit to Martinique several years earlier—a much easier task than Bligh's. Contrary to expectations, however, the breadfruit never has enjoyed the same popularity among the inhabitants of the Caribbean region and Central America that it did, and still does, in the East; wherever bananas and plantains are available in the New World, the breadfruit, although completely adapted, is neglected as a food.

Butternuts

THE BUTTERNUT, *Juglans cinerea*, is the most northern and cold-resistant member of the walnut family. Indigenous to eastern North America and growing mainly in the northeastern quarter of the United States, its native range extends northward well into Canada. A deciduous tree, attaining a height of some thirty to sixty feet, with a diameter of two to three feet, it has a broad, open crown and compound leaves made up of eleven to seventeen rather sticky leaflets. The fruits are oblong, cylindrical, sharp-pointed at the apex, about two and one half inches in length, and with a rough, jagged surface. They occur alone or in clusters and contain a single kernel which is thin, not plump. Since the shell is bony and thick, it is generally difficult to crack the nuts without shattering the kernels. The flavor of the kernel is delicious, yet distinctive.

American Indians gathered butternuts and ate them raw, cooked or ground up into a meal for baking in cakes or to thicken porridge. The Iroquois extracted the seed oil and used it in cooking as well as for dressing the hair. Young, tender butternuts, gathered in the summer while still green, can be pickled like walnuts have been pickled traditionally in

BUTTERNUT

279

BUTTERNUT FRUITS (*Juglans cinerea*)

civilians and sympathizers of the Confederate cause in the North were consequently frequently referred to as "butternuts."

The close-grained, satiny wood of the butternut—often called "white walnut"—is softer and lighter in color than that of the black walnut. It is utilized in making furniture, boat construction and is highly regarded by wood carvers.

Commercially, demand for the butternut has lagged far behind the Persian walnut and the eastern black walnut. For the most part, its popularity is limited to home consumption, primarily in New England and southern Canada. Some selection of butternuts has been carried out by horticulturists in this country, with emphasis on nut size and ease of cracking; about twenty-five cultivars have been named. Despite this research, there seems to be little interest in establishing commercial butternut orchards and in fact, none exist.

There are valid reasons for this apathy: the butternut is slow-growing and has the reputation of being short-lived. It is subject to "butternut dieback," caused by the fungus *Melanconis juglandis*, thought to be of oriental origin. This insidious disease starts as twig dieback, then, while defoliation occurs, slowly spreads

England. Butternuts are highly nutritious, with about 3,000 calories per pound. The protein content of 23.7 per cent is among the highest in the edible nuts. The fat content of 61.2 per cent is also high, which may account for the common name. Butternut trees can be tapped for their sweet sap, like sugar maples. In New England, particularly in Vermont, the nuts are combined with maple sugar to prepare a tasty maple-butternut candy.

Young butternut twigs, leaves, buds and fruits are covered with a sticky, hairy fuzz and, when boiled or distilled, yield a light brown dye. During the early part of the Civil War, the uniforms of Confederate soldiers from West Virginia, Kentucky and Tennessee were frequently dyed a tan color by means of butternut dye. Confederate troops, southern

BUTTERNUTS

to larger branches until the tree eventually dies. Pruning to sound wood will only temporarily delay the spread of the fatal fungus. Another problem is that butternut varieties are difficult to propagate. Furthermore, the nuts of most butternut cultivars are hard to crack, in such a way as to obtain satisfactory kernel extraction. In conclusion, it seems that the butternut, despite its delectable flavor, is destined to remain a minor nut for a prolonged period of time.

The souari is a huge, oily, tropical nut, *Caryocar nuciferum*, native to the Guianas, which is known also as butternut. It is not related to the northern butternut, *Juglans cinerea*, and should not be confused with it. The souari nut will be described in a separate chapter.

BUTTERNUTS
Butternut Cake (XLI)

1-1/2 cups (350 ml) sugar	1 teaspoon (5 ml) vanilla
1/2 cup (125 ml) butter	2 cups (500 ml) flour
3/4 cup (175 ml) sweet milk	2 teaspoons (10 ml) baking powder
1 cup (250 ml) butternuts, broken	Whites of 4 eggs, stiffly beaten
Pinch of salt	

Cream the sugar and butter, add milk, then nut meats, salt, vanilla, flour and baking powder. Fold in the egg whites. Bake in a 350° F (175° C) oven until done.

Yield: 28 large cupcakes or two 9-inch (23-cm) layers

Chilean Wild Nuts

THE CHILEAN WILD NUT, *Gevuina avellana*, also known as the Chilean nut and the Chilean hazel, is a member of the Protea family (Proteaceae), to which the macadamia nut also belongs. The tree is a handsome evergreen, up to fifty feet in height, with a large, conical head and shiny, dark-green, pinnate leaves. The leaflets are ovate in shape with toothed margins. The natural habitat of the tree is the cold region of southern Chile, extending from

the snowline on the Pacific slopes of the Andes down to the seacoast.

The inflorescence consists of racemes similar to those of the macadamia, and the white flowers also superficially resemble macadamia flowers. The fruits are fleshy drupes, about the size of cherries, which become coral-red when ripe and contain a single seed, somewhat smaller than the macadamia nut, which is enclosed within a hard, woody shell. Practically all nut production comes from wild trees, which, when mature, yield about ten pounds of nuts annually. These nuts are pleasant-tasting, similar in flavor to the European hazelnut—so their common name in Chile is "avellano." The kernels may be eaten fresh, but they are usually roasted and sold in small paper bags like peanuts.

The wood of the tree is pale brown, light, strong and easily worked; it is employed in Chile to make picture frames, furniture, oars and roof shingles.

Chilean wild nut trees, symmetrical in form, are sought after as ornamentals due to their attractive, glossy foliage, showy racemes of small, snow-white flowers, and the conspicuous, reddish color of their maturing fruits.

Efforts to establish this tree outside of Chile have been only moderately successful as the weak root system of the plant causes it to be extremely sensitive to transplanting in other climatic zones. Experimental plantings in southwest England and Ireland have done better than trials in California.

The tasty Chilean wild nut, although popular in its native land, is in reality a minor nut, virtually unknown elsewhere in the world nut trade.

CHILEAN WILD NUT (*Gevuina avellana*)

Cola Nuts

THE COLA OR KOLA "nut," *Cola acuminata* (also *C. nitida*), is a masticatory like the betel nut, which is chewed but usually not eaten. Along with cacao (cocoa), cola belongs to the family Sterculiaceae. Native to the rain forests of tropical West Africa, the cola tree has been planted in other regions of the tropics throughout the world. The name "cola" comes from Temne, a tribal tongue of Sierra Leone. The fresh cola nut contains caffeine,

COLA NUT (*Cola acuminata*)

van routes which passed from Kano and So- koto in Nigeria to Timbuktu, a crossroads for camel trade routes across the Sahara. During the seventeenth century the cola tree was in- troduced to Jamaica and Brazil, but the nut never has enjoyed the local popularity in the Caribbean and Latin America accorded it in western and central Africa. Cola-chewing seems to be an acquired habit; generally Euro- peans and other non-Africans do not care for the initial bitter, quinine-like taste associated with it.

The cola nut, in addition to about two per cent caffeine, contains a trace of the alkaloid theobromine, as well as a glucoside, kolanin, which is a heart stimulant. It is also composed of 74 per cent carbohydrates, 9 per cent pro- tein, 2 per cent fat and 2 per cent fiber. As a medicine it is reputed to be an effective stimu- lant—a tonic which will allay thirst, promote digestion, give strength and stave off a por- ter's exhaustion during a forced march in the heat of the tropics while bearing an eighty- pound head load. It will prevent sleep, but will not induce a drug habit. It has been found useful medicinally to cure diarrhea and pre- vent vomiting in cases of high fevers. There is a belief in West Africa that cola's medicinal power can render putrid drinking water wholesome, but this has never been substan- tiated.

In the wild, medium-sized cola trees, which resemble apple trees, are part of the understory of tropical rainforests, commonly reaching heights of thirty to forty feet. The leaves are evergreen, broad, leathery and ovate, measuring six to eight inches in length, often twisted at the tip; the flowers are yel- low, streaked with purple. At about seven years of age, the tree starts to bear bunches of rough, green, bean-like pods, each of which contains six to ten nuts, roughly the size of walnuts, red, pink, or white in color, enclosed within a white seed coat. When full produc- tion is reached at about twenty years, each tree under cultivation should bear 200 to 400 good quality nuts annually. The white nuts are most highly regarded for chewing, while

which accounts for its popularity as a mastica- tory stimulant. At first it has a bitter taste, but after chewing the cola nut for a while, a sense of well-being is said to spread through the body, leaving a more pleasant taste in the mouth which causes any food or drink con- sumed immediately thereafter to seem sweet. Small pieces of the nut, when masticated, are supposed to benefit the chewer by increasing his mental activity, reducing his fatigue, dulling his appetite and counteracting intoxi- cation.

The origin of cola chewing is uncertain. Some 800 years ago, cola was known to the Moslems in northern Nigeria; it gradually be- came as important to them as betel among the Hindus. Moslems consider the cola nuts to be a sacred food granted to them by the Prophet.

Domestication of the cola tree took place in West Africa as its use increased. In times long past, the cola trade flourished on ancient cara-

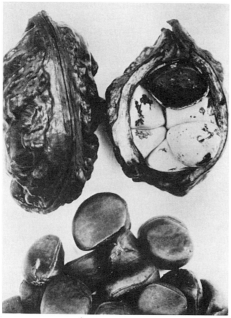

COLA NUTS, BELÉM, BRAZIL

must be changed; with proper care, the nuts can be stored for several months. Cola nuts are collected from the wild, and also from cola plantations, which have been established for the most part in Nigeria. In addition to such typical pests as weevils and moth larvae, cola plantings are damaged occasionally by elephants which like to devour the pods.

Among a number of tribal groups in West Africa, the cola nut is a symbol of hospitality, given to the guest either on arrival or departure. In addition, sharing and partaking of cola is an integral part of many social ceremonies. It plays a significant role in early morning worship, childbirth, child naming, marriage, installation of chiefs and at funerals. Prayers are generally said over the cola nut before it is shared; it is not looked upon as a luxury, but as a vital necessity of life. If the host does not present his guest with a cola nut, it is considered to be a serious breach of etiquette in many Nigerian communities. The hawker of cola nuts is a regular feature today in many Nigerian streets, where the nuts are still very much in demand.

the red nuts provide a natural food colorant worthy of further research.

Following the harvest, the nuts are removed from the pods, fermented for a few days, then washed, cleaned, sun-dried and stored in baskets lined with rot-resistant green leaves. From time to time the leaves

Although there are some cola plantations in Jamaica and Brazil, the crop has not been grown on a large scale outside of West Africa. Nigeria is the world's leading producer of cola nuts, producing annually an estimated 120,000 tons—about two-thirds of total world production. Most of the Nigerian crop is con-

COLA NUTS

284

sumed within Nigeria itself and in neighboring West African countries. The Ivory Coast, Ghana, Sierra Leone, Liberia, Jamaica and Brazil also produce cola nuts, which are utilized in non-alcoholic, cola-type beverages, in pharmaceutical tonics, and as a source of caffeine.

Pulverized and boiled in water, cola nuts formed part of a traditional, stimulating, West African beverage. This accounted for the origin of the word "cola" in several of today's popular soft drinks. During the 1880's, Coca-Cola started out as a powerful, caffeine-rich, patent medicine, containing carbonated water mixed with a powder of ground cola nuts and an extract of coca (*Erythroxylon coca*) leaves from Peru. The coca leaves, which contain several alkaloids including cocaine, have been chewed for centuries by Peruvian and Bolivian Indians to impart endurance. Cocaine, of course, is not an ingredient today in any of the cola beverages in the United States. Concentrated extracts of the cola nut, however, are utilized for natural flavor in many cola-type soft drinks. Some 3,000 tons of dried cola nuts are imported annually from West Africa and Jamaica; the extraction of cola concentrate is then carried out in several plants in New Jersey.

Basically, the cola nut is a preeminent masticatory rather than an edible nut. "Monkey" cola (*Cola caricaefolia*) and "slippery" cola (*C. verticillata*) produce edible kernels of minor importance in West Africa.

Ginkgo Nuts

THE CELEBRATED GINKGO TREE, *Ginkgo biloba*, was called a "living fossil" by Charles Darwin. A relic of the distant past, it is the only surviving member of the Ginkgoaceae, a tree family dominant in the vegetation of the Northern Hemisphere 125 million years ago when dinosaurs were still roaming about. Its original home was probably northern China, and ginkgo is the Chinese name for the tree. It is also known as the maidenhair tree, because its crowded, delicately veined, fern-like leaves, notched at the tips, resemble the leaflets of the maidenhair fern.

Unknown in the wild, the ginkgo tree has been cultivated as a sacred tree in Buddhist temple courtyards in China for over 1,000 years. A slender conical tree, it grows commonly to a height of sixty to eighty feet, with a trunk diameter of two to three feet, although larger and more massive trees remain near

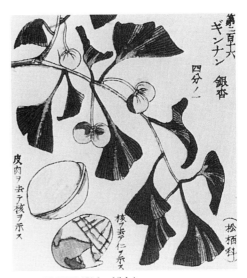

GINKGO NUT (*Ginkgo biloba*)

285

GINKGO LEAVES AND
FRUIT

old Chinese temple shrines. Sparsely branched, its distinctive fan-shaped leaves are broad, short and thick, measuring two to three inches across, with a wavy margin. Due to this unusual leaf shape, the ancient Chinese called it "Ya-chio," meaning duck's foot. The tree is deciduous. Its green leaves become a striking, clear yellow and drop very rapidly in the autumn to form a beautiful, temporary golden carpet on the ground. It is dioecious, that is, male and female flowers are borne on separate trees; to obtain fertile fruits, both sexes must be grown close together.

In about thirty-five to forty years, the fe-

GINKGO NUTS

286

A MATURE, HANDSOME GINKGO TREE

feasts and weddings as an oriental delicacy called "silverfruits."

The edible portion of the ginkgo nut has a high starch content of 62.4 per cent, but a very low fat content of 2.6 per cent. Its energy value is only 940 calories per pound.

The ginkgo nut has been employed in Chinese medicine as an expectorant, sedative and vermifuge. The astringent fruit pulp, although irritating to the skin, has served as a Chinese remedy for tuberculosis, asthma and bronchitis, as well as a wound dressing. In Japan, the ginkgo leaf, inserted between the pages of books has been utilized to prevent insect damage. The leaf is also a widely-used traditional Japanese art motif. It frequently turns up on jewelry, kimonos and family crests and it is the official emblem of Tokyo University.

Ginkgo wood is light, soft, satiny-white in color, and has insect-repelling properties. Occasionally employed in China to make chessboards, bas relief wood carvings, toys and implements, its use is constrained by a limited supply of timber.

Introduced from China in the eighteenth century, the ginkgo is a popular ornamental tree which lines the streets of many European and North American cities. It transplants easily, and although often a slow grower, possesses many desirable characteristics. It is distinctively handsome, has an upright growth habit, is resistant to cold, drought and urban air pollution, and has a very long life span. It requires good drainage, however, and does not grow well in the tropics. Because of the unpleasant smell of the fruits, the nursery trade has selected and developed male ginkgo cultivars to avoid the odor problem. Dwarf bonsai ginkgoes make beautiful indoor plants.

Americans do not fancy ginkgo nuts, which are consumed for the most part in this country by Chinese and Japanese people who enjoy them as appetizers and cook them with meat or fowl. Boiled, canned, imported ginkgo nuts are available in food shops and markets in metropolitan Chinatowns.

male trees start to bear fruits resembling plums, orange-yellow in color and about one inch in diameter. The fruit is drupe-like. Its fleshy, foul-smelling pulp encloses a cream-colored, oval, pointed seed, one-half to three-quarters of an inch long, within a smooth, white, thin shell. When gathered, the fruits are either fermented in vats of water to remove the pulp, with its stinking odor suggestive of rancid butter, or buried to hasten the pulp's decay. They are then washed and dried in the sun. Roasting or boiling the nuts, either shelled or in the shell, completes the task of getting rid of the unpleasant taste. The soft, inner kernel, when cooked, is edible, with a pleasant flavor similar to mild Swiss cheese; it is said to promote digestion and diminish the effects of too much drinking. Ginkgo nuts have a ritual significance in China and Japan, where they are consumed at

287

Heartnuts

THE HEARTNUT, *Juglans ailanthifolia*, which has also been classified as *J. sieboldiana* var. *cordiformis*, is one of the "other walnuts" which belong to the walnut family (Juglandaceae). Its common English name is derived from the shape of the nut, before and after hulling. In England, it is called the cordate (heart-shaped) nut. Native to Japan, it is known also as the Japanese walnut and the Siebold walnut.

Heartnuts rarely grow larger than apple trees, although in exceptional cases they may reach a height of fifty to sixty feet. The tree is deciduous, its crown broad and symmetrical; the leaves are three to six inches long and are composed of a dozen or more leaflets. The nuts, about one inch in diameter, are smaller than the butternut, and are easily cracked to remove the kernel; the flavor is mild and pleasant, resembling that of the butternut.

Introduced into the United States from Japan in the 1860's, the heartnut did well for a time, but in the early twentieth century was

HEARTNUT (*Juglans sieboldiana*)

HEARTNUT

288

nearly decimated by the walnut bunch disease. Its average life span in this country is relatively short—about thirty years. It has been replaced, for the most part, by the Persian walnut. Heartnuts are still grown on a noncommercial basis in the northeastern part of the United States and in lower Ontario—regions where the climate is too severe for the Persian walnut.

The wood of the heartnut is light, soft and dark brown in color; in Japan it is utilized for gun stocks and cabinet making. The heartnut is chiefly valued in North America for its use in ornamental plantings. The low, spreading trees with abundant foliage and unusually long strings of nuts are suitable for planting in yards of ranch-type homes.

A number of heartnut cultivars and heartnut hybrids have been developed which should prove to be useful for cross-breeding purposes. Heartnuts and butternuts cross readily and tend to produce vigorous hybrids which have been called "buartnuts"—combining the desirable kernel flavor and superior climatic adaptability of the butternut, with the higher yield and better crackability of the heartnut.

Hickory Nuts

The squirrel on the shingly shagbark's bough
Now saws, now lists with downward eye and ear
Then drops his nut.

James Russell Lowell

THE HICKORIES, members of the walnut family (Juglandaceae), are widespread throughout the temperate regions of eastern and central North America from the Canadian border to northern Mexico. The only commercially important hickory is the pecan (*Carya illinoiensis*), which is covered in a separate chapter of this book. There are several other American hickories worthy of mention which produce edible nuts: the shagbark (*C. ovata*); the shellbark (*C. laciniosa*); the mockernut (*C. tomentosa*; the pignut (*C. glabra*); and the bitternut (*C. cordiformis*). Another species, *C. cathayensis*, is indigenous to eastern China.

During the pre-glacial Pliocene period, hickories were abundant in Europe but were subsequently exterminated during the last Ice Age on that continent; the hardy genus survived in North America.

The Algonquin Indians in Virginia in the mid-seventeenth century called the nuts *pohickery*, which the colonial settlers shortened to hickory. The Indians pounded hickory kernels and shells in a mortar until they were finely powdered; water was added, the mixture passed through fine strainers, and the process continued until a nourishing, milky drink called *pawcohiccora* or "hickory

HICKORY NUTS

289

SHAGBARK HICKORY FRUITS (*Carya ovata*)

SHAGBARK HICKORY

Left: growth habit of young tree.
Right: closeup of shaggy bark.

milk'' was produced. This rich, creamy concoction was added to venison broth, or used to prepare hot corn meal cakes, hominy and roasted sweet potatoes.

The early settlers in North America held the hickories in high esteem. They savored the sweet, pleasant flavor of the nuts, which could be kept for two years or more in a cool cellar without deterioration; while the tough, elastic timber was an ideal wood for making tool handles and agricultural implements and was also the best firewood available. Nevertheless, in the course of time, the hickories have remained among the least developed of the native North American nut trees. Although there is a fair demand for hickory nuts, especially in the midwestern states, no large scale orchards have been established. There are several valid reasons: the hickories are difficult to transplant, slow-growing, late-bearing and low-yielding; furthermore, although the nuts may be flavorsome, their shells are generally thick and difficult to crack.

The most abundant and popular is the shagbark hickory, so named because of the peculiar, shaggy, unkempt appearance of the bark of mature trees of this species. The trees are moderately tall, reaching sixty to eighty feet in height, with trunks one to two feet in diameter. The crowns are open, and the branches large. The glossy, dark green leaves are deciduous, eight to fourteen inches in length, and are usually made up of five leaflets. Seedling trees may not begin to bear until they are about fifteen years of age, while grafted trees start to produce much earlier. Shagbark nut yields, like other hickory yields, are low—much less than that of pecans for example. The shagbark fruits, commonly about one and one-half inches long, contain a single, compressed, creamy-white kernel, resembling that of the Persian walnut in its shape, with a sweet flavor similar to the pecan.

The shellbark hickory, which also has a rather shaggy bark, grows mainly on lowlands and river-bottom lands, while the shag-

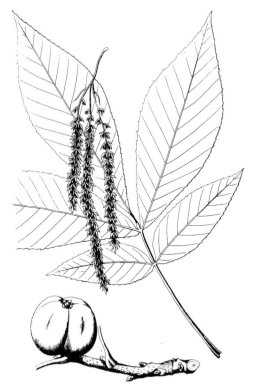

SHELLBARK HICKORY

bark prefers upland soils. The leaves of the shellbark are much larger than those of the shagbark; there are usually seven leaflets instead of five. The shellbark's fruits are much plumper than that of the shagbark—and are about two to two and one-half inches long; the shells are thicker, light brown, hard and bonelike. Shellbark nuts are delicious, in fact, they are considered by some connoisseurs to be the sweetest of the hickories.

The mockernut, an upland species, is abundant in the southern states and rare in the north. Its hairy leaves are large, up to a foot long, and highly aromatic when crushed. The shells of the mockernut are so thick and hard to crack that even squirrels cannot cope with them. These pale brown nuts have little commercial value.

291

The bark of pignut hickories is smooth. The fruits are usually pear-shaped, and about one inch long. The nuts are small, but of uncertain flavor as some are sweet, while others are astringent; their quality is inferior to other hickory nuts. In fact, the common name appears to originate from the use of pignuts for hog feed. Although of no value as a commercial nut source, the trees have excellent wood and are attractive as ornamentals even in winter when they lack their leaves.

The bitternut, the hardiest of the hickories, is widely distributed from Canada to Florida, and westward to Oklahoma, occurring in both uplands and lowlands. Its trunk is smooth, the husks and shells are thin, but the round, heart-shaped nuts are so bitter they are not commonly eaten.

Hickories hybridize freely with one another. Natural hybrids—crosses between the shagbark or shellbark hickory and the pecan, or between the bitternut and the pecan—are known as "hicans." Some of these hicans turn out to be very handsome ornamental trees. Considerable plant breeding research would be necessary, however, before any hybrid hican clones could be developed which would be suitable for commercial nut production. In the meantime, the hickories provide an excellent source of food for squirrels and other wildlife, and tasty nuts on a limited scale for humans.

Although a neglected, minor nut, the hickory is a part of traditional American lore. To refer to something as being "as tough as hickory" was a common expression among our early settlers. President Andrew Jackson's nickname "Old Hickory" was given to him by his frontier militiamen in 1813 when he was an Indian fighter, on account of his unyielding toughness. In days gone by, reading, writing and arithmetic were "taught to the tune of the hickory stick."

HICKORY NUTS

Hickory Nut Seafoam Candy (XLII)

2 cups (500 ml) brown sugar	Whites of two eggs, stiffly beaten
1/3 cup (75 ml) corn syrup	2/3 cup (150 ml) chopped hickory nuts
1/2 cup (125 ml) water	

Boil sugar, syrup and water together until the mixture forms a hard ball when dropped into cold water (about 250° F/122° C). Cool the mixture slightly and slowly pour it over the egg whites. Beat until it loses its gloss. Add the hickory nuts. Drop by spoonful on a buttered plate or waxed paper and allow to set.

Yield: about 60 candies

Jack Nuts

THE JACK NUT or jack fruit, *Artocarpus heterophyllus*, formerly called *A. integrifolia*, belongs to the mulberry family (Moraceae) along with the breadfruit. The tropical, evergreen tree is native to rain forests from India to the Malay Peninsula, and has been cultivated since ancient times in India and Malaysia.

The name *jack* was given to it by the Portuguese in the sixteenth century since it sounded like the Malayan word *tsjaka*.

The jack tree is medium-sized, some fifty to sixty feet in height, with dense foliage. The large, dark green, smooth, leathery leaves are about nine inches long. Flowering

JACK NUTS

Tsjakamaram.inc. Pilau. lat.
Δειλ...αι Mal.
Penoffou पणस, bram.
Πέλι. Arab.

JACK TREE

JACK FRUITS GROWING ON
TRUNK AND LARGE BRANCHES

293

JACK FRUITS ARE AMONG THE LARGEST OF ANY CULTIVATED TROPICAL PLANT; THEY MAY WEIGH 70 POUNDS OR MORE.

taste of the pulp is aromatic and agreeable—something like that of the pineapple. The versatile pulp is consumed in a variety of ways: it may be eaten fresh, cooked with scraped coconuts and spices, mixed in curries as a vegetable, included in fruit salads, boiled and dried for storage, or preserved in syrups. Jack nuts or seeds are almost as adaptable, although they are not generally eaten in raw form. A slightly unpleasant flavor is removed by boiling or roasting, following which the nuts taste very much like European chestnuts. Jack nuts have an unusually low fat content of less than one per cent, even lower than chestnuts. When boiled, the nuts can be

and fruiting take place on the trunk and large branches, a somewhat unusual habit called "cauliflory," which also occurs in the cacao tree. The huge jack fruits—which are among the largest of any tropical plant—measure up to three feet in length by eighteen inches wide and weigh on the average forty to fifty pounds although some extraordinary specimens have weighed over 100 pounds. Under normal conditions, a tree may bear 150 to 250 fruits per year. The massive jack fruit is filled with a sweet, golden, fleshy pulp and several hundred kidney-shaped seeds about one by one and one-half inches in size. Both the pulp and seeds are edible.

When the ripe fruits fall to the ground and rot under the trees, the odor is offensive and disgusting. Nevertheless, when fresh, the

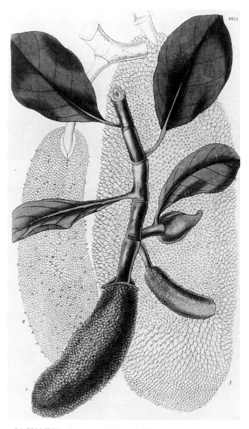

JACK NUT. *Artocarpus heterophyllus.*

294

added to soups, stewed with meat, or made into a starchy flour.

The jack tree has been introduced throughout the world's tropical lowlands, where it thrives in warm, wet regions in well-drained soils at elevations of less than 3,000 feet. In addition to its outstanding food value, the tree yields an excellent yellow timber, almost as valuable as teak, which is employed to make fine furniture, musical instruments, door and window frames and for general building purposes. Jack wood chips are distilled in Burma and Sri Lanka to produce a yellow pigment used to dye the fabrics for the robes of Buddhist priests. The bark yields a fiber from which clothing can be fashioned. A juice ex-

tracted from the roots is reputed to cure fevers in Malaysia.

The jack fruit is consumed in large quantities throughout southern Asia; in south India it forms a regular part of the diet during some seasons of the year. One of the most useful and productive of tropical trees, the jack is worthy of further research to develop its full nutritional and agricultural potential. Currently, there are few large jack orchards. Much scientific work needs to be done with respect to the selection of promising jack varieties and improvement of propagation techniques. Jack fruits and jack nuts could in time provide more food for the hungry in many developing tropical countries.

Jojoba Nuts

JOJOBA, *Simmondsia chinensis*, is a desert shrub native to an extensive arid area in the Sonora Desert, including parts of Arizona, California and adjoining northwestern Mexico. It is usually found at elevations of between 2,000 and 4,000 feet. It belongs to its own family: Simmondsiaceae. The evergreen, bushy plant, two to fifteen feet tall, has oval, gray-green leaves about two inches long. It thrives in hot, dry, inhospitable regions with an annual rainfall of only fifteen to eighteen inches. Like many desert plants, it develops a deep root system. Jojoba is dioecious: pollen is produced on "male" plants; while "female" plants, when their flowers are pollinated—mostly by wind—bear fruit capsules which contain one to three oily, chocolate brown seeds or nuts, about the size of small hazelnut kernels. Mature plants yield from three to twelve pounds of seed (dry weight) per year; the average yield is about five pounds. The plants start to bear after about five years. The lifespan of the hardy jojoba, which does not

appear to be subject to serious damage by insects or disease, is 50 to 200 years. The plants require good drainage, however, and are sensitive to frost.

When the British naturalist, H. F. Link, landed in Baja California in 1822 and gathered botanical specimens of jojoba, he named the plant *Simmondsia* in honor of another British botanist, T. W. Simmonds, who had died several years earlier in Trinidad. Subsequently, Link visited China to carry out further plant exploration. When he shipped a box of Chinese botanical specimens back to England, his Mexican jojoba was accidentally mixed in with his Chinese botanical collection. Thus the plant was erroneously given the specific name *chinensis*.

Some of its vernacular names indicate the earlier utilization of jojoba: "wild hazel," "goatnut," "sheepnut," and "pignut." Its fruits and leaves are devoured with avidity by goats, sheep and deer. Indians of the desert Southwest gathered jojoba nuts and ate them,

JOJOBA BUSH, PRUNED
FOR HARVEST

raw or roasted; their flavor is reminiscent of the hazelnut, but more bitter. Indians prepared a nourishing beverage by roasting jojoba nuts, grinding them with the yolk of a hard-boiled egg, then boiling the pasty mass in water with milk and sugar. Jojoba nuts contain about fifty per cent oil and thirty per cent protein. The Indians employed jojoba fruits medicinally to treat sores and as a cure for wounds. They utilized the oil as a remedy for kidney disorders, as a hair dressing, and even as a salad and cooking oil, since it has a mild, pleasant taste.

Today, the use of jojoba nuts for human consumption is mainly of historic interest. The plant is now the object of a major crop development program because jojoba seed oil is the only natural substitute for sperm whale oil. Banning the importation of sperm whale oil into the United States in 1970, in an attempt to save that endangered species from extinction, was the major impetus for the current research in jojoba oil. The unsaturated, clear, liquid wax, readily extracted from jojoba seeds closely resembles sperm whale oil in its chemical composition. Jojoba oil has many potential uses as a substitute for sperm

whale oil in cosmetics, drugs, plastics, waxes, leather processing and industrial lubricants. Cosmetic companies are marketing jojoba shampoos, soaps, and ointments as well as body moisturizers that are supposed to leave the skin supple and soft but not oily.

Jojoba seed meal, a by-product of the extraction of jojoba oil from the seed, might prove useful to livestock producers in arid regions. A source of concentrated vegetable protein, the meal has one drawback which might be serious: it contains an unusual toxic material "simmondsin," which suppresses the appetites of laboratory rodents, but has no noticeable influence on the appetites of squirrels, chipmunks, deer and rabbits. If jojoba meal is to become acceptable as a livestock feed in the United States, requirements of the Food and Drug Administration will have to be met.

Since 1971, the National Research Council of Washington, D.C., the United States Department of Agriculture, various other governmental agencies and several United States corporations, have been carrying out scientific and technical assessment of the practical uses of jojoba. Continuous research is being

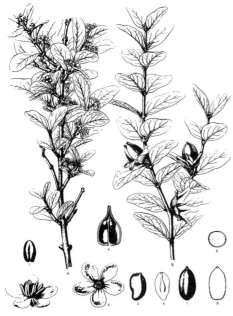

JOJOBA

California at Riverside, the University of New Mexico, the University of Sonora in Mexico and Ben-Gurion University in Israel. It is hoped that arid and semi-arid, marginal regions in many countries, not suitable for conventional crops, might be utilized productively if planted with jojoba.

In addition to the United States, Mexico and Israel, some ten other countries are experimenting with jojoba cultivation, including Costa Rica, Egypt, Australia, Sudan, India, Venezuela, South West Africa, Libya, Kuwait and Thailand. At the present time, an estimated 30,000 acres of jojoba have been planted in the United States in Arizona, California, New Mexico, Texas, Florida and Nevada. In addition, some 3,500 acres have been planted in Costa Rica; 2,000 acres in Mexico; and hundreds of acres of experimental plantings in the other countries mentioned above. These plantings are all relatively new. Since it takes at least eight to twelve years for a plantation to reach full production, the supply of jojoba will remain very limited for at least a decade.

sponsored in arid countries throughout the world to study jojoba planting as well as the production and processing of jojoba oil. Programs on the domestication of jojoba for plantation cultivation are being conducted at the University of Arizona, the University of

Quite apart from this serious research and systematic planting activity, there has been some irresponsible ballyhoo extolling the virtues of jojoba, especially in the southwestern part of the United States. Such promotion may be intended to raise the presumable

JOJOBA SEEDS OR NUTS

PRESENT AND POTENTIAL USES FOR JOJOBA

Liquid Wax	*Lubrication*—substitute for sperm whale oil; see below. *Cosmetics*—present use as a base in the manufacture of cosmetics, hair oil, shampoo, face creams, sunscreen compounds and virtually every type of cosmetic product. *Pharmaceuticals*—suitable carrier or coating for some medicinal preparations; penicillin production; inhibitor to growth of tubercle bacilli; potential treatment for acne; historical use as a hair growth restorer. *Food-related*—cooking oil; low calorie additive for salad oil, vegetable oil, and shortening.	Alcohol and Acid Derivatives	*Preparation of*—disinfectants, surfactants, detergents, lubricants, driers, emulsifiers, resins, plasticizers, protective coatings, fibers, corrosion inhibitors, and bases for creams and ointments.
		Hydrogenated Wax (Solid)	*Polishing Wax*—as a carnauba wax substitute for floors, furniture and automobiles. *Protective Coating*—on fruit, food preparations, candies and confectionaries, and paper containers. *Cosmetics*—for lipsticks. *Candles*—as a beeswax substitute, burns with bright, essentially smokeless, flame; high-melting point, and low ash content. *Textiles*—sizing for yard goods.
Sulfurized Liquid Wax	*Factice*—potential in the manufacture of adhesives, printing ink composition, varnishes, candalilla wax substitute in chewing gum and new rubber-like compounds. *Lubrication*—requires little or no refining for use with high-speed machinery or machinery operating at high temperatures and pressures; serves well as cutting or grinding oil additive to other lubricants; may be suitable as a transformer oil. *Leather Processing*—potential use as a fat-liquoring agent for the production of soft non-greasy leathers, sheen on suede surfaces, an ability to be polished in full-grain leathers; imparts "run" to leather, a property particularly important in the manufacture of high quality gloving leathers.	Oil-Extracted Meal	*Animal Feed Supplement*—potential use if possible toxin is denatured; 30-35% protein. *Fertilizer*—possible use if high nitrogen content can be utilized.
		Seed Hulls (Capsules)	*Soil or Mulch Amendment*—protective ground cover to reduce evaporation, erosion, weed growth, and enrich soil which is low in organic matter.
		Jojoba Shrubs	*Animal Food*—jojoba foliage is excellent browse for deer, cattle, sheep and goats. *Ornamental*—already in use throughout the south-western United States as an ornamental shrub with a higher resistance to smog than all other landscape plants.

value of arid, rocky, marginal acreage where jojoba is already growing or where it could be grown, so that the land could be sold at inflated prices to gullible buyers. For example, jojoba oil has been referred to as "liquid gold," and like a "tree that gives gasoline instead of maple syrup." Wild, unsubstantiated claims have been made that jojoba will cure baldness; and that when used as an additive, it can improve the gasoline mileage of your car by twenty-five per cent.

The future of jojoba seems to depend on

its development as a cultivated crop. If successful, considerable economic and social benefits could be provided to improve the conditions in several reservations in Arizona and California: Many disadvantaged native Americans might find gainful labor in a new jojoba industry. There are major agricultural problems concerning its cultivation, however, which must be solved. Although jojoba can be propagated asexually by cuttings, no time-tested, high-yielding cultivars are available at present for planting. Furthermore, if jojoba is to be produced on a large-scale, commercial basis, mechanical harvesting will have to be employed and special pruning

techniques improved to make a mechanized harvest feasible. Harvesting is still carried out by costly hand labor and almost all production originates from wild plants. At present, the demand for jojoba exceeds the available supply. The price of good quality nuts is high—about $8 to $10 per pound. Jojoba oil currently costs $60 to $120 a gallon.

It should be pointed out that jojoba development is still in the experimental stage. The future looks promising, however, for this unusual, drought-resistant shrub. The table on preceding page from *Jojoba: The "Super Bean" of the Future*, Part I, 1982, by Jerome F. Smith, summarizes its present and potential uses.

Litchi "Nuts"

THE TREE THAT PRODUCES the litchi or lychee "nut," *Litchi chinensis*—formerly *Nephelium litchi*—has common and scientific names which reveal its origin. "Litchi" is the anglicized Chinese word for the plant, which is native to southern China. It is a member of the Soapberry family (Sapindaceae). A hand-

some, medium-sized, tropical or subtropical tree which grows to a height of fifty feet, the litchi is very sensitive to frost, drought and wind. It has glossy, evergreen, feather-shaped leaves, three to four inches in length; the flowers are small and greenish white. At about ten years of age, the tree begins to bear

LITCHI NUTS

299

Nephelium Litchi
Scytalia Litchi Roxb

blance to the fresh fruit. Canned litchis, with rind and seed removed, do retain at least some of the flavor of the fresh fruit.

Fresh litchis are best, but the fruits must be picked without delay when ripe, and dispatched to the market immediately because they lose their flavor and color after a few days. Litchis may be kept for a year or more in frozen storage, if the temperature is continuously held near zero degrees Fahrenheit. In China, the traditional method of preserving litchis is to hang them in clusters to dry in the sun; sun-dried fruits are considered to have a more delectable flavor than those dried in a kiln. Litchis, a good source of Vitamin C, are very popular indeed in Chinese cuisine—fresh, dried, canned, as ingredients of sauces and jams, or made into wine. To eat the fresh litchi, a piece of the rind is broken off at one end and the pulp and seed are forced into the mouth by pressing with the fingers. The seed is then discarded.

Cultivated for more than 2,000 years in China, the litchi has been introduced to many countries throughout the world, including the United States, but has never become an important crop outside of Asia. It was brought to Florida in the 1880's, and a limited and irregular production of fresh litchis commenced in the 1950's, principally in the central and southern parts of that state.

Many clonal litchi varieties are propagated in China and India. An important variety in Florida is called Brewster, named for the man who introduced it through the United States Department of Agriculture. It came from the Fukien province of China, where it was known as *Chen-tze*. The first litchi variety introduced to Hawaii in 1873 was named *Kwai-Mi*, and still does well there, as does a newer variety called Groff. The most desirable clones have small seeds and a large percentage of fleshy aril.

Seedling trees tend to be highly variable and produce fruits of lower quality, so the litchi is generally propagated vegetatively by air-layering. A branchlet of the clone selected for propagation is ringed, that is, about one-

loose clusters of two to twenty fruits which, on ripening, assume a pinkish crimson tint that turns to a dull brown as the fruit dries. The ripe fruits are nearly round, about one inch in diameter, have a warty rind, and resemble strawberries. The peeled skin reveals a white, juicy, bittersweet, jelly-like pulp or aril, surrounding a single, small, smooth, dark brown seed. The seed and skin are inedible, although the former has reputed medicinal value for intestinal maladies in China. Only the rich pulp is edible; its texture is suggestive of grapes. Litchis are really fruits, not nuts, but when they first became available in this country many years ago, it was in dried form only; the dry peel was a fragile nut-like shell which caused the fruits to look like nuts—an illusion which brought about the confusion in nomenclature. The taste of dried litchis, similar to raisins, bears no resem-

THOUSANDS OF TONS OF LITCHI (LYCHEE) "NUTS"—DRIED AND IN SYRUP—ARE
EXPORTED ANNUALLY FROM CHINA TO CHINATOWNS AND CHINESE RESTAURANTS
THROUGHOUT THE WORLD

half inch of bark is removed and the wood is scraped. The wound and a few inches of bark above it are covered with a mixture of sphagnum moss or other fibrous material (in China, chopped straw and mud) and kept well watered until roots are formed. Subsequently, the branch, with new roots, is cut off and planted in a nursery until strong enough to plant in the field.

A litchi tree takes twenty to thirty years to reach its prime; it may then last for a century, sometimes even a thousand years. A Chinese litchi tree in Fukien province, planted in the eighth century A.D., is still bearing fruit.

In addition to yielding delicious fruits, beautiful, spherically-shaped litchi trees are ideal ornamentals for dooryard landscapes in Florida and Hawaii; for much of the year the foliage is deep green. In China, litchi wood is prized for fine furniture and cabinet work. The versatile litchi is utilized in Kwantung in the preparation of a special tea: dried tea leaves are soaked in fresh litchi juice, dried again in the sun, then made into a fragrant tea which releases the litchi flavor.

Harvesting litchi fruits is more expensive in the United States than in China and India, because of the high cost of labor. Mature trees require ladders to reach the top clusters since mechanical harvesters for litchi cannot replace tedious handpicking; this is performed carefully to avoid tearing the wall of the fruit and causing the pulp to spoil.

The litchi has been traditionally the favorite fruit of southern China. When the Sung dynasty poet, Su Tung-po, was exiled to Hainan Island in the eleventh century, he declared that if he could have 300 litchis to eat every day, he could reconcile himself to banishment anywhere. Modern Chinese are also enthusiastic about litchis: thousands of tons of the dried and canned litchi fruits produced in China every year are exported for consumption throughout the world.

Lotus Seeds

THE LOTUS SEED or nut, *Nelumbo nucifera*, belongs to the water-lily family (Nymphaeceae). *Nelumbo* comes from the name of the plant in Singhalese (Sri Lanka), and *nucifera* means "nut bearing." This handsome water-lily is native to Asia from Iran to China and Japan, and to northeastern Australia. It has been held sacred in the Near and Far East for over 5,000 years. The elegant, sweet-scented lotus flowers have long been regarded with reverence by Buddhists in China, India and elsewhere in the Orient, where they are presented as temple offerings and looked upon as symbols of Buddha. The rhizomes and seeds have been eaten as food for over 3,000 years in China, where there are records of the plant's cultivation dating back to the twelfth century B.C.

An aquatic, perennial herb, the lotus produces large, umbrella-shaped leaves, one to three feet across, which grow on long stalks well above the surface of the water. Easily

LOTUS SEED (*Nelumbo nucifera*)

(also known as "Egyptian Lotus" and "Indian Lotus")

propagated by rhizome cuttings or seeds, the lotus is often found in ponds and lagoons. It develops long, creeping rhizomes with a wide, radial spread, and showy, fragrant flowers which may be white, pink or red. These flowers are considered symbols of pristine beauty throughout the Orient, since the exquisite blossoms grow on tall stalks high above the water—clean and untouched by the muddy pools from which they rise. The seed-bearing structure is a flat-topped receptacle in which many one-seeded carpels are embedded. Shaped like a spinning top, the receptacle matures after the petals fall off; it contains ten to thirty marble-sized, white fruits,

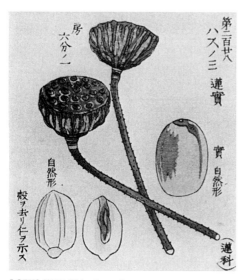

LOTUS SEED (*Nelumbo nucifera*)

LOTUS SEEDS ARE IN DEMAND FOR USE IN MANY ORIENTAL MEAT AND VEGETABLE DISHES, PUDDINGS, PASTES AND CANDIES.

covering has been removed; they are eaten raw, like nuts, before they are fully ripe. At this stage, they have a pleasant, nutty flavor. When mature, the nutritious seeds, rich in Vitamin C, are generally roasted or boiled; they may also be ground into flour, or dried for storage. Roasted and ground lotus nuts make a tolerable substitute for coffee. The starchy lotus seeds are popular ingredients in many oriental meat and vegetable dishes, as well as in puddings, pastes and candies. Analysis has shown them to consist of approximately 58 per cent carbohydrates, 17 per cent protein and 2.5 per cent fat.

The lotus is a multiple-purpose food plant. The thick, cylindrical rhizomes, which taste like artichokes, are more important than the seeds; they can be roasted, sliced and fried as chips, sliced and dried, pickled or candied. The lotus rhizomes, when mature, can usually be recognized in Chinese dishes, since they have air spaces and look like slices of Swiss cheese. A highly digestible starch is prepared from them, as well as a kind of sweet, aromatic "arrowroot," known in China as *ou-fen*. This product is used as a stimulating tonic to increase mental acuteness, as a baby food for infants who cannot be nursed, and as a medicine in the treatment of diarrhea and dysentery. *Ou-fen* is made by crushing the lotus rhizome, washing the starch out with

each of which encloses a single seed. When the receptacle dries out and shrinks away from the hardening fruits, the seeds become loose and rattle in their individual cavities. During the harvest, the edible seeds are taken out of the receptacles and the extremely bitter green embryos removed. The seeds, about a half inch in length, are whitish after the outer

LOTUS SEEDS AND SECTIONS OF THE FLESHY RHIZOMES

303

water, and allowing it to settle until the water can be poured off. In Malaysia, a tea made from the lotus seed embryo is prescribed for its reputed ability to reduce high fever and to treat cholera.

In many parts of the Far East, the young leaves, petioles and flowers of the lotus are consumed as vegetables, and the tender leaves are eaten in salads.

Lotus "root" (or rhizome) is a popular export item from China and Hong Kong, sold at high prices in dried and canned form as a delicacy all over the world.

An interesting aquatic crop, the lotus might be developed as a source of food for the future in the warm wetlands of many countries, including our own Florida Everglades. In its normal habitat, the rhizome lies deep in the mud, so far under water that it is beyond the reach of the occasional frost.

Oyster Nuts

THE OYSTER NUT, *Telfairia pedata*, is a little-known member of the exclusive and significant gourd family (Cucurbitaceae). It is named after Charles Telfair (1778-1833), an Irish botanist and plant collector who lived in Mauritius. Native to tropical East Africa, this large, fast-growing, woody-stemmed, climbing vine reaches a height of sixty to seventy feet as it climbs and scrambles over tall trees; individual branches may attain 100 feet in length, while a single plant can cover an area larger than a tennis court. The main stem of the vine is six to eight inches thick at the base; the roots are stout, fleshy and perennial; the leaves, lobed and dark green. The hardy plant, which may live for fifteen to twenty

A HUGE TWO-YEAR-OLD OYSTER NUT VINE IN TROPICAL EAST AFRICA

Climbing and scrambling over tall trees, the vigorous oyster nut vines, loaded with heavy fruits, often crush the trees which originally supported them.

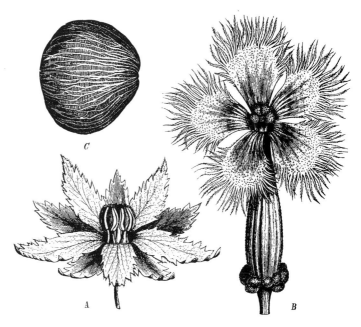

OYSTER NUT (*Telfairia pedata*)

years, grows in a variety of soils in tropical Africa, from sea level to 6,000 feet of elevation. It grows best in sheltered areas due to its sensitivity to cold winds and frost.

The oyster nut is usually propagated by seed and is dioecious: that is, male and female flowers are borne on different plants and both sexes are necessary for fruit and seed formation. It takes eighteen months for the vines to flower, and until that time it is impossible to determine which plants are male and which female. When growing oyster nut plants, numerous seedlings are planted: after flowering, only a small percentage of males should be kept. Artificial pollination is sometimes carried out by collecting male pollen on a clean stick and applying it gently to the stigma of female flowers.

The deeply-ridged fruits, shaped like large footballs, mature in four to five months; they reach one to two feet in length, eight to twelve inches in diameter and weigh up to thirty pounds each. The weight of the huge vines, loaded with these heavy gourds, becomes so great that the trees which originally supported the vines are often smothered and crushed. When the fruits ripen, they burst open, releasing some 100 to 140 pale yellow seeds embedded in a golden yellow pulp. These seeds, or nuts, are protected by a strong, bitter-tasting, fibrous, outer husk; they are large, flat, circular, and about one

OYSTER NUT

305

and one-half inches in diameter by one-half inch thick—roughly the size of a wrist watch. The vernacular name comes from the oyster-like appearance of the seeds; after being washed and dried in the sun for several days, the seeds are opened in a manner much like shucking an oyster: after being cut around the edge, the fibrous shells are pried open with a knife to extract the kernels.

Raw, or roasted, the oyster nut is very palatable. The flavor is pleasant, somewhat similar to that of the Brazil nut. It is important, however, to remove the shell, which contains a bitter principle. In East Africa, the kernels are used to make sweets, cakes, soups, and are prepared with a variety of other foods: in one popular dish, roasted oyster nuts are pounded into a paste which is mixed with fish and cooked in a banana leaf.

In East African medicine, oyster nuts are reputed to be effective as galactagogues, stimulating lactation and increasing the flow of milk in postpartum women.

Oyster nuts are nutritious, both high in fat, approximately 62 per cent; and in protein, 27 per cent. Following the removal of the shells, a rich edible oil may be extracted from the kernels that is useful in cooking, as well as in cosmetics, soap manufacture and in a variety of industrial applications. After extraction of the oil, the residue is an excellent live stock feed.

The oyster nut appears to have a promising future as an expanded food source in tropical regions. Although virtually unknown in the United States, it might in time be more widely used in this country in confectionery, snack-nut chocolates and mixed nuts.

Paradise Nuts

THE PARADISE or sapucaia nut, *Lecythis usitata*, formerly *L. zabucajo*, belongs to the Lecythis family (Lecythidaceae) along with the more important Brazil nut. The common name "paradise" owes its origin to the high quality of the nut, said to be even more delicious than the Brazil nut; "sapucaia" is an Amazonian Indian word meaning "chicken," since the nut was frequently fed to chickens. The generic name *Lecythis* is from the Greek for "oil jar," a rather accurate description of the appearance of the fruit, which looks like a jar complete with a neatly-fitting lid.

Native to the Amazonian rain forests of northeastern Brazil and neighboring Guyana, the paradise nut tree is tall, some 90 to 120 feet in height, with a diameter which may reach five feet. It bears a dense crown of elliptical leaves up to seven inches long which are shed near the end of the dry season. In their natural state, the sapucaia trees generally occur in small groups near the tops of hills in the forest, where little shade exists. There are some fifty species of *Lecythis* in northern South America, of which the Brazil nut and the paradise nut are the most widely known.

The paradise nut tree begins to bear when eight to ten years old, and produces large, woody fruits about eight inches long and ten inches wide which are suspended upside-down from the ends of the branches. When mature, after some eighteen months, the lid of the fruit drops off; the nuts then gradually become detached and fall to the ground. A single fruit contains thirty to forty irregular-oblong, wrinkled seeds (nuts), each about two inches long, resembling Brazil nuts although the paradise nuts are more rounded, have a lighter brown color and a thinner, softer shell. A limited production of paradise

PARADISE NUT—SAPUCAIA NUT

keys and wild pigs. The empty, woody paradise nut shells, urn-shaped receptacles known as "monkey pots," with their lids removed, are sometimes baited with sugar to be used as traps for catching small monkeys which are unable to withdraw their hands or heads when inserted in the small aperture.

Paradise nut kernels are ivory white with a creamy texture. Containing about 62 per cent fat and 20 per cent protein, the nuts are highly nutritious. They may be eaten raw or roasted and are utilized to a limited extent in making candies and cakes. An excellent, pale-yellow, edible oil is expressed from the kernels, which is employed by natives of the Amazon to produce soap and illuminants.

Precautions should be taken in gathering and eating paradise nuts: there are many harrowing reports about the fruits of certain poisonous species of *Lecythis* in tropical America, which, when eaten, can cause severe nausea, diarrhea, dramatic (if temporary) loss of scalp and body hair, and the shedding of finger nails.

Paradise nuts have an unusual, delicate, sweet flavor and are considered by some connoisseurs to be the finest known nut. The mature sapucaia trees are heavy producers: it has been estimated that the average annual yield per tree in the Amazon amounts to about 175

nuts is gathered from wild trees, but since the nuts fall from the fruit—unlike the Brazil nuts which are protected by a closed shell when the entire fruit falls—they are consumed for the most part by forest animals, mainly mon-

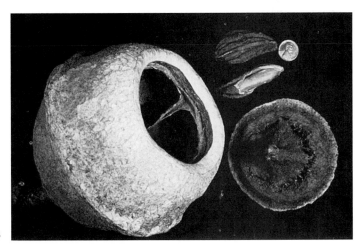

PARADISE NUTS

307

pounds of nuts. Nevertheless, large commercial paradise nut plantations have not yet been developed although a few small plantings exist in Brazil, the Guianas, the West Indies and Malaysia. More than anything else, the high loss of mature nuts to wild animals has been a drawback for the paradise nut and has resulted in more attention being given to the exploitation and development of the Brazil nut.

Pili Nuts

THE PILI NUT, *Canarium ovatum*, is the most important of several nut-bearing species of *Canarium* belonging to the family Burseraceae, which are native to the Old World tropics of southeast Asia. A closely related species, *C. commune*, is known as the Java almond. The pili gets its common name from the Philippines and is indigenous to that island group.

During the eighteenth and nineteenth centuries, an odorous, soft resin or gum was obtained from *Canarium* trees, called Manila or Philippine "gum elemi." For many years this gum, with a texture similar to honey, was in demand in the British and European drug trades as an ointment for healing wounds and for use as a plaster. The Spaniards used to employ it as a sticky pitch to repair their ships. Elemi is not so important a product today as in times past, having been replaced as an antiseptic by antibiotics, and as a plaster by synthetic materials.

The pili tree is of moderate height, reaching sixty to eighty feet, with a trunk diameter of about sixteen inches. It has large, evergreen, feathery leaves, four to eight inches long. It is dioecious, having male and female flowers on separate trees; the female trees begin to produce in the sixth year, but full production is not reached until twelve or fifteen years of age. The oblong, black, smooth fruits, which are about two and one-half inches in length, grow in clusters. Each fruit contains within a fleshy husk a single, slender, triangular, sweet-tasting, cream-colored nut which is pointed at both ends.

The tree is purely tropical; it thrives at low elevations in Luzon and other warm regions of the Philippines where rainfall is abundant. It cannot tolerate even a slight frost.

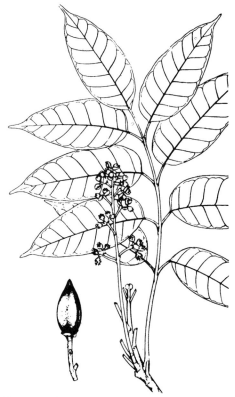

PILI NUT (*Canarium ovatum*)

PILI NUTS

ing in or near coconut and hemp plantations. The thick, bony shell of the nut is hard to crack—so hard in fact, that it may have been an obstacle to pili orchard development, even though the kernels are very popular for local consumption in the Philippines. The pili tree has been introduced to tropical America, where some promising agricultural research has been carried out at the Escuela Agricola Panamericana in El Zamorano, Honduras.

Pili nuts are eaten raw, or roasted and salted; in all cases, the seed coat is removed before eating. The kernels are suitable for the manufacture of nut chocolates and other sweet confections. The pili has a very high oil or fat content. Analysis of the edible portion shows it contains: fat (71.1%); protein (11.4%); and carbohydrates (8.4%). A good quality edible oil, suitable for culinary purposes, is expressed from the kernels; it also serves as a lamp oil in the Philippines.

Early in the twentieth century, pili nuts were being exported from the Philippines to the United States on a fairly large scale, but in recent years this trade has fallen off. The pili seems to be a minor nut with a promising potential, especially if thin-shelled varieties—with easy-to-crack shells—could be selected as sources of scion wood for vegetative propagation in order to establish future orchards.

The pili has a delicious flavor, suggestive of the almond. It is easily digested, in fact, a nutritious emulsion of the kernels is utilized now and then in the Philippines as a substitute for milk for infants. Nevertheless, the tree has not been cultivated on a large-scale commercial basis; production comes mainly from wild trees and scattered plantings grow-

Pine Nuts

THE PINE FAMILY (Pinaceae) is one of the most familiar groups of evergreen trees in North America since it furnishes most of our traditional Christmas trees, provides a strong, excellent softwood timber and is an important source of turpentine and rosin. Less known perhaps is the fact that some members of the genus *Pinus* also bear edible seeds, commonly referred to as nuts. Worldwide, approximate-

ly 100 species of true pines are recognized; of these, about a dozen—all in the Northern Hemisphere—produce nuts of sufficiently high quality and desirable flavor to make them worth gathering.

"Pine nut" denotes any of these edible nuts. Other distinctions should be made, however, depending upon the geographical area involved. The most common designation

309

for the nuts in Europe is "pignolia," a term which refers to pine nuts of the Italian stone pine, *Pinus pinea*, grown for the most part in Spain, Portugal, Italy and North Africa. Nuts of a different species called "piñon," a name derived from the Spanish word for pine nut, are produced in the western United States. These piñon nuts come mainly from the Colorado piñon tree, *P. edulis*, a two-needled pine which grows wild in the states of Colorado, New Mexico, Arizona and Utah.

Piñon nuts of lesser importance are harvested from other nut pines including the single-leaf piñon, *Pinus monophylla*, which oc-curs in mountainous regions of Arizona, Utah, Nevada, California and southward into Baja California; and from the Mexican piñon, *P. cembroides*, found in the Mexican states of Sonora, Chihuahua and Puebla, which is usually two or three-needled, and produces thicker-shelled nuts.

The Swiss stone pine, *Pinus cembra*, growing in the central European Alps and in the Carpathian Mountains, also produces edible nuts. Four other Asian nut pines include: the Chilghoza, *P. gerardiana*, of eastern Afghanistan, portions of Pakistan and northern Himalaya; the Siberian stone pine, *P. sibirica*,

ITALIAN STONE PINE—PIGNOLIA (*Pinus pinea*)
(from the Mediterranean region)

310

extending from the Ural Mountains eastward in the Soviet Union; the Korean nut pine, *P. koraiensis*, native to Korea, China, eastern Siberia and northern Japan; and the Japanese dwarf stone pine, *P. pumila*, found in the Japanese archipelago and on the adjacent Asian mainland. In most cases, these Asiatic pine nuts are popular foods locally, but elsewhere are not commercially important—with the exception of *P. koraiensis* nuts now being exported from mainland China.

In the United States nut trade, "pine nuts" may refer to the European pignolia, the North American piñon or the Chinese pine nut.

To trace the early history of pine nut utilization it is necessary to look to both Europe and North America and to consider separately the two major commercial species, the Italian stone pine and the common North American piñon.

In the Mediterranean region, the Italian stone pine is a familiar conifer. In addition to providing pignolia nuts (known in Italy as "pinocchios") and timber, it is an attractive, picturesque, ornamental tree which adapts well to both urban and rural settings. Easily recognized by its wide-spreading, umbrella-shaped head of foliage—it is often called the "umbrella pine"—the tree grows to a height of eighty feet. Its reddish brown bark is scaly and deeply furrowed, but not resinous like that of the American piñon; it has pairs of rigid, sharp, bright green needles, five to eight inches in length. The brown cones have a broad, ovoid shape, measure up to six inches in length, and are borne singly or in groups of two or three. Each cone contains a hundred or more narrow, cylindrical seeds, one-half to three-quarters of an inch long, with a hard, brown covering. The kernel is whitish-yellow, has a softer consistency than most nuts, and possesses a unique, sweet flavor. Its cones require three years to mature, a trait shared with the American piñon. Unlike the piñon, which crosses freely with other pines to produce natural hybrids and create problems for plant taxonomists, the Italian stone pine is very stable and apparently does

not hybridize with other species of *Pinus*. Based upon historical and paleobotanical evidence, it appears that *Pinus pinea* is indigenous to the Mediterranean region from the Iberian Peninsula to the coast of Asia Minor. It has been found to grow at altitudes ranging from sea level to about 3,000 feet.

The pine nut dates from a remote period in time. Hosea was a minor Hebrew prophet who lived during the eighth century B.C. in the kingdom of Israel. The Old Testament mentions the nut in Hosea 14:8: "I am like a *green fir tree*. From me is thy fruit found." Many Biblical scholars believe that this tree was the stone pine, *Pinus pinea*, and the edible fruit referred to was the pine nut.

The ancient Greeks and Romans appreciated the taste of pine nuts. Among the Greeks, the stone pine was held to be a tree sacred to the god Neptune. Records exist which mention the consumption of pine nuts around the beginning of the Christian era. The kernels were eaten, preserved in honey, during Pliny's time. Archaeologists have found pine nuts among household foodstuffs in the ruins of Pompeii, destroyed by the violent eruption of Mount Vesuvius in 79 A.D. The Roman Legions carried pine nuts among their provisions, evidenced by pine nut shells uncovered in refuse dumps of Roman encampments in Britain which date from the middle of the first century.

The traditional European method of harvesting pine nuts is to cut or break loose the cones by means of a long pole with an iron hook affixed to its end. The harvest is usually carried out during the period from October through the end of March; the harvest time is not critical, however, since the nuts store very well on the tree. Collected from beneath the trees, the cones are transported to open areas and heaped into long, low piles to dry in the sun. Sun drying causes the scales of the cones to open up and loosen the seeds, thereby facilitating their extraction by either manual or mechanical means. The cones are beaten by hand to separate the seeds, or threshed by machine. Once removed, the seeds are dried further before being processed in a milling machine to separate the kernel from its hard outer covering. The kernels and shells are separated by sifting; the testa, or thin skin which still covers the kernel, is then removed. Thereafter, the kernels are graded and sized. Superior, unblemished, shelled kernels, both large and small, are reserved for the export market, while the remaining kernels are sold locally or utilized in prepared foods.

Although pignolia nuts may be eaten out of hand, raw or roasted, they have the distinction of being the only nuts used predominantly as ingredients in cooking. For many centuries in European cookery, they have been blended in combination with lamb, veal, pork, chicken, fish, duck and game birds. They also have appeared in stuffings, sauces, vegetables, soups, stews, sweetmeats, cakes and puddings. To a lesser extent, they are coated with chocolate and eaten as candy. Inferior pignolias, not suitable for use as human food, are expressed in order to yield an oil employed in pharmaceuticals, while the residual cake is fed to livestock. Pine nut shells and cones provide a serviceable fuel in many European communities.

Pine nut development in North America is modest in comparison with that in Europe.

The Italian stone pine tree, with superior timber, is larger and grows faster than the stunted piñon of the southwestern United States. Italian stone pine plantations are well established in Mediterranean Europe, while the American piñon remains neglected and uncultivated.

It is estimated that extensive and sprawling piñon-juniper woodlands occupy some thirty-three million acres, lying between deserts and mountains—stretching from Texas to the Santa Inez Mountains of southern California and from southern Idaho deep into Mexico—primarily at elevations of 5,000 to 7,000 feet. The state tree of New Mexico, *Pinus edulis*, the common piñon, is small, rugged, drought-resistant, bushy and of low stature; it normally grows to a height of about twenty feet. It does not start to bear nuts until it is twenty-five years of age, and full production

PIÑON PINE NUT—*Pinus edulis*

From the Colorado piñon tree, which grows wild in Colorado, New Mexico, Arizona and Utah.

VENERABLE COLORADO
PIÑON

Growing in Roosevelt
National Forest, Colorado,
this tree's age is estimated to
be 600 to 800 years.

is not reached until it is seventy-five; it only bears large crops every third or fourth year. The foliage is made up of dark green needles which are fairly short—about three-quarters of an inch to two inches in length—and are usually borne in pairs. Mature cones of this pine are up to three inches long and contain approximately fifteen to thirty small, edible seeds, about three-eighths of an inch in length, which are the main piñon nuts of commerce. The piñon nuts are slightly darker in color, more ovoid and not so slender in shape as the pignolias.

Well before the domestication of other food plants, the pine nut was a food source for the Indians occupying the lands of the present southwestern United States. Archaeologists have found evidence of piñon nuts—charcoal and seed coats—in the firepits of Gatecliff Shelter, Nevada, carbon-dated at 6,000 years of age, as well as in caves in northwestern Utah in strata over 3,000 years old. Sixteenth-century Spanish explorers in the Southwest observed how the Indians utilized piñon nuts: Álvar Núñez Cabeza de Vaca noted in 1536 that the Indians (in southern New

Mexico) ground up the thin-shelled pine nuts and ate them as meal; in 1540, the chronicler for Francisco Vásquez de Coronado, the discoverer of the Grand Canyon, described how the Zuñis gathered and stored large quantities of the nuts. The piñon tree provided food and fuel for many Indian tribes of the Southwest, including the Navaho, Pueblo, Zuñi, Hopi, Shoshone, Gosiute and Cahuilla. Piñon wood was utilized in various types of construction, while the gum pitch was employed as glue for waterproofing jugs, as a black dye for blankets and to repair pottery. Piñon pitch was used medicinally to dress open wounds, while the fumes of the burning gum were inhaled to treat head colds, coughs and earaches. The piñon was an integral part of the mythology of many Indians of the Southwest: for example, the Navaho smeared piñon pitch on a corpse before burial. Before going out of doors in December, the Hopi applied a dab of the pitch to their foreheads as a protection against sorcerers. Incense for Navaho nocturnal ceremonies was provided by burning piñon gum, and specially selected piñon branches served as ritual wands.

Historically, the harvest of piñon nuts was a traditional family outing among the American Indians. In early autumn, many groups camped in the nut groves, often remaining until snowfall. Hooked sticks were sometimes used to beat down the cones from the trees, although the customary procedure was to pick the seeds off the ground. Some of the early cones, harvested in August and September when still green and tightly closed, were opened immediately by the heat of fires and consumed on the site, but the bulk was taken back to the villages, roasted in the shell, and stored in jars or baskets for winter consumption. (Unshelled, roasted piñon nuts can be stored for a year or more without becoming rancid.) The piñon festival was a high point of the year's activities.

The piñon nuts were consumed by the Indians in various ways: cracked between the teeth, they could be eaten raw or roasted, or, they could be ground into a flour and mixed with cornmeal or sunflower seed to make a nutritious bread. Sometimes the kernels were mashed to prepare a tasty pine nut butter to spread on hot corn cakes, or to make a thick soup.

Despite their importance as a wild food, piñon nuts have never become an important, commercial, domesticated tree crop. Perhaps due to the extensive tree stands and the abundance of wild nuts, cultivation of the piñon has seemed unnecessary. In addition, the excessively long wait—about a quarter of a century after planting—for the first crop may have been an obstacle. There is an additional problem at harvest time: if the cones are allowed to reach full maturity and drop their seeds—which makes them much easier to collect—there is a risk of losing a sizable

FOUR KINDS OF PINE NUTS

Upper left: Portuguese pignolias—
Pinus pinea
Upper right: Colorado piñon
nuts—*P. edulis*
Lower right: Chinese pine
nuts—*P. koraiensis*
Lower left: Mexican piñon
nuts—*P. cembroides*

314

portion of the crop to rats, squirrels and birds such as the jay and nutcracker. The wood rat is notorious for gathering and hoarding piñon nuts for the winter in hidden caches. One theory of how the American Indians first came to utilize piñon nuts holds that they discovered the rodents' caches, found the hidden nuts to be highly edible and thus got the idea of harvesting the nuts themselves. Even today wood rat and squirrel hiding places are plundered by humans for stored piñon nuts on some Indian reservations. Local authorities ask the people involved to replace the nuts they obtain with pinto beans in order to protect the animals' food supply.

Accurate, up-to-date statistics on piñon nuts harvested in the Southwest are not available, since collection is haphazard and large quantities are consumed but not reported. It is estimated that the annual piñon harvest in the United States is approximately two million to four million pounds. Apparently piñon nuts are not so important commercially today as they were fifty years ago: production declined after World War II, when there was a shortage of labor for the harvest, while the cost of available labor spiraled upward. There was also competition from less expensive nuts, especially peanuts.

A look at the nutritional composition of American piñon nuts in comparison with European pignolias, shows that the piñon nuts are higher in fat content, 60 per cent compared to 47 per cent; higher in food energy, with 2,800 calories per pound compared to 2,500; and higher in carbohydrate content, with 20 per cent compared to 12 per cent for the pignolias. In protein content, the pignolias are higher, with 31 per cent compared to 12 per cent for the piñon nuts.

In the United States nut trade, the American piñon ranks in importance behind the imported European pignolia; as a rule, both can be found for sale in well-stocked gourmet, health-food and specialty nut stores. Shelled pignolias, imported from Portugal, Spain and Italy, are generally the second most expensive edible nuts, following the macadamias. The piñon nuts from the Southwest, sometimes called "Indian nuts," are sold mainly in the shell and cost usually thirty to forty per cent less than the imported shelled pignolias. Steady supplies of piñon nuts cannot be relied upon, however, a disadvantage which has hurt their acceptance and sales. One year there may be a bumper piñon crop and the following season practically none may be available. Pignolia imports are far more dependable. During recent years, a new, and commercially competitive nut has arrived in the United States in the form of shelled Chinese pine nuts (*P. koraiensis*), that are imported from mainland China. Cheaper than the more delicate European pignolias, these Chinese pine nuts—whose shape is somewhat similar to that of small American piñones—are of rising importance. Many people still prefer the pignolias, however, in traditional dishes.

There is undoubtedly an enormous potential for increasing piñon nut production in the southwestern United States. Harvesting methods are still primitive and depend entirely on hand labor. Cultivation of the piñon pine in New Mexico, Arizona and Colorado is virtually nonexistent, since nut production comes from wild trees. With improved technical forestry practices, including timely pruning and thinning techniques, and the development of new orchards with selected, high-yielding cultivars, the piñon pine might become commercially important in time, not only in the Southwest but in the nationwide nut trade as well.

Pumpkin Seeds

THE PUMPKIN, *Cucurbita pepo*, of the gourd family (Cucurbitaceae) is most commonly thought of as a delectable pie or a jolly, jack-o'-lantern fruit for Halloween, but it also contains edible seeds. A coarse, annual vine of New World origin, *C. pepo* was widely distributed over central and northern Mexico and the southwestern United States in pre-Columbian times. Archaeological remains of pumpkin seeds, rinds and fruits have been found in the valley of Oaxaca, Mexico, dating back to 8750 B.C.; and in the Ocampo Caves, Tamaulipas, Mexico, dating from 7000 to 5000 B.C. The pumpkin formed an integral part of the corn-bean-squash complex which supplied the main diet of several pre-Columbian civilizations. The species was already widely grown in the Americas when the first Europeans arrived. The long-lasting pumpkin must have been an attractive food for primitive peoples lacking adequate means of food preservation. The fruits, seeds, and even the flowers provided nourishment. Also, the hard rinds of the mature fruits, after removal of the flesh and seeds, served as convenient containers.

During the sixteenth century, the pumpkin was introduced to Europe, where it was planted extensively from England to Italy. Later it was taken to Asia Minor, Africa and the Far East. The crop is now cultivated extensively in many tropical and subtropical regions throughout the world. In addition to *Cucurbita pepo*, other edible, annual species include *C. maxima*—cold-tolerant and of good quality; *C. moschata*, which is quite resistant to humidity and highly esteemed for its squash fruits; and *C. mixta*, of Guatemalan origin, a pumpkin with tasty seeds but stringy fruit flesh. It should be noted that pumpkins are not usually served as table vegetables since they are coarse and strongly flavored, a fact that makes them most appropriate for baking and for pumpkin pie, or for utilization as stock feed for animals. On the other hand,

squash, which generally refers to a fruit with a fine-grained flesh and a milder flavor, is more suitable for use as a vegetable. These popular, non-technical words, pumpkin and squash, are lay terms which have no botanical significance.

Pumpkins have the distinction of being the largest fruits of the plant kingdom, at times reaching weights in excess of 300 pounds, with huge circumferences of five to six feet. The fruits come in many different sizes. The average weight of the variety Connecticut Field, the common, orange-skinned, globular field pumpkin of New England, is

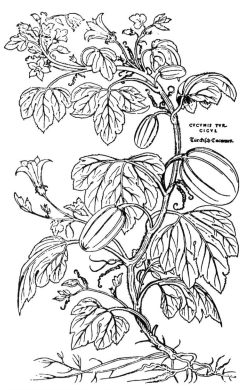

PUMPKIN SEED (*Cucurbita pepo*)

316

LADY GODIVA PUMPKINS
AND SEEDS

eighteen to twenty-five pounds. Small Sugar, the variety utilized for pumpkin pie at Thanksgiving time, weighs about five pounds. There are trailing varieties, producing stems several yards long, and bushy types with compact growth habits. All of them grow quickly.

The seeds are often planted in low mounds, four to five feet apart for the smaller, upright, bush-type vines and eight to twelve feet apart for the trailing, long-running types. Several seeds are planted in each mound, at a rate of three to four pounds per acre. The plants are frost-sensitive, drought-tolerant, and require long periods of warm, dry weather for optimum growth. They cannot tolerate wet, poorly drained, acid soils. Adequate fertilizing is essential. The stems and leaves are rough, hairy and scratchy to the touch. The fruits rest on the ground. The pumpkin has become popular mainly as the fresh vegetable known as summer squash which is harvested while the fruits are immature at about seven to eight weeks after planting—before the rinds begin to harden. Mature fruits, which take three to four months to develop fully, are baked for pies

and jams, canned, or employed as livestock feed. In recent years, the nutritious seeds, rich in fats and protein, have become more important as a health and snack food and as the source of pumpkin seed oil, an edible, unsaturated vegetable oil. The seeds are flat, white, elliptical, three-quarters to one inch in length and about one-half inch wide, with a thin seed coat. The seeds can be separated readily from the pulp, facilitating their use; they contain about forty-seven percent oil, twenty-nine per cent protein and are rich in Vitamin A. The seeds may be eaten like nuts, raw or roasted; fried in deep fat and salted, they are known as "pepitos." In some parts of Central America, the roasted kernels are combined with sticky syrup to form "pepitorio," a sweet confection which resembles popcorn balls. The seeds, ground into pumpkin meal, are sold in health-food stores in the United States and Europe for use in baked goods, as meat extenders and as ingredients of breakfast cereals.

Dried, ripe pumpkin seeds have been utilized medicinally in Latin America, Africa and India as an anthelmintic or verminfuge to expel intestinal worms. Some European physi-

317

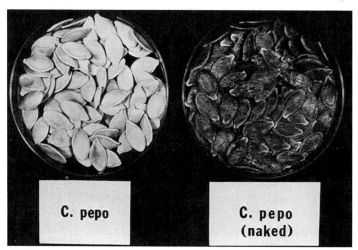

C. pepo

C. pepo
(naked)

PUMPKIN SEEDS

On the left, usual seeds of
C. pepo, enclosed in their
seed coats. On the right,
the Lady Godiva variety,
released by the U.S.D.A.
in the early 1970's, which
is naked, i.e. has no seed
coat.

cians recommend pumpkin seeds, rich in magnesium, to cure prostate troubles in aging men. They point out that there is virtually no incidence of enlarged prostate glands or other prostate disorders in several European regions in Hungary, Bulgaria, Transylvania and the Ukraine, where large quantities of pumpkin seeds are consumed. It is suggested that the seeds may provide regenerative building materials for male hormones to prevent swelling, attrition and deterioration of the prostate gland. Needless to say, this therapeutic recommendation is highly controversial, and further research is required to determine its validity.

In the early 1970's, the United States Department of Agriculture released a new, high-yielding pumpkin cultivar called Lady Godiva, with rounded, dark green, naked seeds that have no seed coat. These attractive, shell-less seeds are suitable for consumption as a snack food.

Apart from their snack value, cucurbit seeds are potentially important as an oilseed crop. For example, the buffalo gourd, *Cucurbita foetidissima*, grows well in desert regions and could be cultivated in dry, unproductive wastelands to provide an additional source of edible oil and protein to support the current geometric increase in the world's population.

Quandong Nuts

THE QUANDONG NUT, *Eucarya acuminata* (formerly *Fusanus acuminatus*), also known as the Australian "native peach," is a member of the sandalwood family (Santalaceae). "Quandong" is the aboriginal name for the small trees or shrubs, native to and abundant in the southwest and central desert regions of Australia, where there is little rainfall.

The quandong tree grows to a height of only twenty to thirty feet. It has thick, leathery, sharply-pointed, light green leaves, two to three inches long. The flowers are whitish

QUANDONG NUT (*Fusanus acuminatus*)

other tree. The quandong root then taps the host plant to drain moisture away from it into its own tissues. Consequently, a quandong tree will not grow well in isolation in an open field with no host plants.

In 1974, an experimental orchard of two hundred quandong plants was established in Quorn, South Australia—a region with a hot, arid climate most of the year, but subject occasionally to winter frosts. Kikuya grass was planted to serve as a host. Some quandong trees commenced fruiting after three years, but there has been considerable variability in the production and quality of the fruits and nuts. Although unusually delectable, the flavor of the quandong kernel tends to be too pungent and overpowering for some palates; efforts are being made to select types with milder-tasting nuts. These superior selections will be clonally propagated for distribution to interested growers in Australia.

From time to time, attempts have been made to introduce the quandong plant to other countries, without much success. Despite its captivating tang, the quandong seems destined to remain a minor Australian nut.

to cream colored. The fruits are globular, about one-half to three-quarters of an inch in diameter, and usually bright red in color. Within the pitted stone, inside the fruit pulp, is an edible, oily seed or nut, with a hard shell which is difficult to crack. The edible pulp, rich in vitamin C, may be eaten raw, used as a pie filling, or made into preserves and jellies with a flavor similar to that of the guava. The kernels, harshly aromatic in flavor, have been prized by the aborigines for many centuries; they are fairly popular throughout Australia, but virtually unknown elsewhere. The nutritious kernels, containing about sixty per cent fat and twenty-five per cent protein, are generally eaten roasted. Apart from their culinary utilization, the nuts are made into necklaces, bracelets and other ornaments. The timber of the tree is hard, durable and close-grained—a high quality wood for cabinet-making and wood-engraving.

The drought-tolerant quandong plant is a root parasite, which sends its roots along the ground until they encounter the roots of some

QUANDONG NUTS

319

Sesame Seeds

Sesame, *Sesamum indicum*, belongs to the sesame family (Pedaliaceae). Native to Indonesia and tropical Africa, the erect annual herb has been cultivated since earliest times in many hot countries of the Old World for its small seeds, which contain a superior vegetable oil employed in cooking. The seeds and leaves have been eaten traditionally as a food in Africa and India, while in most other coun-

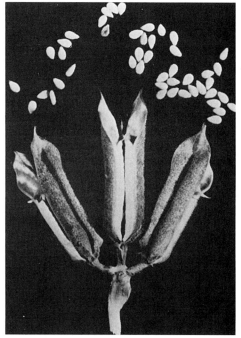

SESAME CAPSULES AND SEEDS

SESAME SEED   *Sesamum indicum* L.

tries sesame has been and still is grown for its oil. The versatile seed is also a spice—one of the oldest condiments known to man: records of its production in the Tigris and Euphrates valleys date back to 1600 B.C. The Egyptian name for sesame, *sesemt,* is found in the list of medicinal drugs recorded in the Ebers Papyrus, dated about 1550 B.C.

In *The Thousand and One Nights,* the story of Ali Baba and the forty thieves, a password was needed to open the door of the robbers' den. The magical command "Open Sesame" may have been chosen because the ripe sesame seeds burst from their pods suddenly with a sharp pop, like the springing open of a lock.

During the first century A.D., sesame oil was imported to Europe from India via the

320

Red Sea. By the Middle Ages, the crop was being cultivated in Egypt and exported to Venice from Alexandria. In 1298, Marco Polo reported that oil of sesame was being utilized in Persia for cooking purposes.

The use of sesame as a food and edible oil became widespread in Africa, where it was known as *benne*. During the seventeenth and eighteenth centuries, benne seeds were brought to America by the slaves, who looked upon them as tokens of good luck. Sesame oil was employed as a laxative and all-purpose medicine, as well as in cooking. Sesame is still known as benne in parts of the American South.

An herbaceous annual, sesame is grown only from seed. It thrives best in sandy, well-drained soils in a warm climate with moderate rainfall. The plants, which grow to a height of two to five feet, need a fairly long growing season of about four months to mature their seed. The seeds are small, glossy, flattish, and oval-shaped, about one-eighth of

SESAME SEEDS

The hulled seeds, on the left and above, are usually pearl white; black, unhulled seeds on the right; crunchy sesame sticks have been introduced in recent years to the nut snack trade.

an inch in length, one-twentieth inch thick, and are available hulled or unhulled. The hulled seed is pearl white in color. The unhulled seed varies in color from white to black though, depending on the cultivar, some are red or brown. The seeds are highly nutritious, containing up to sixty per cent oil and twenty-five per cent protein; when roasted, they have a tasty, nutty flavor reminiscent of the almond.

Total world production of sesame seed is about four billion pounds per year, most of which is converted to oil. India and China are the world's largest producers and users. Other important producing countries include Ethiopia, Nicaragua, the Sudan, Mexico, Guatemala and the United States. The crop is grown extensively in this country in Texas, California, Louisiana and Arizona.

The primary demand for sesame, a leading world oilseed, is for its fixed edible oil, obtained by expression. This pale yellow, nearly tasteless oil rarely becomes rancid; it is of great importance in Europe, the United States

SESAME IS AN ANNUAL PLANT

and elsewhere in the production of margarine, salad oils and good quality cooking oils. The recent emphasis on low-cholesterol diets has resulted in an increased demand for sesame oil as a source of polyunsaturated fats.

Sesame seeds are consumed in a variety of ways throughout many countries. They may be eaten dry; fried and added to soups; used as a garnish on savory dishes; sprinkled atop cakes, bread and pastries; or mixed with sugar to prepare the Jewish candy halvah and other sweet confections. In the Middle East,

sesame paste is spread on bread instead of butter. *Niu bi tang*, a sweet, gummy, malt candy is one of many popular Chinese confections which make use of sesame. In India, sesame oil has been employed traditionally as a substitute for ghee, as well as a medicinal tonic and laxative.

In recent years, sesame seed has been introduced to the snack-nut trade in the United States, where it is featured in crunchy products such as sesame nut mixes and sesame sticks.

Souari Nuts

THE SOUARI NUT, *Caryocar nuciferum*, belongs to the Caryocaraceae, a family of tropical American trees. Approximately fifteen species of *Caryocar* occur, all of which bear edible nuts. The unusual vernacular name, applied to several species, comes from the Cariban Indian word *sawarie*; it is spelled in a number of different ways, including souari, sawari, swarri and souri. To add to the confusion, the British often refer to the tree as "butternut," since the nuts have a high oil content of about sixty per cent. This tropical American butternut is not related to and should not be confused with the other butternut of the walnut family.

A handsome, lofty tree, up to 100 feet tall and four feet in diameter, with a spreading crown, the souari is native to northern Brazil and the adjoining Guianas. It has very large, trifoliate, evergreen leaves; the clusters of brightly-colored, showy flowers are deep purple on the outside and yellow within. They are borne at the ends of the branches, and remain conspicuous for some time after falling to the ground. The fruits are round, soft-wooded capsules, about six inches in diameter; when ripe, they crash to the ground and burst on impact, loosening the nuts they con-

SOUARI NUT (*Caryocar nuciferum*)

322

SOUARI FRUITS AND NUTS

few to several hundred. Harvesting is an arduous and dangerous task due to the density of the tropical undergrowth where deadly fer-de-lance snakes may lurk. The nuts are collected from the ground by natives, who compete with rodents and other animals for the fruits. The thick souari shell offers excellent protection, so the nuts can lie on the forest floor for some time without deterioration. One disadvantage of this solid, bulky shell is that it usually represents about eight per cent of the weight of the nut; freight charges are very high if souari nuts are exported in the shell. Efforts have been made in recent years to dry and shell the nuts in Suriname, prior to shipping the kernels overseas in sealed containers. Souari nuts are virtually unknown in the United States, but small quantities have been exported to England, where they have been well received. Souari timber is very durable and of good quality; it is utilized by the people of Suriname to construct canoes and small boats, but on a limited scale only, since the local inhabitants are aware of the value of the trees as a source of food and refrain from chopping them down.

tain (two to five in number) which are large, brown, kidney-shaped, and about the size of a hen's egg. Surrounding the nuts is an oily, yellow pulp which may be cooked and eaten as a vegetable. The nuts have a hard, woody, warty shell, about one-quarter of an inch thick, which is difficult to crack. The kernels, which are somewhat larger than Brazil nuts, are pure white and soft, with a sweet, almond-like flavor. A food resource of forest-dwelling Indians, souari nuts are eaten raw or roasted and also serve as a source of cooking oil.

Souari nut production comes almost entirely from wild trees in remote forest regions; the trees usually occur in isolated groups of a

Trial plantings of souari have been made in several tropical countries including Suriname, Trinidad, Sri Lanka and Malaysia. If plantations of selected, thin-shelled souari cultivars could be developed, in the course of time this tasty minor nut might become more important as a commodity in the world nut trade, and as a source of edible oil.

SOUARI NUTS

323

Soybeans

THE SOYBEAN, *Glycine max*, a member of the pea family (Leguminosae), is the most important world source of vegetable oil, supplying more than fifty per cent of the world's oilseeds. Native to eastern Asia, the plant was first domesticated in northeastern China about the eleventh century B.C. During the following millenium, its cultivation spread to Japan, Korea, Malaysia, Indonesia and elsewhere in the Orient where animal protein was and still is a luxury. Consumed in many different ways throughout the Far East, soybeans have become a prominent part of the human diet. Fresh, fermented or dried, they are eaten as vegetables. The dried beans, rich in digestible nutrients, are processed to produce soy milk,

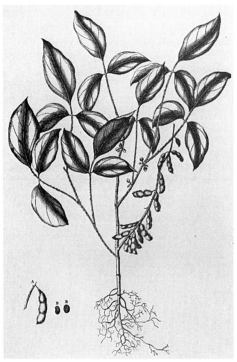

SOYBEAN (*Glycine soja*) (Botanical print, 1747)

a valuable protein supplement for feeding infants and invalids as well as a satisfying beverage for adults. Soy sauce, a dark brown liquid prepared from fermented soybeans, is a foremost flavoring in eastern Asia and a principal ingredient in some pungent Western sauces such as Worcestershire. Soybean sprouts—young seedlings grown in the dark and harvested about a week after germination—are popular in Chinese cookery. Soy flour, which has a high protein and low carbohydrate content, is mixed with wheat flour in Oriental baking. Whole, roasted soybeans are used in cakes and candies.

Long overlooked in the West, the versatile soybean did not achieve commercial status in the United States until the present century, when it was first utilized as a forage and later as an oilseed crop. During the past sixty years, it has made a phenomenal rise to prominence and is now this country's most important cash crop, having overtaken wheat and corn. Soybean acreage in the United States has increased from less than one-half million acres in 1920 to over seventy million acres by 1982. One reason for this vast increase in production is the ease with which the soybean crop can be fully mechanized. The traditional method of harvesting soybeans by hand still prevails in Asia and in many tropical countries where labor is abundant. In the United States on the other hand, harvesting is totally mechanized through combines which harvest and shell the beans, virtually eliminating hand labor. Production comes mainly from the midwestern and southern states; Illinois and Iowa are the leading producers. This country is the world's largest producer of soybeans; other important producing countries include Brazil, mainland China, Argentina, Canada and Mexico.

The soybean is a leguminous, subtropical annual, now grown extensively throughout the middle latitudes of the world. It is an erect

324

SOYBEANS

yield from twenty to twenty-three per cent of an edible oil, which is converted to margarine, shortening and salad oils. This yellowish oil, with fairly good drying qualities, is also important in the manufacture of plastics, paints, pharmaceuticals, soap and numerous other products. The beans contain about thirty-nine to forty-five per cent meal, which serves primarily as a source of high protein animal feed for the production of poultry, eggs, feedlot steer and pork. At the present time, some fifty million bushels, roughly two and one-half per cent of the soybean crop in this country, are employed for human food uses other than oil; the average individual in the United States consumes annually about thirty-five to forty pounds of soybean oil. The protein content of the dry soybean varies between thirty and forty-five per cent. The soy-

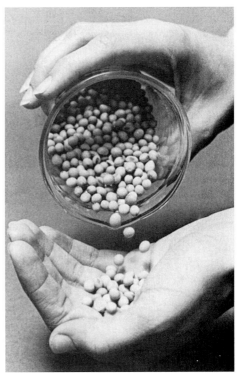

SOYBEANS

plant, twelve to forty-eight inches tall, depending on the cultivar. The leaves are pale and usually trifoliate. The stem, leaves and seed pods are covered with rough, brownish or grayish hairs; the flowers are small, white or light purple. The pods, two to three inches long and about one-half inch wide, commonly contain two to four small, smooth, globose seeds which are usually yellow but may be green, brown, red, black or multicolored. The length of the growing season ranges from 80 to 200 days, depending on the variety and the locality. Average yields of thirty-two bushels of soybeans per acre are obtained in the United States; elsewhere in the world, the yields are generally lower. Following the harvest, the beans are stored at a moisture content of twelve per cent or less.

In the West, the two foremost products, obtained through the processors' "crush," are soybean oil and soybean meal. The beans bean's nutritive value is very high, the proteins being of considerable biological value since they contain a good balance of the essential amino acids and possess as well a high calcium, iron and vitamin content.

The terms "soyfoods" and "soy deli," recent additions to everyday language in the United States, point out the growing interest in a vast array of edible soybean products for human consumption, once strictly East Asian, which are gradually becoming Americanized. Among the most popular of these soyfoods are *tofu, tempeh, miso,* and the more familiar soy sauces. Tofu, sometimes called "soybean cheese," is a bland, low-cost, highly digestible, white cake of pressed curds made from coagulated soymilk; it is as popular in Japan as bread in the United States. Tofu is now being incorporated in lunch programs in the school systems of Georgia, California, New York and Hawaii. Tempeh is a soybean patty with a nutty flavor, prepared from tender, dehulled, cooked soybeans which have been fermented for twenty-four hours; also easily digested, it is a basic food for millions of Indonesians. Miso, a seasoning with a consistency like peanut butter, is a fermented soybean paste composed of *koji*—polished rice which has been inoculated with the mold *Aspergillus*—mixed with cooked soybeans, salt and water, then set to ferment for one month or longer. True soy sauces—dark, liquid condiments *par excellence* known as "shoyu" and "tamari"—require about a year to prepare: soybeans, salt, water, koji (and sometimes wheat) are made into a mash and left to ferment in a vat. The liquid which oozes out of the mash is soy sauce. Some labeled soy sauces for sale in supermarkets, however, have been concocted rapidly in twenty-four hours through a chemical hydrolysis process.

Soy protein is utilized as an ingredient in many different processed foods including baked goods, meat, poultry and fish products, beverages, soups, sauces, confectionery, infant products and snacks. Meat alternates (imitation meats), breakfast strips, vegetarian entrées, whipped toppings and imitation cheese are examples of popular, processed, soy food products, sometimes referred to as analogs. Analogs are products which resemble conventional foods in appearance, color, flavor and texture. The growth in soy protein's acceptance is due to a number of factors including its versatility, nutritive value, low cost, abundance and availability. Its annual consumption in this country now amounts to over one billion pounds—an amount equal to four pounds per person.

These noteworthy advantages have led to the introduction of the soybean not only to the snack-nut trade, but also to the nut trade itself. Soybeans, in the form of "soynuts," are attractive nut substitutes. Like peanuts they belong to the pea family of plants bearing legumes or pods. Soynuts are whole soybeans which have been processed to look like nuts, taste like nuts and to be utilized like nuts. With a crunchy texture, no cholesterol, and more than double the protein content of most tree nuts, they have a low moisture content of two per cent, which allows for an unrefrigerated shelf life of six to eight months. Furthermore, the soynuts are available year-round and are relatively inexpensive since they are competitive in price with peanuts. The soynuts occupy roughly thirty per cent more volume than the same weight of peanuts or tree nuts, a factor which makes their price, per unit of volume, even more economical. On the other hand, many consumers still prefer the taste of tree nuts and peanuts to that of soynuts. Additionally, unlike many other nuts, soynuts cannot be sliced.

The development of soynuts commences with the planting of larger than usual soybeans, with a high protein and low oil content, in the northern part of the soybean belt in regions such as north-central Michigan. These selected, vegetable-type beans are fast maturing and ready for harvesting in eighty to ninety days. Their yield per acre is lower and their price higher than the customary, smaller, commercial, field-type soybeans.

Following the harvest, the soybeans are carefully cleaned and graded; their natural,

FIVE TYPES OF "SOYNUTS"

Clockwise, from middle left: Carob Superjoys; Soyjoys; Dry roasted soynuts; Barbecued soynuts; and Super Soys.

snack mixes, candy bars and various confections; they also serve as toppings for puddings or ice cream. The food service industry makes use of soynuts as a garnish for salads, soups and vegetables.

Oil-roasted soynuts are jumbo soybeans which look like dark-colored, roasted peanuts; preserving the basic nutrients, they retain their physical form and have a satisfying taste. They are marketed under several brand names, including: "Super Soys," "Golden Harvest," "Soy Town," and "Soy Ahoy." Dry-roasted soynuts, lighter in color, resemble dry-roasted, blanched, split peanuts; they are sold under brand names such as "Pro Nuts," and "Soy Nuts."

Tree nuts and peanuts undoubtedly face stiff, future competition in the nut trade from less expensive, readily-available and highly nutritious, processed soynuts.

somewhat overpowering, cereal-like taste—esteemed in the Orient but not pleasing to American tastebuds—is removed during preconditioning (expanding the beans) and processing, either through oil-roasting or dry-roasting. The oil-roasted soynuts are processed with or without the hulls; the dry-roasted are split and dehulled, since the hulls could become too dark or be burned during the roasting process. In either case, the processed, unseasoned soynuts end up with a bland, neutral taste. They are prepared for the market in a variety of flavors, including plain (unsalted), lightly salted, salted, seasoned (with garlic, onion-garlic, pizza, jalapeño, cheese, barbecue), as well as sweetened (butter toffee, carob, yogurt or chocolate-coated). The soynuts are sold in small, transparent packages or vacuum-sealed jars, like peanuts, in supermarkets, health-food stores, vending machines and through other retail outlets. Soynuts, like other nutmeats, can be used as an ingredient in nut bread, granola, trail mixes, cookie doughs, mixed nuts, natural

SOYBEANS

Peach Surprise Muffins (XLIII)

1-3/4 cup (325 ml) all-purpose flour, sifted	1/4 teaspoon (1 ml) nutmeg
1/4 cup (60 ml) soy flour, sifted	1 egg 1 cup (250 ml) soy milk
1/2 cup (125 ml) sugar	2 tablespoons (30 ml) soy oil
3 teaspoons (15 ml) baking powder	4 tablespoons (60 ml) peach preserves
1/2 teaspoon (2.5 ml) salt	

Preheat oven to 400° F (210° C). Sift flour, soy flour, sugar, baking powder, salt and nutmeg together into a mixing bowl. Make a well in the center. In a separate bowl, combine egg, milk and oil; mix thoroughly. Add egg mixture all at once to dry ingredients and stir until flour is moistened. Fill cups in greased muffin pan 1/3 full. Place 1 spoonful of peach preserves in the center of each. Spoon remaining batter into cups, until 2/3 full. Bake 20 to 25 minutes.

Yield: 12 muffins

Tahiti Chestnuts

THE TAHITI CHESTNUT, *Inocarpus fagiferus*, (formerly *Inocarpus edulis*), is a tropical tree in the large pea family (Leguminosae). Also known as the Polynesian chestnut, since it is native to Polynesia, the tree is a moderate-sized, slow-growing evergreen, up to thirty-five feet in height with long, drooping branches and large, shiny leaves. Widely distributed throughout the tropical Pacific islands, it is often cultivated near villages. It prefers a hot, humid, tropical climate at low altitudes, with well-distributed rainfall, and thrives along the banks of streams and even in swamps.

The flowers, borne on the tips of the branches, are small, yellowish-white and

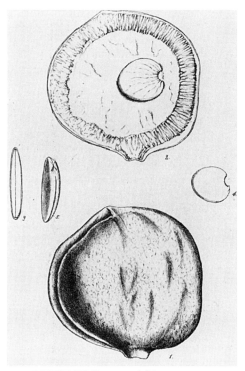

TAHITI CHESTNUT (*Inocarpus edulis*)

TAHITI CHESTNUT (*Inocarpus edulis*)

sourly fragrant; they develop into clusters of stout, kidney-shaped pods, some three inches in length, each of which contains one large, fleshy seed or "nut." Usually gathered when nearly ripe, the seeds are boiled or roasted and taste like chestnuts, accounting for the common name in English. Prevalent in the markets of French Polynesia, where they are sold threaded on twigs like beads, the seeds, known as *mape*, are a staple food in some archipelagoes. A popular Polynesian dish consists of flat cakes prepared from grated Tahiti chestnuts mixed with coconut meat, flavored with coconut cream, wrapped in green leaves and baked in a stone oven. In some Pacific islands the *mape* seeds are allowed to undergo

328

TAHITI CHESTNUT

partial fermentation, following which they are buried in underground pits where they are stored for future use—to be eaten when other native foods, such as breadfruit, become scarce.

Tahiti chestnuts, although quite palatable, are reputed to be somewhat difficult to digest, even when cooked. They are moderately nutritious, the leguminous seeds contain about 41 per cent carbohydrates, 5.6 per cent protein and 1.75 per cent fat. At the present time, it seems unlikely that these Polynesian "nuts" will become popular in the United States and Europe; they appear destined to remain an indigenous food item of southeast Asia.

Tallow Nuts

THE TALLOW NUT, or tallowwood plum, *Ximenia americana*, also known as "false sandalwood," belongs to the family Olacaceae. It is named after Francisco Ximenes, a Spanish friar who translated into Spanish a Latin manuscript describing the Mexican flora and fauna in 1615. This widespread species is found throughout the tropics of the world, equally at home in the East and the West. Its pleasantly scented timber resembles the aromatic, closely grained, true sandalwood for which it is sometimes substituted in India.

A densely-branched shrub or small tree, which is usually deciduous, the tallow nut rarely grows to a height of more than twenty-five feet; its branches are thorny, armed with numerous stout, sharp spines. When crushed, the elliptical, leathery leaves, have an odor similar to that of bitter almonds. The flowers

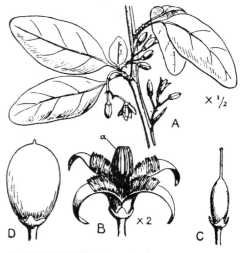

TALLOW NUT (*Ximenia americana*)

329

inches 1 2 3 4

TALLOW NUTS

are small, yellowish-white and fragrant. The juicy, fleshy pulp of the yellow or reddish-colored, egg-shaped fruit is plum-like in character, as suggested by several of its colloquial names such as "hog plum," "seaside plum," and "Spanish plum." Although the fruits have an acid taste like sour apples, they are eaten either raw or cooked, and can be made into an excellent jelly.

The fruits contain a large, oily seed, the kernel of which is white. Reports on the palatability of the tallow nut vary: some extol its flavor, comparing it to the filbert; others warn that the nuts are strongly purgative and should be eaten only a few at a time. The kernels are nutritious, rich in protein and have a high fat content of about sixty-six per cent; they may be eaten raw or roasted. A non-dry-

ing, pale yellow oil, extracted from tallow nuts, is utilized for cooking in southern India, to anoint the body and hair in Angola, and for making soap in many other countries.

In West Africa the pulverized bark and roots are used medicinally as a dressing for sores and ringworm; the freshly crushed leaves and roots are applied locally to treat headaches, while the bark is rubbed on the skin during the treatment of fevers.

The tallow nut is remarkable for its wide altitudinal distribution, from sea level to 7,000 feet, throughout the tropics of the world. Although it would probably lend itself well to cultivation in many regions, even on marginal soils, the tree has not been planted on a large-scale, commercial basis anywhere. It seems likely to remain a nut of minor importance.

Tiger Nuts

THE TIGER "NUT," *Cyperus esculentus,* is a low-growing, perennial, grass-like sedge, one to three feet tall, with stiff, triangular leaves, indigenous to the Mediterranean region and western Asia. A member of the sedge family (Cyperaceae), it is known by various other names, among them chufa, earth almond, earth nut, rush nut and zulu nut; chufa is the

best known name. Tiger "nuts" are not really nuts, but edible, underground tubers of the creeping rootstock of the plant. When dried, these tough-skinned corms, about one inch long by one-half inch in diameter, look like large, wrinkled peas. They possess an agreeable, slightly sweet, nutlike flavor.

Tiger nuts have been cultivated since an-

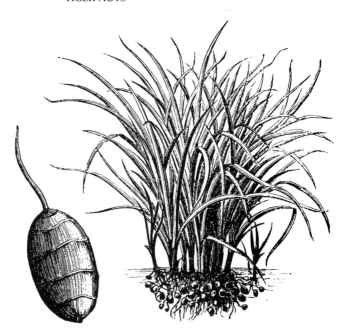

TIGER NUT (*Cyperus esculentus*)

cient times. Remains of tubers have been found in Egyptian tombs of the twelfth dynasty, dating from 2400 to 2200 B.C. Theophrastus, a Greek scientist of the third century B.C., described how the Egyptians harvested the tubers, cooked them in barley juice to add a sweet taste, then ate them as dessert nuts. Cultivation of the plant was spread by the Arabs following their conquests in North Africa, southern Italy and Spain. Although tiger nuts contain no caffeine, they have been utilized in the past as a coffee substitute in Germany and Hungary. The cooked tubers became popular as a vegetable in parts of southern Europe, Thailand and India. In Valencia, where tiger nuts have been cultivated for many years as a food for humans, a cool, refreshing, typically-Spanish beverage called "horchata de chufas" is prepared by mixing the ground tubers in water with spices such as cinnamon or vanilla and adding sugar and ice.

By 1854 the plant was introduced to the United States as a food for swine and the Patent Office distributed tiger nuts for plant-

ing in many states, under the name chufa. The cultivated strain, derived from tropical and sub-tropical Africa, could not be cultivated with success in the northern states. Chufa is grown to a limited extent today in the southeastern part of the country, especially in Florida where the tubers are relished by hogs. The "nuts" are harvested and fed to the animals, or the hogs may be turned loose in the fields to feed themselves. This relatively inexpensive method of feeding hogs does have a drawback, however, in that the meat tends to be fatty and soft compared to that of corn-fed pork.

Extensively cultivated on the west coast of Africa for human consumption, *Cyperus esculentus* has become naturalized in Ghana, Nigeria and Sierra Leone. The plant grows best in sandy loam, and likes medium or light rainfall. The climate should be warm and frost-free. The "nuts" are ready to be harvested in about three to four months after planting; they are washed, then dried in the sun for several days. During the harvest, a number of small tubers are likely to be left in the soil.

331

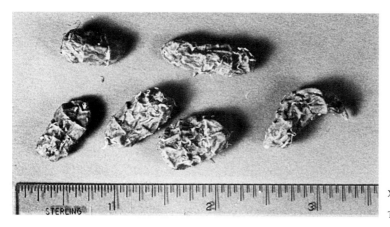

XIII.86

TIGER NUTS

Consequently, once established in some African regions, the tiger nut has become a weed that is difficult to eradicate.

The fibrous "nuts" may be eaten raw out of hand, but they are usually roasted or cooked and added to soups. In Ghana, a popular beverage known as "atadwe milk" is prepared by grinding and straining tiger nuts, then boiling the mash in water and adding wheat flour and sugar to form a milky pap. The grated "nuts" are also made into a chocolate-like paste, or utilized as an ingredient in sherbets and ice cream. In confectionery, the roasted "nuts" may be substituted for almonds. In Sierra Leone there is a native belief that the tiger nut has an aphrodisiac effect. The Zulus chew the tubers to relieve indiges-

tion and to sweeten a foul breath. When a Zulu maiden wants to hasten the inception of menstruation, she eats a porridge in which tiger nuts have been mashed.

Chufa oil, a yellow, transparent edible oil, is obtained from crushed tiger nuts; its pleasant odor is suggestive of burnt sugar. The "nuts" contain about twenty-eight per cent fat and forty-three per cent starch. Chufa oil, considered to be a superior table oil which compares favorably to olive oil, is also employed in soap-making.

In the United States the tiger nut is virtually unknown. Thus, though the crop is an important food in many warm, developing countries—especially in Africa—it seems destined to remain a minor nut in America.

Tropical Almonds

THE NAMES tropical almond, Indian almond and Malabar almond all refer to the tall, tropical, deciduous tree *Terminalia catappa,* a member of the family Combretaceae. The scientific binomial is descriptive, for *Terminalia* refers to the manner in which the leaves are borne in

bunches on the branch ends; while *catappa* comes from a Malayan name for the tree. Native to the sandy coasts of Malaysia and other regions of southeast Asia, the tropical almond has become naturalized throughout the tropics of the Old and New Worlds as an orna-

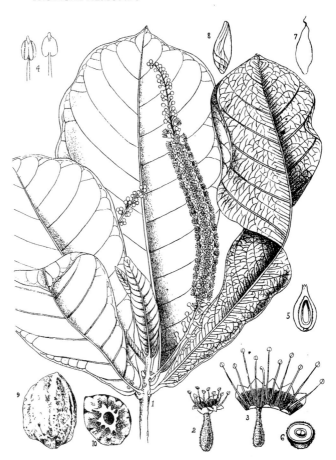

TROPICAL ALMOND (*Terminalia catappa*)

mental and shade tree; Captain Bligh brought it to St. Vincent in the West Indies in 1793, along with the breadfruit. Occasionally reaching a height of eighty feet (but usually less), it has a handsome, spreading, distinctively pyramidal form and branching habit: the relatively few branches are arranged circularly in whorls spreading horizontally on the same plane with one another in tiers, to give the tree a layered or candelabra-like appearance. The large, shiny, leathery leaves, abruptly pointed at the tips, from six to ten inches in length, on very short stalks, turn a striking red before they are shed in the cooler or drier season. Such conspicuous autumn leaves

TROPICAL ALMONDS

333

TROPICAL ALMONDS,
LEAVES AND FRUITS

without frost are very unusual in the tropics. New leaf growth on the tropical almond is tinted with red and purple.

Tropical almond fruits are about the size of a plum and are slightly compressed on two sides. They have a tender skin and a thin layer of edible, juicy pulp surrounding a thick, spongy shell, which is very difficult to crack. The crisp, white nutmeat of the small, slender kernel within the shell has a delicious flavor reminiscent of the true almond, *Prunus dulcis,* to which the tropical almond is not related. The nuts are edible, raw or roasted, and are popular and highly regarded in the Far East, having been described by one writer as "beyond comparison the most delicious nut of any kind India affords." In that country the nuts are often served at meal time, in a plate of water placed on the table. The trees have been widely planted as ornamentals in many fine avenues and parks in southern Florida, the West Indies and Latin America in localities free from frost, since they are easily killed by cold.

The kernels yield about fifty per cent of a sweet, colorless, nondrying, edible oil, "Indian almond oil," which resembles true almond oil in flavor and odor. Highly esteemed as a

GALL NUTS WATER

For sale in Benares, India, about 1820. The nuts, collected from the small Indian timber tree, *Terminalia chebula,* were converted into commercial myrobalans, used for tanning and dyeing. These fruits have also been utilized in Hindu medicine since ancient times as a purgative, and not consumed as an edible nut like *T. catappa.*

334

table oil in India and Malaysia, it does not readily become rancid. The oil cake is considered a good feed for pigs. The oil, leaves and bark have medicinal applications in southeast Asia. The leaves act as a sudorific which produces sweating; they are applied to relieve rheumatic joints. A decoction of the leaves has been utilized in Thailand and Vietnam to treat dysentery.

Several other *Terminalia* species, especially *T. chebula,* have long been important in the Orient because of their fruits, known as myrobalans, which are employed in tanning,

medicine and dyeing. Myrobalans are the source of a dye in demand in some parts of eastern India to color the teeth black, while in Hindu medicine they have traditionally been prescribed as a purgative.

Easily propagated by seed and tolerant of poor soils, the tropical almond seems more likely to gain wider recognition in the Western Hemisphere as a handsome ornamental tree than for its delicious nuts—which are not popular as a food, mainly because of the difficult of extracting the small kernels from their tenacious husks.

Water Chestnuts

TWO SOMEWHAT SIMILAR, although botanically unrelated, plant products are known as water chestnuts. Standing alone, the name usually refers to *Trapa natans,* the European water chestnut, which belongs to the water chestnut family of aquatic plants (Trapaceae). The addition of "Chinese" to the name changes the reference to *Eleocharis dulcis,* an Asiatic sedge of the family Cyperaceae.

Trapa is an abbreviation of the Old English *calcatrippe* or caltrap, an ancient instrument of war which was an insidious iron ball with four sharp-pointed spikes employed to impede and harass the enemy's cavalry. The dark brown, hard-shelled, woody fruit of the water caltrap (or caltrops) has four woody horns or spine-like projections which resemble that dreaded military weapon. The fruits are two to three inches wide from tip to tip of the horns and about one inch in depth. One large, white starchy kernel is enclosed within each fruit. Native to tropical Africa, central Europe and eastern Asia, the edible seed or nut of the water chestnut, raw or roasted, has been consumed in central Europe since Neolithic times. The floating, annual aquatic plants, with beautifully mottled foliage, grow luxuri-

EUROPEAN WATER CHESTNUT (*Trapa natans*)

335

WATER CHESTNUT (lower left); CHINESE WATER CHESTNUT (lower right); LOTUS (upper left).

336

EUROPEAN WATER CHESTNUTS (*Trapa natans*)

boiled, fried like a vegetable, preserved in honey and sugar, candied, or ground into flour for making bread. Another water chestnut, *T. bispinosa*, native to tropical Asia, is extensively cultivated in India, especially in the lakes and pools of Kashmir, where it is known as the Singhara nut. During several months of the year this nut is said to provide the main food for many thousands of Hindus. It is eaten raw, or cooked as a porridge.

Despite their usefulness in China and India, it is doubtful that water chestnuts of the *Trapa* species will become important commercially in the United States. The kernels contain about sixteen per cent starch and three per cent protein, but they are not particularly nutritious when compared with most other nuts.

The Chinese water chestnut, *Eleocharis dulcis*, commonly called "matai" in Cantonese, is more familiar to devotees of Chinese foods. A grasslike, annual plant common to marshy environments, it is a paddy crop which reaches three to five feet in height and

antly in standing water; they strike root in muddy bottoms and float on the surface of ponds, pools, lakes and irrigation tanks. The flowers are small, white and inconspicuous; the fruits are hidden beneath the aquatic foliage until they ripen, drop off and sink to the bottom. During the harvest, the nuts are gathered or scooped up from the depths in small nets. Introduced into the United States about one hundred years ago, the water chestnut has become naturalized in many eastern states to such an extent that in some regions it is now a pest which crowds out other native plants.

Related species have become important staple foods in other parts of the world. *Trapa bicornis*, called "Ling" in Chinese, is grown in China, Japan and Korea. As indicated by the botanical name, the fruits of this species bear only two horns, which resemble in miniature the skull of an ox. In China, the nuts are eaten

CHINESE WATER CHESTNUTS (*Eleocharis dulcis*)

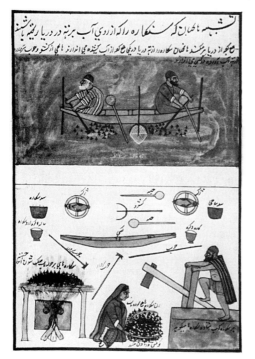

WATER CHESTNUTS IN THE VALLEY OF KASHMIR, NORTH INDIA

Painted by an unknown artist in Srinagar about 1850, these scenes portray the collection,
roasting and pounding of water chestnuts to prepare them for the local market.

spreads by means of horizontal rhizomes along the edges of shallow marshes and lakes. Indigenous to the tropics of the Old World, its range stretches from tropical Africa across to the islands of the Pacific. It is not a true nut as the name might imply, but is the edible, dark brown corm or tuber of an Asiatic sedge. The Chinese characters for matai mean "Horse's hoof," referring to the shape of the tubers. When cultivated, the corms are sprouted in nursery beds, then transplanted to fields which are flooded for six months and drained. After the tops are removed, the tubers are turned up by a plow and harvested by hand. At harvest time, the underground

corms, about an inch and one-half in diameter, are produced on rhizomes down to a depth of some ten inches—forming at times a solid mass of edible material. Under favorable conditions, from ten to twenty tons of corms may be harvested per acre. The Chinese water chestnut has a delicious flavor, reminiscent of sugar cane, sweet corn and coconut; it is starchy, similar to white potatoes in composition, and possesses a unique crisp texture which it retains, even after cooking. Sliced, peeled water chestnuts provide crispness to chop suey in this country, while shredded matai is an ingredient in a variety of Oriental soups, salads, meat and fish dishes. The raw

338

There is a steady demand for Chinese Water Chestnuts from mainland China and Taiwan in overseas Chinatowns.

corms are eaten out-of-hand in China as a substitute for fresh fruits, or frequently cooked alone as a winter vegetable. Minced matai is made into puddings. The edible portion of the Chinese water chestnut contains about 19 percent carbohydrate, 1.4 per cent protein and a very low fat content of 0.2 per cent.

Chinese water chestnuts have been cultivated experimentally, with controlled irrigation, as an annual crop in several temperate regions of the United States which have a lengthy, frost-free growing season of seven months. Promising areas for growing this aquatic vegetable in the future include the Atlantic and Gulf coastal states as far north as Virginia, as well as Puerto Rico and Hawaii.

Whole, peeled Chinese water chestnuts are exported, both in fresh form and canned, from mainland China and Taiwan to the United States and Europe, where there is a brisk demand for them in many overseas Chinatowns.

Watermelon Seeds

A NATIVE of desert areas of tropical and sub-tropical Africa on both sides of the equator, the watermelon, *Citrullus lanatus*, belongs to the gourd family (Cucurbitaceae). This annual, quick-growing, creeping vine was cultivated in Egypt in ancient times dating back to the IVth Dynasty (2900 to 2750 B.C.); its arrival in India was prehistoric. It was introduced to the Greco-Roman world during the beginning of the Christian era, and subsequently taken to China in the twelfth century A.D. where it became very popular in the province of Kwantung. By the end of the sixteenth century, the watermelon was being cultivated in England; it was then carried by Europeans to Brazil, the West Indies, eastern North America, the islands of the Pacific and Australia. It became widely disseminated throughout tropical and sub-tropical regions around the world.

In 1857, the Scottish missionary and explorer, David Livingstone, described the abundance of the watermelon in the vast, dry plateaus of the Kalahari Desert of Bechuanaland in central South Africa. He noted that the fruits were variable—some bitter and others sweet—while the natives and all animals of the region from mice to elephants ate them ravenously. Since they contain ninety per cent water, watermelons are a valuable alternative to drinking water in desert areas.

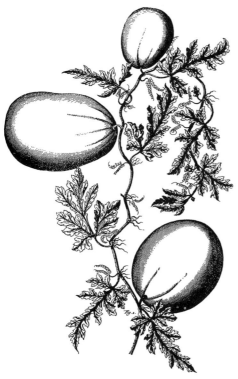

WATERMELON SEED (*Citrullus vulgaris*)

Although we do not usually place watermelon seeds in the category of nuts in this country, in other parts of the world, notably Africa and China, they are eaten out of hand just like peanuts—either raw or roasted—following removal of the seedcoat. In some districts of western tropical Africa, watermelons with bitter flesh are today grown solely for their edible seeds. Following the harvest, the ripe fruits are piled in heaps until their pulp has fermented; the seeds are popular ingredients in native soups and stews, or may be ground into meal to make bread.

Watermelons grow best in hot, dry areas, when exposed to full sunlight in sandy, well-drained soils. Liberal fertilization is recommended, as well as moderate watering every few days. The plants are drought-resistant, but will not withstand waterlogging or frost. The seeds may be sown two to three per hole at a spacing of three to four feet between the holes. Seedlings appear after about a week to ten days. Their stems, leaves and flower stalks are hairy. The flowers are yellow. Female flowers are often hand-pollinated in India and southern China where labor is cheap, but this labor-intensive practice is too expensive for most countries. The flower stalks

CLOSE-UP OF A
WATERMELON ON THE
VINE

340

WATER MELON SEEDS

Variety Charleston Gray.
Acceptable for eating.

gradually thicken and when the ovary begins to swell, bend over to contact the ground. One plant may produce three to five fruits, which are harvested about four to five months after sowing the seed. Depending on the cultivar, there is considerable diversity in the size, shape and color of the fruits, whose juicy flesh may be sweet or bitter, or white, pink, yellow or scarlet. Some fruits weigh ten pounds or less, while others may weigh ninety pounds or more. The edible seeds vary as well: they may be black, white, yellow or reddish. The seeds are smooth, flat, up to five-eighths inch long by one-quarter inch wide. A thin shell encloses an oily, nutritious kernel which contains some 20 to 45 per cent fat, about 35 per cent protein and is free of any poisonous substances. In many parts of Africa, a yellow, edible oil, extracted from the seeds, is employed for table use instead of peanut oil; the oil is also utilized as an ingredient for making soap and as a cheap illuminant. The seed cake can be used as a livestock feed. In tropical western Africa, the whole seeds are frequently chewed as a masticatory. In Nigeria the ground seeds are taken medicinally to treat diarrhea and dysentery.

Watermelon seeds are in demand as edible "nuts" in some countries, mainly Africa and China. Presently, however, the predominant interest in watermelons in the United States is for the sweet flesh of their perishable fruits, which are produced for the most part, in Florida, Georgia, Arizona, Texas and California. The nutritious but neglected seeds might find a modest place in the growing snack-nut trade in the future, although they are not nearly so popular today as sunflower and pumpkin seeds.

WATERMELON SEEDS

On left, shelled from Georgia.
On right, Chinese, roasted in the shell.

341

Glossary

A

Achene A small, dry, indehiscent, one-seeded fruit with a thin shell, whose seed is attached to the outer layer at one point only (example: the sunflower).

Acorn The one-seeded, non-splitting fruit of the oak.

Acre Unit of area commonly used in the United States; equal to 43,560 square feet. An acre is about 0.40 hectare.

Alkaloid An organic, nitrogen-containing, often bitter, constituent found in many plants, usually with marked biological activity.

Amygdalin A white, toxic, crystalline glycoside present in bitter almonds; used as a flavoring agent after hydrolysis and extraction of toxic substances.

Annual An herbaceous plant of one year's duration from seed to death, which flowers and produces seed within one year.

Anther The pollen-producing portion of the stamen.

Antibacterial Any substance that has the ability, even in dilute solutions, to destroy or inhibit the growth or reproduction of bacteria and other microorganisms; used especially in the treatment of infectious diseases of man and other animals and plants.

Antidote A substance that counteracts or negates in animal bodies the effects of poisons.

Antiseptic A substance which prevents sepsis, putrefaction, or decay by arresting the growth or action of noxious microorganisms, either by inhibiting their activity or by destroying them. The term antiseptic generally refers to agents applied to living tissue; the term disinfectant to those used on inanimate objects such as floors, walls, or clothing.

Aphid A small insect which sucks the juice of plants.

Aphrodisiac A drug or food believed to arouse sexual desire.

Aquatic A plant growing or living in or upon water (example: the water chestnut).

Aril An accessory appendage of certain seeds (examples: mace, the red, fleshy cover around the nutmeg seed; the swollen, white, jelly-like pulp around the litchi "nut").

Asexual propagation Producing a new plant by vegetative means, such as grafting, budding, or rooting of cuttings; reproduction without the union of male and female germ cells.

Axil The upper angle formed where a leafstalk (petiole) joins the stem that bears it.

B

Biennial An herbaceous plant of two years' duration from seed to death, usually flowering and fruiting only in the second year.

Binomial nomenclature Provision of a name of two Latinized words; the first is that of the genus, the second is the specific epithet. For example, in the case of the peanut, *Arachis hypogaea* L., *Arachis* is the name of the genus and *hypogaea* identifies the species. (L. is the abbreviation of Linnaeus, the person who first gave the species this binomial.)

Blanch To scald with water or steam in order to remove the skin, as in almonds.

Bud The immature or unopened state of a stem, leaf, or flower.

Bulb A modified underground stem usually consisting of overlapping fleshy scales (example: the onion).

Bur The rough, prickly seedcase or fruit of certain plants including nut trees such as the chestnut. Burs are made up of the matured clusters of small leaves which originally surrounded the flowers.

C

Calorie (large) The amount of heat required to raise the temperature of 1 kilogram of water 1 degree Centigrade; the unit customarily employed by nutritionists for measuring the energy value of foods and the energy needs and expenditures of man.

Calyx The outer circle of the floral envelope, the bracts or cup (usually green) enveloping the flower when in bud. (*See* Corolla.)

Cambium A layer of formative, dividing cells in woody plants between the bark and the wood.

Capsule A dry fruit, composed of two or more carpels, that splits open at maturity (example: sesame).

Carbohydrates Organic compounds, containing carbon combined with hydrogen and oxygen, which take part in the metabolism of plants and animals and include starches, sugars and celluloses.

Carminative A drug that relieves flatulence and assuages the pain associated with it.

Carpel An immature seed vessel; one of the units of the female element (pistil) of a flower. (*See* Gynoecium.)

Cashew apple The fleshy, usually pear-shaped stalk of the cashew fruit; the cashew nut is attached to its end. The cashew apple is nutritive and edible when completely ripe.

Catkin A slender, spikelike inflorescence (example: the chestnut).

Cereals Members of the grass family in which the grain is utilized for food and feed (examples: wheat and corn).

Cholesterol A crystalline fatty alcohol found especially in animal fats, tissues and bile; important in physiological processes and thought to be a factor in atherosclerosis.

Clone All the descendants of common ancestry derived asexually from a single, individual plant by means of vegetative propagation, such as grafting, budding, rooting of cuttings or multiplication of bulbs.

C N S L (Cashew Nut Shell Liquid) The brown, caustic, nut shell liquid found in the shell of the cashew nut. The toxic inner shell substances, which are highly irritating to the skin, are removed by roasting the nuts.

Condiment A substance used to give relish to food; a seasoning.

Conifer A plant species that bears its seeds in cones (example: the pine).

Coppicing The periodical cutting back of trees to near ground level to force the development of sprouts, suckers, or shoots.

Corm A solid, swollen part of a stem, usually underground, protected by a thin layer of scale leaves.

Corolla The inner of the two envelopes of certain flowers, composed of united petals, forming a bell, trumpet, tube, or similar shape. (*See* Calyx.)

Cover crop A crop sown to protect and enrich the soil (especially in orchards).

Cross-pollinate To apply pollen from one flower to the stigma of another flower.

Cultivar A horticultural variety that has originated in cultivation (example: the Nonpareil almond). Newly described cultivars bear modern language rather than Latin names. Within a plant species, a cultivar, or cultivated variety, differs in some measure from the rest of the species.

Cup-bearing Producing a woody, cup-shaped covering of the nut, made up of small, hardened, modified leaves, as in the acorns of oaks.

Cutting A segment of a stem, leaf or root; used in horticulture to propagate plants.

D

Damping-off A disease of germinating seedlings, generally caused by a fungus.

Deciduous Not evergreen. Generally applied to

woody plants (trees and shrubs) that lose all of their leaves annually.

Decoction A flavor or essence extracted by boiling.

Decorticate To remove the bark, husk or peel from stem fibers, fruits or seeds.

Dehiscence The bursting open at maturity of a dry capsule or seed pod. For example, sesame is dehiscent and its pod splits open at maturity; the filbert is indehiscent—its dry, woody shell does not burst open at maturity. Most nuts are indehiscent.

Dioecious Having the male and female flowers on separate plants (example: the pistachio).

Distillation A purification process in which a liquid is converted to vapor by the external application of heat and the vapor is condensed to the purified liquid by some means of cooling, usually a water-cooled condenser.

Domesticate To convert a wild plant species into a cultivated crop through selection and adaptation.

Drupe Usually, a one-seeded, indehiscent fruit with a fleshy (e.g. almond), spongy (e.g. walnut) or fibrous (e.g. coconut) portion covering a hard-shelled stone which contains the seed.

E

Embryo The rudimentary plantlet fully formed within the seed.

Emetic A drug that causes or promotes vomiting.

Emmenagogue A drug or physical measure that induces menstruation.

Endocarp The hardened, inner layer of the wall of a mature fruit (example: the tough shell of the almond).

Enzymes Organic substances, frequently proteins, produced by living cells, that promote chemical reactions in the metabolism of plants and animals. When outside of living cells, many enzymes are still capable of functioning and exerting a catalytic effect, as in fermentation.

Escape A cultivated or introduced plant that has "escaped" from cultivation and grows spontaneously.

Essential oils Volatile oils with a distinctive odor which evaporate readily and usually leave no stain. They occur in various parts of plants, especially in the flowers and leaves, and may be isolated from plants by distillation or extraction (example: peppermint oil).

Evergreen Having green leaves throughout the year (examples: the pine and the Brazil nut).

Expression The extraction or squeezing out of the fatty oils of seeds or nuts by mechanical pressure, as in soybean oil and peanut oil.

F

Family A group of related plants forming a category higher than a genus and lower than an order. The family names in plants usually end in "aceae," such as Anacardiaceae (cashew family), or Juglandaceae (walnut family) among the nuts.

Fat Solid or semisolid, oily or greasy substances found in plant and animal tissues; compounds of various fatty acids and glycerol, insoluble in water. The fat content of some nuts is high, i.e., about seventy percent in pecans and macadamia nuts. However, the fat content in most nuts is highly unsaturated and tends not to elevate blood cholesterol—unlike animal fats which are saturated. Fat may be in solid form, as butter or lard; or in liquid form as peanut oil, soybean oil and other vegetable oils.

Fertilization (1) In biology, the uniting of sperm and egg; (2) in agriculture, the application of manure or nutrient fertilizers on land to increase its productivity.

Fixed oils Fatty oils, usually bland, that leave a stain and do not evaporate (examples: peanut oil and sesame oil); they may be obtained by expression or solvent extraction, but not through steam distillation as with essential oils.

Flower The reproductive part of a plant having a short axis which, when the flower is perfect, bears an outer ring of calyx and corolla, a middle ring of stamens, and a central group of carpels (pistils).

Fruit The ripened or matured ovary of a plant (often with fused associated parts that developed with it from the flower), normally containing the seeds (ripened ovules).

Fungicide A chemical compound used to kill fungi or to check the growth of spores of fungi.

345

G

Genus (plural Genera) A major category of plants ranking above the species, and below the family. Among examples of nut-producing genera are: *Anacardium, Carya* and *Macadamia*.

Geotropic The growth of a plant part downward, responding to the pull of gravity (example: the ripening stalk of the peanut fruit).

Gland A secretory part or organ, such as the nectar gland of a flower.

Glycosides Physiologically active substances found in plants; when treated with acids or enzymes, they yield glucose or other sugars as well as nonsugar components.

Graft The act of inserting a piece of stem or scion with buds attached, of one plant, into the stem of another plant, placing the cambium layers adjacent so that union will take place.

Gynoecium The female parts of a flower collectively, including the carpels; the pistils as a unit.

H

Habitat The home of a plant; where it grows naturally or is indigenous.

Hectare In the metric system, a measure of area equal to 10,000 square meters (about 2.5 acres).

Heliotropic The tendency of certain plants to turn or bend under the influence of sunlight; for example, the movement of the sunflower head during the day to face the sun.

Herb A soft-stemmed plant that dies back to the ground at the end of its growing season; also a plant used for the sweet scent or taste of its herbage or flowers.

Herbaceous Pertaining to herbs. Not woody.

Herbicide A chemical substance utilized to destroy weeds, or to check their growth.

Hull The outer covering, or husk, of certain fruits or seeds.

Hybrid Offspring of mixed parentage, i.e., of two plants of different species or varieties. For example, when pecans and hickories are cross-pollinated, hybrid "hicans" result.

I

Imperfect Refers to a flower which contains the organ(s) of only one sex; that is, lacks either stamens or carpels.

Indehiscent Not splitting open when ripe.

Indigenous Native to a given place.

Inflorescence Flower-bearing branch, or the arrangement in which the flowers are borne.

K

Kernel The inner, edible portion of a nut; usually refers to the seed.

L

Lactiferous Bearing a milky fluid or latex, usually evident during injury to a plant.

Layering or Layerage The asexual propagation of plants by bending down a shoot or twig of the parent plant and partially covering it with earth so that it may take root.

Legume A plant of the pea family or Leguminosae. Beans, peas and peanuts are typical examples. Leguminous plants have the ability to produce nitrogen-fixing nodules on their roots.

M

Masticatory A substance to be chewed but not swallowed, to increase the flow of saliva (example: the betel "nut").

Metric ton A measure of mass equal to 1,000 kilograms (2,204.6 pounds), in the metric system.

Monoecious Having separate male and female flowers, but both types borne on the same plant, often on the same stem (example: the chestnut).

Myrobalans The dried fruits of certain tropical trees of the genus *Terminalia*; used in tanning and dyeing.

N

Nectar A sweetish liquid, secreted by flowers, that attracts pollinating insects. Bees make honey from the nectar and pollen of many flowers and, in so doing, inadvertently carry pollen from one stamen to the pistil of another flower, thus assisting in seed formation.

Nematode Belonging to a class of unsegmented roundworms; many are serious soil parasites of plants.

Node The point on a stem where one or more leaves are attached.

Nut A type of fruit that consists of one, often edible, hard seed, covered with a dry woody shell that does not split open at maturity; the kernel of such fruit, especially when edible.

Nutlet A small or diminutive nut, or nutlike fruit.

O

Ornamental In horticultural parlance, a plant cultivated for decorative purposes.

Ovary The female reproductive organ; in a flower, the basal, swollen, ovule-bearing portion of the carpel or pistil.

Ovoid Egg-shaped.

Ovule The egg-containing organ within the ovary which in a plant, following fertilization, develops into the seed.

P

Parasite An organism living within or on another, the host, at the expense of the host.

Perennial An herbaceous plant of several years' duration, as distinct from annuals (one year) and biennials (two years).

Perfect flower One having both male (staminate) and female (pistillate) parts.

Pericarp The covering of a seed derived from the ovary wall; the wall of a ripened ovary.

Petal One of the segments of the corolla of a flower.

Petiole The stalk of a leaf, absent if the leaf is sessile.

Pigment (as used in this book) Any of various coloring matters found in the cells and tissues of plants or animals.

Pistil The female reproductive portion of a flower, comprised of ovary, style and stigma; sometimes designated the gynoecium.

Pod A general term for a dry fruit that splits open at maturity; commonly applied to the legume of the pea family.

Pollen The male chromosome-bearing grains produced within the anther of a stamen; the basic male element of a flower.

Pollination The transfer of pollen from an anther to a receptive stigma.

Polygamous Having both perfect and imperfect flowers on the same plant (example: the cashew).

Protein Any of a large class of nitrogenous substances which are complex combinations of amino acids. An essential constituent of the protoplasm of all living cells.

Prune To remove vegetative parts of a plant to increase flower or fruit production or to improve its form.

Pubescent Covered with minute, soft, short hairs.

R

Raceme An elongated, unbranched flower cluster with individual flowers attached by short stems.

Repellent A substance which causes insects to react by staying away; employed to prevent insect attacks.

Resistant A plant which is able to grow and produce a crop even though infected with a disease. There are various degrees of resistance: a plant that grows in spite of the disease is called tolerant; one that is killed is classified as completely susceptible; complete resistance is known as immunity.

Rhizome A creeping, underground, fleshy stem, usually with scale-like leaves, which commonly produces roots at the nodes. When detached, or cut into sections, rhizomes can usually produce new plants. Rhizomes may store food material (example: the chufa or tiger "nut").

Rootlet A small root.

Rootstock In horticulture, a plant onto which a bud or scion of another plant is grafted.

Runner A slender, horizontal, trailing stem or branch, usually above ground, that may take root and produce new plants at the nodes.

S

Scion A detached stem or bud of a plant (usually a cultivar) that is transferred to a rooted part of another (the rootstock) in the horticultural practice of grafting.

Seed The ripened or matured ovule, consisting of two protective coats, an embryo, and a nourishing supply of reserve food, needed in the earliest stages of seed germination.

Seed leaf The first seedling leaves (technically called cotyledons) to appear after germination. They are preformed within mature seeds as a part of the plant embryo. Monocotyledons have a single seed leaf, whereas dicotyledons have usually two seed leaves.

Seedling A plant grown from seed, as distinguished from one propagated asexually by grafting, budding or rooting of cuttings. Plants grown from seeds (including trees) do not duplicate themselves exactly due to genetic differences within the seeds. For this reason, nut orchards are usually established with grafted trees of selected varieties or cultivars, and not with seedling trees. For example, seedling trees grown from seeds of the desirable Nonpareil almond variety will not produce more Nonpareil almonds, but smaller and different nuts that may be worthless; on the other hand, grafted trees of Nonpareil almond will bear nuts true to variety.

Self-fruitful Plants whose flowers pollinate themselves without need of pollen from another plant.

Sessile Without leafstalk or petiole, said of a leaf.

Shell (1) The relatively tough wall of the fruit which protects the seeds, as in the peanut; (2) the inner portion of the fruit wall, called the endocarp, as in the almond and in the pistachio. The shell itself, in many nuts, is protected by another outermost covering which is known as the hull or husk, as in the chestnut or filbert.

Species A category of plants subordinate to a genus but above a variety. For example: *Pistacia vera* is the botanical name for the pistachio; *Pistacia* is the genus, and *vera* is the species.

Stamen The male, pollen-bearing unit of a flower, usually comprised of filament (stalk) and anther (the pollen sacs).

Staminodium or Staminode A sterile stamen: that is, one that produces no pollen, often a filament only, or an abortive stamen.

Stigma The terminal part of the carpel or pistil that receives the pollen.

Stimulant Any substance, natural or synthetic, which exerts a stimulating effect upon the central nervous system and thereby promotes wakefulness.

Stomachic A drug, herb, or extract that acts as a tonic for the stomach and promotes gastric digestion.

Style The usually elongated portion of the pistil between the ovary and the stigma.

Sucker A vigorous shoot, usually originating from the roots or lower portion of the stem of woody plants. Sucker formation is often stimulated by wounding, as by pruning or when a tree is felled.

T

Testa The hard, protective, outer covering of a seed.

Tonic A remedial agent, usually in the form of a palatable liquid, that increases body tone by stimulating the nutrition of tissues within the body.

Topwork To cut back seedling trees and graft scions of selected cultivars on the resulting sprouts or branches.

Tuber A short, thick, fleshy part of an underground stem, serving the plant as a food-storage organ; usually characterized by sunken buds or "eyes," as in the potato.

V

Variety A category of classification subordinate to a species; a subdivision of a species.

Vegetative Synonym for nonsexual reproduction of plants, in contrast to sexual; refers to stem, root or leaf development, not to flower and seed development.

Vermifuge Any agent that expels intestinal worms and similar intestinal parasites upon ingestion or repeated ingestion.

Volunteer plants Plants which grow from seed remaining on the field from a previous crop; often unwanted.

W

Weed A troublesome, generally uncultivated plant which arises unwanted and grows abundantly in cultivated areas, thus becoming a nuisance.

Windrow A loose, continuous row of cut plant material gathered on the surface of the ground for drying and to facilitate the harvest.

Bibliography

Agnolini, Mario and Giuliani, Franco. *Cashew Cultivation.* Ministry of Foreign Affairs. Instituto Agronomico per l'oltremare. Florence, Italy, 1977.

Aldon, Earl F., and Loring, Thomas, J. *Ecology, uses, and management of piñon-juniper woodlands: Proceedings of the workshop.* Albuquerque, New Mexico, March 24-25, 1977. United States Department of Agriculture Forest Service General Technical Report RM-39; Rocky Mountain Forest and Range Experiment Station, Fort Collins, Colorado.

Allan, P. "Macadamia Nut Production Overseas, Part I." *Farming in South Africa,* No. 367. (March, May and June 1969).

Almeida, Carlos Pinto de. *Castanha do Pará.* Estudos Brasileiros No. 19. Ministerio de Agricultura. Rio de Janeiro, Brazil, 1963.

Almond Production Costs in California. Leaflet 2231. Division Agricultural Sciences. Compiled by A.D. Reed and L.A. Horel. University of California, 1979.

Almonds for goodness sake. Sacramento, California: Almond Board of California, May 1980.

Almond Facts. Sacramento, California: California Almond Growers Exchange, March/April 1979.

Almonds Health Nut. Sacramento, CA: Almond Board of California, September 1980.

The Almond Industry of Spain. Foreign Agriculture Service, FAS M-287. United States Department of Agriculture. Washington, D.C.: U.S. Government Printing Office, 1979.

American Soybean Association. *Contemporary Soybean Recipes.* St. Louis: 1980.

Ames, Oakes. *Economic Annuals and Human Cultures.* Cambridge, Mass.: Botanical Museum of Harvard University, 1939.

"An American Succeeds with Pecans in Australia." *Pecan South.* June 1981.

Andres, Cal. "The Versatile Soybean." *Food Processing,* May 1981.

Angrist, Stanley W. "Sunflower Seed Fuel?" *Forbes.* July 21, 1980.

Arber, Agnes. *Herbals, Their Origin and Evolution.* Darien, Conn.: Hafner Publishing Co., 1970.

Armour, R.P. "Kernel Weight in Relation to Fruit Size in the Pili Nut (*Canarium ovatum* Engl.)" Proceedings of American Society for Horticulture Sciences 9. Kingston, Jamaica: July 1965.

Asher, Sandra Fenichel. *The Great American Peanut Book.* New York: Grosset & Dunlap, 1977.

Ashworth, Fred L. "Butternuts, Siebold (Japanese) Walnuts and their Hybrids." *Handbook of North American Nut Trees.* Edited by Richard A. Jaynes. Northern Nut Growers Association, 1969.

Audas, James W. *Native Trees of Australia.* Melbourne: Whitcombe and Tombs, Ltd., 1952.

Axer, Jack. "Competitive Tree Nuts, Friend or Foe?" *Almond Facts.* Sacramento, California: California Almond Growers Exchange, March/April 1980.

_____. "World Cashew Production . . . in Review." *Almond Facts.* Sacramento, California: California Almond Growers Exchange, January/February 1980.

_____. "The World of Nuts." *Fruit Grower.* November 1980.

Bailey, L.H. *The Standard Cyclopedia of Horticulture.* I, II and III. New York: The Macmillan Company, 1963.

_____. *Hortus Third: A Concise Dictionary of Plants Cultivated in the United States and Canada.* New York: Macmillan Publishing Co., Inc., 1976.

351

BAKER, B.T. *World Almond Study, Tour Report 1980.* Department of Agriculture, South Australia, 1980.

BEARD, BENJAMIN H. "The Sunflower Crop." *Scientific American.* May 1981.

BECKMAN, DAVID L. "The Nutritious Nibble." *The Givaudan Flavorist.* No. 3 (1975).

BERRY, EDWARD W. "Notes on the Geological History of the Walnuts and Hickories." *The Plant World.* Vol. 15, No. 10 (October 1912).

THE BIBLE (authorized King James Version).

BLACK, JOHN M. *Flora of South Australia,* Part II. Adelaide: K.M. Stevenson, Government Printer, 1948.

"Blackline Disease Headlines Walnut Grower Event." *Fruit Grower,* June 1982.

BLOCH, FELIX and BREKKE, JOHN E. "Processing of Pistachio Nuts." *Economic Botany.* Vol. 14, No. 2 (April-June 1960).

Blue Diamond Almonds. Sacramento, California: California Almond Growers Exchange. (Undated).

Blue Diamond Bulletin. Sacramento, California: California Almond Growers Exchange, January 1982.

BOOMSMA, C.D. "Native Trees of South Australia." Woods and Forest Department, South Australia, 1981.

"Brazil nuts: another wonderful fruit (and a tasty one) of the Amazon jungle." *Brazil Trade and Industry.* August 1980.

BRISON, FRED R. *Pecan Culture.* Austin, Texas: Capital Printing, 1978.

Brooklyn Botanical Garden. Leaflets, May 17, 1922, Series X, No. 4, "Brazil Nuts."

BROTHWELL, DON and PATRICIA. *Food in Antiquity.* New York: Frederick A. Praeger, Publishers, 1969.

BROUK, B. *Plants Consumed by Man.* London: Academic Press, 1975.

BROWN, WILLIAM H. *Useful Plants of the Philippines.* Vol. 2 (Technical Bulletin No. 10), Manila: Department of Agriculture and Natural Resources, 1954.

BROWN, JUDY. "Soyfoods: Catching On in the U.S. Diet." *National Food Review.* Winter 1981.

BURKILL, I.H. *A Dictionary of the Economic Products of the Malay Peninsula.* London: Crown Agents for the Colonies, 1935.

BUSH, CARROLL D. *Nut Growers Handbook.* New York: Orange Judd Publishing Company, Inc., 1941.

"The California Walnut." Third Edition. Stock-ton, California: Diamond Walnut Growers, Inc., 1980.

CANTRELL, GEORGIA E. *Cashew Nuts.* War Food Administration. Washington, D.C., June 1945.

Cashew. Monograph on Plantation Crops - 1. Central Plantation Crops Research Institute. Kerala, India, March 1979.

CASTAÑEDA, RAFAEL ROMERO. *Frutas Silvestres de Colombia Vol. I.* Bogotá: Rafael Romero Castañeda, 1961.

Castanha do Brasil: Levantamento Preliminar. Ministerio da Agricultura. Belem, Pará, Brazil, 1976.

CAVALCANTE, PAULO B. *Frutas Comestíveis da Amazônia I.* Pub. No. 17, Museu Goeldi, Belém, Brazil.

CHANDLER, WILLIAM HENRY. *Deciduous Orchards.* Philadelphia: Lea & Febiger, 1957.

————. *Evergreen Orchards.* Philadelphia: Lea & Febiger, 1958.

CHAPMAN, STEPHEN R. and CARTER, LARK P. *Crop Production: Principles and Practices.* San Francisco: W.H. Freeman and Company, 1976.

Chestnut Blight and Resistant Chestnuts. Farmers' Bulletin No. 2068. United States Department of Agriculture. Washington, D.C.: U.S. Government Printing Office, 1954.

CHILD, REGINALD. *Coconuts.* London: Longmans, 1964.

CHILDERS, NORMAN FRANKLIN. *Modern Fruit Science.* New Brunswick, New Jersey: Horticultural Publications, Rutgers University, 1975.

China Reconstructs, August 1978. "The Lychee."

CHRISTISEN, DONALD M. "Nut Trees for Wildlife." *Nut Tree Culture in North America.* Edited by Richard A. Jaynes. Northern Nut Growers Association, 1979.

CLARK, MORTON GILL. *A World of Nut Recipes.* New York: Avenel Books, 1967.

COBIA, DAVID and ZIMMER, DAVID E. "Sunflower: Production and Marketing"; Extension Bulletin 25. (Revised) North Dakota State University, Fargo, North Dakota, July 1978.

COOK, O.F. "The Maya Breadnut in Southern Florida." *Science.* Vol. 82, No. 2139, December 27, 1935.

The Complete World of Mr. Peanut. Planters® Nuts. (Undated).

Composition of Foods. United States Department of Agriculture. Agricultural Handbook No. 8. Washington, D.C.: United States Department of Agriculture, 1975.

CORNER, E.J.H. *The Natural History of Palms.*

352

Berkeley: University of California Press, 1966.

————. *Wayside Trees of Malaya.* Singapore: Government Printing Office, 1952.

COUNCIL OF SCIENTIFIC & INDUSTRIAL RESEARCH. *The Wealth of India.* Vols. 1, 2, 3, 7 and 9. *Raw Materials.* New Delhi: Council of Scientific & Industrial Research, 1948, 1950, 1952, 1966 and 1972.

CRANE, H.L., REED, C.A., and WOOD, M.N. "Nut Breeding." *Yearbook of Agriculture.* Washington, D.C.: United States Department of Agriculture, 1937.

CRANE, JULIAN C. "Pistachio Nuts." *Tree Nuts: Production Processing, Products.* 2nd Edition. Woodroof, J.G. Westport, Conn.: Avi Publishing Company, 1979.

CRANE, JULIAN C. and DUNNING, J.J. "Separation of Blank Pistachio Nuts by Mechanical Harvesting." *California Agriculture.* November 1975.

CRANE, JULIAN C. and NELSON, M.M. "The Unusual Mechanism of Alternate Bearing in the Pistachio." *HortScience.* Vol. 6 (5) (October 1971).

CRIBB, A.D. and CRIBB, J.W. *Wild Food in Australia.* Sydney: William Collins, Pub., 1975.

CRITCHFIELD, WILLIAM B. and LITTLE, JR., ELBERT L. *Geographic Distribution of the Pines of the World.* Misc. Pub. No. 991, Forest Service. Washington, D.C.: United States Department of Agriculture, 1966.

————. *Subdivisions of the Genus PINUS (Pines).* Misc. Pub. No. 1144, Forest Service. Washington, D.C.: United States Department of Agriculture, 1969.

DAHLGREN, B.E. *The Coco Palm.* Chicago: Field Museum of Natural History, 1922.

————. *Tropical and Subtropical Fruits.* Chicago: Chicago Natural History Museum, 1947.

DALZIEL, J.M. *The Useful Plants of West Tropical Africa.* London: Crown Agents for the Colonies, 1948.

DASTUR, J.F. *Useful Plants of India and Pakistan.* Bombay: D.B. Taraporevala Sons & Co., 1951.

DE CANDOLLE, ALPHONSE. *Origin of Cultivated Plants.* New York: Hafner Publishing Company, 1964.

DENGLER, HARRY WILLIAM. "The Folklore of Walnuts." *Northern Nut Growers Association, 49th Annual Report.* 1958.

DICKSON, JOHN D. "Notes on Hair and Nail Loss After Ingesting Sapucaia Nuts (*Lecythis elliptica*)," *Economic Botany.* Vol. 23, No. 2 (April-June, 1969).

DILLER, JESSE D. *Chestnut Blight.* Forest Pest Leaflet 94. United States Department of Agriculture,

Forest Service. Washington, D.C.: U.S. Government Printing Office, March 1965.

DOYLE, ROGER P. and REDDING, JAMES L. *The Complete Food Handbook.* New York: Grove Press, Inc., 1976.

DUKE, JAMES A. *Handbook of Legumes of World Economic Importance.* New York: Plenum Press, 1981.

The Edible Nut Market, A Marketing and Economic Study. Merrick, New York: The Morton Research Corporation. (February-March 1982).

EFFERSON, J. NORMAN. "Lethal Yellowing is Cause of Alarm." *World Farming.* March 1979.

ELLACOMBE, HENRY N. *The Plant-Lore & Garden-Craft of Shakespeare.* Exeter, England: William Pollard, 1878.

ELLISON, E., HARDEN, J., and COLE, C. "Peanut Production in the U.S." *BASF Agricultural News.* No. 3 (1978).

ENGLER, A. *Die Pflanzenwelt Ost-Afrikas und der Nachbargebiete.* Berlin, 1895.

EPPERSON, J.E. and ALLISON, J.R. *The Pecan Producing Industry—A Two Region Analysis.* Research Report 320. Athens, Georgia: The University of Georgia College of Agriculture, July 1979.

ERICHSEN-BROWN, CHARLOTTE. *Use of Plants for the Past 500 Years.* Aurora, Ontario, Canada: Breezy Creeks Press, 1979.

FANSHAWE, D.B. *Forest Products of British Guiana.* Georgetown: Forest Department, 1950.

FAO Production Yearbook. FAO Statistics Series, Vol. 33. Rome: 1980.

————. *FAO Statistics Series.* Vol. 35. Rome: 1982.

FERNALD, MERRITT L. and KINSEY, ALFRED C. *Edible Wild Plants of Eastern North America.* Cornwall-on-Hudson, New York: Idlewild Press, 1943.

FLÜCKIGER, FRIEDRICH A., and HANBURY, DANIEL. *Pharmacographia: A History of the Principal Drugs of Vegetable Origin, Met With in Great Britain and British India.* London: Macmillan and Co., 1879.

FOGG, GEORGE G. "The Pinyon Pines and Man." *Economic Botany.* 20(1) (1966).

FORDE, HAROLD I. "Walnuts." *Advances in Fruit Breeding.* Edited by Jules Janick and James N. Moore. West Lafayette, Indiana: Purdue University Press, 1975.

————. "Persian Walnuts in the Western United States." *Nut Tree Culture in North America.* Edited by Richard A. Jaynes. The Northern Nut Growers Association, Inc., 1979.

FULLER, ANDREW S. *The Nut Culturist.* New York: Orange Judd Company, 1912.

FUNK, DAVID T. "Black Walnuts for Nuts and Timber." *Nut Tree Culture in North America*. Edited by Richard A. Jaynes. The Northern Nut Growers Association, Inc., 1979.

GARARD, IRA D. *The Story of Food.* Westport, Connecticut: The Avi Publishing Company, Inc., 1974.

GARNER, MARY L. "New Horizons for Soybeans." *Sunshine State Agricultural Research Report*. Florida Department of Agriculture, Winter 1979.

GASKILL, GORDON. "The Coconut Palm: A Living Supermarket." *Readers Digest*. August 1968.

GENTRY, HOWARD SCOTT. "The Natural History of Jojoba (*Simmondsia chinensis*) and its Cultural Aspects." *Economic Botany*. 12 (July-September 1958).

GIBBONS, EUELL. *Stalking the Wild Asparagus*. New York: David McKay, Inc., 1962.

GODFREY-SAM-AGGREY, W. "Cola Production in Ghana." *World Crops*, Vol. 21 (1969).

GOLDBECK, NIKKI and GOLDBECK, DAVID. *The Supermarket Handbook*. New York: New American Library, 1976.

GOOR, ASAPH and NUROCK, MAX. *The Fruits of the Holy Land*. Jerusalem: Israel Universities Press, 1968.

GORTON, LAURIE A. "Soy 'nuts' improve yield/lb 30-40%." *Baking Industry*, January 1977.

GOWDA, M. "The Story of Pan Chewing in India." *Botanical Museum Leaflets, Harvard University*, Vol. 14, No. 8 (January 15, 1951).

GREGORY, W.C. and GREGORY, M.P. "Groundnut." *Evolution of Crop Plants*. Edited by N.W. Simmonds. London: Longman Group Ltd., 1976.

GRIMWOOD, BRIAN E. *Coconut Palm Products: Their Processing in Developing Countries*. FAO Agricultural Development Paper No. 99. Rome: FAO, 1975.

GROFF, G. WEIDMAN. "The Introduction into the United States and the Culture of *Eleocharis dulcis*, the 'Matai' of China," *Proceedings Florida State Horticultural Society*. 1950.

GROVE, WILLIAM R., JR. and VAN SICKLER, D.R. "The Lychee in Florida Today." *Proceedings Florida State Horticultural Society*. Vol. 87 (1974).

Growing Filberts in Oregon. Oregon State University Extension Service. Extension Bulletin 628. Revised March 1978.

HAMILTON, R.A. and FUKUNAGA, EDWARD T. *Growing Macadamia Nuts in Hawaii*. Bulletin 121.

Honolulu: Hawaii Agricultural Experiment Station, University of Hawaii, January 1959.

HAMILTON, R.A. and NAKAMURA, MASAO. "*Kau*," a Promising New Macadamia Variety. No. 334. Honolulu: Hawaii Agricultural Experiment Station, Journal Series. May 1971.

HAMILTON, R.A. and STOREY, W.B. "Macadamia Nut Production in the Hawaiian Islands." *Economic Botany*. Vol. 10, No. 1 (January-March 1956).

HAMILTON, RICHARD A., YEE, WARREN and ITO, PHILIP. *Macadamia: Hawaii's Dessert Nut*. Revised, Circular 485. Honolulu: University of Hawaii at Manoa, March 1980.

HAMMONS, ROY O. *Early History and Origin of the Peanut. Peanuts . . . Culture and Uses*. A Symposium—American Peanut Research and Education Association, Inc. Stillwater, Oklahoma, 1973.

HARRAR, E.S. and HARRAR, J.G. *Guide to Southern Trees*. New York: McGraw-Hill Book Co., 1946.

HARRIES, H.C. "The Evolution, Dissemination and Classification of *Cocos nucifera* L." *The Botanical Review*. Vol. 44, No. 3 (July-September 1978).

HARRIS, THISTLE Y. *Australian Plants for the Garden*. Sydney: Angus and Robertson, 1953.

HARRISON, S.G., MASEFIELD, G.B., and WALLIS, MICHAEL. *The Oxford Book of Food Plants*. London: Oxford University Press, 1969.

HARTLINE, BEVERLY KARPLUS. "Fighting the Spreading Chestnut Blight." *Science*. Vol. 209 (August 22, 1980).

HAY, ANDREW MACKENZIE. *A Century of Coconuts*. New York: Calvert, Vavasseur & Co., Inc., 1972.

HAYTER, C.N. *The Oyster or Kueme Nut*. Bulletin No. 1560. Salisbury, Rhodesia: Minister of Agriculture and Lands, 1950.

HEISER, CHARLES B., JR. *The Gourd Book*. Norman, Oklahoma: University of Oklahoma Press, 1979.

————. *Seed to Civilization: The Story of Man's Food*. San Francisco: W.H. Freeman and Company, 1973.

————. "Sunflowers." *Evolution of Crop Plants*. Edited by N.W. Simmonds. London: Longman Group Ltd., 1976.

————. *The Sunflower*. Norman: University of Oklahoma Press, 1976.

————. "The Sunflower Among the North American Indians." *Proceedings of the American Philosophical Society*. Vol. 95, No. 4 (August 1951).

HENNING, RONALD J. "In a Nutshell." *Leaflet 312*,

Cooperative Extension Service. Athens, Georgia: University of Georgia, College of Agriculture, November 1978.

HEPTING, GEORGE H. "Death of the American Chestnut." *Journal of Forest History.* July 1974.

HERKLOTS, G.A.C. *Vegetables in South-East Asia.* London: George Allen & Unwin, Ltd., 1972.

HESS, JERRY. "Missouri Firm has 'open Sesame' to Snack Market." *Snack Food Magazine.* October 1981.

HEYERDAHL, THOR. *Kon-Tiki, Across the Pacific by Raft.* Chicago: Rand McNally & Company, 1950.

HILL, ALBERT F. *Economic Botany.* New York: McGraw-Hill Book Company, Inc., 1952.

HODGE, W.H. "Chinese Water Chestnut or Matai—A Paddy Crop of China." *Economic Botany.* Vol. 10, No. 1 (January-March 1956).

HOGAN, LeMOYNE; LEE, CHI WON; PALZKILL, D.A.; and FELDMAN, W.R. "Jojoba: A New Horticultural Crop for Arid Regions." *HortScience.* Vol. 15, No. 2 (April 1980).

HOROSCHAK, THEODORE. *The Walnut Industries of the Mediterranean Basin.* Foreign Agricultural Service Report No. M-245. Washington, D.C.: U.S. Government Printing Office, April 1972.

HOWES, F.N. *Nuts.* London: Faber and Faber, Limited, 1948.

HUNGER, F.W.T. *COCOS NUCIFERA.* Amsterdam: Scheltema & Holkema's Boekhandel, 1920.

HYMOWITZ, T. "On the Domestication of the Soybean." *Economic Botany.* Vol. 24, No. 4 (October-December 1970).

INFORMATION PLEASE ALMANAC 1982. New York: Simon and Schuster, 1982.

IRVINE, F.R. *West African Crops.* London: Oxford University Press, 1974.

————. *Woody Plants of Ghana.* London: Oxford University Press, 1961.

JACKS, T.J., HENSARLING, T.P. and YATSU, L.Y. "Cucurbit Seeds: I. Characterizations and Uses of Oils and Proteins. A Review." *Economic Botany.* Vol. 26, No. 2 (April-June 1972).

JANICK, JULES; SCHERY, ROBERT W.; WOODS, FRANK W.; and RUTTAN, VERNON W. *Plant Science, An Introduction to World Crops.* San Francisco: W.H. Freeman and Company, 1969.

JAYNES, RICHARD A. "Chestnuts." *Advances in Fruit Breeding.* Edited by Jules Janick and James N. Moore. West Lafayette, Indiana. Purdue University Press, 1975.

————. "Chestnuts." *Nut Tree Culture in North America.* Edited by Richard A. Jaynes. The Northern Nut Growers Association, Inc., 1979.

————. "The Late, Great American Chestnut." *Horticulture.* May 1978.

JOHNSON, DENNIS V. "The Botany, Origin and Spread of the Cashew, *Anacardium occidentale* L." *Journal of Plantation Crops.* Vol. 1, Nos. 1 & 2, (1973).

————. "Cashew Cultivation in Brazil," *Agronomia Moçambicana.* Lourenco Marques, Brazil. (July-September 1973).

————. "Cashew Nut Processing in Brazil." *Indian Cashew Journal.* Vol. XII, No. 2 (1979).

————. "Palm Fruit Products from Southeast Asia." *Principes.* Vol. 24, No. 1 (January 1980).

JOHNSON, F. ROY. *The Peanut Story.* Murfreesboro, North Carolina: Johnson Publishing Co., 1964.

JOHNSTON, RICHARD W. "A Marketing Man goes to work on the Macadamia Nut." *Fortune,* October 1976.

JOLEY, LLOYD E. "Pistachios." *Nut Tree Culture in North America.* Edited by Richard A. Jaynes. The Northern Nut Growers Association, Inc. 1979.

KADANS, JOSEPH M. *Encyclopedia of Fruits, Vegetables, Nuts and Seeds for Healthful Living.* West Nyack, New York: Parker Publishing Company, Inc., 1973.

KENNARD, WILLIAM C. and WINTERS, HAROLD F. *Some Fruits and Nuts for The Tropics.* Miscellaneous Publication No. 801, Agricultural Research Service. Washington, D.C.: United States Department of Agriculture, March 1960.

KERDEL-VEGAS, FRANCISCO. "The Depilatory and Cytoxic Action of 'Coco De Mono' (*Lecythis ollaria*) and its Relationship to Chronic Seleniosis." *Economic Botany.* Vol. 20, No. 2 (April-June 1966).

KESTER, DALE E. "Almonds." *Nut Tree Culture in North America.* Edited by Richard A. Jaynes. The Northern Nut Growers Association, Inc., 1979.

KESTER, DALE E. and ASAY, RICHARD A. "Almonds." *Advances in Fruit Breeding.* Edited by Jules Janick and James N. Moore. West Lafayette, Indiana: Purdue University Press, 1975.

KILLINGER, G.B. and STOKES, W.E. *Chufas in Florida.* Bulletin 419, Agricultural Experiment Station. Gainesville, Florida: University of Florida, February 1951.

KING, SETH S. "Sunflower Emerging as a Commodity." *The New York Times.* July 4, 1981.

KIRKBRIDE, DIANA. "Beidha, An Early Neolithic Vil-

355

lage in Jordan." *Archaeology Magazine.* Vol. 19, No. 3 (June 1966).

————. "Beidha: 1965 Campaign." *Archaeology Magazine.* Vol. 19, No. 4 (October 1966).

KRAPOVICKAS, ANTONIO. "Evolution of the Genus Arachis." *Agricultural Genetics.* Jerusalem: National Council for Research and Development, 1973.

KRAUS, BEATRICE H. and HAMILTON, RICHARD A. *Macadamia Nomenclature.* Bibliography of Macadamia. Research Report 176. Part I, Author's Index. Honolulu: Agricultural Experiment Station, College of Agriculture, University of Hawaii. June 1970.

KRUTCH, JOSEPH WOOD. *Herbal.* New York: G.P. Putnam's Sons, 1965.

KUZIO, WALTER. "Peanut Update." *Candy and Snack Industry.* February 1981.

LAGERSTEDT, HARRY B. " 'Ennis' and 'Butler' Filberts." *HortScience,* Vol. 15, December 1980.

————. "Filberts." *Nut Tree Culture in North America.* Edited by Richard A. Jaynes. The Northern Nut Growers Association, Inc., 1979.

————. "Filberts." *Advances in Fruit Breeding.* Edited by Jules Janick and James N. Moore. West Lafayette, Indiana: Purdue University Press, 1975.

LAMBOURNE, J. *The Brazil Nut in Malaya.* Kuala Lumpur: Department of Agriculture, Straits Settlements and Federated Malay States, March 1930.

LANE, FERDINAND C. *The Story of Trees.* Garden City, New York: Doubleday & Co., Inc., 1952.

LANNER, RONALD M. *The Piñon Pine: A Natural and Cultural History.* Reno: University of Nevada Press, 1981.

LEE, SHUN-CHING. *Forest Botany of China.* Shanghai: Commerical Press, Ltd., 1935.

LEHMAN, W.F.; ROBINSON, F.E.; KNOWLES, P.F.; and FLOCK, R.A. "Sunflowers in the Desert Valley areas of Southern California." *California Agriculture.* August 1973.

LEHNER, ERNST and LEHNER, JOHANNA. *Folklore and Symbolism of Flowers, Plants and Trees.* New York: Tudor Publishing Company, 1960.

LEIGH, D.S. *The Macadamia Nut.* Fifth Edition. Bulletin H 3.1.6. Division of Horticulture, New South Wales, Dept. of Agriculture, Australia: 1975.

LEVER, R.J.A.W. *Pests of the Coconut Palm.* FAO Agricultural Studies No. 77. Rome: FAO, 1969.

LEVITON, RICHARD. *Tofu, Tempeh, Miso and Other Soyfoods.* New Canaan, Connecticut: Keats Publishing, Inc., 1982.

LEYEL, MRS. C.F. *The Magic of Herbs.* New York: Harcourt Brace & Company, 1926.

LI, HUI-LIN. "Ginkgo—The Maidenhair Tree." *American Horticultural Magazine.* Vol. 40, No. 3, July 1961.

LOFGREN, JAMES R. "Sunflower for Confectionery Food, Birdfood, and Petfood." *Sunflower Science and Technology.* Edited by Jack F. Carter. Madison, Wisconsin: American Society of Agronomy, Agronomy No. 19, 1978.

LOWENSTEIN, ROGER. "Latest Riddle: When is a Shrub a Hedge? When it is a Jojoba." *The Wall Street Journal.* January 27, 1981.

MACDANIELS, L.H. "Hickories." *Nut Tree Culture in North America.* Edited by Richard A. Jaynes. Northern Nut Growers Association, 1979.

MACDANIELS, L.H. and PINNOW, DAVID L. "Walnut Toxicity, An Unsolved Problem." *Northern Nut Growers Association Proceedings.* 1976.

MACMILLAN, H.F. *Tropical Planting and Gardening.* London: Macmillan & Co., Ltd., 1962.

MADDEN, GEORGE. "Pecans." *Nut Tree Culture in North America.* Edited by Richard A. Jaynes. The Northern Nut Growers Association, Inc. 1979.

MADDEN, GEORGE D. and MALSTROM, HOWARD L. "Pecans and Hickories." *Advances in Fruit Breeding.* Edited by Jules Janick and James N. Moore. West Lafayette, Indiana: Purdue University Press, 1975.

MAIDEN, J.H. *The Forest Flora of New South Wales.* Vol. I. Sydney: Government Printer, 1904.

MASSAL, EMILE and BARRAU, JACQUES. *Food Plants of the South Sea Islands.* Technical Paper No. 94, South Pacific Comm., Noumea, New Caledonia, 1956.

McCONACHIE, IAN. "The Macadamia Story." *California Macadamia Society Yearbook.* Vol. XXVI. 1980.

McDANIEL, J.C. "Other Walnuts including Butternut, Heartnut, and Hybrids." *Nut Tree Culture in North America.* Edited by Richard A. Jaynes. Northern Nut Growers Association, 1979.

————. "Yankee Pecans." *American Fruit Grower.* May 1973.

McGraw Hill Encyclopedia of Science and Technology. New York: McGraw Hill, Inc., 1966.

McKAY, JOHN W. and CRANE, H.L. "Chinese Chestnut—a Promising New Orchard Crop."

Economic Botany. Vol. 7, No. 3 (July-September 1953).

MEDSGER, OLIVER PERRY. *Edible Wild Plants.* New York: The Macmillan Co., 1939.

MENNINGER, EDWIN A. *Edible Nuts of the World.* Stuart, Florida: Horticultural Books, Inc., 1977.

MERRIAM, C. HART. "The Acorn, a possibly neglected source of Food." from *National Geographic Magazine.* Vol. XXXIV. (1918).

MEYER, FREDERICK G. "Carbonized Food Plants of Pompeii, Herculaneum, and the Villa at Torre Annunziata." *Economic Botany.* 34 (October-December 1980).

MICKE, WARREN C. and KESTER, DALE E. *Almond Orchard Management.* Publication 4092. Division of Agricultural Sciences, University of California, 1978.

MILLER, MADELEINE S. and MILLER, J. LANE. *Harper's Bible Dictionary.* New York: Harper & Brothers, Publishers, 1956.

MILLIKAN, D.F. "Beeches, Oaks, Pines and Ginkgo." *Nut Tree Culture in North America.* Edited by Richard A. Jaynes. Northern Nut Growers Association, 1979.

————. "Oaks, Beech, Pines and Ginkgo." *Handbook of North American Nut Trees.* Edited by Richard A. Jaynes. Northern Nut Growers Association, 1969.

MIROV, N.T. *The Genus Pinus.* New York: The Ronald Press Company, 1967.

————. "Simmondsia or Jojoba—A problem in Economic Botany." *Economic Botany* 6, 1952.

MOLDENKE, HAROLD N., and MOLDENKE, ALMA L. *Plants of the Bible.* New York: The Ronald Press Company, 1952.

MOORE, THOMAS and AYRES, WILLIAM P. "Sacred Botany—The Terebinth—Nuts." *The Gardeners' Magazine of Botany.* Vol. 1. London, 1850.

MOORE, OSCAR K. "The Coconut Palm—Mankind's Greatest Provider in the Tropics." *Economic Botany.* Vol. 2, No. 2 (April-June 1948).

MORRIS, ROBERT T. *Nut Growing.* New York: The Macmillan Company, 1924.

MORTON, JULIA F. "The Cashew's Brighter Future." *Economic Botany.* Vol. 15, No. 1 (January-March, 1961).

————. "Further Associations of Plant Tannins and Human Cancer," *Quarterly Journal of Crude Drug Research.* Vol. 12, No. 1 (1972).

MORTON, JULIA F. and SNYDER, GEORGE H. "Aquatic Crops vs. Organic Soil Subsidence." *Proceedings Florida State Horticultural Society.* 89, 1976.

MORTON, JULIA F. and VENNING, FRANK D. "Avoid Failures and Losses in the Cultivation of the Cashew." *Economic Botany.* Vol. 26, No. 3 (July-September 1972).

MORTON, KENDAL and JULIA. *Fifty Tropical Fruits of Nassau.* Coral Gables, Fla.: Text House Inc., 1946.

MÜLLER, CARLOS HANS. *Castanha-Do-Brasil: Estudos Agronómicos.* EMBRAPA. Belem-Pará, Brazil, 1980.

NABHAN, GARY PAUL. "Southwestern Indian Sunflowers." *Desert Plants.* Vol. 1, No. 1 (August 1979).

NAIR, P.K. RAMACHANDRAN. *Intensive Multiple Cropping with Coconuts in India.* Berlin: Verlag Paul Parey, 1979.

NATIONAL PEANUT COUNCIL. *The Peanut Story.* Washington, D.C.: National Peanut Council, 1980.

————. *1981 Peanut Buyers Guide.* Washington, D.C.: National Peanut Council, 1981.

NATIONAL SOYBEAN PROCESSORS ASSOCIATION. *Soybean Processing in the United States.* Washington, D.C.: National Soybean Processors Association, 1981.

The New Encyclopaedia Britannica. Micropaedia. Vol. VII, 1980.

The New Treasury of Almond Recipes. Sacramento, California: California Almond Growers Exchange. (Undated).

Noncitrus Fruits and Nuts. Report FrNt 1-3 (81). United States Department of Agriculture. Washington, D.C.: U.S. Government Printing Office, 1981.

Nut Culture in the United States. United States Department of Agriculture, Division of Pomology. Washington, D.C.: U.S. Government Printing Office, 1896.

Nuts. Foreign Agriculture Circular FN 3-79, United States Department of Agriculture. Washington, D.C.: U.S. Government Printing Office, November 1979.

NZEKWU, ONUORA. "Kola Nut," *Nigeria Magazine.* Vol. 71, 1961.

OCHSE, J.J.; SOULE, JAMES; DIJKMAN, M.J. and WEHLBERG, C. *Tropical and Subtropical Agriculture.* I and II. New York: The Macmillan Company, 1970.

OGUTUGA, D.B.A. "Chemical Composition and Potential Commercial Uses of Kola Nut, *Cola*

357

nitida. . ." *Ghana Journal of Agricultural Science.* Vol. 8 (1975).

OHLER, J.G. *Cashew.* Communication 71. Department of Agricultural Research. Koninklijk Institut voor de Tropen. Amsterdam, 1979.

OPITZ, KARL W. "The Pistachio Nut." *Leaflet 2279. Division of Agricultural Sciences.* University of California, June 1975.

PALMER, E. LAURENCE. "Nuts." *Nature Magazine.* Vol. 33 (1940).

PARDO-TEJEDA, E. and SÁNCHEZ-MUÑOZ, C. *Brosimum alicastrum. Recurso Silvestre Tropical Desaprovechado.* Instituto de Investigaciones sobre Recursos Bioticos. Xalapa, Mexico, 1980.

PARK, J.W. "Gifts of the Americas. The Pecan." *Agriculture in the Americas.* Washington, D.C.: United States Department of Agriculture, Office of Foreign Agricultural Relations, August 1946.

PATIÑO, VICTOR MANUEL. *Plantas Cultivadas y Animales Domésticos en América Equinoccial*—Tomo I, Frutales. Imprenta Departamental, Cali, Colombia, 1963.

PAYNE, JERRY A. "Chinese Chestnut Production in the Southeastern United States: Practice, Problems and Possible Solutions." *Proceedings of the American Chestnut Symposium,* West Virginia University. January 4-5, 1978.

PAYNE, JERRY A.; JAYNES, RICHARD A.; and KAYS, STANLEY, J. "Chinese Chestnut Production in the United States: Practice, Problems and Possible Solutions." *Economic Botany.* 37(2)(1983).

PAYNE, JERRY A.; MALSTROM, HOWARD L.; and KENKNIGHT, GLENN E. "Insect Pests and Diseases of the Pecan." ARM-S-5. New Orleans: Agricultural Research (Southern Region), Science and Education Administration, Washington, D.C.: United States Department of Agriculture, November 1979.

Peanuts: Background Information and Program Alternatives. National Economics Division, United States Department of Agriculture. Washington, D.C.: U.S. Government Printing Office, February 1981.

Pecans: Handling, Storage, Processing and Utilization. Department of Food Science. Research Bulletin 197. Georgia Station: University of Georgia College of Agriculture, March 1977.

Pecans in Georgia. Bulletin 609. Cooperative Extension Service. Athens, Georgia: University of Georgia College of Agriculture, July 1975.

Pecan Nuts: Their Production and Marketing. T.P.I.

Report No. 27/62. London: Tropical Products Institute, 1962.

PENNINGTON, T.D. and SARUKHAN, JOSÉ. *Arboles Tropicales de Mexico.* F.A.O. & Instituto Nacional de Investigaciones Forestales, Mexico, D.F., 1968.

PETERS, CHARLES M. and PARDO-TEJEDA, ENRIQUE. "*Brosimum alicastrum* (Moraceae): Uses and Potential in Mexico." *Economic Botany.* 36(2) (1982).

PHILLIPS, HENRY. *Pomarium Britannicum.* London: Henry Colburn & Co., 1821.

Planters Pep. Planters ® Nuts. Suffolk, Virginia, October 1978.

POOLE, GRAY JOHNSON. *Nuts from Forest, Orchard and Field.* New York: Dodd, Mead & Company, 1974.

POPE, W.T. *The Macadamia Nut in Hawaii.* Bulletin No. 59. Honolulu: Hawaii Agricultural Experiment Station, November 1929.

POPENOE, JOHN and FISHER, JACK B. "Lethal Yellowing of Coconuts." *American Horticulturist,* Vol. 53, No. 3 (Late Summer 1974).

POPENOE, WILSON. *Manual of Tropical and Subtropical Fruits.* New York: The Macmillan Company, 1920.

PORTERFIELD, W.M., JR. "The Principal Chinese Vegetable Foods and Food Plants of Chinatown Markets." *Economic Botany.* Vol. 5, No. 1 (January-March 1951).

PRANCE, GHILLEAN T., and MORI, SCOTT A. *Flora Neotropica.* Monograph No. 21. Lecythidaceae—Part I. The New York Botanical Garden, New York, August 15, 1979.

Products from Jojoba: A Promising New Crop for Arid Lands. Washington, D.C.: National Academy of Sciences, 1975.

PURSEGLOVE, J.W. *Tropical Crops: Dicotyledons 1 and 2.* New York: John Wiley and Sons, 1968.

————. *Tropical Crops: Monocotyledons 2.* New York: John Wiley and Sons, Inc., 1972.

RAGHAVAN, V. and BARUAH, H.K. "Arecanut: India's Popular Masticatory—History, Chemistry and Utilization," *Economic Botany.* Vol. 12, No. 4 (October-December 1958).

RECORD, S.J. and HESS, R.W. *Timbers of the New World.* New Haven: Yale University Press, 1948.

REED, CLARENCE A. and DAVIDSON, JOHN. *The Improved Nut Trees of North America.* New York: The Devin-Adair Company, 1958.

ROBBINS, WILFRED W., and RAMALEY, FRANCIS. *Plants*

Useful to Man. Philadelphia: P. Blakiston's Sons & Co., Inc., 1937.

ROBINSON, R.G. "The Sunflower Crop in Minnesota." Bulletin 299. Agricultural Extension Service, University of Minnesota, 1973.

ROCK, JOSEPH F. *Leguminous Plants of Hawaii.* Honolulu: Hawaiian Sugar Planters' Association Experiment Station, 1920.

RODALE PRESS EDITORS. *Nuts and Seeds, The Natural Snacks.* Emmaus, Pa. Book Division, Rodale Press, Inc., 1973.

ROSENGARTEN, FREDERIC, JR. *The Book of Spices.* Wynnewood, Pennsylvania: Livingston Publishing Company, 1969.

SANBORN, R.R.; MIRCETICH, S.M.; NYLAND, G.; and MOLLER, W.J. " 'Golden Death,' a new leaf scorch threat to almond growers." *California Agriculture.* December, 1974.

SANCHEZ, LUIS and STOREY, W.B. "The Chilean Wild Nut or Avellano." *California Macadamia Society Yearbook.* Vol. 16, 1970.

SARGENT, CHARLES SPRAGUE. *Manual of the Trees of North America.* Vols. 1 and 2. New York: Dover Publications, Inc., 1965.

SAUNDERS, CHARLES FRANCIS. *Useful Wild Plants of the U.S. and Canada.* New York: Robert H. McBride & Co., 1934.

SCHERY, ROBERT W. *Plants for Man.* Englewood Cliffs, New Jersey: Prentice-Hall, Inc., 1972.

SCHREIBER, WALTER R. *The Amazon Basin Brazil Nut Industry.* Foreign Agriculture Report No. 49. Washington, D.C.: United States Department of Agriculture Office of Foreign Agricultural Relations, June, 1950.

————. *Filberts in Turkey.* United States Department of Agriculture, Foreign Agricultural Report No. 73. Washington, D.C.: U.S. Government Printing Office, June 1953.

SEDGLEY, M. "Technical notes: Preliminary Assessment of an Orchard of Quandong Seedling Trees." *The Journal of the Australian Institute of Agricultural Science.* Adelaide, 1982.

Seeds. 1961 Yearbook of Agriculture. United States Department of Agriculture, Washington, D.C.: U.S. Government Printing Office, 1961.

SHEPARD, RICHARD F. "The Favorite Nosh of the Queen of Sheba." *The New York Times Magazine.* October 21, 1979.

SHURTLEFF, WILLIAM "Soynuts. The Soybean's Answer to the Peanut." *Soyfoods.* Number 5 (Summer 1981).

SKEAT, WALTER W. *An Etymological Dictionary of the English Language.* Oxford: Oxford University Press, 1963.

SKIRVIN, ROBERT M. and CHU, MEL C. "Ginkgo: A Beautiful Tree with Edible Seeds." *Illinois Research.* Vol. 21, Number 4 (Fall 1979).

SMITH, J. RUSSELL. *Tree Crops: A Permanent Agriculture.* Old Greenwich, Connecticut: Devin-Adair Co., 1950.

SMITH, JEROME F. *Jojoba: The "Super Bean" of the Future.* Part I, 1982. San José, Costa Rica.

SOUZA, AMARO ENRIQUE DE. *Castanha do Pará.* Estudos Tecnicos No. 23. Rio de Janeiro, Brazil: Ministerio de Agricultura, 1963.

SOUZA-NOVELO, NARCISO. *Plantas Alimenticias y Plantas de Condimento.* Merida, Yucatán: Instituto Técnico Agricola Henequenero, 1950.

SOY PROTEIN COUNCIL. *Soy Protein: Improving our Food System.* Washington, D.C.: Soy Protein Council, 1982.

SPRECHER VON BERNEGG, ANDREAS. *Tropische und subtropische Weltwirtschaftspflanzen.* Stuttgart: Verlag von Ferdinand Enke, 1929.

STANDLEY, PAUL C. *Flora of the Lancetilla Valley, Honduras.* Chicago: Field Museum of Natural History, 1931.

————. "Trees and Shrubs of Mexico." *Contributions U.S. National Herbarium.* Vol. 23, Pt. 3. Washington, D.C.: Smithsonian Institution, 1923.

STANDLEY, PAUL C. and STEYERMARK, JULIAN A. "Flora of Guatemala." *Fieldiana: Botany.* Vol. 24, Pt. 4 Chicago: Chicago Natural History Museum, 1946.

Statistics of Hawaiian Agriculture 1979. Hawaiian Agricultural Reporting Service. Honolulu: Hawaii Department of Agriculture and United States Department of Agriculture, June 1980.

STEVENSON, TOM. "Plight of the Palms." *American Forests.* October 1976.

STOREY, J. BENTON. "Zinc Nutrition." *Texas Pecan Orchard Management Handbook.* Compiled at Texas Pecan Orchard Management Shortcourse. College Station, Texas: Texas A&M University, January 1981.

STOREY, W.B. "History of the Macadamia Nut." *California Macadamia Society Yearbook.* Vol. XXIII. 1977.

————. "Macadamia Facts and Fallacies." *California Macadamia Society Yearbook.* Vol. XXV. 1979.

359

STUCKEY, H.P. and KYLE, EDWIN JACKSON. *Pecan-Growing*. New York: The Macmillan Company, 1925.

STURTEVANT, E. LEWIS *Sturtevant's Notes on Edible Plants*. Edited by U.P. Hedrick. Albany, New York: J.B. Lyon Company, State Printers, 1919.

SYKES, J.T. "The Influence of Climate on the Regional Distribution of Nut Crops in Turkey." *Economic Botany*. 29 (April-June 1975).

TANNAHILL, REAY. *Food in History*. New York: Stein and Day, 1973.

TERRELL, EDWARD D. and WINTERS, HAROLD F. "Changes in Scientific Names for Certain Crop Plants." *HortScience*. Vol. 9(4) (August 1974).

TERRY, SARA. "Psst! Mister! Wanna buy a jojoba plantation, cheap?" *The Christian Science Monitor*. July 3, 1981.

TESCHE, WILLIAM C. *The Walnut and Filbert Industries of the Mediterranean Basin*. United States Department of Agriculture, Foreign Agriculture Report No. 93. Washington, D.C.: U.S. Government Printing Office, October 1956.

THAMPAN, P.K. *Handbook on Coconut Palm*. New Delhi: Oxford & IBH Publishing Co., 1981.

THEISS, LEWIS and THEISS, MARY. "By all Means Plant Nut Trees." *The Garden Magazine*. October 1921.

THOMAS, C.A. "Jackfruit, *Artocarpus heterophyllus* (Moraceae), as a Source of Food and Income." *Economic Botany*. Vol. 34, No. 2 (April-June 1980).

THOMSON, PAUL H. "Macadamia." *Nut Tree Culture in North America*. Edited by Richard A. Jaynes. The Northern Nut Growers Association, Inc., 1979.

TIPPO, OSWALD and STERN, WILLIAM LOUIS. *Humanistic Botany*. New York: W.W. Norton & Company, Inc., 1977.

TOWLE, MARGARET A. "The Ethnobotany of Pre-Columbian Peru." *Current Anthropology*. New York: Wenner Gren Foundation, 1961.

TURNER, NANCY J. and SZCZAWINSKI, ADAM F. *Edible Wild Fruits and Nuts of Canada*. Ottawa: National Museum of Natural Sciences, 1979.

UDUPA, K.N. and TRIPATHI, S.N. *Natürliche Heilkräfte*. Eltville am Rhein: Rheingauer Verlagsgesellschaft, West Germany, 1980.

UPHOF, J.C. *Dictionary of Economic Plants*. 2nd. ed. Würzburg, West Germany: Verlag von J. Cramer, 1968.

UNITED STATES DEPARTMENT OF AGRICULTURE.

"Growing Pumpkins and Swashes." *Farmer's Bulletin 2086*. Washington, D.C.: 1955.

VELAPPAN, E. and PAULOSE, T.T. "Present Position of the Arecanut Industry in India." *Arecanut and Spices Bulletin*, Vol. 6, No. 2 (October-December 1974).

Walnut Production in California. Leaflet 2984. University of California, Division of Agricultural Sciences, November 1978.

WARD, ARTEMAS. *The Encyclopedia of Food*. New York: Artemas Ward, 1923.

WATT, SIR GEORGE. *The Commercial Products of India*. New Delhi: Today & Tomorrow's Printers & Publishers, 1966.

WATT, JOHN M. and BREYER-BRANDWIJK, MARIA G. *Medicinal and Poisonous Plants of Southern and Eastern Africa*. Edinburgh: E. & S. Livingstone, Ltd., 1962.

Webster's Biographical Dictionary. Springfield, Massachusetts: G. & C. Merriam Co., 1961.

Webster's Geographical Dictionary. Springfield, Massachusetts: G. & C. Merriam Co., 1962.

WESTER, P.J. *Food Plants of the Philippines*. Bulletin No. 39. Manila: Department of Agriculture and Natural Resources, 1924.

WESTWOOD, MELVIN N. *Temperate-Zone Pomology*. San Francisco: W. H. Freeman and Company, 1978.

WHITAKER, THOMAS W. and CUTLER, HUGH C. "Prehistoric Cucurbits from the Valley of Oaxaca," *Economic Botany*. Vol. 25, No. 2 (April-June 1971).

WHITAKER, THOMAS W. and KNIGHT, JR., ROBERT J. "Collecting Cultivated and Wild Cucurbits in Mexico," *Economic Botany*. Vol. 34, No. 4 (October-December, 1980).

WHITEHOUSE, W.E. "The Pistachio Nut—A New Crop for the Western United States." *Economic Botany*. Vol. 11, No. 4 (October-December 1957.)

WILLIAMS, A.K. and LEEPER, GEORGE F. *Chinese Waterchestnut Culture*. United States Department of Agriculture. Information Sheet. Horticultural Crops Laboratory. Athens, Georgia: January 1976.

WILLIAMS, E.G.C. "Ginkgo." *Popular Gardening*. January 1953.

WILLIS, J.C. *A Dictionary of the Flowering Plants and Ferns*. 7th ed. Edited by H. K. Airy Shaw. Cambridge, England: Cambridge University Press, 1966.

WILSON, ROGER J. *The market for edible groundnuts*. G 96. London: Tropical Products Institute, 1975.

360

_____. *The market for cashew-nut kernels and cashew-nut shell liquid.* No. G 91. London: Tropical Products Institute, April 1975.

WOOD, MILO N. *Almond Culture in California.* Circular 103. California Agricultural Extension Service. Berkeley: The College of Agriculture, University of California, January 1937.

WOODROOF, J.G. and YOUNG, CLYDE T. "Nuts." *Kirk-Othmer Encyclopedia of Chemical Technology.* New York: John Wiley & Sons, Inc., 1967.

WOODROOF, JASPER GUY. *Coconuts: Production, Processing, Products.* 2nd ed. Westport: Avi Publishing Company, Inc., 1979.

_____. *Peanuts: Production, Processing, Products.* Westport: Avi Publishing Company, Inc., 1973.

_____. *Tree Nuts: Production, Processing, Products.* 2nd ed. Westport: Avi Publishing Company, Inc., 1979.

Yearbook of Agriculture. United States Department of Agriculture. Washington, D.C.: U.S. Government Printing Office, 1937.

YOUNG, W.J. "The Brazil Nut." *The Botanical Gazette.* University of Chicago Press, September 1911.

Recipe Acknowledgments

The author is most grateful to the following companies and other organizations for permission to use selected recipes:

Almond Recipes: I, California Almond Growers Exchange, Sacramento; II, Reprinted by permission of the Pillsbury Company *Goin' Nuts Cookbook*, © 1978; III, Sun Giant, Tenneco West, Inc.; IV, Almond Board of California.

Brazil Nut Recipes: V, Association of Food Distributors, Inc., New York; VI, *The Nut Jar*, Michigan Nut Growers Association; VII, *Brazilian Cookery*, by Margarette de Andrade. Published by A Casa do Livro Eldorado, Rio de Janeiro, 1978.

Cashew Recipes: VIII, Courtesy of Nabisco Brands, Inc. ("PLANTERS," "MR. PEANUT," and "MR. PEANUT DEVICE" are trademarks owned and used by Nabisco Brands, Incorporated); IX, Reprinted by permission of the Pillsbury Company *Goin' Nuts Cookbook*, © 1978; X, The Cashew Export Promotion Council, Ernakulam, Cochin, India.

Chestnut Recipes: XI, Southeastern Chestnut Growers Association, Atlanta, Georgia; XII, *The Nut Jar*, Michigan Nut Growers Association; XIII, Harriet Healy.

Coconut Recipes: XIV, Red V Coconut Products Company, Inc.; XV, Reproduced courtesy of General Foods Corp., owner of the registered trademarks BAKER'S, ANGEL FLAKE, JELL-O, POST, GERMAN'S, TOASTIES and GRAPE-NUTS.

Filbert Recipes: XVI, Oregon Filbert Commission, Tigard, Oregon; XVII, *The Nut Jar*, Michigan Nut Growers Association; XVIII, Harriet Healy.

Macadamia Nut Recipes: XIX, Mauna Loa Macadamia Nut Corp.

Peanut Recipes: XX, Courtesy of Nabisco Brands, Inc. ("PLANTERS," "MR. PEANUT," and "MR. PEANUT DEVICE" are trademarks owned and used by Nabisco Brands, Incorporated); XXI, Georgia Peanut Commission; XXII, National Peanut Council; XXIII, Georgia Agricultural Commodity Commission for Peanuts.

Pecan Recipes: XXIV, Imperial Sugar Company; XXV, National Pecan Marketing Council; XXVI, Reprinted by permission of the Pillsbury Company *Goin' Nuts Cookbook*, © 1978; XXVII, National Pecan Shellers & Processors Association; XXVIII, H.M. Thames Pecan Company, Inc., Mobile, Alabama; XXIX, Nut Tree Pecan Company; XXX, Georgia Pecan Growers Association.

Pistachio Recipes: XXXI, Sun Giant, Tenneco West, Inc.; XXXII, Courtesy of California Pistachio Association.

Sunflower Seed Recipes: XXXIII, Sigco Research, Inc.; XXXIV, Reprinted by permission of the Pillsbury Company *Goin' Nuts Cookbook*, © 1978; XXXV, Fisher Nut Company; XXXVI, North Dakota Sunflower Council.

Walnut Recipes: XXXVII, *The Nut Jar*, Michigan Nut Growers Association; XXXVIII, Reprinted by permission of the Pillsbury Company *Goin' Nuts Cookbook*, © 1978; XXXIX, Courtesy of Nabisco Brands, Inc. ("PLANTERS," "MR. PEANUT," and "MR. PEANUT DEVICE" are trademarks owned and used by Nabisco Brands, Incorporated); XL, Diamond Walnut Growers, Inc.

Other Edible Nut Recipes: XLI, Butternuts, *The Nut Jar*, Michigan Nut Growers Association; XLII, Hickory Nuts, *The Nut Jar*, Michigan Nut Growers Association; XLIII, Soybeans, American Soybean Association.

Illustration Acknowledgments

End papers in color, Lewis & Neale, Inc., New York; XIII, Robert Chip Vincent, American School of Classical Studies at Athens; XIV, The Mansell Collection, London; XV left, Julian C. Crane; XV right, *Gray's Anatomy*, Churchill, Livingstone, Edinburgh; XVI, Bobbi Angell, New York Botanical Garden; XVIII, United States Department of Agriculture; XIX, *The Nut Gatherers*, Painting by Edward Henry Wehnert, London, 1850. (Courtesy of The British Library); 2, *Icones plantarum medicinalium*. Nürnberg: Johannes Zorn, 1790; 4 top, *Kräuterbuch*. Basel: D. Jacobi Theodori, 1731; 4 bottom, Lübecker Bibel of Arndes. Lübeck, 1494; 5 top, Frederick G. Meyer; 5 bottom, Royal Ontario Museum, Toronto; 6, *De Crescentiis Commodorum ruralium libri*. Speyer: Peter Drach, 1493; 7, Courtesy, Field Museum of Natural History, Chicago; 8 top and 8 bottom, T. M. Duché Nut Co., Inc.; 9 top, California Almond Growers Exchange, Sacramento; 9 bottom, Julian C. Crane; 10 top and 14, Elmer W. Smith Stamp Collection; 10 bottom, South Australian Department of Agriculture; 12, Warren T. Johnson. From *Nut Tree Culture in North America*, 1979; 13, California Almond Growers Exchange, Sacramento; 15, The Five Forms of California Almonds. From *The Art of Almond Cookery*, Blue Diamond, California Almond Growers Exchange, Sacramento; 16, 17, and 18, California Growers Exchange, Sacramento; 22, *Plantae Aequinoctiales*. Tubingae: Alexander von Humboldt and Aimé Bonpland, 1808. (Courtesy of the Linnean Society of London); 24 top, *Revue Horticole*. Paris, 1867; 24 bottom left, Ghillean T. Prance; 24 bottom right, *Annals of Botany*, Volume XV. London, 1901; 25, U.S.D.A., Office of Foreign Agricultural Relations; 26 and 28, *Tipos e Aspectos do Brasil*. Illustrations by Percy Lau. Rio de Janeiro: I.B.G.E., 1975; 27, Courtesy, Field Museum of Natural History, Chicago; 29 top, United States Department of Agriculture; 29 bottom and 30 top, Lewis E. Nordlinger; 31 top, United States Department of Agriculture; 31 bottom, Ghillean T. Prance; 34, Association of Food Distributors, Inc., New York; 36, *Selectarum stirpium americanarum*. Nicolaus Joseph Jacquin. Mannheim, 1788; 38 top left, *Historia Natural do Brasil ilustrada*. Guilherme Piso. Amsterdam, 1648; 38 top right, Elmer W. Smith Stamp Collection; 38 bottom, *Singularidades da Franca Antartica*. A. Thevet, 1558; 39, United Press International photo; 40 top, United States Department of Agriculture; 40 bottom, Botanical Museum, Harvard University; 41 and 43, The Cashew Export Promotion Council, Ernakulam, Cochin, India; 42, *Tipos e Aspectos do Brasil*. Illustration by Percy Lau. Rio de Janeiro: I.B.G.E., 1975; 45, United Press International photo; 46, Valbolan, Cia., Ltda., Quezaltenango, Guatemala; 47, *Tipos e Aspectos do Brasil*. From an illustration by Percy Lau. Rio de Janeiro: I.B.G.E., 1975; 48, "PLANTERS," "MR. PEANUT," and "MR. PEANUT Device" are Trademarks owned and used by Nabisco Brands, Inc.; 50, *The Herball or Generall Historie of Plantes*. John Gerarde. London, 1636; 52, Illustration by Winslow Homer. From *Every Saturday*, October 29, 1870. (Courtesy of Princeton University Library); 53 left, *North American Sylva*. F. A. Michaux. Philadelphia, 1865; 53 right, Forest Hill Society, Santa Cruz, California; 54 left, *Nut Culture in the United States*. U.S.D.A. 1896; 54 right, United States Department of Agriculture; 55, National Park Service, Longfellow National Historic Site; 56 left, *The Nut Culturist*. Andrew S. Fuller. New York: Orange Judd Co., 1912; 56 right, The Arnold Arboretum of

Harvard University; 57, Richard A. Jaynes; 58, Jerry A. Payne; 59 left, *The Nut Culturist*. Andrew S. Fuller. New York: Orange Judd Co., 1912; 59 right, 2 stamps, Elmer W. Smith Stamp Collection; 60, H. Armstrong Roberts, Inc.; 61, *A History of the Vegetable Kingdom*. William Rhind. London: Blackie & Son, 1857; 64 and 91, *Recueil de Planches de Botanique de l'Encyclopedie*. Paris, 1823; 66 top, *A Monograph on the Coconut Palm*. John Shortt. Madras, India, 1885; 66 bottom, The Malay States Information Agency; 67, 68 and 71, *COCOS NUCIFERA*. F. W. T. Hunger. Amsterdam: Scheltema & Holkema's Boekhandel, 1920; 69 left, *De Kokospalm of Klapperboom*. L. Th. Maijer. Batavia, Java, 1917; 69 right, *La Noix de Coco*. Octave-J.-A. Collet. Paris, 1913; 70 and 90, Crown Copyright, Courtesy of the Tropical Products Institute, London; 72, *Het Amboinish Kruid-boek*. G. E. Rumphius. Amsterdam, 1750; 73, 74, 75, 87 and 88 bottom, Elmer W. Smith Stamp Collection; 76, Courtesy, Field Museum of Natural History, Chicago; 77 and 78, Red V. Coconut Products Company, Inc.; 80, *Tipos e Aspectos do Brasil*. Illustration by Percy Lau. Rio de Janeiro: I.B.G.E., 1975; 81, *A Practical Guide to Coco-nut Planting*. R. W. Munro and L. C. Brown. London: John Bale, Sons & Danielsson, Ltd., 1920; 82 top and 88, *The Prince of Palms*. W. P. Treloar. London, 1884; 83, *The Cult of the Coconut*. London: Curtis Gardner & Co., Ltd., 1912; 82 bottom, 84, 85 top and bottom, 86 top and bottom and 93, Reproduced courtesy of General Foods Corp., owner of the registered trademarks BAKER'S, ANGEL FLAKE, JELL-O, POST, GERMAN'S, TOASTIES and GRAPE-NUTS; 89, *All About Coconuts*. Roland Belfort and Alfred Johannes Hoyer. London: The St. Catherine Press, 1914; 94, *The Herball or Generall Historie of Plantes*. John Gerarde. London, 1636; 96, *Kreutterbuch*. Hieronymus Bock (1489-1554). Strassburg (undated); 97, From a painting by Albrecht Dürer, 1512. The Mansell Collection, London; 98, *Icones Plantarum Medicinalium*. Johannes Zorn. Nürnberg, 1781; 99 top, 101, 103 top, 105 and 111, United States Department of Agriculture; 100 and 115, *Die Haselnuss*. Franz Goeschke. Berlin, 1887; 102, Findik Tarim, Satis Kooperatifleri Birligi. Giresun, Turkey; 103 bottom, 104 top and bottom, Elmer W. Smith Stamp Collection; 106, 107 top and bottom, 108 bottom and 110 top, Harry B. Lagerstedt; 108, Frederic Rosengarten, Jr.; 109, Harry B. Lagerstedt and American Fruit Grower; 110 bottom and 113,

Oregon Filbert Commission, Tigard, Oregon; 116 and 141, *Revue Horticole*, Paris, 1891; 118, 129 bottom, 130 top and bottom, 131 top and bottom, 133, 136, 137, 138, 139 top and bottom and 142, C. Brewer & Co., Ltd. (Mauna Loa Macadamia Nut Corp.); 119 top and bottom, 125, 126, 127, 128 and 134, A. Gutt, Guatemala; 120 top and bottom, Mitchell Library, New South Wales, Australia; 121, Ian McConachie, Brisbane, Queensland, Australia; 122, *The Cultivation of the Australian Nut*. F. Turner. Dept of Agriculture, New South Wales, Australia. 1893; 123, Sherwood Greenwell and Richard A. Hamilton; 129 top, William B. Storey; 144, *Köhler's Medizinal-Pflanzen*, Band III. Berlin-Lichterfelde, 1898; 146, American Museum of Natural History, New York; 147, *Indiae Utriusque re Naturali et Medica*. Gulielmi Pisonis. Amsterdam, 1658; 148, *Frank Leslie's Illustrated Newspaper*. December 5, 1885; 149, *Scientific American*. December 29, 1894; 150, Arizona Historical Society, Buehman Collection Photo; 151, The Carver Research Foundation of Tuskegee Institute; 152 left and right, 153 and 166, "PLANTERS," "MR. PEANUT," and "MR. PEANUT DEVICE" are Trademarks owned and used by Nabisco Brands, Inc.; 154, 160, 161 and 163, United States Department of Agriculture; 155, *El Maní en Venezuela*. Bruno Mazzani. Ministerio de Agricultura y Cria. Maracay, Venezuela. Diciembre de 1961; 156, Courtesy, Field Museum of Natural History, Chicago; 157 top and bottom, ICRISAT, Andhra Pradesh, India; 158, *The Peanut Plant*. B. W. Jones. New York: Orange Judd Company, 1920; 164, Elmer W. Smith Stamp Collection; 170, George D. Madden; 172, U.S. Forest Service photo; 173, *The Silva of North America*. Charles Sprague Sargent. Cambridge, Mass.: The Riverside Press, 1895; 174, Reproduced by permission of the publisher from THE STANDARD CYCLOPEDIA OF HORTICULTURE, edited by L. H. Bailey. Copyright 1914, 1915, 1916, 1917 by Macmillan Publishing Company. Copyright renewed; 175, J. B. Storey; 176 top, Gold Kist, Inc.; 176 bottom, Ewing Galloway; 178, J. G. Woodroof; 179, Jerry A. Payne; 180, 189, 191, 192 and 193, *Nut Culture in the United States*. U.S.D.A., 1896; 181 top and 185 right, *Pecan-Growing*. Stuckey, H. P. and Kyle, E. J. New York: The Macmillan Company, 1925; 181 bottom, Jerry A. Payne; 182, 184 and 187, J. B. Storey; 183, Warren T. Johnson in *Nut Tree Culture in North America*, 1979; 185 left, U.S.D.A. photo. U.S. Pecan Field

Station, Brownwood, Texas; 186 top and bottom, Bernard L. Lewis and Stahmann Farms; 190, National Pecan Marketing Council; 196, *North American Sylva*. F. A. Michaux. Philadelphia, 1865; 198, Diana Kirkbride Helbaek; 199 left, *Kreuterbuch*. Adamo Lonicero. Franckfurt, 1679; 199 right, Courtesy, Field Museum of Natural History, Chicago; 200 and 205 bottom, United States Department of Agriculture; 201 top, Frederic Rosengarten, Jr.; 201 bottom and 202 bottom, Ira S. Agress; 202 top, Kavir Pistachio Export Co.; 204 bottom, 205 top, 206 and 208, Julian C. Crane; 207 and 212, California Pistachio Association; 214, *The Herball or Generall Historie of Plantes*. John Gerarde. London, 1636; 216 top and bottom, David J. Hetland, Ltd.; 217, R. G. Robinson; 218 left, *The Queensland Agricultural Journal*. Vol. VII, 1917; 218 right, 224, 225 and 234, Elmer W. Smith Stamp Collection; 219, Theodor de Bry. *Historia Americae*. Frankfurt, 1590. (Courtesy of Princeton University Library); 221, *The Sunflower*. Charles B. Heiser, Jr. Copyright 1976 by the University of Oklahoma Press; 222 and 223, Charles B. Heiser, Jr.; 226, Gerhardt N. Fick; 227, Photo courtesy of Dahlgren and Company, Crookston, Minnesota; 228, Avitrol; 229, Cargill, Inc.; 230, Sunflower and Grain Marketing; 232, Sigco Research, Inc.; 238, *The Herball or Generall Historie of Plantes*. John Gerarde. London, 1636; 240, *Gewächse*. Friedrich Gottlob Hayne's. Berlin, 1837; 241 top, Ewing Galloway; 241 bottom, Frederick G. Meyer; 242, 257, 258 and 260, *Cosmographia Universalis.*. Sebastian Münster. (Mary Evans Picture Library); 243, Courtesy of Princeton University Library; 245, *Icones plantarum rariorum*. Nicolaus Joseph Jacquin. Wien, 1781-1793; 246, United States Department of Agriculture; 247 top and bottom, 253, 254 top and bottom and 261, Diamond Walnut Growers, Inc.; 248, Courtesy, Field Museum of Natural History, Chicago; 244 and 249, Elmer W. Smith Stamp Collection; 250, Covello Photography; 251, Julian C. Crane; 252, Ramacher Manufacturer Co.; 255, T. M. Duché Nut Co., Inc.; 256, P. Liu, National Arboretum; 265, *Album of Water-Colour Drawings of Flowers and Fruit*. Jacques Le Moyne de Morgue. London, 1585. (Courtesy of the British Library); 266, *A Report on the Trees and Shrubs*. Vol. I. George B. Emerson. Boston: Little Brown & Co., 1887; 267, Courtesy, Field Museum of Natural History, Chicago; 268, Elmer W. Smith Stamp Collection; 269, *Monographiae Phanerogamarum*. Vol. Quartum. Alphonso et Casimir de Candolle. Paris,

1883; 270, Edwin A. Menninger; 271, *The Herball or Generall Historie of Plantes*. John Gerarde. London, 1636. (Courtesy of Princeton University Library); 272 left, Andrew S. Fuller. *The Nut Culturist*. New York: Orange Judd Co., 1919; 272 right, Terence O'Driscoll; 273, Lamarck: *Encyclopédie Méthodique Botanique*. Paris, 1823; 274 top, Terence O'Driscoll; 274 bottom, Courtesy of the British Library; 275 left, United Press International photo; 275 right, Edwin A. Menninger; 276, *Flore Pittoresque et Medicale des Antilles*. M. E. Descourtilz. Tome Huitieme. Paris, 1829. Courtesy of British Museum (Natural History); 277 top, Edwin A. Menninger; 277 bottom, Courtesy, Field Museum of Natural History, Chicago; 278, John Apai; 279, *American Medical Botany*. Vol. I. Jacob Bigelow. Boston, 1817; 280 top, Courtesy, Field Museum of Natural History, Chicago; 280 bottom, Terence O'Driscoll; 281, Terence O'Driscoll; 282, *Sinopsis de la Flora Chilena*. Carlos Muñoz Pizarro. Ediciones de la Universidad de Chile, 1959; 283, *The Gardeners' Chronicle*. Vol. XLVII. London, 1910; 284 top, Ewing Galloway; 284 bottom, John Apai; 285, *Useful Plants of Japan*. Tanaka, Yoshio and Ono, Motoyoshi. 1895; 286 top and bottom, U.S. Forest Service photo; 287, Crown Copyright, reproduced with the permission of the Controller of Her Majesty's Stationery Office, and of the Royal Botanic Gardens, Kew; 288 top, Reproduced by permission of the publisher from THE STANDARD CYCLOPEDIA OF HORTICULTURE, edited by L. H. Bailey. Copyright 1914, 1915, 1916, 1917, by Macmillan Publishing Company. Copyright renewed; 288 bottom and 289, Terence O'Driscoll; 290 top, Courtesy, Field Museum of Natural History, Chicago; 290 bottom, L. H. MacDaniels in *Nut Tree Culture in North America*. 1979; 291, *A Report on the Trees and Shrubs*. Vol. I. George B. Emerson. Boston: Little Brown & Co., 1887; 293 top, *Hortii Indici Malabarici*. Pars Tertia. Heinricum van Reede. Amsterdam, 1682. (Courtesy of the Linnean Society of London); 293 bottom, *Three Visits to Madagascar*. Rev. William Ellis. London, 1859. (Courtesy of the Linnean Society of London); 294 top, Courtesy, Field Museum of Natural History, Chicago; 294 bottom, *Curtis's Botanical Magazine*. Vol. II. London, 1828; 296 and 297 bottom, Noel D. Vietmeyer; 297 top, *Report on the United States and Mexican Boundary Survey. Botany of the Boundary*. Part I, Vol. II. William H. Emory. Under the Direction of the Secretary of the Interior. Washington, 1859; 299, Botanical Museum,

Harvard University; 300, *Icones Plantarum India e Orientalis*. Robert Wight. Madras, India. 1840. (Courtesy of the Linnean Society of London); 301, John Apai; 302 top, Courtesy, Field Museum of Natural History, Chicago; 302 bottom, *Useful Plants of Japan*. Tanaka, Yoshio and Ono, Motoyoshi. 1895; 303 top and 305 bottom, John Apai; 303 bottom, Julia F. Morton; 304, *The Gardeners' Chronicle*. January 19, 1907; 305 top, *Deutsch-Ost-Afrika*. Band V. A. Engler, Berlin, 1895; 307 top, *Histoire des Plantes de la Guiane Francoise*. Tome Quatrieme. M. Fusée Aublet. London & Paris, 1775; 307 bottom, W. H. Hodge; 308, *Philippine Resins, Gums, Seed Oils and Essential Oils*. West, Augustus P. and Brown, William H. Bureau of Forestry, Philippine Islands. Bulletin No. 20. Manila, 1920; 309, Botanical Museum, Harvard University; 310, *The North American Sylva*. F. W. Michaux. Paris, 1865; 311, Elmer W. Smith Stamp Collection; 312, L. H. MacDaniels; 313, 317, 318, 320 top and 321 bottom, United States Department of Agriculture; 316, *De Historia Stirpium*. Leonhard Fuchs. 1542; 319 top, *The Forest Flora of New South Wales*. Vol. I. Joseph Henry Maiden. Sydney, Australia. 1904; 320 bottom, *Curtis's Botanical Magazine*. Vol. 41. London, 1815; 322, *Histoire Naturelle des Végétaux*. M. Edouard Spach. Paris, 1846; 323 top, W. H. Hodge; 323 bottom, Edwin A. Menninger; 324, *Herbarium amboinense*. Georg Eberhard Rumphius. Amsterdam, 1747; 325 top, American Soybean Association, by Bob Elbert; 325 bottom, Cargill, Inc.; 327, 339 and 341 bottom, John Apai; 328 left, *The Philippine Agricultural Review*. Manila. November, 1912; 328 right, *Hooker's Icones Plantarum*. Vol. IX. Sir Joseph Dalton Hooker. London, 1889; 329 top, Edwin A. Menninger; 329 bottom, *Flora of Jamaica*. Vol. III. William Fawcett and Alfred B. Rendle. London, 1914; 330 and 333 bottom, Terence O'Driscoll; 331 *Le Potager d'un Curieux*. A. Paillieux and D. Bois. Paris, 1892; 332, Ara Der Marderosian; 333 top, Crown Copyright, reproduced with the permission of the Controller of Her Majesty's Stationery Office, and of the Royal Botanic Gardens, Kew; 334 top, W. H. Hodge; 334 bottom, By Courtesy of the British Library; 335, *The Botanical Register—of Exotic Plants*. Vol. III. Sydenham Edwards. London, 1817; 336, *The Oxford Book of Food Plants*. Text by S. G. Harrison, G. B. Masefield and Michael Wallis. Illustrations by B. E. Nicholson. Copyright by Oxford University Press, 1969; 337 top, Botanical Museum, Harvard University; 337 bottom, Julia F. Morton; 338, By Courtesy of the British Library; 340 top, *Herbarium amboinense*. Georg Eberhard Rumphius. Amsterdam, 1747; 340 bottom, United States Department of Agriculture; 341 top, Hollar & Co., Inc.

Recipe Index

General Index

(**Boldface** numerals indicate principal references in the text.)

Achene, xvii
Acorns (*Quercus alba*), xiii, 51, 265-69
Aesculus carnea, see Red horse chestnut
Aesculus hippocastanum, see Horse chestnut
Afghanistan, 14, 198, 200, 239, 310
Aflatoxin, 160
Africa, 44, 146, 320-21, 331, 339-41
   See also East Africa; North Africa; West Africa;
      specific countries
Alabama, 154, 175, 177
Aleurites fordii, see Tung nuts
Aleurites triloba, see Candlenuts
Algeria, 14
Alkaloids, xvii, 274, 283, 285
Almond butter, 14
Almondettes (*Buchanania lanzan*), **269-70**
Almonds (*Prunus dulcis*), xiii, xvi-xviii, xxii-xxiv,
   2-21, 321
   blanched, xxii, 7, 14, 15
   composition of (tables), xx-xxi, 233
   See also Java almonds; Tropical almonds
Amazon Basin, 23, 25, 28-32, 158, 306-8
American filberts (*Corylus americana*), 95
Amygdalin in bitter almonds, 3
Anacardiaceae (family), 37, 197, 198, 269
Anacardium occidentale, see Cashew nuts
Angola, 46
Animal feed, *see* Feed
Antoine (slave), 173-74
Arachis hypogaea, see Peanuts
Arachis villosulicarpa, 145
Archaeology, nuts in, xiii, 96, 145-46, 197, 198, 218,
   239-41, 313, 316
Areca catechu, see Betel nuts
Argentina, 148, 156, 225, 324
Arizona, 177, 182, 218, 232, 295, 297, 299, 310, 315,
   321, 341

Arkansas, 177, 246
Arrack, 87
"Arrowroot," 303
Artichokes, 217
Artocarpus altilis, see Breadfruit
Artocarpus heterophyllus, see Jack nuts
Australia, 10, 32, 117-23, 133, 179, 243, 255, 297,
   318-19, 339
   aborigines of, xiv, 117, 122-23

Bacteria, 188, 252
Bakery products, nuts in, 44-46, 60, 83, 163, 188,
   189, 207, 232, 256, 271-72, 307, 317, 322, 324,
   327, 337, 340
Barnum, Phineas T., 150
Bartram, John, 172
Bauple nuts, *see* Macadamia nuts
Beaked filberts (*Corylus cornuta*), 95
Bean family (pea family; Leguminosae), 145, 324,
   328
Beaumont, J. H., 135
Beech family (Fagaceae), 51, 265, 270
Beechnuts (*Fagus grandifolia*), xvii, **270-72**
Belém (Brazil), 27, 30, 32, 284
Benne, 321
Bertholletia excelsa, see Brazil nuts
Betel nuts (*Areca catechu*), xviii, **273-75**, 282
Beverages from nuts, 46, 65, 66, 70, 189, 277-78,
   285, 287, 331
   See also Milk, nut
Biblical references to nuts, xiii, 4, 197, 241, 265, 311
Bitternut hickory nuts (*Carya cordiformis*), 289, 292
Black walnuts, *see* Walnuts—black
Blake, William, quoted, 215
Blanching, 32, 162
   of almonds, xxii, 7, 14, 15
Bligh, Captain William, 75, 278-79, 333

375

377

A CATALOG OF SELECTED DOVER
BOOKS IN ALL FIELDS OF INTEREST

CONCERNING THE SPIRITUAL IN ART, Wassily Kandinsky. Pioneering work by father of abstract art. Thoughts on color theory, nature of art. Analysis of earlier masters. 12 illustrations. 80pp. of text. 5⅜ x 8½.   23411-8

ANIMALS: 1,419 Copyright-Free Illustrations of Mammals, Birds, Fish, Insects, etc., Jim Harter (ed.). Clear wood engravings present, in extremely lifelike poses, over 1,000 species of animals. One of the most extensive pictorial sourcebooks of its kind. Captions. Index. 284pp. 9 x 12.   23766-4

CELTIC ART: The Methods of Construction, George Bain. Simple geometric techniques for making Celtic interlacements, spirals, Kells-type initials, animals, humans, etc. Over 500 illustrations. 160pp. 9 x 12. (Available in U.S. only.)   22923-8

AN ATLAS OF ANATOMY FOR ARTISTS, Fritz Schider. Most thorough reference work on art anatomy in the world. Hundreds of illustrations, including selections from works by Vesalius, Leonardo, Goya, Ingres, Michelangelo, others. 593 illustrations. 192pp. 7⅛ x 10¼.   20241-0

CELTIC HAND STROKE-BY-STROKE (Irish Half-Uncial from "The Book of Kells"): An Arthur Baker Calligraphy Manual, Arthur Baker. Complete guide to creating each letter of the alphabet in distinctive Celtic manner. Covers hand position, strokes, pens, inks, paper, more. Illustrated. 48pp. 8¼ x 11.   24336-2

EASY ORIGAMI, John Montroll. Charming collection of 32 projects (hat, cup, pelican, piano, swan, many more) specially designed for the novice origami hobbyist. Clearly illustrated easy-to-follow instructions insure that even beginning papercrafters will achieve successful results. 48pp. 8¼ x 11.   27298-2

THE COMPLETE BOOK OF BIRDHOUSE CONSTRUCTION FOR WOODWORKERS, Scott D. Campbell. Detailed instructions, illustrations, tables. Also data on bird habitat and instinct patterns. Bibliography. 3 tables. 63 illustrations in 15 figures. 48pp. 5¼ x 8½.   24407-5

BLOOMINGDALE'S ILLUSTRATED 1886 CATALOG: Fashions, Dry Goods and Housewares, Bloomingdale Brothers. Famed merchants' extremely rare catalog depicting about 1,700 products: clothing, housewares, firearms, dry goods, jewelry, more. Invaluable for dating, identifying vintage items. Also, copyright-free graphics for artists, designers. Co-published with Henry Ford Museum & Greenfield Village. 160pp. 8¼ x 11.   25780-0

HISTORIC COSTUME IN PICTURES, Braun & Schneider. Over 1,450 costumed figures in clearly detailed engravings–from dawn of civilization to end of 19th century. Captions. Many folk costumes. 256pp. 8⅜ x 11¾.   23150-X

PHOTOGRAPHIC SKETCHBOOK OF THE CIVIL WAR, Alexander Gardner. 100 photos taken on field during the Civil War. Famous shots of Manassas Harper's Ferry, Lincoln, Richmond, slave pens, etc. 244pp. 10⅝ x 8¼.   22731-6

FIVE ACRES AND INDEPENDENCE, Maurice G. Kains. Great back-to-the-land classic explains basics of self-sufficient farming. The one book to get. 95 illustrations. 397pp. 5⅜ x 8½.   20974-1

SONGS OF EASTERN BIRDS, Dr. Donald J. Borror. Songs and calls of 60 species most common to eastern U.S.: warblers, woodpeckers, flycatchers, thrushes, larks, many more in high-quality recording.   Cassette and manual 99912-2

A MODERN HERBAL, Margaret Grieve. Much the fullest, most exact, most useful compilation of herbal material. Gigantic alphabetical encyclopedia, from aconite to zedoary, gives botanical information, medical properties, folklore, economic uses, much else. Indispensable to serious reader. 161 illustrations. 888pp. 6½ x 9¼. 2-vol. set. (Available in U.S. only.)   Vol. I: 22798-7
Vol. II: 22799-5

HIDDEN TREASURE MAZE BOOK, Dave Phillips. Solve 34 challenging mazes accompanied by heroic tales of adventure. Evil dragons, people-eating plants, blood-thirsty giants, many more dangerous adversaries lurk at every twist and turn. 34 mazes, stories, solutions. 48pp. 8¼ x 11.   24566-7

LETTERS OF W. A. MOZART, Wolfgang A. Mozart. Remarkable letters show bawdy wit, humor, imagination, musical insights, contemporary musical world; includes some letters from Leopold Mozart. 276pp. 5⅜ x 8½.   22859-2

BASIC PRINCIPLES OF CLASSICAL BALLET, Agrippina Vaganova. Great Russian theoretician, teacher explains methods for teaching classical ballet. 118 illustrations. 175pp. 5⅜ x 8½.   22036-2

THE JUMPING FROG, Mark Twain. Revenge edition. The original story of The Celebrated Jumping Frog of Calaveras County, a hapless French translation, and Twain's hilarious "retranslation" from the French. 12 illustrations. 66pp. 5⅜ x 8½.
22686-7

BEST REMEMBERED POEMS, Martin Gardner (ed.). The 126 poems in this superb collection of 19th- and 20th-century British and American verse range from Shelley's "To a Skylark" to the impassioned "Renascence" of Edna St. Vincent Millay and to Edward Lear's whimsical "The Owl and the Pussycat." 224pp. 5⅜ x 8½.
27165-X

COMPLETE SONNETS, William Shakespeare. Over 150 exquisite poems deal with love, friendship, the tyranny of time, beauty's evanescence, death and other themes in language of remarkable power, precision and beauty. Glossary of archaic terms. 80pp. 5³⁄₁₆ x 8¼.   26686-9

THE BATTLES THAT CHANGED HISTORY, Fletcher Pratt. Eminent historian profiles 16 crucial conflicts, ancient to modern, that changed the course of civilization. 352pp. 5⅜ x 8½.   41129-X

THE STORY OF THE TITANIC AS TOLD BY ITS SURVIVORS, Jack Winocour (ed.). What it was really like. Panic, despair, shocking inefficiency, and a little heroism. More thrilling than any fictional account. 26 illustrations. 320pp. 5⅜ x 8½.
20610-6

FAIRY AND FOLK TALES OF THE IRISH PEASANTRY, William Butler Yeats (ed.). Treasury of 64 tales from the twilight world of Celtic myth and legend: "The Soul Cages," "The Kildare Pooka," "King O'Toole and his Goose," many more. Introduction and Notes by W. B. Yeats. 352pp. 5⅜ x 8½.
26941-8

BUDDHIST MAHAYANA TEXTS, E. B. Cowell and others (eds.). Superb, accurate translations of basic documents in Mahayana Buddhism, highly important in history of religions. The Buddha-karita of Asvaghosha, Larger Sukhavativyuha, more. 448pp. 5⅜ x 8½.
25552-2

ONE TWO THREE . . . INFINITY: Facts and Speculations of Science, George Gamow. Great physicist's fascinating, readable overview of contemporary science: number theory, relativity, fourth dimension, entropy, genes, atomic structure, much more. 128 illustrations. Index. 352pp. 5⅜ x 8½.
25664-2

EXPERIMENTATION AND MEASUREMENT, W. J. Youden. Introductory manual explains laws of measurement in simple terms and offers tips for achieving accuracy and minimizing errors. Mathematics of measurement, use of instruments, experimenting with machines. 1994 edition. Foreword. Preface. Introduction. Epilogue. Selected Readings. Glossary. Index. Tables and figures. 128pp. 5⅜ x 8½.
40451-X

DALÍ ON MODERN ART: The Cuckolds of Antiquated Modern Art, Salvador Dalí. Influential painter skewers modern art and its practitioners. Outrageous evaluations of Picasso, Cézanne, Turner, more. 15 renderings of paintings discussed. 44 calligraphic decorations by Dalí. 96pp. 5⅜ x 8½. (Available in U.S. only.)
29220-7

ANTIQUE PLAYING CARDS: A Pictorial History, Henry René D'Allemagne. Over 900 elaborate, decorative images from rare playing cards (14th–20th centuries): Bacchus, death, dancing dogs, hunting scenes, royal coats of arms, players cheating, much more. 96pp. 9¼ x 12¼.
29265-7

MAKING FURNITURE MASTERPIECES: 30 Projects with Measured Drawings, Franklin H. Gottshall. Step-by-step instructions, illustrations for constructing handsome, useful pieces, among them a Sheraton desk, Chippendale chair, Spanish desk, Queen Anne table and a William and Mary dressing mirror. 224pp. 8⅛ x 11¼.
29338-6

THE FOSSIL BOOK: A Record of Prehistoric Life, Patricia V. Rich et al. Profusely illustrated definitive guide covers everything from single-celled organisms and dinosaurs to birds and mammals and the interplay between climate and man. Over 1,500 illustrations. 760pp. 7½ x 10⅛.
29371-8

Paperbound unless otherwise indicated. Available at your book dealer, online at **www.doverpublications.com**, or by writing to Dept. GI, Dover Publications, Inc., 31 East 2nd Street, Mineola, NY 11501. For current price information or for free catalogues (please indicate field of interest), write to Dover Publications or log on to **www.doverpublications.com** and see every Dover book in print. Dover publishes more than 500 books each year on science, elementary and advanced mathematics, biology, music, art, literary history, social sciences, and other areas.